W9-BXP-608

Understanding Adulthood

Barbara M. Newman
Ohio State University

Philip R. Newman

Holt, Rinehart and Winston
New York Chicago San Francisco
Philadelphia Montreal Toronto London
Sydney Tokyo Mexico City Rio de Janeiro
Madrid

Library of Congress Cataloging in Publication Data

Newman, Barbara M.
Understanding adulthood.

Includes bibliographies and index.
1. Adulthood—Psychological aspects. I. Newman, Philip R. II. Title.
BF724.5.N48 1983 155.6 82-15784
ISBN 0-03-046576-1

Address correspondence to:
383 Madison Avenue
New York, N.Y. 10017

Printed in the United States of America
Published simultaneously in Canada
3456 038 987654321

CBS COLLEGE PUBLISHING
Holt, Rinehart and Winston
The Dryden Press
Saunders College Publishing

Credits

Cover photo, Phoebe Dunn; **p. 3,** David Burnett/CONTACT: **p. 8,** UPI Photos; **p. 10** (top) Joanne Leonard 1978/Woodfin Camp; **p. 10** (bottom) Forsyth from Monkmeyer; **p. 11** (top) Michael Hayman/Stock, Boston; **p. 11** (bottom) © Thomas S. England 1982/Photo Researchers; **p. 22,** Sigmund Freud Copyrights, Ltd.; **p. 37,** Photo by William Carter. Courtesy of Viking Press; **p. 40,** Omikron/Photo Researchers; **p. 49,** courtesy Bernice Neugarten; **p. 65,** Gloria Karlson Portogallo, Inc.; **p. 72,** Douglas Kirkland 1980/CONTACT; **p. 87,** © Eve Arnold/Magnum Photos; **p. 94,** copyright © Michael Philip Manham 1976/Photo Researchers; **p. 100,** Omikron/Photo Researchers; **p. 104,** Copyright Stephen Shames 1981/Woodfin Camp; **p. 113,** © Geoffrey Coxe/Rapho/Photo Researchers; **p. 120** (top), Public Relations Department, Lenox Hill Hospital; **p. 120** (bottom), from Goodell Savonarola, 1547; Eucharius Rhodius, 1544; Deventer, 1701; Stein, 1805; **p. 126** © Thomas S. England 1975/Photo Researchers; **p. 129,** Michael Weisbrot and Family/Stock, Boston; **p. 131,** Peter Menzel/Stock, Boston; **p. 133** (top), Mimi Forsyth/Monkmeyer; **p. 133** (bottom), Wide World; **p. 156,** photo by Van Bucher, Courtesy Wagner College, Department of Psychology/Photo Researchers; **p. 169,** © Teri Leigh Stratford 1982/Photo Researchers; **p. 172,** copyright Leif Skoogfors 1978/Woodfin Camp; **p. 194,** photo by Steve Kagan/Photo Researchers; **p. 210,** reproduced from the Collection of the Library of Congress/Photo Researchers; **p. 214,** Anestis Diakopoulos/Stock, Boston; **p. 229,** © Beryl Goldberg; **p. 237,** © Tony Howarth/Woodfin Camp; **p. 241,** photo by Paul Fortin/Stock, Boston; **p. 274,** © Alice Kandell/Photo Researchers; **p. 284,** The Museum of Modern Art/Film Stills Archive; **p. 300,** copyright by Richard Frieman/Photo Researchers; **p. 318,** photo by Arthur Tress/Photo Researchers; **p. 334,** photo by Bill Anderson from Monkmeyer; **p. 337,** © Marcia Weinstein 1976; **p. 343,** Jeff Albertson/Stock, Boston; **p. 346,** Paul Conklin from Monkmeyer; **p. 352,** © Freda Leinwand from Monkmeyer; **p. 362,** © Dick Hanley/Photo Researchers; **p. 364,** copyright Timothy Eagan 1980/Woodfin Camp **p. 368,** Maude Dorr/Photo Researchers.

Preface

As children, we looked forward to becoming adults. As authors, we have looked forward to writing about adulthood. This book is about the challenges and opportunities for growth that occur during adulthood. It is an attempt to integrate the many thoughtful perspectives that psychologists, sociologists, anthropologists, physicians, and educators have brought to the understanding of adult life. The book combines a view of the inner experiences of adult development including health, sexuality, cognitive abilities, and personality, with a view of the powerful and dynamic contexts that most adults encounter including friendship and intimacy, family relationships, and the world of work.

Adulthood lasts for a long period of time, perhaps as long as sixty years. For those of you who are in your twenties now, adulthood even may last for eighty years. Increasingly large numbers of people are experiencing the full span of adult life. This fact is providing new opportunities to understand the potential for development during adulthood. More time means greater opportunity to devise a variety of life stories. It also means a more complex family system with many intergenerational relationships. Finally, it poses challenges to our current thinking about the typical pattern of involvement in major life roles, especially the roles of spouse and worker.

As we look over the chapters of the book, some of the implications of a long and healthy adulthood are clear. With respect to physical health, we see a new outlook on the role of exercise and the potential for fitness in later adult life. We are beginning to see that some aspects of aging are the consequences of a sedentary, post-industrial lifestyle. While some biological changes that accompany aging may be irreversible, others can be minimized through exercise and diet. In the area of sexuality, we see that it is possible to retain active, satisfying sexual functioning throughout life. These facts contradict myths that many people believe about what happens to us as we get older.

The study of cognition reveals that the idea that intellectual functioning declines with age must be reevaluated. Studies show that while some ability areas show decline, others do not. Also whether or not a skill is exercised seems to influence performance with age. In some areas, adulthood brings on new cognitive competences and perspectives that are not often observed in childhood or adolescence. In the study of personality, we discover that the impact of childhood characteristics, while important, is clearly not the final word on development. Adults can reinterpret their past. Choices they make influence the direction of their life story.

The study of intimacy indicates that there are a number of lifestyles emerging that begin to provide alternatives to the traditional nuclear family as a context for achieving intimacy. The loss of intimacy for older women when their spouse dies is an especially critical concern, in that many women can anticipate a period of ten years or more during later adulthood when they will be without a partner.

Within families, a long adult life has several consequences. There are more complex intergenerational relationships. The frequency of divorce and remarriage introduces complex networks of enduring family relationships. Middle-aged adults are increasingly involved in the care of their aging parents. The family seems to be facing many new frontiers of redefinition and reorganization as choices and life span increase.

The world of work reflects the impact of a long, healthy, adulthood in several ways. Many people experience a discontinuous work history where several different types of work constitute their work career. The concept of retirement is being redefined, and we are taking a second look at the wasted resources of our older workers. In some cases, the world of work has become a tense battleground among the generations for scarce resources.

The study of adulthood raises many important questions about the normal course of development and the impact of our environment on healthy growth and adjustment. At the heart of this area is the ultimate question of what it means to live a meaningful life and to fulfill one's human potential. The many patterns of adult experience provide us with a composite map of the paths that are possible and the strategies adults use to traverse these paths.

We have surveyed the literature in each of the topic areas in the book in order to provide a picture of the current findings, questions, and directions in the study of adulthood. We have also made use of case examples to heighten the focus on individual lives and to provide some common ground for the application of theoretical concepts. Professionals from many disciplines are turning their attention to the study of adult life, becoming increasingly aware that adulthood brings its own unique changes and challenges. If this book fulfills its purpose, it will sensitize its readers to a more complex analysis of the course of adult development. We hope that some of you will be challenged to continue the needed research that will clarify questions about the regularities and uniqueness of adulthood. We hope that some of you will find opportunities to apply the ideas and information you read here to the creation of programs, educational material, and settings that more adequately meet the needs of our diverse population of modern adults.

We are fortunate to have had assistance from a number of skillful and thoughtful people in the preparation of this book. We would like to thank the following people who read part or all of the manuscript.: Sandra Candy, University of Kentucky, Lexington; Ruby Gingles, University of Nebraska, Lincoln; Peter Murk, Ball State University; Suzanne Prescott, Governors State University; Freda Rebelsky, Boston University; Jean Romaniuk, Virginia Commonwealth University; Gamal Zaki, Rhode Island College.

We want to thank Dan Loch, our Maxwell Perkins, who has carefully guided the development of the manuscript. Others at Holt, Rinehart and Winston, especially Ruth Stark, Vic Calderon, Gloria Gentile, Cheryl Mannes, and Annette Mayeski, have worked their magic to transform the manuscript into a book.

We would like to thank Judy Woodall and Sue Cross who typed early drafts of the manuscript. We are also deeply grateful to our "word pro," Lyn Akers, who managed all the final phases of manuscript coordination and production.

No book we write can be accomplished without the loving support and encouragement of our children: Sam, Abe, and Rachel. They make our adulthood the time of our lives.

B.N.
P.N.

Contents

1 Introduction

Any fulfillment of the individual life cycle, far from being simply a matter of finding terminal clarity, can only fulfill what is given in the order of things by remaining responsible and by contributing continuous solutions to the ongoing cycle of generations.

Erik H. Erikson, *Adulthood,* 1978, p. 29

The word "adult" derives from the Latin adolescere, "to grow up." The concept "adult" often carries with it the sense of someone who is fully developed, physically and psychologically. Yet this is a conception of adulthood that this book will attempt to reject. The focus of the book is on development. Our goal is to understand the continuous growth that occurs during the adult years. In adulthood, as in every earlier period of life, the status quo is not a real alternative for living beings. One either changes and grows or deteriorates and dies. In this book, you will encounter a conception that views adulthood as continuing adaptation to an increasingly complex social environment and to an increasingly complex sense of self. The physical, emotional, social, and intellectual aspects of the person have the potential for change. The psychological growth of the person during adulthood is in the direction of expanded consciousness.

The Study of Adulthood

The study of adult development raises three questions: (1) What is normative? (2) What is possible? 3) Why does change occur?

What Is Normative?

The first question refers to a general description of patterns of change during adult life. You have probably read books that describe the typical behaviors of infants, toddlers, or school-age children. You know that the study of child development focuses on such topics as language development, perception, social relationships, and cognition. In each area, data has been collected to describe the levels of competence we expect at each age. The search for a normative guide to adulthood seeks the same kinds of information. What do we expect of adults at different ages in their cognitive, emotional, social, or physical characteristics?

What Is Possible?

The second question focuses on individual differences. We can talk about an average height in adulthood, but many people are shorter or taller than average. We can talk about a normal pattern of acquisition and change in social roles, such as marriage partner, parent, or worker. Yet some people remain single, some do not have children, and some are unemployed.

The diversity of life patterns expands dramatically in adulthood. In contemporary American society, adults have many choices to make. Among other things, they can choose a place to live, a type of work, whether to marry, whether to have children, how to enact the male or female role, and what religion to believe in. The more education people have, the more they are aware of life choices. The greater the quantity of

The study of adulthood requires an appreciation of individual differences. Each person has a unique life story.

economic resources people have, the more freedom they have to select from the array of life-styles that exist in this country.

Individual differences are especially important to an understanding of adult development since adults have the capacity to contribute to their own development. People can choose to encounter diversity, to engage in demanding work roles, to participate actively in their community, or to devote time, money, and energy to improving the quality of life for others. They can also choose to screen out diversity, to select a minimally demanding form of work, to spend time alone, or to devote time, money, and energy to their own leisure. The differences in people's life choices are a reflection of a variety of psychological differences in motivation, personality, and intelligence. Once the choices are made, the environments that people encounter will continue to shape their psychology. The study of adult development must include an examination of the interaction of individual differences and the kinds of settings where significant life events take place.

Why Does Change Occur?

The third question involves the search for explanation. How can we explain the fact that some people continue to function in a creative, productive

FIGURE 1.1 Factors That Contribute to Psychological Development in Adulthood

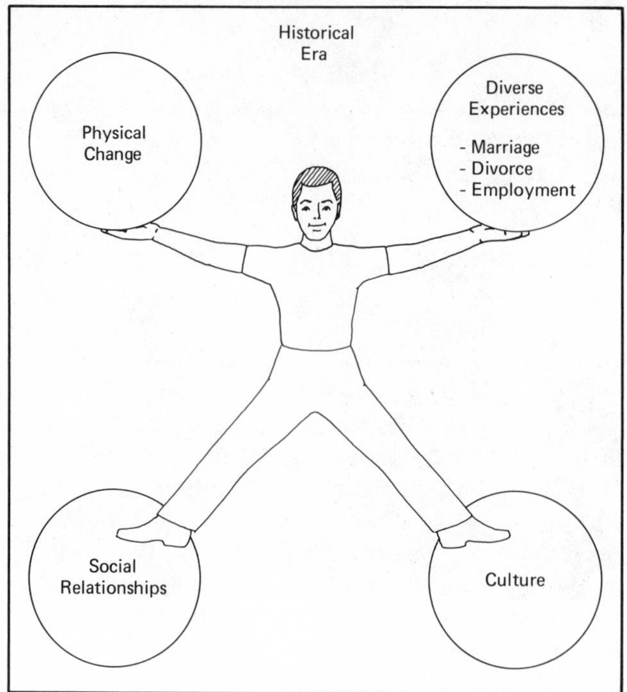

fashion throughout adulthood, while others stagnate? Why do some men become more interested in their families after the age of 40, while others become less interested? Why do some women become depressed after their children leave home, while other women confront this transition with enthusiasm? The study of adult development includes a concern for causal relationships. This search requires an interdisciplinary approach. Psychological development in adulthood is a product of physical changes, diverse experience, social relationships, historical era, and culture (see Figure 1.1). Our study of adulthood makes use of ideas and information from psychology, biology, sociology, history, and anthropology in order to fully appreciate the ways that adults conceptualize their experiences and change.

When Is Adulthood?

When a teacher is confronted by a difficult question, one good strategy is to throw the question back to the class. When do you think a person is an adult? What time period should a text on adult development cover? The period of adulthood and its meaning differ from culture to culture. In some societies, adult status and responsibilities begin at puberty with the completion of rituals, celebrations, and formal rites of passage. In other societies, entry into adulthood does not occur until the early twenties after a long period of education, role experimentation, and gradual involvement in complex roles. In the traditional Chinese society, the female did not attain the respect and status of a full adult until her own sons were married. Before that time, she was treated as a servant and subordinate to her mother-in-law. In that culture, full adult status was not attained until the woman was in her forties or fifties.

We want to draw a distinction among three ways of approaching the definition of the time period of adulthood. First, adulthood has a legal definition (see Table 1.1). There is an age at which society recognizes that a person is legally responsible for his or her actions and legally entitled to certain rights and privileges. In American society this age hovers between 18 and 21, with some states reflecting one position and some the other. A person might enlist in the army at the age of 18 but still not be served an alcoholic beverage in a hometown restaurant.

Second, there is a social definition. We view certain life roles as the domain of adulthood. People who work to support themselves, marry, and have children are considered adults. We find some people precariously straddling the line between adolescence and adulthood. A 15–year-old girl may have a baby. She may view the entry into motherhood as a sign of being an adult. At the same time, she may expect her family to support her, shelter her, and care for her baby while she attends school. A graduate student who is in her twenties may be unmarried, living in her parent's home, not earning enough money to support herself, and still in the student role. Are these people adults? In some ways yes and in some ways no.

The questions left by these examples suggest the need for a third definition of adulthood, a psychological definition. Psychologically, adulthood is a way of thinking, feeling, and relating to others. In adulthood, people are capable of abstract, logical thought (Piaget, 1972). Adults can conceptualize the future in a realistic, probabilistic way. This means that they understand that some future events are likely, but that nothing is certain. They can hypothesize about events that have not yet occurred. From a psychosocial perspective, in adulthood, people make commitments to values (Erikson, 1963). Adults have an integrated view of them-

TABLE 1.1 Three Ways of Defining Adulthood

Legal	Age at which society assumes a person is responsible for actions and entitled to certain rights and privileges.
Social	When person acquires social roles appropriate to adulthood.
Psychological	When person is capable of certain ways of thinking, feeling, and relating to others.

selves, existing into the future. They make life decisions based on personal goals and their commitments to others.

The end of adulthood is the end of life. In today's world, one can expect 60 or more years of adult life (from about 20 to 80). At the turn of the century, an adult's life expectancy was about 50. People who are born today can expect to live to age 69 if they are male or 77 if they are female. People who are already 65 can expect to live to 79 for males or 83 for females (U.S. Bureau of the Census, 1981b). The period of adulthood has doubled in length during this century. The implications of this dramatic increase in life expectancy are discussed throughout this book. This fact accounts in part for the great increase in research on adulthood as well as for the growing number of courses on adult development. Most likely, if the period of adulthood had not changed so markedly, we would not be writing this book and you would not be reading it.

Stages of Adult Development

The concept of stages is a component of many theories of development. It refers to periods of time during which particular competences are achieved or a unique orientation toward people and objects dominates experience. The stages may refer to a variety of content areas, including cognitive growth, emotional development, social skills, orientations toward work, phases of family life, or even phases of grief after separation or loss. The assumptions of *every* stage analysis are: (1) that each stage is qualitatively different from the others; and (2) that movement from stage to stage occurs in an orderly progression with the achievements of an earlier stage serving as a prerequisite for subsequent development. Usually, stage theories assume that the accomplishments of earlier stages are not lost, but reintegrated into new strategies or new competences.

What differentiates adulthood from the earlier life stages? As a result of biological development, the adult's body has a different appearance and a different capacity for physical and sexual behavior than does the body of an infant, a child, or an adolescent. In childhood and adolescence there is usually an expectation that one can count on others to provide the resources necessary for survival, especially food and shelter. In adulthood, one is expected to provide these resources for oneself and others. The stages of infancy, childhood, and adolescence are often viewed as periods of preparation and training. Adulthood is the period for which this preparation is intended. It is the game rather than the practice. Even though we see adulthood as a period of continued growth and new learning, the sense of adulthood as a time of responsibility and decision-making puts greater emphasis on the adequacy of each performance. In contrast to earlier life stages, adulthood is the time when one's own decisions and actions are likely to influence subsequent generations. This influence may come through parenting, through work activities, through programmatic changes in community resources, and/or through individual acts of creative accomplishment. As a result, adult thought is characterized by greater use of abstractions, hypothesis-raising, and anticipation.

Three Psychosocial Stages of Adulthood

The stage theorist who has had the most impact on our thinking about adult development is Erik Erikson. Erikson (1963, 1978) has described three stages of adulthood that he views as universal. In young adulthood (approximately 21 to 30 years old) the focal theme is intimacy versus isolation. Adults are expected to form intense commitments with age mates. Usually these commitments blend emotional closeness with sexual closeness. The capacity for intimacy requires an ability to regulate one's own needs in order to satisfy the needs of another person. In order to achieve intimacy, two people must be able to respond to one another in a mutually satisfying way. Isolation is the negative outcome of repeated failures to achieve intimacy. Isolation may result from an inability to move close to another. For some young adults, emotional closeness threatens to overwhelm them. Isolation may also result from repeated rejection.

The stage of middle adulthood (from approximately 30 to 50 years old) brings a focus on generativity versus stagnation. Generativity is a commitment to the quality of life for future generations. People may express their generativity in many ways, including childrearing, teaching, inventing, public service, or the creative arts. A sense of generativity means that a person attaches meaning to life after his or her own death. People become invested in hopes for a future that may not directly benefit them. Stagnation is a preoccupation with oneself and one's immediate needs. People who experience stagnation may be so depressed that they do not believe they are capable of making a worthwhile contribution to others. Stagnation may also be an expression of complete self-involvement. In this case, people are so preoccupied by their own importance that they cannot become invested in the lives of others.

The stage of later adulthood (from age 50 to death) focuses on the theme of integrity versus despair. In this period there is a need to integrate one's life history and one's values. Each person must come to terms with his or her successes and failures, with the decisions and the pains of his or her life. Integrity is achieved when a person can accept the past without intense regret. Once integrity is achieved, the possibility of death is also accepted as another of life's experiences. Despair refers to a deep sense of failure or longing for another chance. People who experience despair cannot resolve their bitterness or frustration about the disappointments of their lives. In their own eyes, their successes do not seem to overshadow their failures. The sense of despair blocks the way to an acceptance of death, since death would prevent any further opportunity to set things

Development during adulthood involves both continuity and change. Here we see Sir Winston Churchill at four stages of development: as a young cadet at Sandhurst Military Academy; as First Lord of the Admiralty at the end of World War I; as Prime Minister of England during World War II; and, at the age of 80, attending a political conference.

right. The last phase of life is focused on the articulation of a philosophy of life that permits an acceptance of one's past and one's future.

Erikson's view of adult development provides a global, thematic structure within which to follow transitions of focus in thoughts and relationships. The concept of a polarity of issues at each stage suggests that there is a developmental tension at every phase of a experience some of the negative pole at each stage as to resolve the conflicts of that stage. The issues of each at the other periods of life. Young children and adolescents the concern about intimacy in their relationships with peers. Y anticipate the theme of generativity as they make a decision children. Once a stage has passed, the theme loses its predominant qua but the issues may still be problematic. In later adulthood, for example, concern about intimacy continues. For adults who did not achieve intimacy in young adulthood, the conflict may be quite intense. There may be serious questioning about the absence of meaningful relationships. For adults who have lost an intimate partner through widowhood, the question that is raised is not whether they are capable of intimacy but whether there are ways to restore the satisfactions of an intimate relationship at this period of life.

The theory also suggests that the same themes that are relevant for the individual are also relevant for the society. Societies require that adults achieve intimacy in order to permit procreation. Generativity is essential so that powerful adults do not use up or destroy the resources that will be needed for the next generation. Integrity among the old makes the struggle of life seem worthwhile to those who are younger. When the oldest members of the society appear to have achieved a sense of wisdom, their struggles can be interpreted by younger members as necessary and valued. The growth of individuals through adult life is entwined with the continuation of the culture. In this sense, the meaning of development in adult life takes on heightened importance. Societies must provide the context for continued growth in adulthood, not only for the enhancement of the members of the group but for the survival of the culture itself.

Life Events and Adult Development

Not all scholars of adult development agree with Erikson's stages. Some theorists, whose ideas you will read about in Chapter 2, have identified other stages of adulthood. Other theorists do not even apply the stage concept to adulthood. One approach that has been very influential in stimulating research on adult development is the life-events analysis of adulthood (Atchley, 1975; Neugarten and Datan, 1973). Life events are significant experiences. Usually they involve role gain or role loss. Examples of life events are marriage, entry into the labor force, and retirement. From this perspective, adult development is a product of adaptation to life events that occur in areas of personal importance, including work, marriage, parenting, and family of origin.

For any given population, we can describe a normative or average pattern of life events (see Figure 1.2). We know the age at which most

Life events like marriage, childbirth, moving, or death of a loved one require continuous coping and adaptation.

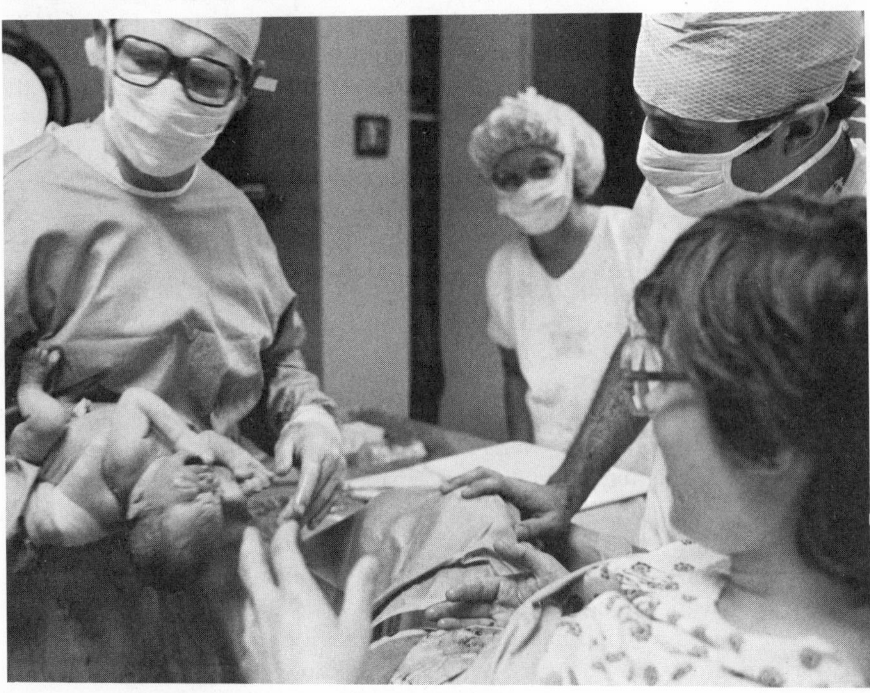

U-HAUL
U-HAUL
ONE-WAY AND LOCAL RENTALS
U-HAUL

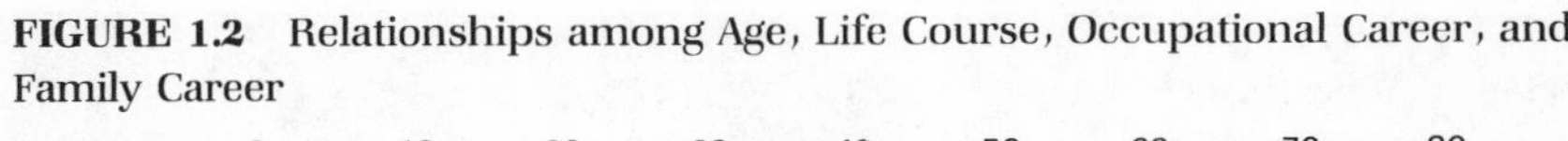

FIGURE 1.2 Relationships among Age, Life Course, Occupational Career, and Family Career

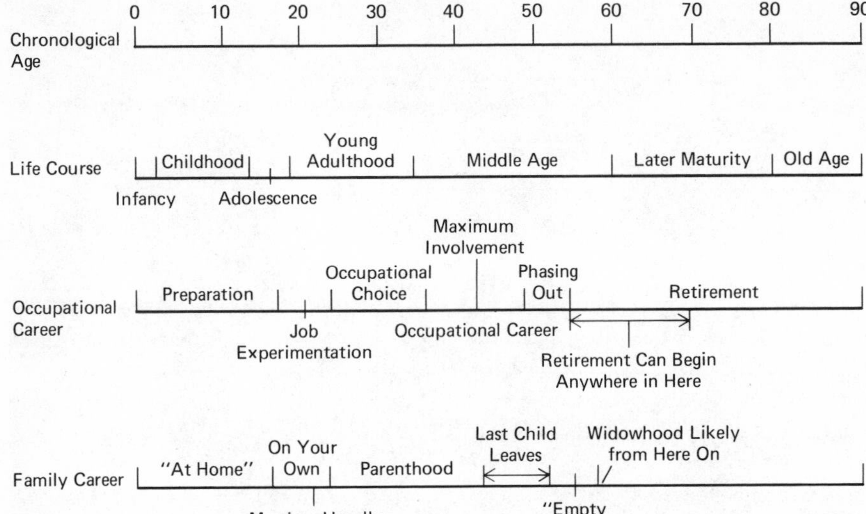

Source: Adapted from "The Life Course, Age Grading, and Age-Linked Demands for Decision Making" by R. C. Atcheley, in N. Datan & L. H. Ginsberg (Eds.), *Life-Span Developmental Psychology: Normative Life Crises* (New York: Academic Press, 1975), p. 264.

people get their first job, leave school, get married, or die. These patterns provide a picture of what people can expect during adulthood. They also provide a frame of reference against which people judge the timing of their own life course. A man may perceive himself as on-time or off-time with respect to his work-related achievements. The timing of life events can be viewed as a source of pride or stress depending on the normative framework against which the event is compared.

The life-events perspective does not assume any necessary order of development. Rather, development is described as a continuous process of coping with the challenges of life. Crisis or conflict can occur when several life transitions take place during the same period of time. There is no assumption that adulthood is stable. However, many of the events can be viewed as predictable. We do not know when our own parents will die. But we know that they will die and that we will most likely be alive to experience that loss.

For example, from 1970 to 1980 we have seen a trend toward more women remaining single during their twenties. In 1980, half the women in the age range 20–24 were single. This was an increase of 40 percent since 1970. The proportion of women remaining single in the age range 25–29 doubled from 1970 to 1980, from 10.5 percent to 20.8 percent (U.S. Bureau of the Census, 1981a). This change toward delaying marriage alters our perception of the normative pattern of life events. It also reflects a change in women's perceptions of marriage as a choice among life events in adulthood rather than a "requirement." When the timing and pattern of life events changes for a society, we can expect accompanying changes in roles, aspirations, and behaviors.

The Approach of This Book

The approach of this book is a blend of the developmental stage analysis and the life-events analysis. We believe that development is a product of the interaction between the competences and orientation of the person at each life stage with specific situations and settings. In order to understand adulthood, we must try to keep these two perspectives in mind.

On the one hand, at each life stage, a person brings a certain perspective to life events. A young adult may experience an event, like the death of his wife, as a direct challenge to his capacity to open up to an intimate relationship. An older adult who has experienced 25 or 30 years of marriage may interpret the death of his spouse as a challenge to his sense of life meaning.

On the other hand, each life story is a complex array of meaningful choices and events. Some events are predictable and make use of existing competences. Other events are sudden, unpredictable, and require competences the person may not yet have developed. The pattern of life events provides a way of describing the prompts and barriers to new growth during adulthood.

Three of the chapters in the book focus on major life-event areas, including intimate relations, family roles, and work. Within these chapters, we will consider changes of emphasis across the three broad periods of early, middle, and later adulthood. Four other chapters focus on aspects of biological and psychological change, including health, sexuality, intellectual functioning, and personality. In those chapters, we will consider the evidence for change and stability across the three periods of adulthood.

The power of the two perspectives is in bringing subjective reality and objective reality together. Life events can be described objectively. However, their interpretation depends on the person's inner conceptualization. Any event like job transfer, divorce, or the birth of a child may be interpreted as an opportunity or a problem, depending on the person's stage of development and past experience. People can grow through encounters with new life transitions. The direction of that growth depends on both the resources and demands of the situation and the person's conceptualization of the experience. At each life stage, the relevant developmental themes will influence the conceptualization of the experience.

References

Atchley, R. C. The life course, age grading, and age-linked demands for decision making. In N. Datan & L. H. Ginsberg (Eds.), *Life-span developmental psychology: Normative life crises.* New York: Academic Press, 1975.

Erikson, E. H. *Childhood and society* (2nd ed.). New York: Norton, 1963.

Erikson, E. H. Reflections on Dr. Borg's life cycle. In E. H. Erikson (Ed.), *Adulthood.* New York: Norton, 1978.

Neugarten, B. L., & Datan, N. Sociological perspectives on the life cycle. In P. B. Baltes & K. W. Schaie (Eds.), *Life-span developmental psychology: Personality and socialization*. New York: Academic Press, 1973.

Piaget, J. Intellectual evolution from adolescence to adulthood. *Human Development,* 1972, *15,* 1–12.

U.S. Bureau of the Census. Current Population Reports, Series P–20, No. 363. *Population Profile of the United States:* 1980. Washington D.C.: U.S. Government Printing Office, 1981(a).

U.S. Bureau of the Census. Current Population Reports, Series P–23, No. 111. *Social economic characteristics of Americans during midlife.* Washington, D.C.: U.S. Government Printing Office, 1981(b).

2 Theories of Adult Life

In the early stages of the development of any science different men confronting the same range of phenomena, but not usually all the same particular phenomena, describe and interpret them in different ways. What is surprising, and perhaps also unique in its degree to the fields we call science, is that such initial divergences should ever largely disappear.

Thomas Kuhn, *The Structure of Scientific Revolutions*, 1970, p. 17

You know that light is faster than sound. Do you also know that theory is faster than research? It takes far less time to identify a meaningful relationship than it does to prove its relevance or to determine its origins empirically. In this sense, theories of development lead the way, while researchers run desperately to catch up. In this chapter, we will introduce an array of theories and theoretical concepts about adult development. They will help orient you to ways that are used to think about adulthood. Early in the chapter, we are going to ask you to read a case study about people in a contemporary American family. The family has just moved because of the husband's job transfer. After presenting the basic concepts of each theory we will make an interpretation of the case based on that theoretical perspective. This will help make the theory clear to you as well as giving you a sense of how to work with it.

What Is a Theory?

It is important to think for a moment about what a theory is before you read on. A theory is a system of general concepts that provides a framework for organizing and interpreting observations. The role of theory is to identify the orderly relationships that exist among the many and diverse events of life. Theories provide a guide to the factors that will have explanatory power and those that will not. In the area of personality development, for example, one theory might direct our attention to dreams and slips of the tongue as data worth observing. Another theory might direct our attention to goals and aspirations as data worth observing.

Theories can address the same observation from a variety of perspectives. In the study of adulthood, we have theories that emphasize social roles, some that emphasize culture, others that emphasize motivation, and still others that emphasize cognition. The same behavior may have quite a different meaning depending on the theoretical framework that is applied to understand it. For example, in the case study that is presented a man's decision to take a new position and to require his family to move can be interpreted as a need for self-fulfillment, a means of meeting cultural expectations, a learned response to an existing reinforcement schedule, or an expression of unconscious hostility toward his wife. The reality of adult experience is an integration of many levels of analysis. We might guess that some aspects of development are more closely tied to social roles, and others are more closely tied to strategies for solving problems and organizing information. One could also suggest that the theories are differentially accurate for different people. For some adults it may be the cognitive processes that best explain characteristics of behavior, while for others, adult development is best explained by looking at emotional processes. In fact, the diversity of life patterns experienced during adulthood makes the search for a single unifying theory or explanation likely to end in frustration.

In evaluating any theory one can ask three questions. First, what phenomena is the theory trying to explain? If a theory is offered as an explanation of intellectual development, it might include hypotheses about the evolution of the brain, the growth of logical thinking, or the capacity for symbolism. We are less likely to expect insights about fears, motives, or friendship from such a theory. Understanding the focus of the theory helps to identify its range of applicability. This is not to say that principles from one theory will have no relevance to another area. However, one must begin by evaluating the accuracy of the theory for the events it was intended to explain.

Second, what assumptions does the theory make? Assumptions are the guiding premises that provide the logic of the theory. Einstein assumed that the speed of light was a constant in deriving his famous equation. Darwin assumed that there was "progress" from lower to higher life forms in developing his theory of evolution. Freud assumed that all behavior was motivated. This led him to theorize about the unconscious as a "storehouse" of motives and wishes. The assumptions of any theory may or may not be correct. They may be influenced by the cultural context, by the sample of observations from which the theorist draws inferences, by the current knowledge base of the field, or by the intellectual capacities of the theorist. Often, the assumptions are not clearly stated. It is up to the student to stop and reflect on the underlying logic of each theoretical position.

The third question, which is really at the heart of understanding the theory, is, what does the theory predict? What are the essential explanatory elements of the theory? If the theory adds new levels of understanding, it does so by clarifying relationships, by unifying observations through the application of integrating processes, or by identifying events that had gone unnoticed.

The Case Study

The case of the Klaskin family described in the *Wall Street Journal* (Ramirez, 1979) is our point of entry for a consideration of the theories of adult development. Read the case. Think about possible explanations for why family members are experiencing the kinds of stress reported (see Box 2.1).

Now that you have read the case, stop and try to list some explanations for the behaviors that were described. Why is Barbara shouting at her father? Why did the Klaskins decide to move? Why has Leona given up her career goals for her husband's career? Why did Roy react to the move by becoming depressed?

Let's look at a variety of theories from psychology, sociology, and anthropology. At the end of each section, we will use concepts from the theory to interpret parts of the case.

BOX 2.1 Family on the Move: A Manager's Transfers Impose Heavy Burden on His Wife, Children

AUSTIN, Texas—Barbara Klaskin stares hard at her left tennis shoe and talks about her moves from Hyattsville, Md., to Beltsville, Md., to Tujunga, Calif., to Wheaton, Md., to Randolph Township, N.J., to the Marshall Islands, to Potomac, Md., to here. She is 13 years old.

"I don't feel I have a home anywhere," she says, sitting stiffly on her living-room sofa, "because I've grown up in so many different places, y'know? And I don't really want to go back anywhere because I don't think that would feel too great."

Her father, Roy Klaskin, 42, holds a middle-management job at International Business Machines Corp., which transferred him here last spring. He knows that the numerous transfers he has made in his career have wounded his family. "There's a loss," he says. "I can't measure it."

Mr. Klaskin and his wife, Leona, were born and raised in Brooklyn. The move here was the seventh for Barbara, the eighth for her 16 year old brother, Howard, and the ninth for Mr. and Mrs. Klaskin since their marriage 20 years ago. As has always been true, the Klaskin family is having difficulty adjusting to its latest move.

Every year, companies transfer hundreds of thousands of employees. Many, like Roy Klaskin, are relatively young men with school-age children. The Employee Relocation Council, a Washington consulting firm, says 96% of transferred employees are men; about half of them are in their 30's, and about one-third have children aged six to 18. Almost 40% of the transferred employees have moved at least four times in their careers.

Generally, of course, a transfer benefits both the company and the employee. It usually means a promotion, resulting in increased status, more challenging work and a bigger paycheck. For companies, transfers are a way to season young executives by giving them varied management experience and familiarizing them with the company's operations in the field.

A Heavy Price

But the nomadic existence of America's managers sometimes exacts a heavy price, and most of it is paid by the wives and children of the men who are transferred.

Ronald Raymond, a Wilton, Conn., psychologist who specializes in helping such families, says a basic problem is the "loss of credentials" that wives and children undergo in moving. The husband enters the new community as a success, his status enhanced by his new job. Wives and children lack such symbols. "Suppose a teen-aged football player has rushed for 1,000 yards in a season," says Mr. Raymond. "How does he apply that credential in a new community without sounding like a braggart?"

For a close look at the stresses arising in a family because of a transfer, a reporter visited the Klaskins here and talked with each of them about the experience.

Barbara

After a painful adjustment in the fifth grade, Barbara seemed to blossom in the sixth and seventh grades. She had a lot of friends. Now she recalls fondly the times in Potomac when she always had someone to talk to, go to the movies with, or just "hack around" with at a nearby shopping mall, wandering among the shops and munching junk food.

For several months here in Austin, she didn't have any friends. She tells of boys taunting her at school, ripping up her papers, knocking over her books. She became especially angry after school officials fumbled some paper work from Maryland and thus forced her to repeat a three-hour standardized test. She turned sullen and withdrawn, and she dumped most of her anger on her father.

"It's all your fault," she would shout at him. When he tried to encourage her to form friendships in Austin, she shouted: "I have all the friends I'm ever going to get. There's no way I'm ever going to get any more. Leave me alone." Although she hadn't strongly opposed the move in the discussions back in Potomac, she now felt she had been "cornered" by other family members into acquiescing.

Mrs. Klaskin says it took Barbara nearly six months to find a close friend. The two girls started going to movies together, and Barbara seemed happier.

But Barbara still hasn't adjusted to the different atmosphere at the junior high school she attends here. In Potomac, girls her age dressed much like the boys, which suited her just fine. She favors tennis shoes, blue jeans and rolled-up sleeves. In Austin, however, girls her age attend school in stockings, high heels, below-the-knee dresses and fake furs. They have elaborate "Farrah Fawcett" hairdos, and they're learning to use makeup, sometimes to excess.

Barbara has been bothered for months by a stomach problem. She believes it is probably "from living here." A doctor says she may be getting an ulcer, but her mother, although genuinely worried, doubts that diagnosis. On one point, however, Barbara's mother says she does agree with the doctor. "He said it's hard to be 13 anywhere, but it's particularly hard when you're where you don't want to be."

Howard

To hear Howard Klaskin tell it, a 16 year old boy's life is pretty much the same wherever he lives. "There's nothing here that's really that much different from back East," he says. "The teen-age mind is programmed to do the same thing everywhere, I feel."

He acknowledges differences between the high school here and the one in Potomac. There, for example, drugs were prevalent at school. "I could just walk into the hall and see kids giving each other money and drugs. It got so open I couldn't believe it. In every class there was somebody who was a drug freak. He wore the same clothes every day, and he stunk. The kid stunk like one big cigarette."

At L. C. Anderson High School here, Howard says, there's hardly any drug use. But there is a lot of chewing tobacco. He says that either students have wads of it in their mouths or they have spit it in a variety of places: in water coolers, the corners of classrooms and garbage cans. "They even have announcements in class: 'Don't chew tobacco in class.'"

Howard gives the impression he is taking these changes and various others in stride. He doesn't want to talk much about the first few months here, but other family members say he found the move about as troubling as the rest of them.

His parents recall that shortly after he arrived in Austin, he became depressed. Like the other family members, he had difficulty adjusting to Austin life and finding friends. It is his nature to clown and joke a lot, they say, but in those first months he was hostile and withdrawn.

After weeks of relative silence, says his mother, one night at the dinner table, Howard suddenly announced in a bitter tone—and using a graphic teen-age slang term—that he had decided he disliked Austin. Each night for a while, he repeated the basic conclusion, wording it a bit differently each time and enumerating fresh examples of what he found objectionable about Austin life.

Leona Klaskin

Mrs. Klaskin sips coffee at her kitchen table here and recalls that distant afternoon when she and her husband drove from Brooklyn to what now is Elmwood Park, N.J.—their first move. "It seemed like we were going to the other end of the world," she says; when she was a youngster, "to go to the Bronx was an adventure."

Nine moves later, she is tired of moving. She says the moves probably have worsened an ailment she has had since childhood: She grinds her teeth. "Other people get upset," Mrs. Klaskin says. "They throw things or they yell and scream. I have a fairly even temperament, and I just grind my teeth." It has taken a year of painful gum and root-canal work, as well as 13 caps, to restore her mouth. While she is sleeping or when she is working intently at something like painting a chair, she wears a retainer to preserve her teeth.

There have been other costs for her. "I've given up personal things," she says, "in the sense of a career, for example. You really can't do that when you move around." Her husband tends to blame himself for that. "In a way," he says, "I deliberately sacrificed her career." (She holds teacher certificates from two states and the Marshall Islands.) "Now it would be very hard for her to compete with the new teachers coming out of college," Mr. Klaskin says.

The stresses of setting up a new household fell most heavily on Mrs. Klaskin. In the move, lamps were shattered, sofas were ripped, dresser legs were broken, bikes were bent. Barbara's piano, a gift from Mrs. Klaskin's parents, arrived in pieces. Additionally, the movers lost the family's station wagon. When it was retrieved six weeks later, it was saturated with the putrid odor of 50 house plants that had rotted while stored inside.

The Klaskin home here is an old house, in an established neighborhood, and those factors turned out to have a depressing effect on her. The house was so dirty that during the lengthy cleanup period, she tacked a beach towel to the wall behind her bed so her pillow wouldn't touch the dirt. She believes the neighborhood's established character contributed to her difficulty in finding friends.

Mrs. Klaskin recognizes the importance of the moves to her husband, but she believes he would be more content if he accepted the viewpoint she expressed to him during those first weeks here. "I told him that in his own way, he'd reached some sort of success," she says—"that he's never going to be president of the company and that he ought to accept that. If he could accept that, he could be happier."

As for future moves, Mrs. Klaskin says, "I would go anyplace with my husband, truthfully." But later, as they are joking together, she declares, "Roy's got one more move left, and that's it." Then she turns to her husband and playfully brandishes a fist.

Roy Klaskin

It began with job frustration. In late 1977, while living in Potomac, Mr. Klaskin started feeling that his work as an IBM senior programmer wasn't sufficiently interesting. Mrs. Klaskin says she noticed signs of boredom: He stopped working as late, and he rarely brought work home.

But when IBM mentioned the possibility of making him manager of the systems assurance department here, he was hesitant, despite the more challenging work at a higher salary. He thought immediately, he recalls, of the problems his family already had suffered because of what he calls his "restlessness."

Eventually, though, he decided he wanted the job, and he began discussing it with his family. None of the family members knew much about Austin, but each could think of reasons that the move was appealing. The Klaskins had never become attached to Potomac, the Washington suburb where they lived. Life there was hectic, and they disliked the showy affluence of the community. Several of their friends had moved away, further reducing the Klaskins' attachment to the area. With Howard acting as Austin's chief advocate in these family councils—a role he soon regretted—the Klaskins finally agreed to make the move.

A year later, Mr. Klaskin sits in his comfortable three-bedroom home here on a picturesque acre of land, and reflects on the decision. "You wonder," he says, "whether the move you make is really good for your family. You wonder what the trade-offs are." He regrets that his children never really got to know his father, who died recently. "To never know one's grandparents very well is a shame," he says.

And he is especially sensitive about his daughter's moodiness—her hair-trigger temper, crying spells and tendency to bolt into her bedroom when she is upset. He suspects that she plays on his sensitivity. "It's a little trick that little girls innately understand," he says.

The first few weeks after the move were especially hard for him because that's when his family seemed to have the roughest time. He became, "quite lethargic," he recalls. "I would just sit on that beautiful porch there and watch that beautiful sunset. I felt that I'd really fouled up the family this time. The job wasn't worth it. What's the use of succeeding at work when I've screwed up my family?"

Psychoanalytic Theory

Psychoanalytic theory as it was formulated by Sigmund Freud focuses primarily on emotional and personality development (Freud, 1953–1974).

Sigmund Freud (1856–1939)

For our purposes, five concepts are of special interest in understanding adult development. First, this theory views all behavior, except perhaps some events that are the product of fatigue, as an expression of two primary motives: sexuality and aggression. When we try to understand behavior we must look beyond the overt, literal action to its symbolic meaning for the person. While these motives guide behavior, their influence is indirect. For most adults, sexual and aggressive motives are satisfied through a process called sublimation. Sublimation refers to the direction of energy from infantile or socially unacceptable desires to socially acceptable behaviors. Examples of sublimation might include chopping wood as an outlet for aggression, or writing romantic novels as an expression of sexual impulses.

A second concept is the idea of the unconscious. Even though all behavior is motivated, we are not always readily aware of these motives. Frequently, we think our behavior has one purpose when, in fact, it satisfies many needs. Psychoanalytic theory suggests that the original wishes and motives that emerge intensely during childhood, especially during the first five or six years of life, continue to influence behavior because they become part of the unconscious. Wishes and fantasies about sexuality and aggression are frightening and difficult for children to understand. They may also be treated as unacceptable by parents, and, therefore, they become unacceptable to the child. Strong desires and restrictions against expressing these desires become too much for the child to cope with emotionally. In order to protect the child from being overwhelmed by these conflicts they are kept from awareness through the mechanism of repression. Repression pushes thoughts out of awareness and holds them in the unconscious. While the unconscious guides behavior, it does so indirectly. Direct expression of impulses is not possible, distortions of unconscious conflicts slip through the barrier created by repression and are admitted into consciousness in symbolic forms. Only through slips of the tongue, free associations, the content of dreams, and interpretation of psychological symptoms can these conflicts be identified.

Adult behavior continues to be guided by an array of childhood desires and fears that remain in the unconscious. Even conscientious introspection will not reveal these "unacceptable" motives. Only through psychotherapy can these wishes and fears be uncovered. The implication is that there is a predictable quality of irrationality in every adult. No matter how self-aware one may be, the content of the unconscious continues to generate behaviors that may not make sense to the objective observer.

The third concept is Freud's model of the structure of personality (see Figure 2.1). All people are influenced by the interaction among three components of personality: id, ego, and superego. Id is the source of all impulse. Id is present at birth and provides a specific energy level that maintains all psychological functioning. The content of id is wishes or impulses. Most of the id's content remains in the unconscious. *Ego* is the reality-oriented function. Ego is capable of many functions, including perceiving, remembering, planning, and negotiating. Ego's primary function is to figure out ways of meeting id's demands or expressing id's wishes without bringing harm to the person or upsetting superego.

FIGURE 2.1 Freud's Model of the Structure of Personality

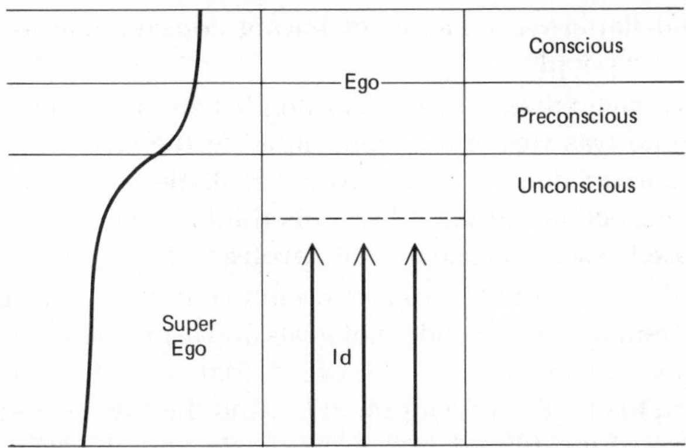

Superego is conscience plus the ego ideal. It serves an affirming, positive role in the form of the ego ideal and a punishing or threatening role as conscience. The ego ideal is a composite of all those qualities the person most admires and strives to become. Conscience comprises all those prohibitions related to moral wrongdoings. As id impulses press for expression, superego sends an alert if the behavior is going to violate a moral standard. This alert is usually in the form of anxiety and guilt. Ego's job is to try to find ways of expressing id impulses without arousing superego.

The fourth concept is the notion of identification. Psychoanalytic theory suggests that beginning in childhood and continuing through adulthood, we incorporate the observable characteristics and personal values of people whom we either love, admire, or fear. Whether it is due to one or all of these motives, we modify our own behaviors and beliefs in order to become more similar to significant others. Identification may take place consciously in adulthood, as we shape our life-style after the example of an admired hero. It may also take place unconsciously through our desire to have the kinds of gratifications that we think another person is enjoying.

Almost the opposite of identification is transference. Whereas in identification we take characteristics of another as our own, in transference we project characteristics of our relationship with one person onto another. The concept of transference is central to the process of psychoanalysis. Because of transference, qualities of the patient's family relationships unfold in the way the patient relates to a therapist. A therapist can then use the content of these interactions to help the patient recognize aspects of his or her own unconscious constructs.

The concepts of identification and transference are important not only because adults experience them, but because adults are the objects for these processes in others. As teachers, community leaders, bosses, or parents, adults are the "significant others" for many younger people. In this sense, one becomes sensitive to the burden of responsibility to provide an admirable model. For identification one can also be drawn into the attractive and flattering situation of having considerable influnce in the lives of younger people.

Psychoanalytic theory has been extended and revised by a number of theorists. Freud was very much committed to the basic principles of the theory as he formulated them. He was not at all pleased when a member of his circle of colleagues deviated from his thinking. One of the most bitter conflicts arose between Freud and his protégé Carl Jung.

Jung's theory differed from Freud's in two major respects. First, Jung (1960) saw personality as a product of goals and aspirations as well as needs and past experiences. Jung emphasized that a search for a sense of wholeness led to creative development beyond the satisfaction of primitive needs. Second, Jung placed major emphasis on the racial and species

Carl Jung (1875–1961)

inheritance as factors influencing personality. He described what he called the *collective unconscious* as a reservoir of predispositions. He argued that each person has both a personal unconscious that is a product of his or her own life experiences and a collective unconscious inherited from previous generations.

Jung (1953) equated the self with the striving for unity or totality. The symbol of the mandala or magic circle is Jung's analogy for the integration and balance of many opposing forces into one unified whole. The self is not fully developed until middle age. Before that time, the many elements of personality require time to emerge and be expressed. During midlife, the goal of the self is to find some balance among the diverse components of personality—one's masculine and feminine qualities; one's dominant and submissive qualities; one's good and evil qualities. This process of personal integration requires confronting many of the myths, fears, and wishes of the unconscious and bringing them into conscious thought.

Case Application

What are some of the elements of the Klaskin case that might be clarified through psychoanalytic theory? We want to emphasize that these interpretations are our applications of the theory to the case. They are presented to illustrate how one might use theoretical concepts to answer questions about a set of observations. The different theories will lead to different interpretations. This fact should serve to alert you to the idea that complex social behavior must be understood from many perspectives or levels at once.

Perhaps the most puzzling question is why Mr. Klaskin continues to accept offers to move, even when he realizes these moves place stress on his family. Several hypotheses might be suggested from a psychoanalytic perspective. First, we might assume that for Mr. Klaskin, the corporation symbolizes the loved parent. Through active efforts to socialize its employees, the corporation dangles the promises of approval, companionship, and security. As a corporate executive, Mr. Klaskin has come to identify with the corporation; its goals have become his goals. When he learns of a new corporate need he becomes more and more motivated to try to satisfy that need. At the same time, Mr. Klaskin has transferred certain feelings about his parents to the corporation. He assumes that the corporation is benevolent, that it looks out for his best interest, and that it is really committed to meeting his needs.

As a parent substitute, the corporation places a barrier in the way of Mr. Klaskin's ego development. It continues to confront him with standards and expectations that are external to his own needs. It reinforces the unrealistic demands of both the superego and the ego ideal by creating an image of the ideal executive toward which Mr. Klaskin is striving. In this sense, the corporate executives exploit the strength of Mr. Klaskin's identification and his transference by encouraging him to put the promises of corporate advancement above commitments to family.

A second hypothesis is that the moves are motivated by unconscious hostility toward his wife and children. This view would argue that Mr. Klaskin perceives the strains that each move place on his family and that he is unconsciously gratified by their pain. Insofar as the moves are initiated by his career goals, one might argue that he has split his feelings directing all the loving, productive energy to the corporation and the hostile, destructive energy toward the family. The fact that there are so many examples of hostility in the rest of the family members would support the interpretation that Mr. Klaskin's choices have had a hostile, frustrating quality.

Turning to Mrs. Klaskin, one might ask why she accepts the frustrations of this life situation. The psychoanalytic view would emphasize females' underlying feelings of inferiority. Freud (1953) argued that at a very early age, young girls are sensitive to the discrepancy in the male and female anatomy. He called this the Electra conflict. Girls feel envious about the penis, seeing this body part as a vital source of satisfaction and power. The early consequence of penis envy is the rejection of the mother and desire for the father. Through marriage and the bearing of male children, women achieve the penis they never had. Through their identification with males women achieve vicarious completion of the great loss they have suffered because of their femininity. The psychoanalytic view suggests that the female can never forgive her mother, whom she blames for her deficiency, nor can she ever feel fully accepting of herself. Therefore, women are likely to enact a life of self-derogation and masochism that is both punishment for their continuous desire to have a penis and for their self-hate for not having one. Mrs. Klaskin's self-sacrifice and anger can be interpreted in this way. Because she doesn't value herself, she subordinates her needs to the needs of her husband. Her sense of worth is enhanced vicariously through identification with her husband's achievements.

Barbara Klaskin is in the period of early adolescence, a time when Electra conflicts and strong sexual impulses are reawakened. Barbara's anger at her father can be viewed as a defense against her strong sexualized fantasies of an exclusive relationship with him. Both children show evidence of identification with the same-sex parent in their reaction to the move. Barbara is angry and stews inside like Leona. Howard is depressed and withdraws like Roy.

Psychosocial Theory

Like Jung, Erik Erikson was strongly influenced by Freud's work. Erikson (1963) developed a theory in which development is viewed as a product of the interactions between personal competences and motives, and the social expectations for accomplishments at each stage of development. The word "psychosocial" emphasizes the idea of the person and the society. In this orientation, culture contributes significantly to growth. Cultures impose restrictions on the expression of certain motives and emotions. Cultures establish patterns of social relationships to which the person must adapt. The development of the person is intimately connected with the society. Psychosocial theory differs from the psychoanalytic tradition by emphasizing a strong role for the person in contributing to his or her development. Through the exercise of competences and through the life choices that are made, people shape the course of their lives. The theory also directs our attention to the entire life span, emphasizing the possibility for new growth throughout adult life.

Psychosocial theory is based on five organizing concepts: (1) stages of development; (2) developmental tasks; (3) the psychosocial crisis; (4) the central process for resolving crisis; and (5) coping behavior. The concept of stages was introduced in Chapter 1. The *stages* refer to periods of life when behavior is dominated by a particular organization or perspective. An assumption of this and other stage theories is that the development that takes place at one stage will have significant impact on subsequent stages. The achievements of each stage are necessary for the next phase of

Erik Erikson (1902–   )

development to occur. Erikson described the life span in eight stages from infancy through old age. Newman and Newman (1979) have added a ninth stage, dividing adolescence into an early phase with a focus on group identity and a later phase with a focus on personal identity. These stages are listed in Table 2.1.

Other theorists working within a psychosocial framework have differentiated additional psychosocial stages during adulthood. Robert Peck (1955) attempted to refine Erikson's stages by proposing seven stages during the years from 30 to death. In his work, the process of ego development during adulthood is given greater emphasis (see Table 2.2).

Work by Daniel Levinson (1977; Levinson Darrow, Klein, Levinson, & McKee, 1978) and Roger Gould (1972, 1975, 1978) has also added detail to Erikson's stage analysis. Their research focused on the adult years from about 20 to 50. In different research projects with different subjects, both researchers identified five transition points of early and middle adulthood (see Table 2.3). The characteristics of Levinson's adult stages focus heavily on the interaction of the person with the world of work. There is a strong goal-oriented focus to his description. This may be a reflection of the fact that Levinson's subjects were all males. Gould's stages focus more heavily on changes in self-insight and personal philosophy. Gould's stages reflect

TABLE 2.1 The Nine Stages of the Life Span

Life Stage	Developmental Tasks	Psychosocial Crises
Infancy (birth to 2 years)	1. Social attachment 2. Sensorimotor intelligence and primitive causality 3. Object permanence 4. Maturation of motor functions	Trust versus mistrust
Toddlerhood (2–4)	1. Self-control 2. Language development 3. Fantasy and play 4. Elaboration of locomotion	Autonomy versus shame and doubt
Early school age (5–7)	1. Sex role identification 2. Early moral development 3. Concrete operations 4. Group play	Initiative versus guilt
Middle school age (8–12)	1. Social cooperation 2. Self-evaluation 3. Skill learning 4. Team play	Industry versus inferiority
Early adolescence (13–17)	1. Physical maturation 2. Formal operations 3. Membership in the peer group 4. Heterosexual relationships	Group identity versus alienation
Later adolescence (18–22)	1. Autonomy from parents 2. Sex role identity 3. Internalized morality 4. Career choice	Individual identity versus role diffusion
Early adulthood (23–30)	1. Marriage 2. Childbearing 3. Work 4. Life style	Intimacy versus isolation
Middle adulthood (31–50)	1. Management of the household 2. Child rearing 3. Management of a career	Generativity versus stagnation
Later adulthood (51–)	1. Redirection of energy to new roles 2. Acceptance of one's life 3. Developing a point of view about death	Integrity versus despair

Source: Based on E. Erikson, *Childhood and Society Second Edition.* (New York: Norton, 1963); and B. Newman & P. Newman, *Development through Life* (Homewood, Ill.: Dorsey, 1979).

changing feelings of depression and self-worth as the person confronts his or her own personality during adulthood.

Developmental tasks refer to a set of skills and competences that are

TABLE 2.2 Robert Peck's Psychosocial Stages for the Second Half of Life

Middle Age

1. Valuing Wisdom vs. Valuing Physical Powers—The emphasis on using one's good judgment and wisdom rather than physical strength and "good looks" to solve problems and to define one's self-worth.
2. Socializing vs. Sexualizing in Human Relationships—The emphasis in interpersonal relationships shifts from viewing others as sex-objects to viewing others as valued individuals.
3. Cathectic Flexibility vs. Cathectic Impoverishment—The emphasis on flexible emotional commitments reflects the reality that many middle adults experience at the death of their parents, loss of and loosening of ties with friends or relatives through death or moving, and loosening of ties with children. The conflict is between expanding investment to a new and wider circle of associates or becoming increasingly isolated.
4. Mental Flexibility vs. Mental Rigidity—A tension between retaining an open, questioning mind and relying on the experiences and lessons of the past.

Old Age

1. Ego Differentiation vs. Work-Role Preoccupation—The ability to develop a set of valued activities and attributes separate from the primary roles of worker or parent.
2. Body Transcendence vs. Body Preoccupation—The emphasis is on finding pleasure and satisfaction in social interactions and intellectual activities that are not hindered by the discomforts of aging and illness.
3. Ego Transcendence vs. Ego Preoccupation—The capacity to find satisfaction in contributing to the lives of others so that one's own death feels less important, less a final close to one's impact.

Source: Adapted from "Psychological Developments in the Second Half of Life" by R. C. Peck, in B. L. Neugarten (Ed.), *Middle Age and Aging* (Chicago: University of Chicago Press, 1968), pp. 88–92.

acquired as the person gains increased mastery over the environment. The concept of developmental tasks was developed by Robert Havighurst (1972). The tasks reflect gains in physical skills, intellectual skills, social skills, and emotional skills. Mastery of the tasks of later stages often depends on successful acquisition of earlier and simpler skills. Generally, developmental tasks are linked to the specific expectations of the culture. Thus, while marriage is a matter that Americans do not usually become involved in until young adulthood, some cultures expect marriage to occur during early adolescence. Similarly, team play may not be a task of every society. Developing a point of view about death may be a task of a much earlier stage in cultures where the spirits of dead persons play a large role in daily life activities.

The *psychosocial crisis* refers to the person's psychological efforts to adjust to the demands of the social environment at each stage of development. The word *"crisis"* in this context refers to a normal set of stresses and strains rather than to an extraordinary set of events. The theory postulates that at each stage of development the society within which one lives makes certain psychic demands upon the individual. These demands differ from stage to stage. The demands are experienced as mild but persistent guidelines and expectations for behavior. Near the end of a

TABLE 2.3 Phases of Adult Life

Levinson	Ages[1]	Gould
Early adult transition: Moving out of preadult world Experimenting and choosing adult roles	17–22 (18–21)	Growing independence from family, openness to new ideas
Entering the adult world: Exploring options Developing a stable life structure	22–28 (22–28)	Stabilization of concerns, autonomous, engaged in work, confident
The age 30 transition: Making efforts to improve or correct the life structure Peaking of marital problems and occupational shifts	28–33 (29–36)	Increasing dissatisfactions, more self-reflection, dissatisfaction with marriage, increasing investment in children
Settling down: Establishing a niche and "making it" Identifying the steps on the ladder of success; strives to achieve authority and independence Reappraising goals and achievements	33–40 (37–43)	Quiet desperation, time is finite, concerns about health increase, concerns arise about one's own parents
Midlife transition: Neglected areas of self press for expression and the life structure is modified	40–45 (44–50)	Stabilization of personality, increased involvement with spouse, children and friends; an acceptance of the way things are

[1]Ages on top from Levinson, in parentheses from Gould.

Source: Adapted from R. Gould, *Transformations* (New York: Simon and Schuster, 1978); and D. J. Levinson, C. M. Darrow, E. B. Klein, M. H. Levinson, & B. McKee, *The Seasons of a Man's Life.* (New York: Knopf, 1978).

particular stage of development, people are forced to make some type of resolution. They strive to adjust to the demands of society while simultaneously translating the societal demands into personal terms.

This process produces a state of tension within the individual that must be reduced in order for the person to proceed to the next stage. It is this tension state that is called the psychosocial crisis. The psychosocial crisis of a stage forces the person to utilize developmental skills that have only recently been mastered. There is, therefore, an interrelationship between the developmental tasks of each stage and the psychosocial crisis of that stage. In addition, resolutions of previous crises influence resolutions of current and future crises.

The crisis of each stage of development, from infancy through later adulthood, is expressed as a polarity—trust versus mistrust, autonomy versus shame and doubt—suggesting the nature of a successful or unsuccessful resolution of the crisis. The likelihood of a completely unsuccessful resolution is quite small. However, some element of the negative pole is expected to be experienced by each person in an effort to confront and resolve the crisis of each stage. We see the negative poles of each crisis as offering important opportunities for understanding oneself and one's social environment. For example, one would not recommend a steady diet of mistrust, yet it is important to be able to evaluate situations and people for their trustworthiness. One must be able to recognize the cues that are being sent about the safety or benevolence of an encounter. It is an advantage to be able to anticipate that in some settings or some relationships others may not be concerned for one's own needs or welfare. In every psychosocial crisis, the experiences that are relevant to the negative pole contribute to the total range of adaptive capacities that the person acquires.

Coping behavior refers to active efforts to resolve stress and to create new solutions to the challenges of each developmental stage. White (1974) identified three components of the coping process: (1) the ability to gain and process new information; (2) the ability to maintain control over one's emotional state; and (3) the ability to move freely within one's environment (see Figure 2.2). Coping can be understood as behaviors that allow for the development and growth of the individual, not merely the maintenance of equilibrium in the face of threat. Consider the example of coping with retirement. Adults who begin to plan for their retirement by getting information about senior-citizen programs, by developing new areas of interest and skill, or by talking with friends who have retired about the problems they have encountered are all showing evidence of coping that will increase their information and their sense of control when the change in work pattern takes place.

Individuals create their own strategies for coping with life challenges. The variation in coping styles reflects the talents and motives of the person as well as the responses of relevant others toward a particular strategy. Think of the first day of school for a group of 5–year-old kindergartners. Some children sit shyly watching the teacher and other children. Other children are clambering over all the equipment and chasing around to touch new toys. Still other children are talking to the teacher or to the other children, finding out names, making friends, or telling about the bus ride to school. Each of these strategies can be understood as a way of

FIGURE 2.2 Three Components of Coping

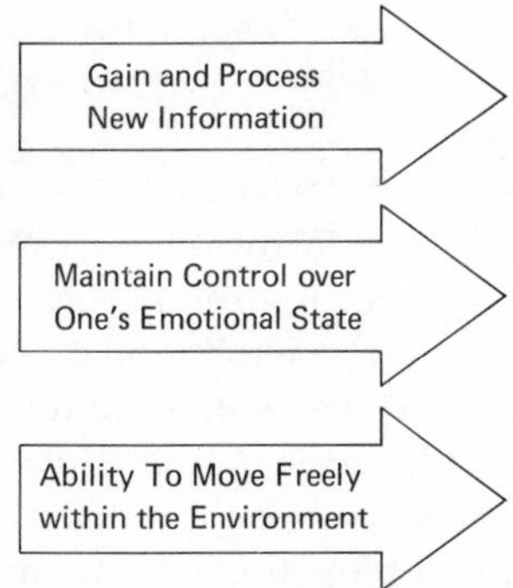

gathering information while preserving a degree of autonomy and integrity in a new and potentially threatening environment. No one way is right or even best except insofar as it serves the person, allowing access to information, freedom of movement, and some control over the emotions evoked by the new challenge. This same diversity of coping strategies continues into adulthood. Adults may feel stronger pressures to cope in ways that appear effective or socially acceptable. They strive to appear independent, decisive, or brave rather than anxious, dependent, or timid. Adults can, however, cope by choosing to leave a situation or by refusing to be influenced by certain authority figures, where a child may be forced to remain in a situation and absorb the realities as best as possible.

Case Application

In the case of the Klaskins we see four family members, two at the stage of middle adulthood, one at the beginning of early adolescence, and one at the end of early adolescence. The parents, Leona and Roy, are clearly involved in the crisis of generativity versus stagnation. They are engrossed in some serious questioning about the purpose or meaning of their lives. Leona is confronting the reality that she has given up certain opportunities for making important contributions beyond the family in order to achieve the intimacy of early adulthood. Roy is asking himself about the value of these career moves. To what extent have they benefited anyone? Most important, to what extent have they benefited or harmed his offspring?

These are normal, if somewhat painful, questions that emerge from the crisis of generativity versus stagnation. They reflect these two adults' appreciation of the "bigger picture" of life's purpose. The moves, especially this recent one, may have precipitated the probing and questioning. However, psychosocial theory would suggest that a certain amount of tension is predictable during middle adulthood as adults strive to confront the society's expectation that they make a contribution to the quality of life for the next generation. We can interpret the feelings of discouragement and frustration as part of the process of evolving a philosophy of life within the very real framework of particular commitments to work, spouse, and children.

Given that every life situation is dotted with difficulties and conflicts, the pain that the Klaskins are experiencing can be viewed as normal developmental anxiety. It reflects their realization that there is a need to clarify life goals and reevaluate priorities. Life does not go on forever. If the choices that have been made in the past are not bringing fulfillment, then there is a feeling of urgency about making certain that future life choices will bring them closer to their aspirations.

For the adults in the Klaskin family the crises are due to the adults' own desire to change and grow. Bringing life choices to the light for examination and evaluation creates an instability that can be extremely troubling. In the Klaskins' case, seeds of doubt about the value of the life they have led are the prods to new growth. While we do not see it in the case, we can expect that the questioning that is going on might lead the way to new, more creative, and more authentic definitions of family, marriage, and work commitments.

Fulfillment Theory

A number of theorists take the idea of people's contributing to their own development a step further than psychosocial theory. They emphasize the purposive, goal-oriented strivings that characterize adult life. People do not always behave in order to reduce tension or to achieve an equilibrium. They seek out challenges, give up security for risk, and impose new and difficult standards on themselves in pursuit of some illusive quality that we call fulfillment.

Charlotte Buhler was one of the earliest and most continuously productive of the humanistic or fulfillment theorists. Her work emphasizes the centrality of life goals and intentionality through the life course (Buhler & Massarik, 1968). In her view, each person experiences life within a complex orientation to past, present, and future time. It is the hope for meeting future goals and for achieving a sense of fulfillment that prompts psychological growth. Buhler saw the years of early and middle adulthood (from about 25 to 50) as a time of setting definite goals and striving to achieve them. Toward the end of middle adulthood, there is focused preoccupation with the assessment of goals and an analysis of successes and failures. This process ends with a sense of fulfillment, partial fulfillment, or despair in later adulthood (at 60 or 65).

The last phase of life (after age 65) is seen as a reaction to this assessment. People may resign themselves to their successes and failures (as Erikson suggests in the concept of integrity). However, some people may be motivated to return to an earlier phase of striving to achieve unfulfilled goals or to undo past failures. Some people end their lives in a despondent state of unfulfillment. They feel that existence has not been meaningful.

Three concepts are of special interest as we think about the Klaskins from the point of view of the fulfillment theories: competence, self-acceptance, and self-actualization. Robert White (1960, 1966) has used the term "competence motivation" to explain behaviors that are motivated toward growth. *Competence* refers to any area of skill that increases one's control over self or over the environment. Every person strives to increase his or her competence through repetition and practice or skills, by gaining new information, through education and training, and through feedback from earlier efforts at mastery. The competence motive can be seen in an infant's efforts at self-feeding even when those efforts result in less food

Carl Rogers (1902–

making the way from dish to mouth. The competence motive can be seen in the determination of an adult to learn to ski despite the cold, the expense, and the muscle pain. It can be seen when retired persons enroll in adult education courses. Often, these adult students seek no degree but express a commitment to new learning for its own sake. In general, the competence motive is used to explain the considerable effort and energy that is expended in the acquisition of new skills. The reward for those efforts is the new achievement and its accompanying contribution to a sense of personal effectiveness.

The second concept, *self-acceptance,* comes from Carl Rogers' (1959, 1961) theory of personality development. An essential component of continued growth is to experience and accept the authentic self. This means achieving a sense of trust in one's ideas and impulses rather than denying or constantly disapproving of them. It means fostering acceptance and trust in relationships with others so that people bring their most authentic selves to interactions. Self-acceptance is a product of the positive feelings that come from being direct and from the acceptance one receives from others. In Rogers' view, barriers to self acceptance come largely from the conditions others place on their love or approval. If others will only give approval when you say certain things or act in a certain way, then you quickly learn to modify your behavior so that it conforms to those conditions. These modifications, however, are made at the price of self-acceptance. They lead a person into a pattern of inhibiting or rejecting new thoughts and relying more and more on the opinions of others. The greater the discrepancy between the authentic self as the person perceives it and daily experience, the more the person is likely to experience life as threatening and stressful. The greater the harmony between the authentic self and experience, the more likely the person is to experience a sense of trust, freedom, and creativity in daily functioning.

The third concept in a fulfillment theory is Abraham Maslow's (1968) notion of *self-actualization*. Self-actualization is a powerful, growth-oriented motive that sits atop a pyramid of needs (see Figure 2.3). In Maslow's view, humans are always in a state of striving. Primary human motives concern physiological needs and safety needs. As those are satisfied and maintained at a relatively comfortable level, belongingness needs and self-esteem needs emerge. If those needs are also satisfied, if the person experiences both love and respect, then energy is focused on self-actualization. This motive is a press toward making optimal use of one's fullest potential, toward becoming the most effective and creative life participant possible. The self-actualization motive continuously urges the person to become more, even to the point of risking lower needs in order to maximize one's potential.

Case Application

What does one learn by applying the perspective of fulfillment theories to the case of the Klaskins? Perhaps Roy's restlessness at work and his desire for a more challenging position can be understood as expressions of the need to experience competence and self-actualization. We can assume that the work domain is the primary realm where Roy Klaskin will attempt to satisfy his growth-oriented motives. Roy's achievement strivings are not being unconditionally rewarded either at work or at home. Roy does not seem to be able to arrive at clear feelings of self-acceptance. There is continuing discrepancy between his own pleasure and pride in work activities and the realities of both the corporation that has placed some

FIGURE 2.3 Maslow's Hierarchy of Needs

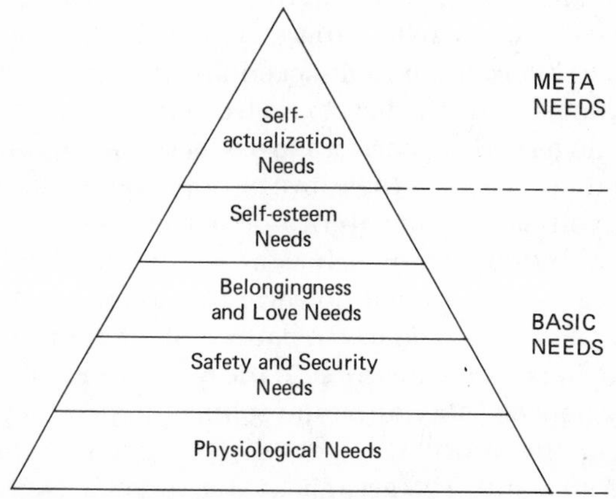

Abraham Maslow (1908–1970)

limit to his success and the family that resents the imposition of constant moving on their life pattern.

For Leona, the importance of belongingness needs appear to have preempted self-actualization. Although we can assume that she finds outlets for competence in her activities in the household and in childrearing, it is clear that she perceives herself as having "given up" some important personal goals in order to preserve her marriage. Ultimately, that choice also interferes with self-acceptance. It creates a continuous tension between what Leona must believe she is truly capable of achieving and what she actually experiences day to day.

Barbara's belongingness needs have clearly been disrupted. She has lost her peer group as a result of the recent move. The sense of unconditional acceptance that was an important part of her peer relationships in Maryland is deeply missed. Barbara is caught in a situation of needing peers to support her self-acceptance, but rejecting the peer values of her new cohort.

Both Leona and Roy are involved in an assessment of the extent to which their life-style is inhibiting or fostering personal fulfillment. Their children's unhappiness may be an important symptom prompting this reassessment. Roy is becoming more sensitive to the impact his choices

Ivan Pavlov (1848–1936)

have had on his wife and children. Leona is becoming more uncomfortable with the restrictions she has placed on her own strivings. With the children emerging into adolescence, there are growing concerns about values, commitments, and life goals. It becomes increasingly important for Leona and Roy to have their life goals specified so that they can facilitate the actualization of their children. The entire family can be seen as on the verge of a new commitment to personal fulfillment through the exercise of competence, the reaffirmation of self-acceptance, and the commitment to opening up new avenues for self-actualization.

Behavioral Learning Theory

Behavioral learning theories assume that behavior is learned in response to conditions in the environment. Three theories of learning have important implications for adult development: classical conditioning; instrumental conditioning; and social learning theory.

The principles of classical conditioning were developed by Ivan Pavlov (1960). When two events occur very close together in time, they come to have similar meaning and to produce similar responses. If you normally eat dinner at six o'clock, you begin to feel hunger pangs at that time of the day. The time six o'clock and the feeling of hunger become associated. If you are busily working and you lose track of time, then when you look up and see that it is six o'clock, you will suddenly feel hungry. When we switch from daylight savings time to standard time, six o'clock remains the time when you feel hungry, even though six o'clock comes an hour later.

Classical conditioning can account for a great deal of the associational learning that occurs throughout life. When a specific symbol is paired with an image, an emotional reaction, or an object, that symbol takes on new meaning. The associations that are made through classical conditioning may involve labels and concepts, but they do not necessarily require language skills. During infancy and toddlerhood, a variety of positive and negative emotional reactions are conditioned to people, objects, and environments. The reactions we retain about the taste of a certain type of food or the feel of a certain material are a result of conditioned learning that is preserved through adulthood. Similarly, certain fears can be a result of classical conditioning. Many people recall one frightful experience of a near drowning or falling from the top of a slide. The association of fear or pain with a specific target can lead to systematic avoidance of that object throughout life.

Operant or instrumental conditioning focuses on the function of reinforcement and punishment on learning. When the learner makes a desired response, it is reinforced. The reinforcement can be anything that increases the likelihood that the response will be repeated. B. F. Skinner (1938, 1974) has developed many of the theoretical principles that explain the conditions under which behavior can be changed through the systematic use of reinforcement.

According to this view of learning, the learner is highly flexible and adapts readily to the reinforcement conditions of the environment. Behaviors that are systematically reinforced are likely to be repeated. Behaviors that are ignored or punished are less likely to occur.

Behaviors can be learned under different schedules of reinforcement. Schedules of reinforcement refer to the frequency and regularity with which reinforcement is provided. A new response can be learned very quickly if it is reinforced every time it occurs. This is a 100 percent reinforcement schedule. Responses that are developed under a 100 percent reinforcement schedule are very vulnerable to extinction. This means that when no reinforcement is provided, the tendency toward that response weakens. In contrast, responses that are learned under variable conditions of reinforcement take longer to learn. However, these responses are more resistant to extinction. When reinforcement comes periodically and unpredictably, the tendency to make the response remains strong.

This condition of variable reinforcement is most like real life. We are not reinforced every time we make a desired response. A young girl learns to make her bed, wash her face, or say thank you under conditions of partial reinforcement. Even though many days go by when no one smiles

B. F. Skinner (1904–)

or praises her for making her bed, she continues to make it as long as she is praised once in a while. Of course, after some time, she can administer her own praise. She sees the well-made bed, admires its attractive appearance, and feels pleased at the outcome. Conditions that are repeatedly associated with reinforcements can become reinforcers themselves.

Both classical conditioning and operant conditioning include the concepts of generalization and discrimination as elements of learning. Generalization means that responses that are made to one stimulus will also be made to similar stimuli. A person who is conditioned to fear bees may also fear other flying insects like wasps, hornets, or horseflies. If the words "thank you" are reinforcing, they will be reinforcing regardless of the tone of voice, pitch, or even the dialect in which the words are spoken. Different words like "thanks," "thanks a lot," or "much obliged" can all serve the same reinforcing function. We do not need to learn the meaning of every situation separately. We use the capacity for generalization to apply previous learning to new, similar situations.

Discrimination is the opposite of generalization. Discrimination permits us to make very fine distinctions among similar stimuli. A child learns that "sit" is an acceptable word but "shit" is not. An adolescent learns that putting his hand on a girl's shoulder is acceptable but putting his hand a few inches lower is not. An adult learns that she can say "yes" to two cocktails and still function normally, but not to the third. Through a process of contingent reinforcement, people learn to respond to some situations and to inhibit responses to others.

We know that much of what we learn takes place without the deliberate manipulation of punishments and rewards. People learn a lot by observing the other important people in their lives (Bandura & Walters, 1963). In fact, if you think about all the things a young child of four can say and do, it is apparent that it would be impossible to deliberately teach all of it. Parents would have no time left in the day to eat, work, or sleep. Even then, it is doubtful that everything could be taught directly.

The concepts of social learning theory have been developed by Albert Bandura (1971, 1977). We tend to imitate models who have status or whose behavior has been reinforced by others. Much of this learning is motivated by the vicarious expectation that the rewards or status achieved by the models will also apply to us if we imitate their behavior. Sarah goes to a party and notices that another woman who is wearing an especially attractive outfit is the center of many men's attention. The next time Sarah is invited to a party, she gives more thought to her outfit and tries to create a look that is similar to the one she saw. You work in an office where the boss is very much concerned about maintaining close contact with his family. He calls home frequently, brings his children to the office from time to time, and frequently talks about his family. As a result of his modeling family commitment, the other workers in the office also try hard to let their families know about their work and try to bridge the gap between home and work.

In adulthood, the process of social learning is important for two reasons. First, adults continue to imitate the behaviors of others who are in positions of status. Second, adults are often key models for adolescents and young children. Their behaviors become a focus of intense interest. The adage "Do as I say, not as I do" simply flies in the face of social learning theory. Children watch what adults do, and imitate the behaviors that appear most effective. These may not always be the behaviors of which the adult is most proud!

Case Application

Let us turn to the case of the Klaskins to see what concepts from behavioral learning theory might apply. Why do the Klaskins continue to move? We can see moving as an example of an approach-avoidance conflict. On the positive side, moving is associated with increases in salary and status, two important reinforcements in our culture. Mr. Klaskin is being directly rewarded through more money and increased corporate benefits. Moving has also taken on secondary reinforcing properties. Earlier moves were followed by important rewards. Moving itself has begun to take on the same meaning as the rewards it brings. On the negative side, moving suddenly removes a person from major portions of reinforcement context.

In a new community, one is a stranger. The friendly smiles and nods of recognition, the gestures of support and appreciation from neighbors, and the self-reinforcing associations with pleasant and familiar surroundings are all removed. This decrease in reinforcement may produce a sense of lethargy or depression.

We do not know the specific reinforcements associated with moving for Mrs. Klaskin. We can assume that she perceives new homes, more money, and all the material objects money provides as some reinforcement. She may also find various reinforcements through her husband's success. Much of this depends on whether she perceives her husband as a source of satisfaction and pleasure. If she finds interactions with him rewarding and he is more reinforcing when his work activities are satisfying, then his success can have an indirect reinforcing impact on Mrs. Klaskin. On the other hand, if Mr. Klaskin's job transfers lead to less satisfying interactions with Mrs. Klaskin, or if the transfers do not provide Mrs. Klaskin with noticeable material rewards, then the strength of the habit that has been established for moving from one community to the next will weaken. In this specific instance, the move had many punishing consequences. Valued things were broken, the car was lost, and the new house was dirty. Many of the conveniences of life in Maryland were not accessible in their Texas community. It is quite possible that one reason for the Klaskins' unhappiness is the relative absence of material, social, or work-related reinforcements present in this new move as compared to the setting they had left.

Another possible source of dissatisfaction is that Mr. Klaskin's company was trying to modify his behavior by changing the reinforcement schedule. Early in his career, rewards came from solving simpler problems and taking fewer responsibilities. Now, every increment in salary and status requires that Mr. Klaskin increase his energy and assume greater responsibility.

We also see some evidence of modeling in this case. Barbara Klaskin is more openly angry about the move. She expresses her anger in part by shouting at her father, but she also lets it stew inside much the way her mother does. Howard Klaskin appears very cool about the move. His reaction to the stress was to become depressed and withdrawn much as his father did. It appears that the two children are imitating some of the stress-related behaviors they see in their same-sex parent.

Cognitive Theory

Human beings shape their experience. They select certain elements of the environment to attend to. They block out other aspects. The cognitive approach to psychology emphasizes the person as *knower*. The capacities to interpret meaning, to solve problems in a creative way, to synthesize

Jean Piaget (1896–1981)

information, and to critically analyze a statement are all examples of cognition.

The modern cognitive approach is heavily influenced by the work of Jean Piaget. Knowing, according to Piaget (1952), is a product of continuous interaction between the person and the environment. We approach new situations using the expectations that have been developed in the past. Each new experience changes those expectations somewhat. Our ability to understand and interpret experience is constantly changing as we encounter diversity and novelty in the environment.

Piaget (1950, 1970, 1971) views intelligence as following lawful, predictable patterns of change (see Table 2.4). Infants rely totally on sensation and motor activity to achieve knowledge. Adolescents and adults have the capacity to generate hypotheses, to anticipate consequences, and to formulate logical systems of reasoning.

The earliest stage of *sensorimotor intelligence* begins at birth and lasts until approximately 18 months of age. Through the formation of increasingly complex sensory and motor schemes, infants begin to organize and control their environments.

The second stage, called *preoperational thought,* starts when the child begins to represent actions with symbols, that is, images, words, or drawings, and ends at about age 5 or 6. During this transitional stage, children develop the tools for representing schemes internally through language, imitation, imagery, symbolic play, and symbolic drawing. Their knowledge is still very much tied to their own perceptions. They find it difficult to hold more than one perspective at a time.

The third stage, *concrete operational thought,* begins at about age 5 or 6 and ends in early adolescence, at about age 11 or 12. During this stage, children begin to appreciate the logical necessity of certain causal relationships. They can manipulate categories, classification systems, and hierarchies of groups. They are most successful at solving problems which have a clear tie to physical reality and less skilled at generating hypotheses about purely philosophic or abstract concepts.

The final stage of cognitive development in Piaget's theory, *formal operational thought,* begins in adolescence and continues through adulthood. Piaget (1970) uses the term "formal operations" to suggest that the adolescent's thoughts are governed more by logical principles than by perceptions and experiences. Normal thought permits the person to conceptualize about many simultaneously interacting variables. It allows for the creation of a system of laws or rules which can be used for problem-solving. Formal operational thought is the quality of intelligence upon which science and philosophy are built.

Several new conceptual skills are established during the stage of formal operations that are not commonly observed in the reasoning of younger children. These include:

1. The ability to manipulate more than two categories or variables at the same time.
2. The ability to think in probabilistic terms about how things might change in the future.
3. The ability to hypothesize about a causal sequence that has not yet taken place.
4. The ability to anticipate the consequences of actions.
5. The ability to detect logical inconsistencies.
6. The ability to think in a relativistic way about oneself and one's society.

Questions have been raised about how well the stage of formal operational thought applies to adult cognition. Are there any new charac-

TABLE 2.4 Piaget's Four Stages of Cognitive Development

Age	Stage	Characteristics
Birth to 18 months	Sensorimotor	Schemes are formed through direct sensory and motor experience.
18 months to 6 years	Preoperational	Children acquire systems to represent experience through imagery, symbols, and language.
7 years to 11 years	Concrete operations	Schemes for specific logical and causal relations emerge. Logic can be applied must be adequately to the observable environment
12 years to adult	Formal operations	Thought is governed by principles of logic that are more powerful than direct experience.

teristics of thought in adulthood? Do adults use formal operational thought as their primary mode of problem-solving? Research on adult thought has shown considerable variability in the use of abstract hypothetical reasoning among adults. Variables such as occupation, social class, and educational level are associated with different degrees of formal operational reasoning (Buck-Morss, 1975). Adults are more inclined to use pragmatic reasoning as opposed to pure logic. Their real-world experiences impose a complexity that interferes with the direct application of abstract reasoning.

Piaget (1967) sees a final modification of formal thought in adulthood. The early phase of this stage places unrealistic faith in the power of logical schemes to explain and alter reality. In adulthood, formal thought is brought into the service of the goals of prediction and interpretation of experience.

> Adolescent egocentricity is manifested by a belief in the omnipotence of reflection, as though the world should submit itself to idealistic schemes rather than to systems of reality. It is the metaphysical age par excellence; the self is strong enough to reconstruct the universe and big enough to incorporate it.
>
> Then just as the sensorimotor egocentricity of early childhood is progressively reduced by the organization of schemata of action and as the young child's egocentric thinking is replaced with the equilibrium of concrete operations, so the metaphysical egocentricity of the adolescent is gradually lessened as a reconciliation between formal thought and reality is effected. Equilibrium is attained when the adolescent understands that the proper function of reflection is not to contradict but to predict and interpret experience. (Piaget, 1967, pp. 63–64)

The criteria for evaluating a decision or solution may change in adulthood. Erikson has hypothesized a shift from a preoccupation with identity in adolescence to a concern about commitments to others in early and middle adulthood. The adult puts his or her reasoning to work in the service of work, family, and community. A decision that might be made with an eye toward personal gain at an earlier stage may be made with an eye toward survival of the organization or the family group at a later stage. For example, a young employee might make a work-related decision with concern for anticipating the consequences for his own career advancement. An older worker might define the problem in terms of a coordination of the resources of the total organization in order to maximize the gains for the larger system (Birren, 1969).

In adulthood, then, we might expect an increasing pragmatism, and perhaps increasing conservatism, that reflects the older person's appreciation of the complexity of the social network of which he or she is a part (Labouvie-Vief, 1980). Through increasing encounters with the inherent conflicts, the unpredictabilities, and the interdependencies of system, adults achieve a new level of adaptation. Labouvie-Vief describes it as "autonomous submission to social roles." Adults realize the limits of the power of their own minds and actions. Through commitment to a social system, they give up some degree of individuality in exchange for the ability to contribute through the system to a broader potential impact. The enthusiasm for speculation and innovation that characterizes the early phase of formal thought is transformed into a commitment to social system maintenance.

The cognitive view alerts us to the potential for new levels and approaches to problem-solving in adulthood. It also highlights the fact that children and adults do not approach problem-solving with the same kinds of reasoning. Adults can appreciate that children may approach problems from a different perspective. Young children probably are not able to take their parents' point of view into account. This is not due to a stubbornness on the part of the child, but to an inability to manage the flexibility of perspective-taking. In an overall view of the resources and competence for decision-making one can see an adaptive advantage in the different orientations toward knowledge and logic that coexist in a human group. For example, the sensory explorations and discoveries of the sensorimotor infant evoke inspiration and awe from the adult. The formal operational adult is capable of anticipation and a sense of logical consequences that protect the infant and create an environment for further growth.

Case Application

In the case of the Klaskin family we see how the members of a family react when they no longer agree about their conception of the future. The parents had believed that the "company" would continue to provide the opportunity for transfers of residence and employment. They also believed that these transfers would be enhancing for each individual family member. Now they are questioning whether the move to Texas was good for them or their children, especially their daughter, Barbara.

In her conceptualization of the future, Mrs. Klaskin thinks her husband has advanced as far as he is likely to in his career. She wants the family to stay put. Mr. Klaskin holds a different view of the future. He believes that should he become more ambitious he might be able to move the family again. He has also hypothesized a causal relation between the move and his daughter's depressed mood. He thinks another move to a better setting might lift her spirits. Mr. and Mrs. Klaskin hold different perceptions about the future, and these differences will be incorporated into subsequent judgments.

Parenting is a role that brings persistent demands to anticipate and respond to the needs of others. Especially during the period when children are infants, without speech, parents are forced to learn to interpret and respond to a whole array of needs that cannot be expressed verbally. At each developmental stage, children make new demands on parental competences and stimulate parents toward new conceptualizations about what would be healthy, enhancing, or appropriate for their children. Work settings can also foster this kind of thinking, especially when adults are responsible for supervising training or educating younger workers. In many settings, adults are responsible for the safety and well-being of either younger or older people. In all of these experiences, there are forces toward increased empathy, perspective-taking, and responsiveness. Active thinking about the needs of others promotes a new level of cognitive complexity.

We see the impact of this new cognitive complexity in the conflict the Klaskins are experiencing. If we compare Barbara's reaction at age 13 with Roy's reaction, the difference is clear. Barbara feels angry at her parents, especially her father, because of how the move has hurt her. Roy feels confused and discouraged because of how the move may be hurting his children. He is worried about the feelings of another person for whom he feels responsible. Barbara's current and future happiness is of great concern to Roy. He must try to infer from his observations and interactions whether his decisions have in fact been detrimental to her growth.

Social-Cultural Theory

Triandis (1977) defines the cultural system as the "man-made" part of the environment. This includes both *objective culture* (roads, tools, factories, etc.) and *external subjective culture* (norms, roles, and values as they exist outside the individual). The external subjective culture is influenced by participation in role relationships and most specifically through the socialization process. It is also influenced by the content of shared myths and fantasies that describe certain characteristics and life goals as heroic, others as deviant, and others as feared.

Social-role theorists trace the process of socialization and personality development through the person's participation in increasingly diverse and complex social roles. A *role* can be defined as any set of behaviors that have some socially agreed-upon function and for which there exists an accepted code of norms (Biddle & Thomas, 1966; Brown, 1965). In infancy the person has few roles, such as those of child, sibling, or grandchild. There are minimal expectations for role enactment in infancy. At successive life stages the person plays a variety of roles within the family, as well as playing roles and engaging in role relationships within the context of other social institutions.

The concept of role highlights the importance of the social context in the developmental process. People bring their own unique temperaments, skills, personal philosophies, and value orientations to bear on the interpretation and enactment of the roles they play. Nonetheless, most roles exist independently of the individuals who play them. For example, we have expectations about the role of a teacher that operate to guide our evaluation of each new teacher we meet. These same expectations influence the way people who perform the role of teacher behave in this role. Knowledge of the functions and norms associated with any given role will influence the performance of the person in the role and the responses of a whole network of people who are associated with the performer (Biddle, 1979).

From the moment one is old enough to conceptualize one's place in a family group, one becomes aware of a cultural "plan" for the life span. The society has a road map for development that exists as a source of norms and guidelines for lifelong participation in the culture. This cultural life plan includes the status of the very young infant, the child, the adolescent, the young adult, and the older adult in the society. It includes the roles that are expected or offered at particular life stages. It includes powers, rights, and responsibilities associated with age. It includes expectations about the ways mothers and fathers should behave toward their children, about the ways grandparents should perform their role, about the attitudes of children toward teachers, and about the attitudes of apprentices or young workers toward leaders, bosses, or experts. In many societies the life plan is differentiated by sex. The culture may establish different expectations for the behaviors of young boys and young girls, of mothers and fathers, or of old men and old women. Thus, even as each of us is engaged in the challenges of a particular life stage, we are aware of the life plan as a cultural backdrop for our immediate activities. We may use it to inspire greater effort to achieve a new level of maturity. We may use it to evaluate the growth that has taken place thus far. We may curse it for demanding us to relinquish behaviors and relationships that have grown comfortable. We may lean on it to help us anticipate some of the uncertainties of our own future.

Figure 2.4 shows the pattern of movement through the family career for men and women at five periods of history. You can see the differences in the pattern for men and women. Women begin parenting at a younger age than men and are younger when the children leave the home. Women have a defineable period of widowhood that is not experienced to any noticeable degree by men. The timing of these transitions has also seen historical change. There has been earlier entry into parenthood in recent years as well as an expanding postparental phase.

One of the ways culture makes its impact on adult development is through age-related norms and expectations. Age norms operate across the life span. They foster some behaviors and restrain others. "He's old enough to be supporting himself." "He's old enough to be married." These are prompts to new behaviors. "She's too old to wear that kind of outfit." "She's too old to want another baby." These are norms that restrict behavior. Bernice Neugarten referred to the impact of age norms on behavior as the "social clock" (Neugarten, Moore, & Lowe, 1965). Within a society, people learn about age-related expectations not only for their own age group but

FIGURE 2.4 Shifts in Median Age for the Husband and Wife at Various Family Transitions for Selected Years from 1890 to 1980

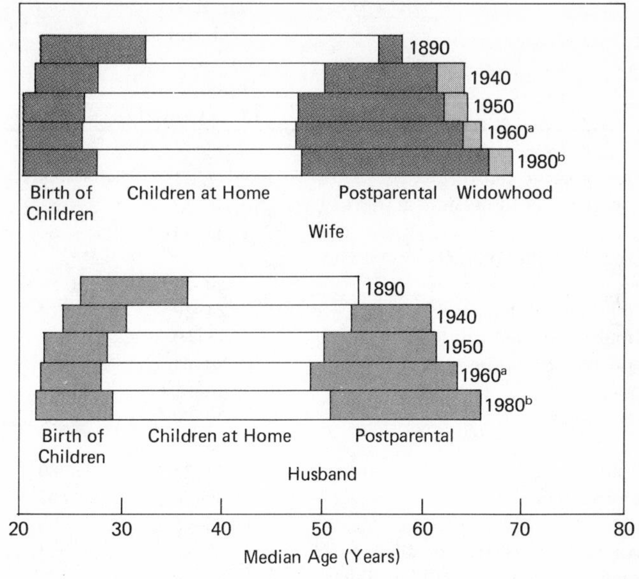

Source: Adapted from E. M. Duvall, *Family Development,* 4th ed. (Philadelphia: Lippincott, 1971), p.73. Reprinted with permission of J. B. Lippincott Company. Copyright 1971.

for the behavior of people younger and older. Table 2.5 shows the responses of middle-class men and women, aged 40 to 70, to questions such as "What do you think is the best age for a man to finish school?" You can see that there was considerable agreement about age-related expectations. In some cases, the agreement is especially surprising since the age range is so small (less than five years).

People do not apply the age norms quite so strictly to their own behavior as they believe others do. People in three age groups—20–29 (young), 30–55 (middle-aged), and 65+ (old)—were asked about their perceptions of age norms. They were asked to give their own opinions and then to say what they thought other people believed. The young and middle-aged groups were more flexible when describing their own opinions. They were less likely to impose strict age limits on behavior, but they believed that others held more restricting views. The older group expressed greater similarity between their own views and the views of others. They were also more restrictive about age norms. It is possible that younger people, who have not yet experienced the major life choices, do not have a clear sense of the costs of decisions that are off the time line. On the other hand, older people who have already made life choices no longer have the luxury of flexibility in those choices.

TABLE 2.5 Consensus in a Middle-class Middle-aged Sample Regarding Various Age-related Characteristics

	Age Range Designated as Appropriate or Expected	Percent Who Concur	
		Men (N=30)	Women (N=43)
Best age for a man to marry	20–25	80	90
Best age for a woman to marry	19–24	85	90
When most people should become grandparents	45–50	84	79
Best age for most people to finish school and go to work	20–22	86	82
When most men should be settled on a career	24–26	74	64
When most men hold their top jobs	45–50	71	58
When most people should be ready to retire	60–65	83	86
A young man	18–22	84	83
A middle-aged man	40–50	86	75
An old man	65–75	75	57
A young woman	18–24	89	88
A middle-aged woman	40–50	87	77
An old woman	60–75	83	87
When a man has the most responsibilities	25–40	93	91
When a woman has the most responsibilities	25–40	93	91
When a woman accomplishes most	30–45	94	92
A good-looking woman	20–35	92	82

Source: "Age Norms, Age Constraints, and Adult Socialization" by B. L. Neugarten, J. W. Moore, and J. C. Lowe, *American Journal of Sociology,* 1965, *70,* p. 712.

Some of the most important life roles endure across several stages of life (see Figure 2.4). We are, for example, someone's child from infancy until death. We may be someone's parent from young adulthood until death. We may be a partner in an intimate, sexual relationship from adolescence through later adulthood. In all of these roles there is both continuity and change (Feldman & Feldman, 1975). In some respects, the expectations for the role performance remain the same, but in other respects the performance of the role changes. We can begin to see how social roles provide a thread of consistency to life experience, and also how they prompt new learning. As the number of simultaneous roles that people perform increases, individuals must learn some skills of role-playing, role differentiation, and role integration. With each new role the individual's self-definition changes and the potential for influencing the world increases.

Case Application

The Klaskin family illustrates several ways in which social-cultural patterns influence adult development. At one level the Klaskins are participants in a

Bernice Neugarten (1916–

technological civilization that values innovation, hard work, and industriousness. They share the values and benefit from the technology of American postindustrial society. Part of their conflict is the result of the cultural expectations for the adult male to strive for success and occupational status within a complex organization.

The theme of culture relates to another aspect of the Klaskins' experience as they compare their life in Texas to their previous community outside of Washington, D.C. They refer to such things as the pace of life, the norms for dress in high school, the differences in interest in artistic and cultural events, and differences in the customs or habits observed among high school boys. These signs of regional cultural differences are part of what makes any move difficult. Despite the continuity that exists across the country, there are numerous regional idiosyncracies to which newcomers must adapt. These regional differences make the transient members of a community feel more on the outside. Similarly, they serve as a source of solidarity for the more stable members of the community.

Another source of conflict experienced by the Klaskins is role strain. Mr. Klaskin is trying to balance commitments to the managerial role in a large corporation with commitments to family and spouse. Leona has consented to support Roy's career role by enacting a traditional wife role. The children, especially Barbara, are less willing to subordinate their role enactment as friend to their father's work activities. In fact, Barbara openly blames her father and his career ambitions for her feelings of loneliness. The early-adolescent role of peer group member and the middle-adult role of nomadic manager bring father and daughter into direct conflict.

We also sense that Leona is beginning to feel a strong need to redefine her maternal role and to redirect her energy toward new roles outside the family. As Barbara and Howard move on to college or leave their home to take a job in another community, Leona will feel greater need to establish alternative activities. If, as the case suggested, each move results in a loss of credentials or equity for community involvement, Leona is likely to want to become credentialed or to resume her former career as a teacher. The stability of the Klaskins' marriage relationship is maintained through a willingness on the part of Leona to play out the complementary role of "housewife" to Roy's "executive." This stability may be disrupted if Leona chooses to go back to school or to look for full-time employment. Subsequent moves would then seriously disrupt her career role and, therefore, would have to be negotiated more carefully. Roy is already beginning to sense that his devotion to career has deprived his wife of pursuing a career of her own. Whether this life pattern was the only choice open to them cannot be ascertained. Now, however, the reality of shifting role demands for Leona will likely impose an alteration of Roy's enactment of his managerial role.

Culture influences the pattern of roles and responsibilities associated with the various family members. The living arrangement, the relationship between parents and children, the distribution of resources within the family, the leadership or authority of husband and wife, the style of discipline or socialization efforts are all components of a cultural pattern of family relationships. To some extent, the Klaskins' family situation is created by the cultural ground rules that the Klaskins and most other American family groups take as givens. These givens include such obvious facts as the following: (1) The parents, not the adolescent children, are the primary decision makers. (2) The children stay with the parents when the parents decide to move. (3) At this stage of family development, all the family members live in the same dwelling. (4) The children have only two adults who function as caregivers and guardians. These and other characteristics of the Klaskins' family organization binds them in to a certain way of perceiving their reality. Some possible options do not appear as options because they are so far removed from the culturally accepted norms for the enactment of family roles. The family is struggling to continue within a rather traditional definition of family roles despite the pressures from a competing commitment to the culture of the organization.

Chapter Summary

Six theoretical orientations were applied to the case of the Klaskin family in order to introduce many of the basic theoretical ideas that have guided thinking about adult development. These ideas will be elaborated in subsequent chapters as we consider the significant events and develop-

TABLE 2.6 Basic Concepts of the Six Theoretical Approaches to Adult Development

1. Psychoanalytic Theory
   All behavior is motivated. The primary motives are sexuality and aggression.
   The unconscious is a reservoir of unexpressed wishes and conflicts.
   The personality is a product of a dynamic tension among id, ego, and superego.
   Through a process of identification, people take in the values and beliefs of those whom they admire, love, or fear.
   Through the process of transference, people project characteristics of important relationships to new adult relationships.
2. Psychosocial Theory
   Development is conceptualized in terms of stages across the life span.
   At each stage, new developmental tasks must be mastered. The discrepancy between developmental competences and social expectations results in a psychosocial crisis.
   Each crisis is resolved though a unique psychological process.
   Coping behavior is the active effort to resolve stress and create new solutions to life challenges. Through coping, individuals contribute to their own development.
3. Fulfillment Theory
   Purposive, goal-oriented striving is a central characteristic of human growth.
   The competence motive energizes growth-oriented behavior. People exert energy in order to increase their sense of control and effectiveness.
   Self-acceptance means achieving a sense of trust and value in one's ideas and impulses.
   Self-actualization is a motive toward making optimal use of one's potential. As survival, belongingness, and self-esteem needs are met, people continue to strive toward a creative realization of their talents.
4. Behavioral Learning Theory
   Classical conditioning: When two events occur close together in time they come to have similar meaning and to produce similar responses.
   Instrumental conditioning: Behaviors that are systematically reinforced will be repeated. Behaviors that are not reinforced or that are punished are less likely to be repeated. Conditions of variable, unpredictable reinforcement produce behaviors that are most resistant to extinction.
   Social learning: Learning can take place through observing and imitating the behaviors of others.
5. Cognitive Theory
   Human beings interpret and shape their experiences.
   Knowing is a product of continuous interaction between the person and the environment.
   Piaget described the growth of intelligence as following a lawful pattern of change from infancy through adolescence.
   Formal operational thought permits flexible, probabilistic, hypothetical, and abstract reasoning.
   In adulthood, there is a merging of abstract, hypothetical reasoning with the constraints and demands of reality. Adults become more aware of the interdependence of roles and the coexistence of conflicting realities.
6. Social-Cultural Theory
   Culture includes the objective culture (tools, roads, etc.) and the external subjective culture (norms, rules, values).
   Roles are behaviors that have an agreed-upon function and an accepted code of norms.
   Cultures have age-graded expectations for behavior.
   Many cultural roles endure across life stages. There may be both continuity and change in the expectations for these roles.

mental changes of adult life. In order to appreciate any theory, it is essential to ask three questions: (1) What is the theory trying to explain? (2) What are the basic assumptions of the theory? (3) What does the theory predict about behavior? Each of the theoretical perspectives focuses on somewhat different aspects of adult life, is built on a different array of assumptions, and emphasizes different areas for prediction. Taken as a whole, they alert us to the complexity of experience and growth during adulthood. They also prompt a complex, dynamic approach to interpretation and prediction.

The basic concepts of each theoretical perspective are summarized in Table 2.6. Some theories see the potential for change in adulthood as prompted by the environment. This would include the learning theory's emphasis on reinforcement and the social-cultural theory's emphasis on changing roles, role expectations, and role conflicts. Other theories emphasize change that is a result of inner experiences and restructuring of concepts about experience. This would include the psychoanalytic theory's focus on inner wishes and conflicts, the fulfillment theory's focus on inner strivings for competence, self-acceptance and self-actualization, and the cognitive theory's focus on new cognitive structures that emerge to direct and interpret behavior. The psychosocial perspective has the strongest interactionist orientation, emphasizing the reciprocity between personal competences and societal resources and expectations. All six theories recognize both the person and the environment as important realities, but each emphasizes a somewhat different set of dynamics as the force for change.

Several observations might be made in preparation for future chapters. First, in contrast to the study of child development or development during adolescence, the theories tend to emphasize biological change far less than cognitive and social change in adulthood. Second, even those theories that do not focus primarily on cognition assume that adults are making use of greater cognitive capacities and that there is movement toward increased cognitive complexity in adulthood. Third, there is a repeated theme of exposure to cultural, social, or organizational incongruities in which the adult is forced to impose priorities and meaning on objectively conflicting or inconsistent demands.

Perhaps the most puzzling question about adulthood is whether the person's development is the product of the life roles and settings in which he or she participates, or if the person can indeed impose direction, vision, and value on adult experience. What is your own view on this matter? Is it possible that some adults do impose their inner reality on the events of adulthood while others are more continuously shaped by life's events?

References

Bandura, A., & Walters, R. H. *Social learning and personality development.* New York: Holt, Rinehart and Winston, 1963.

Bandura, A. (Ed.). *Psychological modeling.* Chicago: Aldine-Atherton, 1971.

Bandura, A. *Social learning theory.* Englewood Cliffs, N.J.: Prentice-Hall, 1977.

Biddle, B. J. *Role theory, expectations, identities, and behaviors.* New York: Academic Press, 1979.

Biddle, B. J., & Thomas, E. J. *Role theory: concepts and research.* New York: Wiley, 1966.

Birren, J. D. Age and decision strategies. In *Interdisciplinary topics in gerontology* (Vol. 4). Basel: Karger, 1969.

Brown, R. *Social psychology.* New York: Free Press, 1965.

Buck-Morss, S. Socioeconomic bias in Piaget's theory and its implication for cross-culture studies. *Human Development,* 1975, *18,* 35–49.

Buhler, C., & Massarik, F. *The course of human life: A study of goals in the humanistic perspective.* New York: Springer, 1968.

Erikson, E. *Childhood and Society* (2nd ed.). New York: Norton, 1963.

Feldman, H., & Feldman, M. The family life cycle: Some suggestions for recycling. *Journal of Marriage and the Family,* 1975, *37,* 277–284.

Freud, S. *The standard edition of the complete psychological works.* J. Strachey (Ed.), London: Hogarth Press, 1953–1974.

Freud, S. Three essays on the theory of sexuality. In J. Strachey (Ed.), *The standard edition of the complete psychological works of Sigmund Freud* (Vol. 7). London: Hogarth Press, 1953 (1st ed., 1905).

Freud, S. New introductory lectures on psychoanalysis. In J. Strachey (Ed.), *The standard edition of the complete psychological works of Sigmund Freud* (Vol. 22). London: Hogarth Press, 1964 (1st ed., 1933).

Gould, R. L. The phases of adult life: A study in developmental psychology. *American Journal of Psychiatry,* 1972, *129,* 521–531.

Gould, R. L. Adult life stages: Growth toward self-tolerance. *Psychology Today,* February 1975.

Gould, R. L. *Transformations.* New York: Simon and Schuster, 1978.

Havighurst, R. J. *Developmental tasks and education* (3rd ed.). New York: McKay, 1972.

Jung, C. G. The psychology of the unconscious. In *Collected works.* (Vol.7). Princeton: Princeton University Press, 1953 (First German edition, 1943.)

Jung, C. G. Instinct and the unconscious. In *Collected works.* (Vol. 8). Princeton: Princeton University Press, 1960 (First German edition, 1948.)

Kuhn, T. S. *The structure of scientific revolutions* (2nd ed.). Chicago: University of Chicago Press, 1970.

Labouvie-Vief, G. Beyond formal operations: Uses and limits of pure logic in life-span development. *Human Development,* 1980, *23,* 141–161.

Levinson, D. J. The mid-life transition: A period in adult psychosocial development. *Psychiatry,* 1977, *40* (2), 99–112.

Levinson, D. J., Darrow, C. M., Klein, E. B., Levinson, M. H., & McKee, B. *The seasons of a man's life.* New York: Knopf, 1978.

Maslow, A. H. *Toward a psychology of being* (2nd ed.). Princeton, N.J.: Van Nostrand, 1968.

Neugarten, B. L., Moore, J. W., & Lowe, J. C. Age norms, age constraints and adult socialization. *American Journal of Sociology,* 1965, *70,* 710–717.

Newman, B. M., & Newman, P. R. *Development through life: A psychosocial approach (rev. ed.).* Homewood, Ill.: Dorsey, 1979.

Pavlov, I. P. *Conditioned reflexes.* New York: Dover, 1960. (Unabridged and unaltered republication of the translation first published in 1927 by the Oxford University Press.)

Peck, R. Psychological developments in the second half of life. In J. E. Anderson (Ed.), *Psychological aspects of aging.* Proceedings of a conference on planning research, Bethesda, Md.: April 24–27, 1955. Washington D.C.: American Psychological Association, 1956.

Peck, R. C. Psychological developments in the second half of life. In B. L. Neugarten (Ed.). *Middle Age and Aging.* Chicago: University of Chicago Press, 1968.

Piaget, J. *The psychology of intelligence.* New York: Harcourt, Brace, 1950.

Piaget, J. *The origins of intelligence in children.* New York: International Universities Press, 1952. (Originally published in French in 1936.)

Piaget, J. *Six psychological studies.* New York: Random House, 1967.

Piaget, J. *Biology and knowledge.* Chicago: University of Chicago Press, 1971. (Originally published in French in 1967.)

Piaget, J. Piaget's theory. In P. H. Mussen (Ed.), *Carmichael's manual of child psychology* (3rd ed.) vol. 1. New York: Wiley, 1970, 703–733.

Ramirez, A. Family on the move. *The Wall Street Journal,* February 28, 1979, *59* (94), 1; 31.

Rogers, C. R. A theory of therapy, personality, and interpersonal relationships as developed in the client- centered framework. In S. Koch (Ed.), *Psychology: A study of a science* (Vol 3). New York: McGraw-Hill, 1959. 184–256.

Rogers, C. R. *On becoming a person.* Boston: Houghton Mifflin, 1961.

Skinner, B. F. *The behavior of organisms.* New York: Appleton-Century-Crofts, 1938.

Skinner, B. F. *About behaviorism.* New York: Knopf, 1974.

Triandis, H. C. Cross-cultural social and personality psychology. *Personality and Social Psychology Bulletin,* 1977, *3,* 143–158.

White, R. W. Competence and the psychosexual stages of development. In M. R. Jones (Ed.), *Nebraska Symposium on Motivation.* Lincoln: University of Nebraska Press, 1960.

White, R. W. *Lives in progress* (2d ed.). New York: Holt, Rinehart and Winston, 1966.

White, R. W. Strategies of adaptation: An attempt at systematic description. In G. V. Coelho, D. A. Hamburg, & J. E. Adams (Eds.), *Coping and adaptation.* New York: Basic Books, 1974.

why

do the fingers

of the lit
tle once beau
tiful la

dy (sitting sew
ing at an o
pen window this
fine morning) fly

instead of dancing
are they possibly
afraid that life is
running away from
them (i wonder) or

isn't she a
ware that life (who
never grows old)
is always beau
tiful and
that nobod
y beauti

ful ev
er hur

ries

3 Health, Illness, and Death

How can you tell how old someone is? For most people, the standards by which they judge another person's age are the physical signs of aging. Graying hair, wrinkled skin, flabby muscles, sagging breasts, and stooped shoulders are common physical characteristics that identify a person as elderly. These outward signs are signals to the person as well as to others that the life course is moving along. Depending on the person's attitudes about getting older and the culture's attitudes toward older members, these signs may be met with discouragement, acceptance, or even pride.

The focus of this chapter is on the continuum of health, illness, and death. What can we expect to be the normal physical resources of adult life? This is an area that is clouded with myths and uncertainty. As we grow older, do we lose our ability to enjoy the world through our senses? What is the course of declining agility and muscle strength in adulthood? Why do older people seem to walk so slowly or to have trouble climbing stairs? Are the declines in physical stamina irreversible? Are they a product of life-style, a kind of illness, or a normal consequence of growing older?

Biological Theories of Aging

The basic building blocks of all living organisms are the cells. The capacity of the organism to function, to adapt to the environment, and to grow is intimately tied to the healthy functioning of the cells. Biological theories of aging are theories of what may be taking place at a cellular level that would explain the changes associated with aging. These theories focus on normal alterations in cellular functioning, not on the impact of disease. The biological explanations of aging are referred to as theories because they attempt to account for a variety of observations by making reference to some specific underlying process. Each theory has its critics. At the present time, the greatest limitation of these explanations is a lack of evidence about the behavioral consequences of the cellular changes. The cells may be altered as a theory suggests, but the change may not result in any clear observable decrement in behavior. Without exception every age-related change is subject to individual variation that depends on environmental conditions, physical activity, health, and an unknown contribution of genetic resilience. All of these contribute to longevity.

Aging as a Result of the Accumulation of Genetic Error

One theory suggests that with age there is an accumulation of errors in the production of DNA, RNA, and protein synthesis. Over time these errors influence metabolism, enzyme activity at the synapses between neurons, and the homeostatic balance of the central nervous system.

The process of producing, replacing, and maintaining proteins within the cells involves a series of steps including "DNA replication, translation (protein assembly with RNA), and the active process of positioning and maintaining the protein in the cell" (Jarvik & Cohen, 1973). At any or many points in this chain, errors might occur. Woolhouse (cited in Jarvik & Cohen, 1973) has argued that with age there are "creeping errors" that disrupt the cell system.

In opposition to this argument, several criticisms might be raised. First, cells have mechanisms for eliminating error. Molecules persist for only a limited time. Then they are broken down and resynthesized. Molecules produced in error might not endure long enough to be included in cell division. Second, tissues age differently, with specific enzymes showing different patterns of activity. Without knowing the specific course of each enzyme within each tissue it is difficult to determine whether errors have occurred (Denny, 1975). Third, and most important, we do not yet know the exact relation between changes at the cellular level and changes in learning and memory. While we can link cellular errors to changes in protein synthesis, metabolism, and the transmission of impulses at the synaptic membrane, the connection between these changes and the complex mental configurations necessary for learning and remembering has not been demonstrated.

Aging as a Result of Cell Loss

This theory points out that with age, there is a gradual loss of cells. This loss differs with different tissues. Cell renewal takes place at different rates in different tissues. The neurons and the cardiac muscle cells do not replace themselves. Most theorists believe that humans have an overabundance of neurons in the central nervous sytem. The number of neurons decreases from childhood to maturity. The number of cardiac cells does not decrease over the life span.

Three types of tissues do renew their cells (Cameron, 1971). One type shows complete renewal of cells within about 30 days. Examples of these tissues are the skin, the red and white blood cells, and the cells that line the intestinal tract. These cells experience a high degree of "wear and tear." The second type of tissue renews itself during the life span of the organism but not within 30 days. Examples include liver cells, pancreas cells, and the lining of the respiratory tract. The third type of tissue renews some but not all of its cells over the life span. This type includes smooth muscle cells, bone cells, and glial cells in the brain.

In the tissues that have been studied there is evidence for cell loss with age (Denny, 1975). Two factors are involved. With age, fewer cells reproduce at any given time. Also, the length of time required for the generation of new cells increases. There is an assumed relationship between cell loss and decreased muscle strength, disturbed eating and sleeping patterns, and impaired mental functioning.

Evidence about the impact of cell loss is contradictory. Some investigators have not observed cell loss with aging, others have, and still others have observed cell loss during an early or midlife period rather than in the later phase of development. Diamond (1978) described the change in cell counts of young, adult, and aging rats. Cells in the occipital cortex were counted in rats who were 26, 41, 108, and 650 days old. Neuron density increased during the period from 26 to 41 days. Neuron density decreased markedly, especially in the lower layers of the occipital cortex, from 41 to 108 days. After that time, cell decrease was not significant. Diamond offers the hypothesis that cortical nerve cells are overabundant because they do not divide. The number of cells is greater than necessary for survival, but provides a potential for adaptation to the variety of environmental conditions in which the organism may find itself. When the environment does not stimulate these cells and relevant behavior patterns are not developed, the cells die (see Figure 3.1).

Cell loss itself can be endured without serious impairment. For example, humans can lose whole organs and still not show the signs of impaired mental or muscular functioning that have been attributed to cell loss. Franks (1974) has argued that cell loss is usually counterbalanced by physiological reserves. Compensation of other tissues, or, in the case of the brain, the formation of new neural pathways, permits continued adaptation despite cell loss. These forms of adjustment continue during adulthood and in fact could be viewed as increasing the vigor or the efficiency of functioning (Shelldrake, 1974).

Aging as a Result of Failure of the Immune System to Protect against Disease

With age there is increased susceptibility to disease. The reasons for this increased susceptibility are not fully understood. One theory suggests that the level of immune activity tends to decrease with age. "Antibody response decreases gradually after adolescence and natural antibody fiber decreases. Older individuals are not as responsive to antigens contacted early in life" (Jarvick & Cohen, 1973). Certain glands do not produce the same quantity of hormones in an aging person. For example, the thymus gland shows a decrease in the production of thymosin. This has the consequence of reduced production of cells that synthesize antibodies to fight off disease. Goldstein (1972) has recommended that thymosin injections might prevent some of the chronic illnesses of aging.

The loss of immune capacities is seen in the increase of positive responses to the tuberculin skin test (Smith & Bierman, 1973). Researchers have suggested that the increase in prevalence of some cancers after age 65 is due to a failure of the immune system to eliminate those cells. Disruptions in the immune system also lead to the destruction of healthy cells. Certain diseases, including pernicious anemia and Addison's disease, result when normal tissues are identified as "non-self" and destroyed by normal antibodies (Walford, 1967).

FIGURE 3.1 A new technique called computed tomography (CT) permits an analysis of the volume of tissue in a living brain. In this photograph, *a* and *b* show two levels of a normal brain; *c* and *d* show the same two levels of an atrophied brain. The large dark spots show areas where brain tissue has been replaced by cerebrospinal fluid.

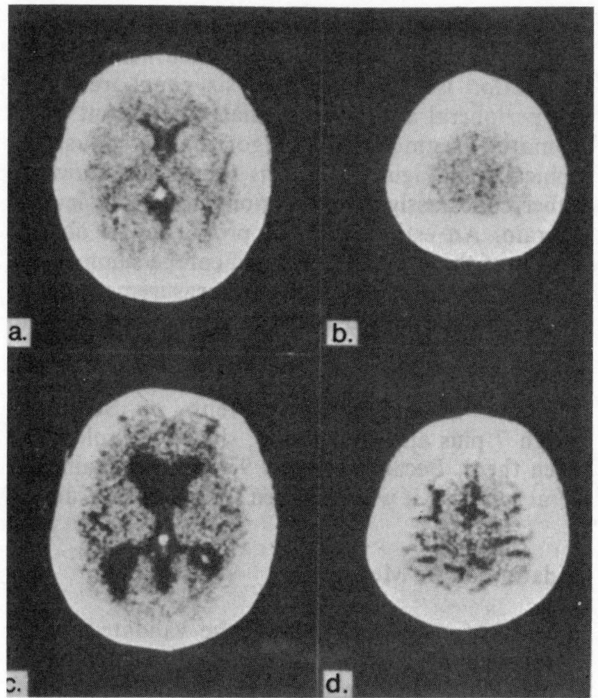

Source: "Measurement of Cerebral Atrophy in the Aged by Computed Tomography" by T. L. Jernigan, L. M. Zatz, I. Feinberg, & G. Fein, in L. W. Poon (Ed.), *Aging in the 1980's* (Washington, D.C.: American Psychological Association, 1980) p.87. Copyright 1980 by the American Psychological Association. Reprinted by permission of the publisher and author.

Aging as a Result of Changes in Cell Structure

In this view, aging is a product of modifications of the cell nucleus or the capacity of neural cells to transmit impulses to one another. One of the major ways of determining the age of an organism is by the accumulation of "age pigment" or lipofuscin in the cells. These pigment granules accumulate in animals throughout the animal kingdom from protozoa to mammals. The amount of lipofuscin is related to the life span of the animal rather than to the passage of time. It is suspected that the pigment is a product of a chemical reaction with a lipid-protein complex. There is some evidence that the age pigment is increased when the diet includes a high amount of polyunsaturated fats. Age-pigment production is decreased with high doses of vitamin E. Even though this relationship between age and lipofuscin is clear, there is no evidence that the accumulation of lipofuscin has any specific behavioral consequences (Denny, 1975).

Other research has found changes in the system of interconnected neurons in the central nervous system. There is evidence of reduced numbers of dendritic spines, resulting in fewer contacts between one neuron and others. There is also evidence of slowing in the conduction of neural impulses. This might be due to a loss of the cells that provide myelination along the axon. Any or all of these changes might account for the slowing of reaction time and the impairment of the coordination-integration functions that have been associated with age (Tomlinson & Henderson, 1976). It is tempting to assume that these cellular changes produce a more global cerebral atrophy or shrinking of brain mass. However, there is no definitive evidence of this causal relation (Jernigan, Zatz, Feinberg, & Fein, 1980).

There are reasons to be cautious about interpreting evidence of neurological deficits among the aged. Neuropsychological tests have been developed to detect types of brain damage. The norms that have been established for those tests have been based on the performance of young adults. These norms may not be appropriate for older adults. Price, Fein, and Feinberg (1980) looked at the relation between performance tests of neuropsychological functioning and intelligence as measured by the Wechsler Adult Intelligence Scale (WAIS) and clinical assessment of daily functioning. Subjects were members of the California Retired Teachers Association. They ranged in age from 66 to 78 years.

On many of the neurological tests, these adults performed at a level that indicated brain damage or neurological impairment. Depending on the specific test, anywhere from 20 to 90 percent of the subjects were evaluated as impaired. Yet these subjects scored in an above-average range on the WAIS. Their daily life activities reflected a high level of competence. The information about neurological deficits was simply not reflected in their behavior.

This kind of finding raises two possible problems in the study of the relation between neurological change and behavior. First, it is possible that the tests accurately identified brain damage but that the impairment was not severe enough to cause behavioral deficits. Second, it is possible that the established norms for the tests need to be revised to reflect more accurately the level of performance of the healthy older adult. We might assume that if healthy adults do undergo a gradual process of neurological change, they also will develop strategies for compensating for those changes.

Aging as a Result of the "Biological Clock"

This theory suggests that cells are programmed to have a specific maximum life span. Such a view would hypothesize some mechanism, presumably in the genetic material, that keeps track of cell divisions within a framework of the species life span. Cells of the nematode, a worm that lives for 28 days, would be programmed to age within that life span. Cells of mice would be programmed for a 3-year span. Cells of humans would be programmed for a 100-year span.

One method for evaluating this theory is to chart the replication of cells in a synthetic growth medium. Human fetal lung cells were placed in bottles and permitted to divide until the entire surface was covered by a single layer of cells. At that point, called confluency, cell division stops. Then the cells are moved to another bottle at a density of one-half confluency. Figure 3.2 shows the cell count at each passage of the cell strain to a new container. The cells seemed to be able to double at a constant rate for 50 doublings. After that, doubling time slowed down until cell division ceased (Hayflick, 1965; Hayflick & Moorhead, 1961).

The number of doublings differs for different species. Chicken and mice embryo cells show 25 doublings before the cells slow their doubling

FIGURE 3.2 Cell Counts at Each Passage of the Cell Strain to a New Container

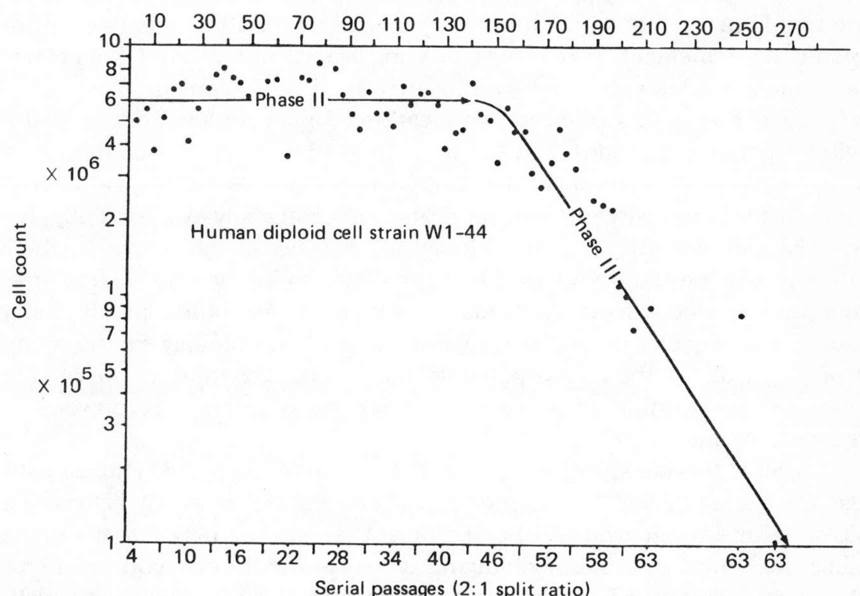

Source: From "The Limited in Vitro Lifetime of Human Diploid Cell Strains" by L. Hayflick, *Experimental Cell Research,* 1965, *37,* 614–636. Courtesy of Dr. Leonard Hayflick, Director Center for Gerontological Studies, University of Florida, 32611.

time. Chickens have a life span of about 10 to 15 years. Mice have a life span of 3 to 4 years. Galapagos tortoises are supposed to have a life span of 150 to 200 years. When the cells of four such tortoises were studied, the number of doublings ranged from 72 to 114 before the growth began to decline (Goldstein, 1974). The specific relation between number of doublings and longevity has not been established. The evidence does suggest that cells have some limit to their growth potential.

Summary of Biological Theories

Five separate biological theories have been advanced to account for the aging process. The first hypothesizes that as an organism ages genetic errors accumulate so that gradually the biological system misfires more often. The increasingly large number of error cells accounts for the aging process. The second theory takes the position that aging results from cell loss. Fewer brain cells, for example, might mean that a person can't think as well as he or she once could. The third theory suggests that aging results from the failure of the immune system to protect the body from disease. Basically, this theory would argue that aging is the result of disease. The fourth theory focuses attention on changes in cell structure as the cause for aging. Changing neural structure is used to account for a slowing of mental processes. Changes in the structure of skin cells might account for the wrinkling of the skin. The fifth theory assumes that cells have a life span that is genetically programmed. Aging is a natural process that occurs as a result of a biological program of the life of the organism.

Each theory has different implications for an understanding of the aging process in humans and for what might be done to alter the aging process. Each of the points of view is controversial. Most of the premises of each theory have spawned counter arguments and analyses. Currently, we would have to argue that the biological theories of aging are in their infancy. The development of the technology to analyze cell structure, genetically coded information, and so on offers the potential for doing research that will lead to an understanding of the biology of the aging process. Thus far, the inability to link cellular changes to more observable biological functioning presents one of the most interesting puzzles to researchers and theorists.

Against this background of potential sources of biological change with age, the remainder of this chapter focuses on the more readily observable biological events that constitute significant factors for new adaptation in adult life. Physical fitness, changing sensory and motor competences, illness, and death are basic elements in the continuum of health and well-being. Each of these areas is relevant to the morale of adults, their self-concept, and the resources they have for engaging new challenges. In each of these areas, we will describe the normal pattern of change and some of the more common psychological responses to these experiences.

Physical Fitness

One aspect of achieving adult status is achieving the height, strength, and endurance of an adult. Many of the tasks that adults perform, including grocery shopping, shoveling snow, and scrubbing the bathtub, require muscle coordination and strength. The leisure activities of adulthood, including golf, tennis, skiing, swimming, and bowling, also require agility and strength. Some adults focus specifically on fitness as a leisure activity. Jogging, body-building, and aerobic dancing are popular hobbies that promote fitness. We are becoming increasingly aware of the need to balance the sedentary nature of our adult work life with some form of physical activity. Of course, there are adults whose daily work and economic survival continue to depend on their muscle strength and endurance. Waiters and waitresses, construction workers, coal miners, dock workers, and professional athletes depend on their strength and physical skills for their livelihood. Our admiration for fitness is expressed in our support of all varieties of professional athletics, our fascination with the circus, and our delight with the ballet as an art form.

For many adults, economic survival depends on physical strength and endurance.

There can be no question that fitness in adulthood requires purposeful commitment. The 3-year-old child's normal day is filled with running, jumping, spinning, and climbing. Young children do not think twice about whether to run across the room. In their eagerness, they move quickly toward their goals. In contrast, many 35-year-olds never run if they can walk and never walk if they can drive. There are few occasions for climbing, jumping, or hopping up and down. The norms of propriety and work demands for concentration and control often prohibit physical exertion.

To bring the challenge of physical fitness into focus, we have included the following excerpt describing the Tennis Grand Masters. The group includes nine players 45 years or older who have been world or national champions. With slowing of reaction time as one of the most frequently mentioned characteristics of aging, it is impressive to see how these masters adjust their game to accommodate changing biological realities. The case points out the variety of biological themes discussed in the chapter, including fitness, behavioral slowing, and illness. It also demonstrates the variety of strategies adults use to respond to biological change. The Grand Masters are models of adult athletes who are struggling to integrate their exceedingly high standards for performance with their changing biological competences. Each of them has to evaluate whether the opportunity to continue playing tournament tennis, with the financial rewards and publicity it brings, is worth the hard work and physical pain involved in staying in shape.

There is no question that the Tennis Grand Masters exemplify the possibility of fitness in adulthood. At 48, Frank Sedgman is probably in better physical condition than most 18-year-olds. What is more, the case illustrates that adult men (and women) can benefit by a program of training and conditioning. Youth itself may bring some advantages, but they only "count" if they are incorporated into a vigorous, active life-style.

Normal Patterns of Change in Physical Fitness in Adulthood

Aging does place obstacles in the way of fitness. The gradual degeneration of tissues limits the speed, endurance, and resilience of adults. In the following discussion we trace the capacities related to fitness from the period between 18 and 30 to the period of 60 and beyond. This description draws primarily from essays by W. A. Marshall (1973).

18–30 During this period the peak in speed and agility is achieved. This is the age of most Olympic athletes. It is a time when muscle strength is still increasing for males, but not for females. Under conditions of prolonged, vigorous exercise, the muscles can produce lactic acid and thereby continue functioning even without an adequate supply of oxygen taken in

BOX 3.1 The Tennis Grand Masters

The Tennis Grand Masters circuit is a dream come true. Nostalgia is big now, or maybe it always was and we were too young to appreciate it. And although the names DiMaggio, Unitas and Cousy are gone from scoreboards forever, by means of the Grand Masters, Sedge and Pancho and Seixas are still on center court, battling one another. Bob Perez, one of the tour's administrators, carries a picture in his wallet of Torben Ulrich and Sven Davidson together when they were 14. They were adversaries then and still are today, 36 years later.

Like everyone else, athletes grow old, except sooner, more conspicuously than mere mortals; they are has-beens at 35. HE CAN'T DO IT ANYMORE is the cruelest headline of all. Look at it this way. At 22, Bjorn Borg's best years may be behind him. No one on the Grand Masters circuit dreamed he would be playing at 50. Perhaps no one dreamed he would ever be 50. But most of them are, and they are playing.

The tour started in 1973. Pancho Segura, one of the first players signed by tour founder Al Bunis, said, "It's tough to run at 50. You either go to Forest Hills or Forest Lawn." Well, this is to report that the Tennis Grand Masters do not have one foot in the grave. They are out there running, no longer to Forest Hills, but to Flushing Meadow and to Wimbledon and Seabrook Island in South Carolina and Quail Ridge in Delray Beach, Fla., where the audience is old enough to know that Jimmy Connors did not invent the two-handed backhand.

The circuit has two segments, spring and fall, with guest appearances in July at Wimbledon and in September at the U.S. Open. The rest of the time, the players work at club jobs. They all keep in shape jogging, doing sit-ups, watching their diets—and playing tennis.

They probably work harder than they did when they were younger and lither. Many people thought Frank Sedgman would retire when he snapped an Achilles tendon playing in a Grand Masters event in 1976. He was 48 years old, the winner of 22 tournaments more than two decades ago, and in his native Australia he had several business ventures that included squash centers and a hotel. Besides, Sedgman previously had injured his other Achilles tendon while playing squash. Instead of retiring, Sedgman recuperated, undertook a vigorous training program and returned to dominate the senior circuit.

Aside from the competition and the fun and the enduring thrill of seeing their names on a scoreboard, the money ain't bad. Sedgman has won $208,000 in his six years on the tour. In 1978 he won 12 singles titles and $59,338 overall. The 1979 schedule includes 18 or 20 stops for an average purse of $15,000, more than was available decades ago when the players looked under the tables for their checks.

But the cash is only part of it. Rex Hartwig had not played in 17 years when Al Bunis called him in 1976. He was on his Czechoslovakian tractor, farming 880 acres of land in Greta, New South Wales, some 150 miles from Melbourne. He played in a TGM event and was surprised and delighted to win the doubles. The following year, with Sedgman still recuperating, Hartwig was the leading money-winner on the tour. Now, he and Sedgman dominate the doubles play; since joining forces, they have won 46 of 52 matches and 20 tournaments, and Hartwig wears a gold necklace that spells out his nickname: sexy. To be a 49-year-old farmer and also a tennis player with a gold necklace, that's something.

The tennis market is split into two distinct groups: those fans who remember and those who wonder. The older crowd turns out because it recalls Sedgman winning the 1952 Wimbledon under overcast skies and through high winds that rendered ineffective the drop shots and lobs of Jaroslav Drobny. The younger audience is curious to see what a tennis player of 50 can do. "People come expecting something like a baseball oldtimers' game," says Vic Seixas, at 55 the tour's oldest competitor. "They don't expect us to be able to play. It's true we've changed. We can't hit the ball as hard. I used to hit it as hard as Connors. We all did, but we can't anymore. So you adjust. The trouble is, your opponent is doing the same thing. We all play the same way."

So the game is minutely slower, enough so that the rallies continue where once they were over in seconds. The tour often plays on clay, which enchances strategy and guile at the expense of speed. Consequently, the best-conditioned players—Sedgman, Ulrich and Davidson—win on stamina as well as ability. By comparison, when Neale Fraser joined the circuit last season as a 45-year-old rookie, his conditioning was only fair and, although he reached the finals of five tournaments, he failed to win one, falling apart in the third set when his legs turned rubbery. The previous year, newly eligible Luis Ayala expected to dominate the old guys and didn't win a match.

There is something attractive about a person who refuses to capitulate to the erosions of age. Ulrich considers the tour his laboratory, a means of experimenting with body and game. Each day the players walk onto the court, wondering—can they do what they could yesterday? The fans view them differently. When Borg defaults it is because he has a blister on his hand. When one of the Grand Masters does, it is because he is old. The seniors take pride in the fact that in the tour's six years, only three matches have been canceled because of injury.

Source: Sports Illustrated, March 12, 1979, 50(11), 34–39.

through the lungs. One of the factors that interferes with fitness is the decrease in physical activity that often comes with a full-time job. During this period the high-calorie diet necessary for adolescent growth is no longer needed. There is a tendency to gain weight during these years because most people continue an eating pattern established in adolescence and participate in less physical activity.

30–40 During this decade there is some loss of speed. The cartilage of the joints begins to degenerate, leading to some decrease in agility. Otherwise, oxygen capacity, efficiency of the lungs, strength, and endurance remain strong. There is a gradual decrease in the elasticity of the aorta and smaller arteries, leading to higher blood pressure. Being overweight increases the likelihood that the normal rise in blood pressure can develop into a health problem.

40–60 The decline in fitness becomes more marked during these years. Muscle strength decreases and it is difficult to maintain maximum strength. Movements take longer to initiate and to accomplish. Vigorous physical exertion is more taxing as the passage of oxygen from the lungs to the blood and from the blood to the muscles becomes less efficient.

> Men in their late fifties can only do hard physical work at about 60 percent of the rate achieved by men of 40. Several different aspects of the aging process account for this change. As a man gets older, thickening of the walls of the minute air sacks in his lungs hinders the diffusion of gases, and he has to increase the amount of air which he breathes in order to pass the same amount of oxygen to his blood. When he is breathing as rapidly and as deeply as he can, he does not oxygenate his blood as well as he did by similar effort when he was younger. (Marshall, 1973, p. 100)

The increased difficulty in doing strenuous activity leads to a more sedentary life. Once life becomes less active, the person is likely to perceive himself or herself as heavier and less agile, leading to even greater reluctance to engage in physical activity. The lack of physical activity itself does contribute to the gradual loss of muscle tone and strength.

After 60. There is enormous variability in fitness after 60 as a life of activity or inactivity, endurance or frailty, illness or health, takes its toll. Strength and capacity for moderate effort are about the same at 70 as they were at 40 (Marshall, 1973). However, the older person is less resilient in the face of exertion and less able to carry out prolonged intense activity. Continued degeneration of the respiratory and circulatory systems makes them less able to provide the heart and the muscle tissue with the needed supply of oxygenated blood. Quick changes in posture may leave an older person feeling "light-headed." A slowed metabolism reduces the need for calories, but there is a new risk that essential vitamins and minerals will be missing from the older person's diet. Malnutrition can contribute to the feelings of weakness and lack of resilience that might be mistakenly attributed to aging.

The picture is one of an increasing number of factors working against maintaining a high level of physical fitness (see Figure 3.3). Yet the consequences of an inactive life, especially obesity and degeneration of muscle strength, will contribute to an even greater decline in physical capacity, especially after age 60. The value of fitness is something to which adults have to be consciously committed. In order to remain in good physical condition, adults must make deliberate efforts to compensate for the sedentary nature of their lives and the increasing reluctance of their bodies.

Fitness is important not only for continued efficiency of the circula-

FIGURE 3.3 Loss of Function with Increasing Age. Graphs show loss as a percentage, with the level of function at age 30 representing 100 percent.

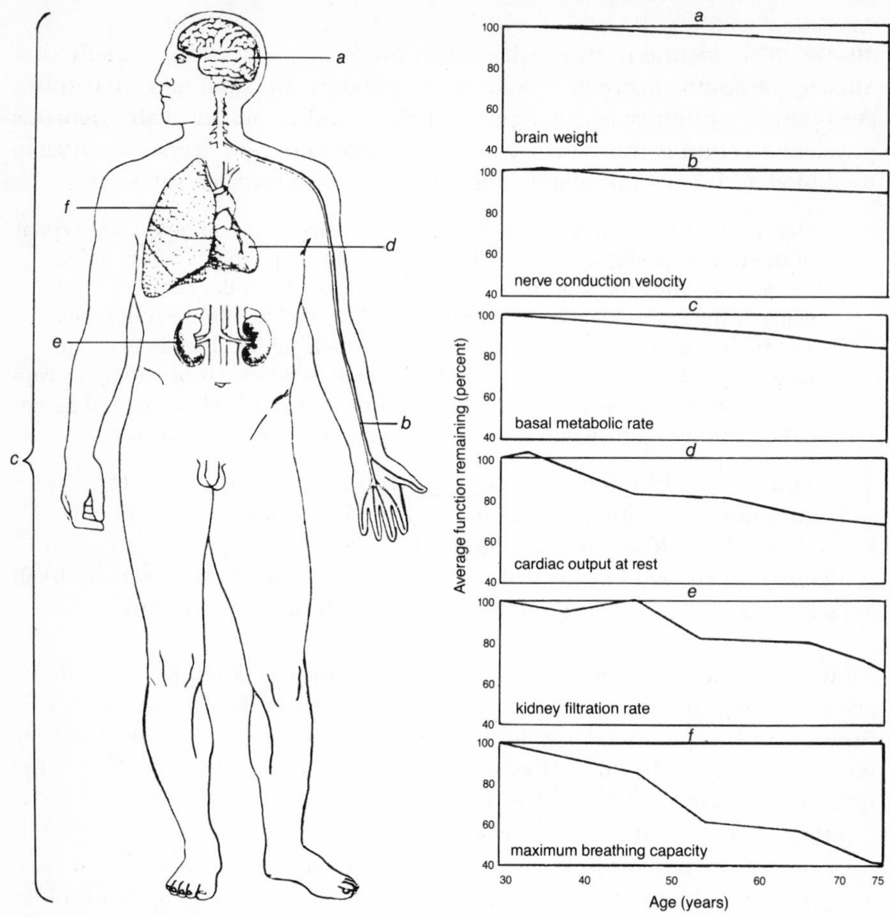

Source: From "Getting Old" by A. Leaf, *Scientific American,* 1973 *229*(3), p.52.

tory, respiratory, and muscle systems. It contributes to a psychological feeling of well-being. As the saying goes: "You're as young as you feel." We take important cues from our bodies that influence self-evaluation and morale.

Exercise

The physical changes of aging are most obviously observed in the difficulties older people have during periods of physical exertion. The consequences of reduced muscle strength, reduced oxygen consumption, or decreased elasticity of the lungs are not so visible or dramatic when the person is at rest. However, when a person is trying to move quickly to engage in athletic activities like running, swimming, or tennis, or to lift and carry heavy loads, the loss of vigor and endurance are more evident. The physiological changes of aging are coupled with two other factors that result in declines in fitness. One is the impact of chronic disease. The other is the impact of chronic disuse.

For some time people were very skeptical about encouraging vigorous activity for older adults. It was believed that the person who is unaccustomed to active physical exercise could be harmed by physical exertion. Recent work on exercise in adulthood suggests quite the opposite interpretation. Not only can adults profit from a program of exercise, but some of the negative consequences of a sedentary life-style can be reversed (DeVries, 1975).

For example, DeVries (1970) reports a program in which men aged 52 to 87 participated in exercise training including calisthenics, jogging, and stretching or aquatic workouts for one hour, three times each week. After six weeks of training, the group showed improvement in the ability to take in and carry oxygen through the blood, an increase in the volume of air that could be drawn in and expelled in a deep breath, a decrease in the percentage of body fat, and improvement in blood pressure. DeVries has argued that middle adult and older adult males can show the same percentage improvement from a program of exercise as younger adult males. Women do not show quite the same large respiratory improvement as the men.

A person's actual program of exercise should be developed in response to his or her level of fitness and capacity to endure vigorous activity. The goal would be to develop a program that would raise the heart rate more than 40 percent of the way from the resting rate to the maximum rate. For men in their sixties and seventies this would mean raising their heart rate above 98 or 95 respectively. Rhythmic large-muscle activities like walking, jogging, running, and swimming are the kinds of exercises most likely to lead to improvement in the cardiovascular-respiratory systems.

Behavioral Slowing

One of the most frequently cited changes in adult functioning is reduced speed in responding to stimuli. This has been called *behavioral slowing* (Birren, Woods, & Williams, 1980). Slowing of behavior is observed in motor responses, in reaction time, in problem-solving, in memory, and in information-processing. There is some evidence that the more complex the response, the more the age-related slowing is observed. Tasks requiring mental processing, especially transformation and encoding of a variety of information, show greater slowing with age than do tasks that require sensorimotor responses (Cerella, Poon, & Williams, 1980).

A program of exercise can significantly improve muscle strength, respiration and endurance.

The slowing of behavior appears to have an impact on a variety of other abilities. Slowing influences the amount of time it takes to retrieve information from short-term memory. Slowing influences the amount of time it takes to decide whether a stimulus has been presented. Slowing of behavior is frequently associated with emotional depression. Behavioral slowing is also implicated as a cause for the increased sedentary life-style of older adults.

There are a variety of hypotheses about why behavior slows with age. Very generally, these explanations point to biological causes, learned or habitual causes, and motivational causes. Biological causes refer to the reduction of neural connections and slowing of neural transmission across the synapse. Research does not show a slowing of reflexive behaviors. However, there is evidence of cell loss and slowing of neural firing in selected higher brain areas (Birren, et al., 1980).

Learned or habitual causes of behavioral slowing refer to the development of *cautiousness* in responding. This view suggests that as people get older, they learn the negative consequences of responding quickly but incorrectly. They develop a habit of taking their time so that they avoid making mistakes as often as possible (Botwinick, 1978).

The third explanation emphasizes the motivational orientation of the adult. Adults may not be paying attention to the task. They may not see the need or special advantage of a fast response. Some of the tasks that provide evidence of slowed behavior may be so routine or mechanical that adult subjects quickly lose interest.

A question that persists is the relevance of behavioral slowing for daily functioning. Some theorists claim that speed of neural firing and speed of information processing give humans a great adaptive advantage.

> Slowness affects a person's chances of survival when critical evasive action must be taken quickly, for example, when faced with a sudden, unanticipated environmental demand. However, at another level, an important theoretical implication of slowness is that the underlying mechanism[s] may limit complex thinking . . .. If it takes too long to complete a task, one may not only forget the elements one is trying to integrate or to reason about, but one may also forget the goal of the task itself. (Birren, et al., 1980, p. 503)

In contrast, one could argue that the magnitude of slowing is not debilitating for normal life situations. For example, one study found that older subjects took about 400 milliseconds longer to retrieve items from short-term memory than younger subjects when there were 7 items in the set of items to remember (Anders, Fozard, & Lillyquist, 1972; see Figure 3.4). Another study showed that the difference between young adults and older adults was about 50 milliseconds for simple reaction-time tasks and about 100 milliseconds for reaction-time tasks involving a choice between two responses (Ferris, Crook, Sathananthan, & Gershon, 1976). How meaningful are these differences in real-life situations? Does it matter if it takes a person a few seconds longer to answer the doorbell or to remember a phone number? Are there many life demands in which declines of this magnitude would seriously impair performance? If the slowing takes place gradually, we might assume that adults would discover ways to compensate or adapt to the changes. In a society where people can survive without

FIGURE 3.4 Age and Response Time to Retrieve Items in Short-Term Memory

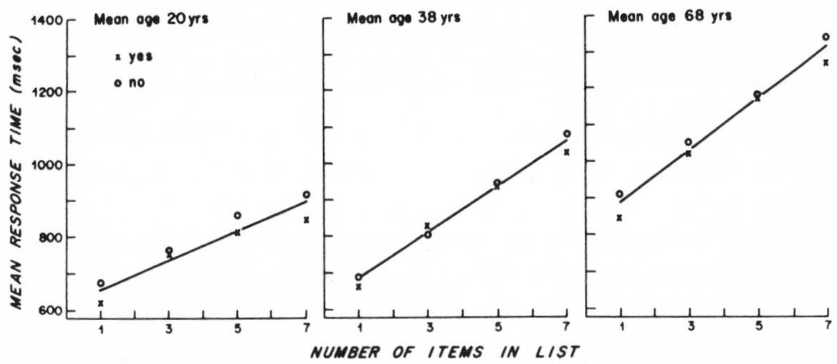

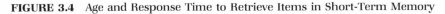

Source: "Effects of Age upon Retrieval from Short-Term Memory" by T. R. Anders, J. L. Fozard, and T. D. Lillyquist, *Developmental Psychology,* 1972, 6, 214–217.

vision or hearing or the use of their hands, some slowing cannot be all that detrimental to effective living. Answers to questions about the magnitude and consequences of behavioral slowing are important for policy decisions about the employment of the elderly, the design of housing for the elderly, and for the development of new technology and products for elderly consumers.

Sensory Modalities

Every sense modality, including hearing, vision, taste, touch, and smell, is vulnerable to age-related changes. In general, with age a higher level of stimulation is needed in order to make an impact on the system.

One adult at age 56 describes it as follows:

> So far I have been able to enjoy a robust health. A strong heart, a good stomach and a healthy back. But I notice my age. My hair gets thinner and grayer. The veins swell. Recently I changed to stronger eye glasses. The sensory impressions get duller. It is as if some taste buds have dried up and part of an octave is broken. Or rather as if perceptions don't make the same impact on my consciousness. Just now the street lights were lit; the window is open a crack; it is a blue and cold spring evening. I don't feel the same happiness and melancholy about this as before. Then there lay a young light upon the world, as well as upon griefs and sorrows. Now I only remember how it felt. Maybe it is unavoidable, and I accept it with composure. I feel there are profits to be gained from a moderate aging, too. (Ulverstam, 1977, p. 2)

The fact that the threshold for stimulation is raised means that older people do not react to the full range of stimuli occuring in the envrionment. This reduced sensitivity may result in a degree of sensory deprivation. From another perspective, the reduction in environmental stimulation opens up more time for private reflection. In the following discussion we will describe some of the changes in vision, hearing, taste, and smell that have been associated with aging.

Vision

In advising his daughter about a career, a father wisely pointed out: "There are two things about which you can be certain—death and taxes." He could have added visual impairment to the list. Research shows declines in the efficiency and effectiveness of the visual system after age 40. Changes in vision occur in four different functions: acuity, accommodation, adaptation to dark and light, and color discrimination.

Vision acuity is the ability to distinguish small details. The standard test of acuity is the size of letters a person can read at 20 feet. Twenty/twenty vision means that the person can see letters as small as the average normally sighted person can see at a distance of 20 feet. Visual acuity is lower for young children, increases up to about age 15, remains stable to the fifties, and then declines (Birren, 1964). The use of large type in children's readers and older adult's newspapers and books helps to compensate for difficulty in detecting small details.

Vision accommodation is the ability to adjust the focus of vision to objects near or far. The hardening of the lens of the eye begins at age 10. There is a gradual loss in elasticity over time that makes it more difficult to focus on near objects (Marshall, 1973). As early as the decade of the thirties this may result in increased difficulty in reading small print. Benjamin Franklin's famous bifocals are a symbol of the human being's determination to compensate for farsightedness.

Vision adaptation is the ability to adjust to changes in the level of illumination. Pupil size decreases with age. This means that less light reaches the retina. It normally takes a few minutes to be able to see well in a dark room after being in the light. Similarly, if you are driving at night and the bright lights of an oncoming car hit your eyes, it takes a few seconds to readjust to the darkness. This flexibility decreases from age 20 to age 60. The result is that older adults need higher levels of illumination to see clearly. They take longer to adjust to changes from dark to light or light to dark. Many older adults find that they are increasingly sensitive to glare. They may draw the shades in their room to prevent the bright light from striking their eyes. Slower adaptation time and sensitivity to glare also explain some adults' reluctance to drive at night.

Vision color discrimination is the ability to distinguish among various hues. The ability to differentiate among shades of blue, blue/green, and violet decreases with age (Bischof, 1976). Color blindness is a genetically determined condition that is not tied to age.

Several physiological conditions may seriously impair vision and result in partial or total blindness in later adulthood. These include cataracts, which are films covering the lens, making them less penetrable by the light; deterioration or detachment of the retina; and glaucoma, which is an increase in pressure from the fluid in the eyeball (Smith, 1976).

Losses in vision pose serious challenges to adult adaptation. There are mechanical devices designed to help compensate for these losses. However, these devices are never as adequate as the healthy function they are intended to replace. What is more, vision loss has the effect of separating adults from contact with their world. Loss of vision is especially linked with feeings of helplessness. Most older adults are not ready to cope with the challenge of learning to function in their daily world without vision. Loss of vision ends up reducing activity level, autonomy, and the willingness to leave a familiar setting.

Hearing

Hearing loss increases with age. The most common effects of hearing loss are reduced sensitivity to high-frequency sounds, reduced sensitivity to low-intensity (quiet) sounds, and some inability to understand spoken messages. These changes may be due to the accumulated effect of exposure to noise, infection, injury to the bones in the ear, damage to the auditory nerve, and changes in the auditory center of the brain, where stimuli are translated into meaningful speech units.

Even though hearing loss is a common characteristic of aging, there are group differences in the magnitude of loss. Women's hearing is better than men's at all ages after 50. Black males have better hearing for low- and high-frequency tones than white males. Rural adults have better hearing than urban dwellers, and certain isolated cultural groups have been noted to have better hearing than adults in our technological society (Bergman, 1971). These findings suggest that other factors besides normal aging contribute to the decreased sensitivity to sound. These factors might include exposure to loud, unpredictable noises or training to differentiate and make use of nonverbal auditory information.

Adults' responses to the hearing test situation may also account for their levels of performance. Older adults are cautious. They will indicate that they hear a tone only if they are quite certain about it. In one study, adults aged 65 to 77 were asked to take a chance on their hearing and to respond to tones even when they were not completely certain. Under these instructions, their tested hearing ability showed significant improvement (Rees & Botwinick, 1971). Thus even in what appears to be a very straightforward area of measurement, the adult's approach to the task may influence the outcome.

Loss of hearing interferes with a basic mode of human connectedness—conversation. Hearing impairment may be linked to increased feelings of isolation and suspiciousness. Hearing things imperfectly or perceiving conversations as a whisper rather than in regular tones may lead to feelings that one is being excluded or ridiculed.

The hearing aid is the device for compensating for hearing loss. This device has some limitations. First, it has to be switched on in order to work. Older adults may not remember to switch it on. Second, for some adults a hearing aid is a stigma, a symbol of degeneration. The negative consequences of being labeled as "deaf" are perceived as worse than the confusion or disorientation that results from impaired hearing. Third, the hearing aid magnifies all sounds in its range equally. The important sounds are made louder, but so are all the background noises. In order to benefit from the hearing aid one must learn to actively screen out the diversions and focus on the significant sounds.

Taste and Smell

The senses of taste and smell become less sensitive with age. By age 70, about two-thirds of the taste buds in the mouth die, and so do a large percentage of sense receptors in the nose (Woodruff, 1975). The loss of taste buds begins at about age 40 to 45 for women and age 50 to 60 for men.

Much of what we experience as delicious to taste or delightful to smell is learned in a cultural context. Even with the decrease in taste receptors, adults maintain food preferences and dislikes. They may tend to heighten the sense of taste by using more sugar, salt, or other spices. The loss of the sense of taste and smell is especially serious in the later years, when adults may neglect to eat. Several factors, including loss of teeth because of gum disease, a decreasing sense of taste and smell, changes in the digestive system, poverty, and loneliness, contribute to a proportionately high frequency of vitamin deficiencies and poor nutrition among the elderly (Berger, 1976).

Table 3.1 summarizes the sensory changes that take place during the adult years. There are two rather different ways to think about these changes. Some people argue that adults gradually lose contact with reality as their sense receptors become less sensitive. The emphasis is on the loss and the resulting decline in reality-testing competences. Another approach is to see these changes as leading to greater body awareness. Woodruff (1972) found that adults over 65 years were able to perform alpha-wave biofeedback conditioning more quickly than young adults. As the changes in sensory acuity occur, middle adults become more sensitive to their body functions and may become more skilled at controlling their internal states. We do not want to suggest that the losses are not real or distressing. On the contrary, these changes are serious challenges to adult functioning, but they are challenges that most adults are able to surmount.

Illness and Recovery

Physical well-being can be viewed along a continuum from a state of fitness and smooth, integrated functioning to serious illness and death. This continuum will be experienced differently by different people. Each person has a potential for certain kinds of optimal states, certain vulnerabilities, and a certain timetable for maturation, aging, and longevity. What is more, the quality of health and the optimum level of performance will depend on developmental age. The muscle strength that might be viewed as optimal for a 10–year-old would be rated as average or even inadequate for an 18–year-old. Failure to menstruate would be viewed as a symptom for a 20–year-old woman but not for a 65–year-old woman. Even among people with the same illness like diabetes or arthritis, there are differences in the severity of the disease, differences in responsiveness to medication, and differences in the influence of that disease on other areas of functioning. A very ill person can create his or her own perception of well-being. The concepts of health and illness are relative concepts. They are best appreciated in the context of the person's own history of well-being or illness, in the context of other people at that life stage, and in the context of normative data about the population as a whole.

TABLE 3.1 Changes in Sensory System in Adulthood

	20–35 Early Adulthood	35–65 Middle Adulthood	65 + Later Adulthood
Vision	Constant decline in accommodation as lenses harden at about age 10.	Sharp decline in acuity after 40. Delayed adjustment to shifts in light and dark.	Sensitivity to glare. Increases in diseases of the eye that produce blindness or partial blindness.
Hearing	Pitch discrimination for high-frequency tones begins to decrease.	Continued gradual loss in pitch discrimination to age 50.	Sharp loss in pitch discrimination after 70. Need greater intensity to hear.
Taste and Smell		Begin loss of taste buds.	About 2/3 of taste buds lost by age 70.

Illnesses can be described as acute or chronic. Acute illnesses have a sharp onset and usually have a brief duration. Examples of acute illnesses are colds, chicken pox, and flu. Chronic illnesses have a long duration or show a pattern of frequent recurrence. Examples of chronic illnesses include arthritis, hypertension, and diabetes. With age, there is a shift to an increased number of chronic diseases. Among people over 65, there are an estimated 4,000 chronic diseases observed per 1,000 population as compared to 400 chronic diseases per 1,000 population under the age of 15 (Schuster & Ashburn, 1980). Many older adults have several chronic conditions. The consequence is that adults cannot conceptualize illness totally in terms of sickness and health. They develop a subjective sense of well-being. It is not uncommon to hear an older person say, "I have good days and bad days."

Self-Perceptions of Health

In a national survey about health, the majority of Americans perceived their health to be good or excellent (see Figure 3.5). They also viewed good health as an important source of life satisfaction (U. S. Bureau of the Census, 1980). The pattern of perceived health varied somewhat for males and females, for younger and older respondents, and for people with different incomes. About 51 percent of males but only 45 percent of females said they were in excellent health. The percent of people who describe their health as excellent decreases with age from 59 percent of the people under 17 years old to 29 percent of the people over 65. At every age level, perceived health is more likely to be rated excellent by the wealthier respondents and more likely to be rated fair or poor by the poorest respondents. This difference by income level is most striking for the age group from 45 to 64. Forty-nine percent of those with an income of less

FIGURE 3.5 Self-Assessment of Health by Age and Income: 1976–1977

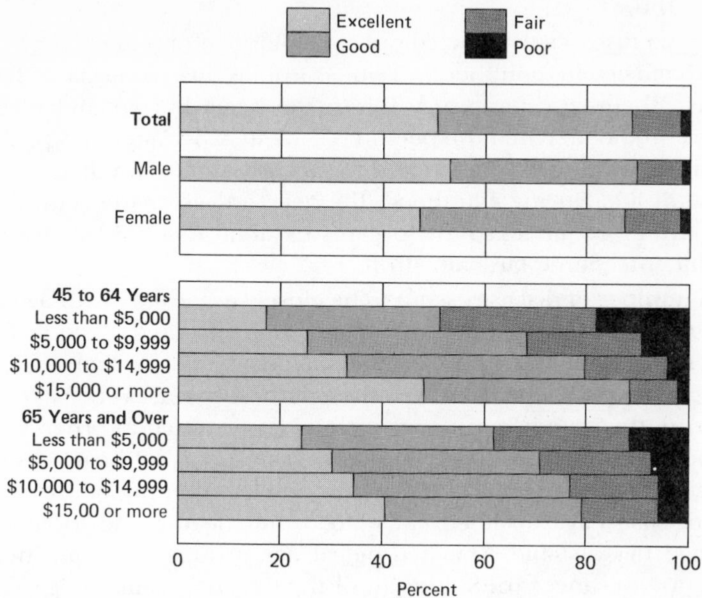

Source: U.S. Bureau of the Census, *Social Indicators III* (Washington D.C.: U.S. Government Printing Office, 1980), p.64.

than $5,000 rated their health as fair or poor. Only 11 percent of those with income above $15,000 rated their health as fair or poor. This appears to be the age range when the increase of untreated chronic ailments can accumulate and markedly disrupt daily functioning. We might expect that the low-income middle adults spend more days incapacitated by illness and feel more oppressed by high illness-related expenses.

Objective Indicators of Health

We all know that illness is an inevitable part of aging. Because the number of illnesses observed during adulthood increases, it is difficult to determine whether it is an aging process that causes this increased proneness to disease or whether the diseases themselves bring on the changes associated with age. We do know that the system that provides immunities to disease becomes less efficient with age. The decline begins during the third decade of life and continues through later adulthood. Two kinds of cells seem to be especially responsible for this decline. B-cells derived from bone marrow form plasma cells that secrete antibodies against disease-producing microorganisms. T-cells derived from the thymus form lymphocytes that attack foreign cells. Changes in the production or activity of these cells is associated with certain diseases in which antibodies are directed at destroying one's own cells. Examples of diseases thought to be due to this process are rheumatoid arthritis and "maturity-onset" diabetes (Marx, 1974).

Some diseases contracted during childhood or adolescence can have delayed effects in adulthood. Two examples are rheumatic fever and syphilis. Rheumatic fever may injure the heart but go undetected until middle adulthood, when the person begins to experience severe shortness of breath. Syphilis may be ignored in its early states and then lie dormant until adult life. During adulthood, the heart valves or the central nervous system may be attacked by organisms that had initially caused the syphilitic infection (Marshall, 1973).

A number of diseases seem to be closely associated with aging. These include arteriosclerosis, hypertension, arthritis, and various forms of cancer. These illnesses have a gradual onset that can go unnoticed or ignored for quite some time. Even though these diseases can be treated and contained, they can become very serious if permitted to progress without treatment. Table 3.2 shows the death rates due to heart disease and malignant neoplasm (cancer) in middle and later adulthood. Deaths due to heart disease have declined since 1950, but deaths due to cancer have remained fairly stable. The two oldest age groups show an increase in deaths due to cancer (U. S. Bureau of the Census, 1980).

Especially with cancers, the treatment as well as the disease itself makes the person susceptible to other diseases. The combination of increasing weakness and lowered resistance leads to a gradual deterioration of the body and vulnerability to a whole array of bacterial and viral infections.

Declining efficiency in the circulatory and respiratory systems is associated with a variety of ailments of adulthood, including heart disease, muscle pain, pneumonia, digestive problems, and kidney ailments. These major life-sustaining systems simply do not continue to provide oxygen and to remove waste as effectively as they had in the past. Once again, degeneration of these systems means the adult must breathe more times and pump more blood in order to get the same job accomplished. The accumulated effects of inefficiency in these systems is gradual decline in many other areas.

A major cause of institutionalization among the aged are the *organic brain syndromes*. These disorders can involve loss of memory for recent as well as past events; confusion or disorientation so that the person does not know the day of the week, the time of year, or the city in which he or she is living; a loss of control over daily functions including toileting, feeding, or dressing; and a loss or inability to focus attention. There are *acute brain syndromes* in which the onset of confusion is sudden. Often this pattern is associated with a severe illness, heart failure, alcoholism, or extreme malnutrition. In these cases, the symptoms of the brain syndrome can be reversed if the accompanying illness can be treated. However, in many instances, the correct diagnosis of these acute symptoms is not made and

TABLE 3.2 Death Rates Due to Heart Disease and Malignant Neoplasm, Persons 40 Years Old and Over, Selected Years: 1950–1976

Age	1950	1960	1970	1976
		Heart Disease		
40 to 44 years	122.5	103.5	90.7	72.8
45 to 49 years	228.7	197.6	174.4	145.7
50 to 54 years	397.5	355.8	308.6	252.5
55 to 59 years	642.2	571.6	514.8	423.2
60 to 64 years	1,007.9	934.2	811.9	701.7
65 years and older	2,844.5	2,823.0	2,683.3	2,393.5
		Malignant Neoplasm		
40 to 44 years	81.2	77.6	76.8	68.9
45 to 49 years	137.0	135.4	139.3	134.4
50 to 54 years	216.9	224.2	229.6	228.4
55 to 59 years	329.6	327.8	357.5	356.2
60 to 64 years	468.5	478.3	498.8	533.5
65 years and older	851.3	870.9	923.4	979.0

Source: Adapted from U.S. Bureau of the Census, *Social Indicators III* (Washington, D.C.: U.S. Government Printing Office, 1980), Table 1/13.

the condition goes untreated (Butler, 1975). Supportive counseling, attention to diet, and skill training in reestablishing certain daily functions can restore the person's normal level of adaptive behavior.

The *chronic brain syndrome* involves a more gradual loss of memory, reduced intellectual functioning, and mood disturbances, especially hostility and depression. Whereas a number of conditions can cause the acute brain syndrome, a smaller number of diseases are associated with chronic brain syndrome. One example is *senile dementia,* a disorder observed in later life, usually after age 75. Patients show confusion, low energy, forgetfulness, slowed motor functions, and difficulty in communicating. Autopsies of these patients show that the brain tissues have shrunk and are filled with tiny twisted fibers. Alzheimer's disease is a disorder that has many of the characteristics of senile dementia, except that it is observed in people who are 40 or 50. Brain tissues deteriorate rather rapidly in this disease, and death usually follows in four or five years. Other diseases that mimic some of the symptoms of senile dementia include Pick's disease, Huntington's Chorea, and Parkinson's disease.

Marjorie Guthrie described the tragic course of her husband Woody Guthrie's struggle with Huntington's chorea. The behavioral symptoms are difficult to cope with and often are misdiagnosed.

> "What confused me, and Woody himself, in the early stage of the illness was that by nature he was a rather moody person. As early as 1948, we began to notice that he was more reflective, and often depressed by trivial things . . . .
>
> [Shortly thereafter] the symptoms of the disease had become more

> obvious. Woody developed a peculiar lopsided walk and his speech became explosive. He would take a deep sigh before breathing out the words. The moods and depressions became more exaggerated and more frequent . . .." [In 1952 the first serious attack occurred. As his wife described it,] "Woody had a violent outburst and foamed at the mouth."
>
> [He was hospitalized for three weeks and diagnosed as an alcoholic. After his release he had another violent seizure which, this time, led to a three-month hospitalization. Later] "the disease was making rapid progress. Woody found it increasingly difficult to control his movements, appearing to be drunk even when he wasn't drinking. Friends watched with apprehension as he dived into traffic, oblivious of danger, Chaplinlike, warding off each car as it sped toward him." (Yurchenko, 1970)

There are no known methods for reversing the course of senile dementia or preventing further deterioration. The treatment usually involves problem-solving to try to cope with the specific forms of disruption as they emerge. It is difficult for people suffering from this disease to adapt to new settings. Every effort should be made to help them retain their optimal level of functioning without overestimating or underestimating their limitations (Davison and Neale, 1982). In many cases, it is the patient's loved ones who need support and counseling about how to best meet the patient's needs and also how to cope with their own emotions as they observe the disruption and decline of a person whom they may have depended on and admired.

The prevalence of disease is one way to assess illness or health. There are other strategies. For example, we might look at visits to physicians and dentists, number of days of hospitalization, expenditures for health care, or the number of days when a person is bedridden or requires restricted activity because of illness. Women have more days per year of restricted activity because of illness than men (21.1 days for women, 16.3 days for men). About 75 percent of the population visits a physician at least once a year. This percentage is fairly constant across age levels. Adults over 65 make an average of 6.5 visits per year, middle adults make 5.4 visits, and young adults make 4.4 visits. A major difference in the pattern of illness can be seen across age groups in the number and length of hospital stays at different phases of adulthood. Table 3.3 shows the number of discharges from the hospital per 100 persons each year and length of stay for males and females at six age periods. The number of discharges is used as an index of the frequency of hospitalization. The high rate for females 17 to 24 and 25 to 34 is due to childbirth. With age, the length of stay and the number of hospitalizations increase (U.S. Bureau of the Census, 1980).

In summary, we see a pattern of more chronic diseases in middle and later adulthood. Many older adults are apt to have more than one chronic disease or disability. The objective consequences of this increase in disease include more days of restricted activity, more visits to physicians, more hospital stays, and longer stays with age. These consequences are reflected in a declining subjective assessment of health with age. We would point

TABLE 3.3 Discharges from Hospitals and Length of Stay by Age and Sex, 1977

Age and sex	Population (thousands)	Discharges per 100 persons per year	Average length of stay (days)
Total	212,153	14.0	7.8
Male	102,384	11.9	8.8
Female	109,769	15.9	7.2
Male			
Under 17 years	30,547	7.1	6.0
17 to 24 years	15,233	7.7	7.8
25 to 34 years	15,608	8.4	8.1
35 to 44 years	11,099	11.3	7.9
45 to 64 years	10,700	17.0	9.9
65 years and over	9,197	30.3	10.9
Female			
Under 17 years	29,362	5.6	5.0
17 to 24 years	16,107	19.4	4.7
25 to 34 years	16,563	22.1	5.2
35 to 44 years	12,009	17.2	7.3
45 to 64 years	22,657	16.2	8.3
65 years and over	13,070	25.4	11.3

Source: Adapted from U.S. Bureau of the Census, *Social Indicators III* (Washington, D.C.: U.S. Government Printing Office, 1980), Table 2/5.

out, however, that in every age category from under 17 to over 65, the vast majority described their health as good or excellent. In one study of adults aged 65 to 93, approximately 25 percent of the sample reported that they were disease-free (Siegler, Nowlin, & Blumenthal, 1980).

The problem with these data on health and age is that they are cross-sectional observations. We do not know if today's youth, raised in a different technological era with different dietary patterns, access to different medications, and awareness of new health-related information will show the same pattern of illness when they reach 65 as do those who are currently 65. It is very possible that some aspects of the pattern of age-related illness are specific to the generation of the subjects being studied and not due to aging alone.

Death

Death may come at any point in the life span. The probability of death peaks in the first year after birth when there are 14 deaths per 1,000 live births (U.S. Bureau of the Census, 1980). This rate is dramatically influenced by life circumstances and access to health-care resources. The infant mortality rate is 21.7 for babies who are not white and 12.3 for white babies. This death rate is not reached again until the age range 55 to 64, when the rate is 15 deaths per 1,000 population. In the 1970s 70 percent of those who were dying were 65 years old or older (Lopata, 1978).

Biological Definitions of Death

The final point on the continuum of well-being is death. Now, even the end point has been called into question as the definition of death is debated. Modern medical technology has provided new strategies for maintaining life. These strategies save the lives of low-birth-weight babies who cannot maintain their own body temperature, respiration, or digestive functions. Similar innovations prolong the lives of those who experience a stroke, severe brain injury, or heart failure. These death-defying technologies require new, technical definitions of death. At what point can we consider a person dead? When should we stop applying the medical technology that maintains basic body functions? Three categories of death have been defined: total brain death, partial brain death, and living death (Robb, 1972). *Total brain death* "involves unreceptivity and unresponsiveness, no movements or breathing, no reflexes, and a flat electroencephalogram (a reading of electrical activity in the brain). These findings must be persistent over a 24–hour period in the absence of intoxicants and hypothermia" (Robb, 1972, p. 33). When a person meets these criteria, any treatment or effort to maintain respiratory or circulatory functions can be ended.

Some argue that this definition is too strict. They suggest that there ought to be a set of criteria described as *partial brain death* which would also permit cessation of treatment. This situation is exemplified in the case of Karen Quinlan. She had lost all capacity for consciousness, but her brain stem continued to function and to maintain breathing. The question is whether a person who is in a permanent coma without the capacity for thought or social experience is really alive. One position holds that "in the absence of the synthesizing function of the cerebral cortex, the person is nonexistent" (Fletcher, 1972).

A third position is that one might preserve life as long as possible in order to make use of the healthy organs contained in the body. This view of the *living corpse* is elaborated in Robin Cook's novel *Coma*. The patient may be declared dead and still be kept alive in order to permit some organs to be transplanted into a needy recipient. Official death could therefore be delayed by hours, days, or theoretically by months if the person's organs could be retained in a healthy state.

Longevity

The desire to prolong life has been a fantasy in many cultures and many historical eras. The ancient Egyptians sought a "rejuvenating elixir." The

Hindus taught the concept of continuous reincarnations. Roger Bacon (1210–1293) described aging as a reversible process that was the result of poor hygiene in his essay "Cure of Old Age and Preservation of Youth." Early in the 1500s Juan Ponce de Leon set out from Spain to search for the Fountain of Youth. He wound up discovering Florida—not exactly the Fountain of Youth, but for many it is a close runner-up.

For people born in the U. S. in 1977, the life expectancy is 69 for males and 77 for females (U.S. Bureau of the Census, 1981; see Figure 3.6). Research by Hayflick described earlier in the chapter suggests that there is a predetermined limit to the life span of cells. The implication is that each species has a finite life span. This view has been supported through population studies. Alex Comfort (1964) showed that improvements in hygiene, nutrition, and medical technology allowed more people to survive infancy and to survive the period from about 40 to 60. About the same

FIGURE 3.6 Life Expectancy at Birth, by Race and Sex: 1900–1977

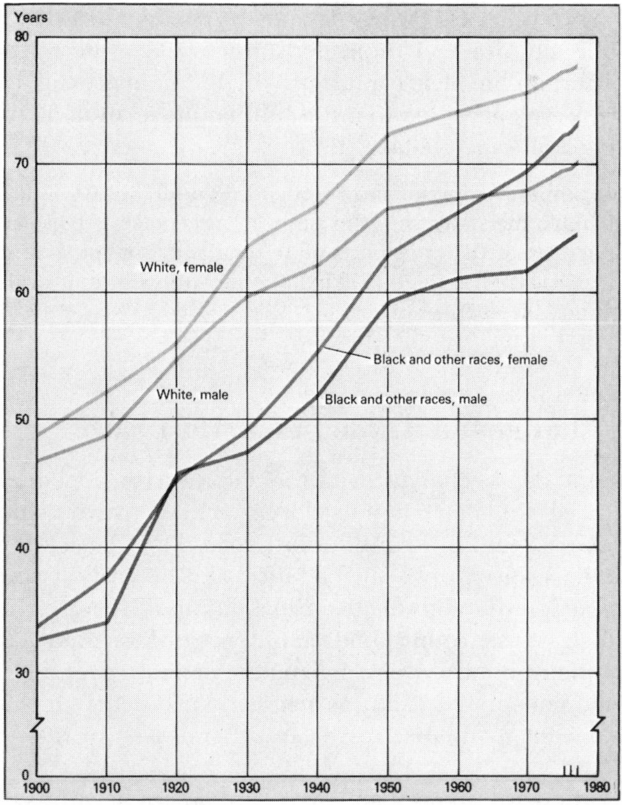

Source: U.S. Bureau of the Census, *Social Indicators III* (Washington D.C.: U.S. Government Printing Office, 1980), p.71.

numbers of people lived to an extreme age of 90 in undeveloped and technologically advanced countries. In other words, technology did not extend the life span. Rather it permitted more people to live out their species potential.

Studies of certain long-lived groups have challenged the view that the human life span is limited. In the areas of Abkhasia in the Georgian Soviet Republic, the Hunza of the Karkorian Range in Kashmir, and the Andean village of Vilcabamba in Ecuador, groups of people have been found who claim that it is common to live to 120 years and not unusual to be as old as 170 (Leaf, 1973; Davies, 1973). Longevity among these special groups has been attributed to qualities of the sparse but adequate life-style. These people work vigorously throughout their lives. They eat a low-calorie diet that is high in fruits and vegetables and low in animal fat and meat. They use little or no alcohol or nicotine. As aged ones they receive honor and respect from others.

Reports of these extremely long-lived humans have been criticized because of the absence of accurate records to support their claims. One man who claimed to be 130 was identified as a World War I deserter who was really only 78 years old (Medvedev, 1974). The high prestige associated with age in his culture had motivated him to elaborate the truth. The claims that a certain life-style can extend the life span are highly questionable. It is pretty well accepted that the human life span of 90 to 100 years has not yet been altered (Wallace, 1979).

> For those still searching for the Fountain of Youth, but unwilling to move to Vilcabamba, the states with the greatest percentage of population over 65 are Kansas, Texas, Missouri, parts of Arizona and Oklahoma, and of course, Florida; however, Mrs. Delina Filkins, the person with the world's longest authenticated life-span—113 years, 214 days, lived in New York. (Kendig and Hutton, 1979, p.19)

Life Span Changes in Thoughts about Death

Thoughts about death change over the life course, depending on our capacity to understand death and its closeness to us. The development of a perspective about death is a continuous process that begins in childhood and is not fully resolved until later adulthood. The earliest concern with death, during toddlerhood, reflects an inability to conceive of an irreversible state of lifelessness. Young children of three or four think a person can be dead and then be alive again. By middle school age, children have a rather realistic concept of death as permanent but they are unlikely to relate that concept to themselves or to others close to them (Anthony, 1972).

Peoples' thoughts about their own death do not become very realistic or focused until some time during later adolescence. Before that time individuals have not yet established an integrated identity. They are unlikely

The elders of Soviet Georgia are honored and respected members of their community.

to project themselves into the distant future or to conceive of their own mortality.

In the process of forming a personal identity, individuals ask questions about mortality, the meaning of life, and the possibility of life after death. During this stage a point of view about death begins to form. Because older adolescents are deeply preoccupied with their own uniqueness, they may tend to have a heightened sense of their own importance. They also see themselves at the very beginning of their adult life. At this stage, death may therefore be anticipated with great fear. Some adults never overcome this fear of death, which is associated with a deep narcissism and sense of self-importance.

During early adulthood, intimate personal bonds are formed which are expected to endure. The individual's concerns about death at this stage include some anxiety about the possible death of the other person and emerging feelings of responsibility for the other person. One's own death has greater consequences once one has linked his or her personal fate with that of another. Thus, a point of view about death must involve some sense of being able to provide for one's partner or to feel confident that the partner can survive in one's absence. One's view about death broadens from a preoccupation with one's own mortality to an appreciation of one's relationships and interdependencies.

During middle adulthood, people recognize that about half of their life has already been lived. They shift from a "time since birth" to a "time until death" perspective. The issue of death also becomes increasingly concrete as parents and older relatives die. At the same time, middle adults begin to have a greater impact on their families and communities. Increased feelings of effectiveness and vitality lessen the threat of death (Feifel & Branscomb, 1973; Fried-Cassorla, 1977). The degree to which individuals gain satisfaction from their own contributions to future generations will determine the extent of their anxiety about death during this stage. Achievement of a sense of generativity should allow them to believe that their impact will continue even after death.

Ideally, during later adulthood the presence of ego concerns with respect to death become minimal. The individual comes to accept his or her own life as it has been lived and begins to see death as a natural part of the life span. Death no longer poses a threat to personal value, to potential for accomplishment, or to the desire to influence the lives of others. As a result of having accepted one's life, one can accept its end without fear or discouragement. This does not imply a willingness to die, but an acceptance of the fact of death. Older adults can appreciate that the usefulness of their contributions does not necessarily depend on their physical presence (Kubler-Ross, 1969, 1972).

There is evidence that attitudes toward death do change during adulthood. Contrary to popular belief, older adults do not seem to be more threatened by death, even though they think about it often. Kalish and Reynolds (1976) surveyed the attitudes of over 400 subjects on attitudes toward death. The sample included blacks, and Japanese-, Mexican-, and Anglo-Americans over the age of twenty. Subjects were from lower- and middle-income families in the Los Angeles area. In describing age differences, they divided their sample into young (20–39), middle-aged (40–59), and old (60+). Death was clearly more salient to the oldest group. Older adults recognized that they were more likely to die in the near future. They knew more people who had died, and they were more likely to have visited cemeteries or attended funerals than the younger groups.

The older group had made more detailed preparations for their own death than the younger groups. They were more likely to have made funeral arrangements, to have made out a will, and to have purchased cemetery space. With the need to make these specific preparations it is not surprising that the oldest group thought about age more often than the younger two groups. Somewhat more surprising is that the middle-aged group claimed to have thought about death least often.

Yet death does not seem to be as frightening to the old as to the young. Table 3.4 shows the responses of the sample to the following question: "Some people say they are afraid to die and others say they are not. How do you feel?" Admitted fear decreased with age and lack of fear or even eagerness increased with age. Bengston, Cuellar, & Ragan (1977) found a similar pattern in their survey of over 1,200 adults. Expressed fear decreased with age. The group aged 45 to 49 had the highest fear of death, the group aged 70 to 74 had the lowest.

There may be several explanations for this finding. First, older people tend to be more religious, and may find more comfort in the religious concepts about life after death. Second, older people may feel more accepting of their lives and the turns they have taken than younger people. This view is supported by the responses of subjects in the Kalish and Reynolds study to the following question: "If you were told that you had a terminal disease and that you had six months to live, how would you want to spend your time?" (see Table 3.5). Older adults were more likely to concentrate on their inner lives or to continue their lives as they were. Young-adult and middle-aged subjects expressed more concern about their relationships with loved ones. The youngest subjects were most likely to want to experience certain things they had not yet done. The idea of death is viewed as less tragic and less disruptive to the old than to the young.

A third explanation is that older people have more experience with death. They have had more opportunities to experience the deaths of others. They have made more preparations for their own deaths. They realistically expect death in the near future. Death is less of an uncertainty. Many people who were over 60 in the mid–1970s never anticipated the healthy old age that they were enjoying. The years after 65 were seen as a gift, an unexpected bonus that their parents and grandparents did not enjoy.

Coping with One's Own Death

Defying the norm for death denial, Elisabeth Kubler-Ross (1969) interviewed dying patients about their feelings, their thoughts, and their needs. Having talked to 400 patients who knew they were dying, she identified five stages of coping with the reality of death. Those stages are summarized briefly in Table 3.6. One of Kubler-Ross's most striking observations is how eager the patients were to share their thoughts with someone and how grateful they were to have someone remove the barriers on this topic.

Not all people move through this sequence of stages in a systematic, orderly way. The pattern of peak anxiety, anger, and grief will depend on many factors, including the circumstances of the illness, the person's age, how certain death is, and how much time the person believes is left to live. We can see a continuum of unpredictability in death. On one end is a healthy person who knows that at some unknown time in the future for some unknown reason death will occur. On the other end is a person who knows he or she has six months or less to live and that death is a clear certainty because of a specific physical ailment (Pattison, 1977). We are beginning to appreciate that individual differences in response to death must be identified in order to help a person achieve a sense of an "appropriate death."

TABLE 3.4 Fear of Death

Some people say they are afraid to die and others say they are not. How do you feel? (Responses in percent)

	Age		
	20–39	**40–59**	**60+**
Afraid/terrified	40	26	10
Neither afraid nor unafraid	21	20	17
Unafraid/eager	36	52	71
Depends	3	3	2

Source: R. A. Kalish, & D. K. Reynolds, *Death and Ethnicity: A Psychocultural Study* (Los Angeles: University of Southern California Press, 1976), p. 209.

Erikson (1950) characterized the stage of later adulthood as the period of conflict between ego integrity and despair. At the heart of this crisis is the capacity to accept one's life and one's death.

> It is the acceptance of one's one and only life cycle as something that had to be and that, by necessity, permitted of no substitutions . . . the lack or loss of this accrued ego integration is signified by fear of death: the one and only life cycle is not accepted as the ultimate of life. Despair expresses the feeling that time is short, too short for the attempt to start another life and to try out alternate roads to integrity. Disgust hides despair. (Erikson, 1950, p. 232)

In order to achieve a sense of integrity, adults must engage in a great deal of deliberate self-evaluation and private thought. The achievement of a sense of integrity results from an ability to introspect about the gradual evolution of life events and to appreciate the significance of each event in the formation of the adult personality. This state can only be reached through individual effort. One may even have to isolate oneself temporarily, shutting out the influences of potentially competitive or resentful associates.

Individuals must engage in repeated soul-searching efforts to sort out

TABLE 3.5 Responses on How Time Would Be Spent before Death (in percent)

	Age		
	20–39	**40–59**	**60+**
Marked change in life-style, self-related (travel, sex, experiences, etc.)	24	15	9
Inner-life-centered (read, contemplate, pray)	14	14	37
Focus concern on other, be with loved ones	29	25	12
Attempt to complete projects, tie loose ends	11	10	3
No change in life-style	17	29	31
Other	5	6	8

Source: R. A. Kalish, and D. K. Reynolds, *Death and Ethnicity: A Psychocultural Study* (Los Angeles: University of Southern California Press, 1976), p. 68.

TABLE 3.6 Stages between Awareness of Illness and Acceptance of Death

Stage 1.	Denial	Unwillingness to accept the reality. Refusal to discuss it.
Stage 2.	Anger	A period of bitterness, nagging, complaining, and criticizing. The dying person is enraged and focuses on various targets as responsible for his or her fate.
Stage 3.	Bargaining	Promises are made (usually to God) in exchange for another year of life or a remission in the illness. Patients focus on specific occasions they want to see or participate in.
Stage 4.	Depression	There are two phases to this stage. First, the patient experiences sadness in talking about the past, things that have been lost, opportunities not taken. Second, the patient mourns his or her own death. It is a more withdrawn, passive period as the person prepares to die.
Stage 5.	Acceptance	A feeling that one is ready to handle the inevitable. This stage is usually accompanied by a period of withdrawal and farewell from those who are loved.

Source: Adapted from E. Kubler-Ross, *On Death and Dying* (New York: Macmillan, 1969).

their lives and to come to terms with some of the discordant events which have inevitably been a part of their history. They must determine whether the essential nature of their personal identity has survived through time. They must evaluate the quality of their close relationships and determine the degree to which they are able to meet the needs of others. They must identify those contributions that represented a serious effort to improve the quality of life for others. Finally, they must determine the extent to which their philosophy of life has been accurately translated into a pattern of significant actions.

Ultimately, the attainment of integrity is a result of thought. Adults' thoughts about their lives will generate a predominant stance toward their feelings of personal contentment and worth. The final outcome of this process of introspection is not a direct translation of the number of positive or negative events in one's life or the number of successes and failures in one's efforts to achieve. There are some adults who have experienced grave, lifelong trauma or who have serious physical handicaps and can still maintain an attitude of contentment with their lots in life. On the other hand, there are adults whose life has been comparatively conflict-free who still view their past with great dissatisfaction and resentment. Resolving the conflict of integrity versus despair is a process of achieving an attitude of self-acceptance through private introspection.

Bereavement and Grief

Adults cope not only with their own illness and death, but with the illness and death of their loved ones. The death of a loved one is called bereavement. It is commonly viewed as a major life stress, accompanied by physical stress, role loss, and a variety of intense emotions including anger, sorrow, anxiety, and depression. The stress of bereavement increases the likelihood of illness and even death among survivors. The depression and confusion accompanied with grieving may decrease the survivors' sensitivity to their own physical health. Those who are deep in mourning may have feelings of uselessness or emptiness that prevent them from seeking help for their own physical or emotional health problems. During the period of grieving, some people try to cope with their grief by increasing their use of medication, alcohol, or tranquilizers which can threaten their own physical health. Loss of appetite and loss of sleep are other symptoms of grief that contribute to the whole pattern of increased vulnerability during this time.

In the face of bereavement, there is a need to "work through" the reality of the loss as well as the feelings that accompany the loss. The experience of the bereaved person who is coping with grief and loss of another is not that different from the experience of the dying person who is coping with his or her own death.

Erick Lindemann is a psychiatrist who worked with many of the bereaved whose relatives died in the Cocoanut Grove fire in Boston. He described the normal grief reaction as involving three phases (Lindemann, 1944). First, the person must achieve "emancipation from the bondage to the deceased." This may include feelings of guilt about ways we have faulted or even harmed the dead person. Second, the person must make an adjustment to all those aspects of the environment where the deceased person is missing. Third, the person must begin to form new relationships. He found that one big obstacle to working through this grief was a desire to avoid the emotions and the intense physical distress of grief. In his analysis, the strategy of avoiding grief only prolonged the person's physical, mental, and emotional preoccupation with the dead person.

A Cultural Comparison In order to appreciate the coping with death, it is helpful to consider the cultural rituals that have emerged for structuring the response to death. The following description of the Amish way of death illustrates the way that death is openly incorporated into every aspect of life. The service and ritual are expressions of the belief in a spiritual immortality and at the same time a recognition of separation. Families customarily care for their aging parents within their own homes. Dying persons are surrounded by their families, who provide reassurance of generational continuity. The bereaved family members experience help and care from community members for at least the first year after a family death. Amish families found six conditions especially helpful for coping with death: "(a) the continued presence of the family, both during the course of the illness and at the moment of death; (b) open communication about the process of dying and its impact on the family; (c) the maintenance of a normal life-style by the family during the course of the illness; (d) commitment to as much independence of the dying person as possible; (e) the opportunity to plan and organize one's own death; (f) continued

BOX 3.2 The Amish Way of Death

The importance that the Amish place on their funeral ceremonies is reflected not only in the familiarity with death but also in an intensified awareness of community. As an Amish man reported in a family interview, "The funeral is not for the one who dies, you know; it is for the family."

At the time of death, close neighbors assume the responsibility for notifying others of the death. The bereaved family has only two tasks: first, the appointment of two or three families to take full charge of the funeral arrangements; second, the drawing up of a list of the families who are to be invited to the funeral.

The Amish community takes care of all aspects of the funeral occasion with the exception of the embalming procedure, the coffin, and the horse-drawn wagon. These matters are taken care of by a non-Amish funeral director who provides the type of service that the Amish desire.

The embalmed body is returned to the home within a day of the death. Family members dress the body in white garments in accordance with the biblical injunction found in Revelation 3:5. For a man, this consists of white trousers, a white shirt, and a white vest. For a woman, the usual clothing is a white cape and apron that were worn by her at both her baptism and her marriage. At baptism a black dress is worn with the white cape and apron; at marriage a purple or blue dress is worn with the white cape and apron. It is only at her death that an Amish woman wears a white dress with the cape and apron that she put away for the occasion of her death. This is an example of the lifelong preparation for death, as sanctioned by Amish society. The wearing of white clothes signifies the high ceremonial emphasis on the death event as the final rite of passage into a new and better life.

Several Amish women stated that making their parents', husbands', or children's funeral garments was a labor of love that represented the last thing they could do for their loved ones. One Amish woman related that each month her aged grandmother carefully washed, starched, and ironed her own funeral clothing so that it would be in readiness for her death. This act appears to have reinforced for herself and her family her lifelong acceptance of death and to have contributed to laying the foundation for effective grief work for herself and her family. This can be seen as an example of the technique of preventive intervention called "anticipatory guidance" (Caplan, 1964, p. 84), which focuses on helping individuals to cope with impending loss through open discussion and problem solving before the actual death.

After the body is dressed, it is placed in a plain wooden coffin that is made to specifications handed down through the centuries. The coffin is placed in a room that has been emptied of all furnishings in order to accommodate the several hundred relatives, friends, and neighbors who will begin arriving as soon as the body is prepared for viewing. The coffin is placed in a central position in the house, both for practical considerations of seating and to underscore the importance of the death ceremonials in Amish society.

The funeral service is held in the barn in the warmer months and in the house during the colder seasons. The service is conducted in German and lasts 11/2 hours, with the same order of service for every funeral. The guests view the body when they arrive and again when they leave to take their places in the single-file procession of their carriages to the burial place.

Viewing the coffin again at the cemetery entrance, the guests gather at the grave dug by neighbors the previous day. As all watch silently, the grave is filled with earth. After scripture reading and prayer, followed by a hymn and the Lord's Prayer, the mourners bow their heads in silent prayer. Following the interment, the family and close neighbors return to the home, where a meal has been prepared by the families in charge of arrangements.

In Amish society, reactions to death are given expression in culturally sanctioned behaviors that are firmly rooted in a belief in life after death for those who remain loyal to the faith. The high visibility and close proximity of the dead are important aspects of the Amish death system; death is real and exerts a powerful influence in this society.

Source: "The Amish Way Of Death" by K. B. Bryer, *American Psychologist*, 1979, *34*, 255–261. Copyright 1979 by American Psychological Association. Reprinted by permission of the publisher and the author.

support for the bereaved for at least a year following the funeral, with long-term support given to those who do not remarry" (Bryer, 1979, p. 260).

We are beginning to appreciate death as a meaningful component of the life course. Scientists are responding more realistically to the needs of the dying, to the process of grieving, and to the need for an ethic that permits us to encounter death as a natural, dignified element of life. As we experience the death of others during adult life, our own lives are clarified. In each death, we reflect on the quality of the relationship we have had with the person, the nature of the person's accomplishments, and the essential

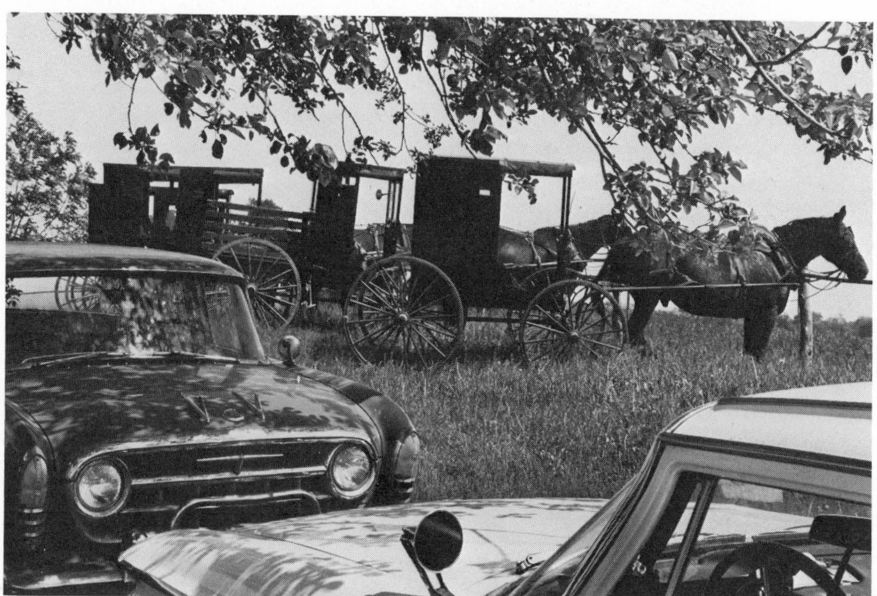

For the Amish, death is an intimate part of life.

value or contribution of that life. The death of each loved or cherished person educates us about the meaning and value of our own life choices. It is with great admiration that we respond to those who confront their own death boldly and with acceptance.

Chapter Summary

Most of the theories of adult development discussed in Chapter 2 do not emphasize the biological changes of adulthood. In fact, some theorists have argued that biological change does not provide the same predictable framework for interpreting adult development as it does for childhood. This is due to the adult's increased capacity to interpret, redefine, and creatively cope with physical change. Nonetheless, there are patterned changes in fitness and health during adulthood. Five biological theories are presented that may account for these changes. They include the accumulation of error, cell loss, failure of the immune system, changes in cell structure, and the genetic program for species longevity (the biological clock). Each of these theories makes use of analyses at the cellular or tissue level. Changes at these levels do not always result in obvious behavioral change.

The continuum of well-being includes varying levels of physical fitness, speed of behavior, sensory sensitivity, illness, and death. These are clearly interrelated. A breakdown in the immune system can increase vulnerability to disease. Decreased visual or auditory sensitivity may limit activity and thus decrease fitness. A loss of muscle strength or respiratory capacity may result in slowing of behavior. With age there are gradual changes in many systems coupled with the increased demands of certain chronic ailments or disabilities. In light of these changes, it is surprising that the great majority of adults at every age perceive themselves to be in good or excellent health.

The theme of death is of growing concern to students of adult development. With the changing medical technology, there are ever-increasing ethical questions about prolonging life or delaying death. The concept of death has different meanings at different periods of development. Young adults are more likely to fear death but to think less often about it. Older adults are likely to think about death often, even to prepare for it in very specific ways. They are less likely to fear death or to see it as robbing them of life chances.

References

Anders, T. R., Fozard, J. L., & Lillyquist, T. D. Effects of age upon retrieval from short-term memory. *Developmental Psychology,* 1972, 6, 214–217.

Anthony, S. *The discovery of death in childhood and after.* New York: Basic Books, 1972.

Bengtson, V. L., Cuellar, J. B., & Ragan, P. K. Stratum contrasts and similarities in attitudes toward death. *Journal of Gerontology,* 1977, *32*(1), 76–88.

Berger, R. Nutritional needs of the aged. In I. M. Burnside (Ed.), *Nursing and the aged.* New York: McGraw-Hill, 1976.

Bergman, M. Changings in hearing with age. *The Gerontologist,* 1971, *11,* 148–151.

Birren, J. *The psychology of aging.* Englewood Cliffs, N.J.: Prentice Hall, 1964.

Birren, J. E., Woods, A. M., & Williams, M. V. Behavioral slowing with age: Causes, organization, and consequences. In L. W. Poon (Ed.), *Aging in the 1980s.* Washington, D.C.: American Psychological Association, 1980.

Bischof, L. J. *Adult psychology.* New York: Harper & Row, 1976.

Botwinick, J. *Aging and behavior.* New York: Springer, 1978.

Bryer, K. B. The Amish way of death: A study of family support systems. *American Psychologist,* 1979, *34,* 255–261.

Cameron, I. L. Cell proliferation and renewal in the mammalian body. In I. L. Cameron and J. D. Thrasher (Eds.), *Cellular and molecular renewal in the mammalian body,* pp. 45–85. New York: Academic Press, 1971.

Caplan, G. *Principles of preventive psychiatry.* New York: Basic Books, 1964.

Cerella, J., Poon, L. W., & Williams, D. M. Age and the complexity hypothesis. In L. W. Poon (Ed.), *Aging in the 1980s.* Washington, D.C.: American Psychological Association, 1980.

Comfort, A. *The biology of senescence.* Boston, Mass.: Routledge and Kegan Paul, 1964.

Cummings, E. E. *Complete poems 1913–1962.* New York: Harcourt Brace Jovanovich, 1968.

Davies, D. A Shangri-la in Ecuador. *New Scientist,* February 1, 1973, pp. 236–238.

Davison, G. C., & Neale, J. M. *Abnormal psychology,* 3rd Edition, New York: Wiley, 1982.

Denney, P. Cellular biology of aging. In D. S. Woodruff and J. E. Birren (Eds.), *Aging: Scientific perspectives and social issues.* New York: D. Van Nostrand, 1975.

DeVries, H. A. Immediate and long-term effects of an exercise exercise training regimen upon men aged 52–88. *Journal of Gerontology,* 1970, *25,* 325–336.

DeVries, H. A. Physiology of exercise. In D. S. Woodruff and J. E. Birren (Eds.), *Aging: Scientific perspectives and social issues.* New York: D. Van Nostrand. 1975.

Diamond, M. C. The aging brain: Some enlightening and optimistic results. *American Scientist,* 1978, *66,* 66–71.

Erikson, E. H. *Childhood and society.* New York: Norton, 1950.

Feifel, H., and Branscomb, A. Who's afraid of death? *Journal of Abnormal Psychology,* 1973, *81,* 282–288.

Ferris, S., Crook, T., Sathananthan, G., & Gershon, S. Reaction time as a diagnostic measure in senility. *Journal of the American Geriatrics Society,* 1976, *24,* 529–533.

Fletcher, J. Indicators of humanhood: A tentative profile of man. *The Hastings Center Report,* November 1972, *2,* 5, 3.

Franks, L. M. Aging in differentiated cells. *The Gerontologist,* 1974, *60,* 51–62.

Fried-Cassorla, M. Death anxiety and disengagement. Paper presented at the American Psychological Association Meetings, San Francisco, 1977.

Goldstein, A. Purification and biological activity of thymosene, a hormone of the thymus gland. *Proceedings of the National Academy of Science,* 1972, *69,* 1800–1803.

Goldstein, S. Aging in vitro. Growth of cultured cells from the Galapagos tortoise. *Experimental Cell Research,* 1974, *83,* 297–302.

Hayflick, L. The limited in vitro lifetime of human diploid cell strains. *Experimental Cell Research,* 1965, *37,* 614–636.

Hayflick, L., & Moorhead, P. The serial cultivation of human diploid cell strains. *Experimental cell research,* 1961, *25,* 585–621.

Jarvik, L. F., & Cohen, D. A biobehavioral approach to intellectual changes with aging. In C. Eisdorfer & M. P. Lawton (Eds.), *The psychology of adult development and aging,* Washington, D.C.: American Psychological Association, 1973.

Jernigan, T. L., Zatz, L. M., Feinberg, I., & Fein, G. The measurement of cerebral atrophy in the aged by computed tomography. In L. W. Poon (Ed.), *Aging in the 1980s.* Washington, D.C.: American Psychological Association, 1980.

Kalish, R. A., & Reynolds, D. K. *Death and ethnicity: A psychocultural study.* Los Angeles: University of Southern California Press, 1976.

Kendig, F., & Hutton, R. *Life spans or how long things last.* New York: Holt, Rinehart, and Winston, 1979.

Kubler-Ross, E. *On death and dying.* New York: Macmillan, 1969.

Kubler-Ross, E. On death and dying. *Journal of the American Medical Association,* February 1972.

Leaf, A. Growing old. *Scientific American,* 1973, *229*(3), 44–53.

Lindemann, E. Symptomatology and management of acute grief. *The American Journal of Psychiatry,* 1944, *101,* 141–418.

Lopata, H. Z. Widowhood: Social norms and social integration. In *Family Factbook (1st ed.).* Chicago: Marquis Academic Media, 1978.

Marshall, W. A. The body: Chapters 1, 4, 7, 10, 13, 16, 19. In R. R. Seas & S. Shirley Feldman (Eds.), *The seven ages of man.* Los Altos, Calif.: William Kaufmann, 1973.

Marx, J. Aging research: Pacemakers for aging. *Science,* 1974, *186,* 4170, 1196–1197.

Medvedev, Z. Caucasus and Altay longevity: A biological or social problem? *Gerontologist,* 1974, *14,* 381.

Pattison, E. M. The dying experience-retrospective analysis. In E. M. Pattison (Ed.), *The experience of dying.* Englewood Cliffs, N. J.: Prentice-Hall, 1977.

Price, L. J., Fein, G., & Feinberg, I. Neuropsychological assessment of cognitive function in the elderly. In L. W. Poon (Ed.), *Aging in the 1980s.* Washington, D.C.: American Psychological Association, 1980.

Rees, J. N., & Botwinick, J. Detection and decision factors in auditory behavior of the elderly. *Journal of Gerontology,* 1971, *26,* 133–136.

Robb, J. W. Death and dying: A search for an ethic. *National Forum,* Fall 1972, *58,* 4, 32–36.

Schuster, C. S., & Ashburn, S. S. *The process of human development: A holistic approach.* Boston: Little, Brown, 1980.

Siegler, I. C., Nowlin, J. B. & Blumenthal, J. A. Health and behavior: Methodological considerations for adult development and aging. In L. W. Poon (Ed.), *Aging in the 1980s.* Washington, D.C.: American Psychological Association, 1980.

Shelldrake, A. R. The aging, growth and death of cells. *Nature,* 1974, *250,* 381–384.

Smith, D. W., & Bierman, E. L. (Eds.). *The biologic ages of man.* Philadelphia: Saunders, 1973.

Smith, M. E. Ophthalmic aspects. In F. U. Steinberg (Ed.), *Cowdry's The care of the geriatric patient.* St. Louis: C. V. Mosby, 1976.

Sports Illustrated, March 12, 1979, *50*(11), 34–39.

Tomlinson, B. E., & Henderson, G. Some quantitative cerebral findings in normal and demented old people. In R. D. Terry & S. Gershon (Eds.), *Aging* (Vol.3). New York: Raven, 1976.

Ulverstam, L. Aging meaningfully. In *Social Change in Sweden.* New York: Swedish Information Service, 1977.

U.S. Bureau of the Census. Current Population Reports, Series P–20, No. 363, *Population profile of the United States: 1980.* Series P–20, No. 363. Washington, D.C.: U.S. Government Printing Office, 1981.

U.S. Bureau of the Census *Social Indicators III.* Washington, D.C.: U.S. Government Printing Office, 1980.

Walford, R. L. Autoimmune phenomena in the aging process. *Symposium of the Society for Experimental Biology,* 1967, *21,* 351–373.

Wallace, D. J. The biology of aging. In J. Hendricks & C.D. Hendricks (Eds.), *Dimensions of aging: Readings.* Cambridge, Mass.: Winthrop, 1979.

Woodruff, D. S. *Biofeedback control of the EEG alpha rhythm and its effect on reaction time in the young and old.* Unpublished doctoral dissertation, University of Southern Calif., 1972.

Woodruff, D. S. A physiological perspective of the psychology of aging. In D. S. Woodruff and J. E. Birren (Eds.), *Aging: Scientific perspectives and social issues.* New York: D. Van Nostrand, 1975.

Yurchenco, H. *A mighty hard read: The Woody Guthrie story.* New York: McGraw-Hill, 1970.

4 Sexuality

The two bodies writhe, unheedingly. The two minds drift into the oblivion of attending only to their own feeling, so perfectly synchronized that the ecstasy of the one is preordained to be the reciprocal ecstasy of the other. Two minds, mindlessly lost in one another. This is the perfect orgasmic experience. This is how an orgasm sighs, moans, exclaims, expires, exhausts itself into exultant repose. No orgasm is the best. They keep getting better and better.

John Money, *Love and Love Sickness*, 1980, p. 119

The Sexual Career

Human sexuality is a many-sided configuration of biological, psychological, and cultural factors. In order to appreciate the sexual experiences and changes of adult life, it is necessary to tell the story from its beginning in the prenatal period of development. We do not arrive at our capacity for adult sexual behavior from a blank past. The sexual aspect of our nature is fostered, inhibited, and continuously socialized from the moment of birth.

The Childhood Origins of Sexuality

Sexuality begins at a genetic level with the presence of the XX or XY chromosome combination in the fertilized zygote. Fetal development during the third month of gestation includes a differentiation of the sex organs. In the presence of the Y chromosome, sperm ducts, testes, penis, and scrotum emerge. In the absence of the Y chromosome, ovaries, fallopian tubes, the uterus, and the vagina develop. If chromosomal material is deleted or if chromosomes fail to separate during cell division, the sexual fate of the fetus is put into jeopardy. It is assumed that the vital function of the X and Y chromosomes is to direct the production of the sex organs and hormones that influence the emergence of secondary sex characteristics.

Freud (1953) pointed out that from infancy children are sexual beings. What is more, he argued that all infants are bisexual, showing the interests,

A 3-month fetus—at this time differentiation of sex organs occur.

responses, and object-selection characteristics of both sexes. Today, we might state that observation differently, suggesting that infants are sexual without reference to the sex of the object or their own sex. They experience sexual stimulation as pleasurable. In infancy, the process of sexual socialization also gets underway. Parents respond to boy and girl babies with varied degrees of physical contact, close fondling, tickling, and gentle rocking. For example, parents are likely to place boy babies at a greater distance from them at an earlier age than girl babies. The history of each person's sexuality begins with the kind of caregiving, handling, and comforting techniques used by important caregivers. If these caregivers make systematic distinctions between the way they handle boys and girls, then those personal histories will very likely be different for males and females.

In childhood, sexuality takes several new turns. First, there is more deliberate masturbation through which children discover the specific sensations associated with genital manipulation. Second, there is peer play during which children may explore each other's bodies, compare sex organs, and even stimulate each other. Third, socialization about sexuality becomes more explicit. In some cultures, sexual play between children is quite open and direct. Adults may use genital stimulation as a way of soothing their toddlers. In our society, children are generally admonished not to masturbate in public and not to explore or touch the sex organs of their playmates. Finally, children have more active thoughts about sexuality. They ask questions about babies and birth, about love, and about why boys have penises and girls don't, and they may wonder exactly what girls do have. The responses to these questions from parents, grandparents, or other adults set the tone for the legitimacy of thinking about sexuality. It may be the child's questions rather than any behavior that creates a stimulus for anger or shaming on the part of parents.

The question of who thinks about sexuality and how often was addressed directly in a study by Cameron and Biber (1973). They surveyed over 4,000 people across the age range 8 to 99 in a variety of settings including home, work, school, church, shopping centers, and parks. In the interview the following questions were included:

> "What were you thinking about over the past five minutes?" "Did you think about sex or were your thoughts sexually colored—even for a moment (perhaps it crossed your mind)?" "What was the central focus of your thought over the past five minutes?"

(One of the 14 possible responses was "about a personal problem—topic concerning sex.")

Table 4.1 shows the percentage of males and females in each age range who had been focusing their thoughts on sex and those for whom sex had been a "fleeting thought." The data suggest that sex is a common fleeting thought across the life span, especially during adolescence and young adulthood. In contrast, as people grow older it is less likely to be a

TABLE 4.1 Thoughts about Sex

	% Sex Crossed Their Mind		% Sex Was a Focus of Thought		
Age Range	M	F	M	F	
8–11	25	27	4	4	N = 116 F 119 M
12–13	50	39	16	11	N = 117 F 146 M
14–15	57	42	10	11	N + 137 F 130 M
16–17	51	42	14	6	N – 207 F 104 M
18–25	48	33	10	6	N – 629 F 541 M
26–39	33	19	8	2	N = 493 F 472 M
40–55	20	9	4	2	N = 366 F 379 M
56–64	19	12	3	0	N = 95 F 97 M
65 and over	9	6	0	0	N – 80 F 82 M

Source: Adapted from "Sexual Thought Throughout the Life-span" by P. Cameron and H. Biber, *The Gerontologist*, 1973, *13*, 144–147.

Reprinted by permission of *The Gerontologist/The Journal of Gerontology*.

focus of concentration, at least so far as people will admit to it. The responses also provide evidence that sexuality is somewhat less prevalent as a focus of thought for females than for males, especially after the age of 11. Boys and girls are about equally likely to have thoughts about sex during the 8–11 age range. We might hypothesize that there are strong socialization factors inhibiting the girls expression of sexual interest during adolescence and thereafter.

Sexuality during Adolescence

Puberty brings not only the adult capacity for reproduction but the secondary sex characteristics associated with adult appearance. For boys, the height spurt, increased muscle mass, growth of pubic, facial, and body hair, and the voice change are all important signs of masculinity. For girls, breast development, the relative broadening of hips in relation to shoulder width, and the redistribution of body fat all converge to produce the more shapely adult female body. These events occur simultaneously with heightened levels of arousal and sensitivity to sexual stimulation. Pictures and thoughts, as well as physical stimulation, can be more arousing than they were in childhood. For males, ejaculation brings a new component to sexual stimulation that separates adolescent sexual experiences from earlier childhood sexual play.

Sullivan (1949) identified one of the conflicts of adolescence as the struggle to integrate sexual impulse (he calls it the lust dynamism) with needs for closeness and emotional support (he calls it the intimacy dynamism). That particular conflict and the desire to resolve it provide the basis for much of adolescent sexual experimentation. There is a search for a partner who can gratify sexual needs and, at the same time, be a good friend.

Learning To Be a Sexual Adult Three kinds of behaviors provide opportunities for developing a sense of one's sexual nature. These are masturbation, sexual encounters with others, and emotional commitment to another person. All of these behaviors take place in a cultural context, so that their meaning derives not only from physical and emotional pleasures but from the extent to which the behaviors fulfill or violate social expectations. The pattern of participation in these three forms of sexual activity are different for males and females.

Masturbation is much more frequent among high-school-age males than females (Francoeur, 1982). In a sample of over 600, 50 percent of the males masturbated by the age of 13, and 80 percent masturbated by age 18. For females, 37 percent had masturbated by age 13 and 59 percent by age 18 (Haas, 1979). Masturbation for males provides an avenue for discovering about orgasm and for reinforcing the pleasure of sexual activity. A survey of adult sexual behavior conducted by the Playboy Foundation (Hunt, 1974) reported that 93 percent of males and 63 percent of females had masturbated to orgasm. About 60 percent of males but only 35 percent of females had experienced orgasm through masturbation by age 13.

Given that sexual maturation begins earlier for females than for males, it appears that sexual activity of a nonsocial nature plays a more important role for males than for females. However, when sexually active girls and boys are compared, girls report more frequent masturbation than boys (Sorenson, 1973; Haas, 1979). For both sexes, masturbation appears to be a primary mode of achieving sexual stimulation and of linking the physical act of orgasm with symbolic fantasies of social encounters. Nonetheless, many adolescents report having negative feelings of guilt or anxiety after masturbating. These feelings reflect the conflict between strong needs to discover and satisfy sexual impulses, and equally strong doubts about the appropriateness of self-stimulation.

The second kind of sexual learning occurs through sexual encounters. These experiences may be homosexual or heterosexual in nature. About 6 percent of females in the age range 13–19 have had at least one homosexual experience (Sorenson, 1973). About 15 percent of males have had at least one homosexual encounter during the age range 12–16, with no subsequent homosexual relationships (Simon & Gagnon, 1967). Often these experiences are the outcome of the strong, close commitment that develops among peers in the early adolescent years. Close physical contact, peer instruction about sexuality, and exploitation of a weaker or younger adolescent by an older adolescent can all be part of the context of early homosexual experiences. Most often, these experiences are discrete events in the pursuit of a heterosexual direction (Gagnon, 1972).

Spanier (1975) has described four stages of heterosexual involvement. These include kissing, light petting, heavy petting, and intercourse. From a national sample of college students, he determined that most people begin with kissing and progress from one level to the next. The process of moving through these levels of involvement is closely related to when persons begin to date and how often they date. The earlier a person begins dating the more likely he or she is to experience premarital intercourse.

In the United States, sexual involvement is well under way during the high school years. A study in Illinois found that 50 percent of boys and 48 percent of girls had experienced light petting by their 15th birthday

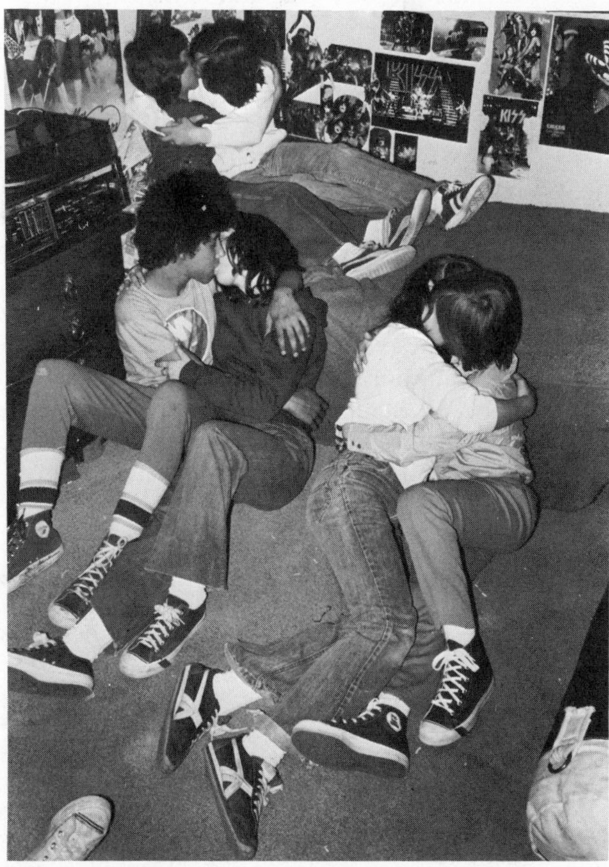

Sexual encounters during adolescence are part of the groundwork for adult sexuality.

(Juhasz, 1976). Sorenson (1973) reported that 59 percent of boys and 45 percent of girls in the age range 13–19 had experienced sexual intercourse. Among this group of sexually experienced adolescents, 13 percent had had their first experience at the age of 12 or under. By the age of 15, 71 percent of males and 56 percent of females who were sexually experienced had had intercourse. These data indicate that a large group of adolescents make the transition to an adult form of sexual behavior through direct experience in sexual intimacy. Although this pattern continues to show females as less active than males in all stages of sexual activity, the pattern is toward increasingly large numbers of sexually active females at young ages (Micklin, Thomson, & Gardner, 1977; Gordon, 1973; Juhasz, 1976).

The third element in the development of adult sexuality is the formation of an emotional commitment to a sexual partner. Intense romantic involvements appear to be a common characteristic of adolescent heterosexual relationships. In a national sample of high school seniors, only 35 percent of the white subjects and 23 percent of the black subjects had never gone steady during the previous three years (Larson, Spreitzer, & Snyder, 1976). White males were the largest group with no experience in a "steady" relationship (40 percent had never gone steady). Sorenson (1973) described the primary expectations of young adolescents in an intimate relationship. Love is seen as mutual participation in a satisfying relationship. Love does not require a long-term commitment. The partners share a feeling of understanding and closeness that is expressed in part through sexual intimacy.

The meaning of sexuality in a relationship seems to differ for two subgroups in Sorenson's sample: the "serial monogamists" and the "sexual adventurers." The serial monogamists do not have sexual relations with other partners while they are involved in a relationship. However, they are likely to move from one close relationship to the next. The sexual adventurers do not make a commitment to the partner in a sexual encounter. They view sex as a pleasurable experience that does not require a context of love or emotional intimacy to be enjoyed. In Sorenson's sample, more of those who experienced intercourse described themselves as serial monogamists than as sexual adventurers. Although the latter had more sex partners, the former experienced intercourse more frequently.

The Double Standard The concept of a double standard refers to a difference in the accepted sexual behavior for men and women. This view was prominent during the Victorian era of the nineteenth century. It was believed that women were asexual, but they put up with their husband's sexual needs out of marital obligation. Men were encouraged to meet their needs elsewhere, especially with servants or prostitutes. The remnants of this double standard are still with us. For example, female virginity is valued more than male virginity. Parents are likely to be more protective about their daughter's social activities than their sons. The data on premarital sexual activity for men and women suggest that women are clearly not asexual. Nonetheless, beliefs about the double standard linger on.

In Table 4.2 the responses of college students from 1965, 1970, 1975, and 1980 are shown. Women who have sexual intercourse with a great many men are more likely to be judged as immoral than men who have intercourse with many women. Another interesting aspect of this data is the trend for students in 1980 to be more critical of multiple sexual relations than their counterparts in 1970 or 1975. These data show that at an attitudinal level, people still express a double standard with respect to the appropriateness of sexual behavior for men and women.

In a sample of over 1,000 students at 12 colleges, Carns (1973) found that males and females were just about opposite in the way they evaluated the nature of the relationship with their first sexual partner. Females were most likely to have intercourse with a person whom they planned to marry or with whom they had a strong emotional involvement. Males were most likely to have intercourse with someone described as a "pickup." When males are involved with casual sexuality, they tend to brag about it or to share it with their male peers. An important part of early male sexual activity is a need for recognition of one's virility among same-sex peers. In contrast, females are more likely to focus on the romantic elements of the relationship. They are more likely than males to keep their sexual experiences to themselves rather than to share them. They are more likely than males to get mixed reactions rather than approval for their sexual activities. In all of these ways, the picture emerges of females carrying on a private dialogue with an old standard of Victorian modesty. In fantasy and

Table 4.2 Percentage of 1965, 1970, 1975, and 1980 College Students Strongly Agreeing with Certain Statements Regarding the Morality of Premarital Sexual Relationships

	Males		Females	
Statement	%	N	%	N
A man who has had sexual intercourse with a great many women is immoral				
1965	35.0	127	56.0	114
1970	15.0	137	22.0	157
1975	19.5	138	30.1	296
1980	26.5	166	38.9	234
A woman who has had sexual intercourse with a great many men is immoral.				
1965	42.0	118	91.0	114
1970	33.0	137	54.0	157
1975	28.5	130	41.0	295
1980	41.8	165	49.6	236

Source: From "Change in Sexual Attitudes and Behavior of College Students from 1965 to 1980: A Research Note" by I. E. Robinson and D. Jedlicka, in *Journal of Marriage and the Family,* 1982, *44,* p. 239.

in reality, females see sexual intercourse as an element of a more elaborate emotional commitment to a partner. Males, on the other hand, begin their movement toward adult sexuality by exploring the satisfactions of sexuality per se. It is only later that they begin to merge sexual interests and social interests into an interpersonal commitment to a partner (Gagnon & Simon, 1973).

The sexual experiences encountered during the period of adolescence have important implications for adult sexuality. They can contribute to feelings of being vulnerable or strong, exploited or in control, attractive or ugly, potent or powerless. The significance of loss of virginity is poorly understood for its contribution to adult sexuality. Clearly sometime during adolescence or young adulthood, we pass across the threshold of sexual experience moving from the state of novice to the state of new initiate. From that point on, there is continuous learning, adaptation, and some degree of frustration associated with the pursuit of sexual intimacy.

Adult Sexuality

The work of Masters and Johnson (1966, 1970) on human sexuality provides a major breakthrough in the study of adult sexuality. They developed a technology for collecting data and making direct observations of the physical changes that accompany masturbation and copulation. Their research has been critical for describing healthy sexual functioning and also for guiding the development of a new form of sex therapy for couples who are experiencing sexual dysfunctions. Masters and Johnson have described four phases to the human sexual response. These include:

1. An *excitement phase* when sexual stimulation leads to clitoral erection and moistening of the vaginal lining for females, erection of the penis and nipples for males.
2. A *plateau phase* when continued stimulation results in muscle tension, rapid breathing, and body flush. For females, the clitoris remains sensitive but retracts and the vaginal opening closes somewhat while the inner two-thirds of the vagina balloon out. For males, the testes increase in size and are pulled up into the scrotum.
3. An *orgasmic phase* of rhythmic muscular contractions. The contractions occur about every 8 second for both males and females. Semen is ejected in five or six spurts. During this phase, heart rate increases, blood pressure rises, and breathing is more rapid.
4. A *resolution phase* when muscle tension, blood pressure, and respiration return to a preexcitement level. Males experience a period when they are not responsive to new sexual stimulation. Females can have further orgasms if stimulated immediately.

Masters and Johnson identified many areas of similarity in the sexual responses of men and women. The subjective experience of orgasm is very similar for men and women. The woman's orgasm is based primarily on clitoral stimulation. With vaginal penetration the orgasm is more diffuse;

with direct clitoral stimulation the orgasm is more rapid and more intense. Women and men both experience feelings of physical discomfort when the plateau phase is not followed by orgasm. A major difference is that women are capable of repeated orgasms whereas men have a built-in resting period before they can respond to sexual stimulation.

The fact that these observations have been made does not necessarily change the way men and women think about sexuality. Hite (1976) found that many women felt guilty about having clitoral orgasm. They also held the idea that women were or were supposed to be less sexually responsive then men. Beliefs about the appropriate roles of men and women in sexuality influence the frequency of intercourse, the frequency with which orgasm is experienced, and the variations in sexual expression that are explored.

Sexuality in Marriage

Information about adult sexuality within the marriage relationship is limited. There are a number of methodological problems that suggest a very cautious approach to the findings of the studies that are available. Kinsey's research was based on data collected from over 11,000 subjects in the period from 1938 to 1951. This means that his data are drawn from a group of people who were born around the turn of the century and later. His sample was a volunteer sample. The subjects represented a wide range of ages, although lower educational levels, rural populations, and nonwhite groups were not adequately represented. The data were collected in carefully conducted face-to-face interviews. One of the most important contributions of the Kinsey research is the far-reaching questions he posed about sexual behavior. The Kinsey data continue to be used as a benchmark against which current trends in sexual behavior are compared.

A more recent study by Westoff (1974) offers data from two probability samples of married women under the age of 45. These data compare frequency of intercourse from 1965 to 1970. The study has the advantage of including a more truly representative sample of the population. It also has some limitations. Only women were studied, and then only in the age range up to 45. Very few questions about sexual behavior were asked.

Several surveys of sexual behavior and sexual attitudes have been published. These include Hunt's (1974) study of sexual behavior that was commissioned by the Playboy Foundation; the *Redbook* survey of its readership; and Bell and Bell's (1972) national survey of married women about sexual values and behavior. Each of these surveys provides a picture of adult sexuality from a slightly different point of view. There are several reasons why these studies cannot be taken to represent the population as a whole. The samples overrepresent well-educated working women. People who are willing to describe their sex life may not have the same pattern of sexual activity as those who are not. The studies by Westoff, *Redbook,* and

Bell and Bell focus exclusively on the woman's perspective. This tendency for sex research to be preoccupied with women's sexual activities and sexual satisfaction is an ironic reverse of the traditional view of women as less sexual or less readily stimulated. These surveys do not address the very real problems of male impotence or questions about satisfactions related to orgasm for men.

In light of the limitations of these data sources, let us consider three questions: (1) What is the frequency of coitus among married couples? (2) How does the pattern of sexual activity change during the marriage? (3) How are sexual activity and sexual pleasure related to marital satisfaction?

Frequency of Coitus among Married Couples. Table 4.3 shows the frequency of coitus as estimated by husbands and wives. The data are based on two sources, the Kinsey reports for the periods 1938 to 1946 (1949 for wives) and the Hunt survey for 1972. Data are compared for white subjects only. These average data suggest that couples are experiencing intercourse an average of 3.3 to 3.7 times weekly at the youngest ages and once per week at the oldest ages. Westoff (1974) reported a change in frequency from

TABLE 4.3 Marital Coitus: Frequency per Week as Estimated by Husbands and Wives

Note: In both tables (Tables 11.3 and 11.4) Kinsey's data have been adapted by recalculating his five-year cohorts into ten-year cohorts to facilitate comparison with Hunt's data. The dates 1938 to 1946 and 1938 to 1949 refer to the years during which the interviews were conducted on which Kinsey's data are based: the Hunt fieldwork was done, as indicated, in 1972. The Hunt data are based on the white sample, since the Kinsey data are only for whites.

Husbands, 1938–1946 and 1972

1938–1946 (Kinsey)			1972 (Hunt Survey)		
Age	Mean	Median	Age	Mean	Median
16–25	3.3	2.3	18–24	3.7	3.5
26–35	2.5	1.9	25–34	2.8	3.0
36–45	1.8	1.4	35–44	2.2	2.0
36–45	1.8	1.4	35–44	2.2	2.0
46–55	1.3	0.8	45–54	1.5	1.0
56–60	0.8	0.6	55 & over	1.0	1.0

Wives, 1938–1949 and 1972

1938–1949 (Kinsey)			1972 (Hunt Survey)		
Age	Mean	Median	Age	Mean	Median
16–25	3.2	2.6	18–24	3.3	3.0
26–35	2.5	2.0	25–34	2.6	2.1
36–45	1.9	1.4	35–44	2.0	2.0
46–55	1.3	0.9	45–54	1.5	1.0
56–60	0.8	0.4	55 & over	1.0	1.0

Source: M. Hunt, *Sexual Behavior in the Seventies* (Chicago: Playboy Press), 1974, p. 190.

6.8 times in a four-week period in 1965 to 8.2 times in a four-week period in 1970. Both data sources suggest that today couples in every age group are having intercourse more frequently than couples were in the past. Westoff (1974) reported that several factors were associated with higher rates of marital coitus. Women who were on the pill, women who worked for professional career reasons, and women who were more highly educated reported more frequent intercourse.

Variability in frequency of intercourse is very great for both men and women. Westoff reported a range in his 1970 data from no intercourse in a four-week period (6 percent) to 21 or more times in a four-week period (3.9 percent). Many life experiences, including illness, work pressures, childbirth, and marital conflict, can temporarily lower the rate of intercourse for a couple.

Another aspect of the pattern of sexual activity is the frequency with which adults achieve orgasm. This question is usually raised with a special interest in women. It is often assumed that men always achieve orgasm, or if male orgasm did not occur, the experience is not "counted" as coitus (Reiss, 1980). Bell (1976) compared the data from his work with that from Kinsey's. Bell found that 90 percent of the women in his sample who were 25 years old had experienced orgasm through coitus. Kinsey had reported that about 75 percent of those who were 25 years old had achieved orgasm. Hunt (1974) compared his data on females in the 15th year of marriage to those of Kinsey. Table 4.4 shows that there has been some increase in the percentage of women who frequently experience orgasm. The change has not been dramatic. The differences in data collection strategies for the two studies leave the matter of real changes open to question.

The historical trends suggest that the cultural context will also influence frequency of intercourse. During the twentieth century there has been a gradual shift toward greater acceptance and value placed on the female sexual experience. The value of mutual orgasm, the rise in frequency of premarital intercourse among women, and the increase in books on making sex a pleasurable experience are all expressions of a changing norm about the importance of sexuality in adult life. More women are expecting to enjoy sex and they are looking to their male partners to provide sexual gratification.

Changes in Sexual Activity over the Course of the Marriage The evidence is rather compelling that frequency of coitus decreases with age. Kinsey, Bell, and Westoff all report a similar pattern of sexual activity declining from about nine times per month at ages 25–30 to six times per month at ages 41–50. Contrary to our contemporary view of the swinging singles, married men reported more frequent rates of orgasm at every age than did single men. Bell (1976) found that two-thirds of the subjects found the frequency of intercourse "just about right," 30 percent wished they would have intercourse more frequently, and only 4 percent thought they had intercourse too often.

TABLE 4.4 Proportion of Marital Coitus Resulting in Orgasm: Married White Females, 1938–1949 and 1972

1938–1949 (Kinsey) Females in 15th Year of Marriage		1972 (Hunt Survey) Females with 15 Years Median Duration of Marriage	
Orgasm Frequency	**Percent of Wives**	**Orgasm Frequency**	**Percent of Wives**
90–100	45	All or almost all of the time	53
30–89	27	About 3/4 to about 1/2 of the time	32
1–29	16	About 1/4 of the time	8
None of the time	12	Almost none or none of the time	7

Source: M. Hunt, *Sexual Behavior in the Seventies* by M. Hunt (Chicago: Playboy Press), 1974, p. 212.

Age does seem to make a difference in the way sexual behavior is enacted (Bell, 1976). Women over the age of 50 are less likely to dress erotically or to choose unusual settings to have sex. They are less likely than younger women to discuss their intimate sexual feelings or fantasies with their husbands. They are also less likely to assume the "aggressive" role, that is, to initiate foreplay. Older women are much less likely to have experimented with oral-genital sex or various sexual positions during intercourse. In general, older women appear to be more restricted in their sex life. Whether this is due to more conventional attitudes or to the establishment of comfortable habits is hard to determine. We will need to wait until the cohort of women who were married in the mid–1970s reaches the age of 50 to learn whether couples who value a variety of sexual experiences retain that imaginative sexuality in a long-term monogamous relationship.

How Are Sexual Activity and Sexual Pleasure Related to Marital Satisfaction? Most people enter marriage with high hopes for a pleasurable sexual relationship. Evidence presented thus far suggests that sexual activity is more frequent early in the marriage and gradually decreases. Does this mean that satisfaction with one's sexual life decreases? Is infrequent sexual activity associated with marital dissatisfaction?

Sexuality is only one element in a marital relationship. We can expect that there is a reciprocal influence between sexual pleasure and marital satisfaction. When the marriage is working and the partners are satisfied in their relationship, their sexual life will be enhanced. Fulfillment in sexual experiences will strengthen the bond between the partners and increase their satisfaction about the marriage.

As we look at evidence about marital satisfaction and sexuality it is important to realize that fewer and fewer adults come to marriage as complete sexual novices. Zelnick and Kantner (1977) reported that 55 percent of unmarried 19–year-old American females had already had intercourse. Among white females, 48.7 percent of 19–year-olds had had intercourse. Among black females, 83.6 percent had had intercourse. Hunt's study found that 95 percent of males and 81 percent of females in the age range 18 to 25 had had premarital intercourse. Tavris and Sadd (1977) found that 96 percent of the respondents to the *Redbook* survey who were under 20 had had premarital intercourse. The implication is that contemporary adults do not marry in order to have sex. There are growing expectations that marriage will integrate sexual satisfaction in an emotionally intimate relationship.

Using Kinsey's data, Gebhard (1966) found that the 60 percent of couples who described their marriage as "very happy" experienced orgasm significantly more often than the other couples. Hunt (1974) found that marital coitus was 50 percent more frequent among couples who described their marriage as "close" rather than "distant." When the quality of the marriage was described as very close, the partners were much more likely to describe their sex life as very pleasurable. This pattern was even more striking for women than for men. The happier couples are together, the more likely they are to see their sexual needs as similar. This would be true whether the couple has frequent or infrequent sexual activity.

Sexual Behavior of Aging Adults

What do we know about the sexual behavior of aging adults? Returning to Table 4.1, there appears to be a decline in thoughts about sex beginning with the 18–25 age group that reaches a lifelong low among the oldest group sampled. If thoughts about sex decrease with age, what about sexual activity?

There is a need to take a balanced approach to this question. One of the most pervasive myths about sexuality is that older people do not have sexual urges. It may even be viewed by some people as inappropriate or disgusting to think of people 70 years old and older as sexual. Many older people themselves hold this view and inhibit or reject their sexual responses. In the face of this myth, Masters and Johnson (1970) made a very strong case for the continued potential for sexual satisfaction during later adulthood.

> Sexually, the male and female can function effectively into their eighties, if they understand that certain physiological changes will occur and if they don't let these changes frighten them. Once they allow themselves to think they will lose their sexual effectiveness, then, for all practical purposes, they will, indeed—but because they will have become victims of the myth, not because their bodies will have lost the capacity to perform. (Masters and Johnson, 1970)

This optimism about sexuality in later adulthood is based on the following facts: Postmenopausal women continue to have a high level of clitoral sensitivity; men over the age of 65 continue to have the capacity for erections and among studies of older adults, in every age group from 60 to

Sexual intimacy can continue to be a rich source of pleasure in later life.

100 there were always some individuals who were sexually active (Pfeiffer, 1978; Weg, 1978). In other words, the evidence supports the idea that there is no biological end point that would prevent further sexual activity.

In contrast to this view, there is evidence that older adults are not as sexually active as younger adults, and that the frequency of sexual relations shows a marked decline from the decade of the fifties to the sixties. Many of the physiological changes of aging that will be described in the section on the climacteric result in more discomfort during intercourse for women and less vigor in the sexual response for men. The early Kinsey reports (Kinsey, Pomeroy, & Martin, 1948) found the incidence of impotence for males to be 2 percent at 35 years, 10 percent at 55 years, and 50 percent at 75 years. In addition to the effects of aging, there may be effects of chronic diseases like diabetes or hypertension that can disrupt sexual functioning. The continued use of tranquilizing drugs can weaken erection or lead to impotence. Finally, the ratio of older women to older men leads to extreme unavailability of sexual partners for women over the age of 65. This may be the primary factor in the decrease in sexual activity for older women.

The key factor for continued sexual satisfaction for both men and women is the presence of a thoughtful, caring partner. For older adults, sex becomes a rich means of experiencing interpersonal closeness, vitality, and reaffirmation of selfhood. A 74–year-old woman expresses these ideas in her perspective on sex:

> Sex isn't as powerful a need as when you're young, but the whole feeling is there; it's as nice as it ever was. He puts his arms around you, kisses you,

> and it comes to you—satisfaction and orgasm—just like it always did . . . don't let anybody tell you different. Maybe it only happens once every two weeks, but as you get older it's such a release from the tensions. I'm an old dog who's even tried a few new tricks. Like oral sex, for instance. . . . We weren't too crazy about it though. . . . We take baths together and he washes my body and I wash his. I know I'm getting old and my skin could use an ironing, but we love each other—so sex is beautiful. (Wax, 1975, pp. 46–47)

The Reproductive Career

The fact that this chapter separates sexuality from the reproductive function sheds some light on where our culture now stands in its view of sexuality. Sexuality can have a reproductive goal, but sexuality can also be a form of playful pleasure in its own right—even within the bonds of marriage! In many traditional societies, sex has been viewed as an obligation the wife performs for her husband. In a survey of 190 cultures, Ford and Beach (1951) found that in nearly all of them, sex was treated as conjugal duty. Sexual pleasure between the couples was not expected, nor was it a key to marital satisfaction. In one society, the Turu of Tanzania, marriages are clearly based on economic considerations. There is minimal expectation for romantic involvement. However, both the husband and the wife are expected to pick a "Mbuya," a lover, who fulfills their romantic needs for sexual pleasure. In that society, there is cultural support for the separation of the reproductive and pleasurable aspects of sexuality (Schneider, 1971).

The reproductive career for women includes menstruation, pregnancy, childbirth, and the climacteric (menopause). For men, the reproductive career includes the production of sperm, impregnation, fatherhood, and the decline in sperm production. As you can see, the physical markers are much clearer for women. The primacy and visibility of the woman's role in reproduction has, for some time, overshadowed the focus on paternity as it affects men and their development.

Menstruation and the Hormone Cycle

With puberty, the increased production of sex hormones has direct impact on the reproductive cycle. Their impact on the desire for sexual activity is less obvious. Research with nonhuman primates has shown that sex hormones act in an on/off fashion to prompt sexual receptivity in the female. Female monkeys are receptive to sexual activity only at one phase of the hormonal cycle, generally a phase that coincides with ovulation. In humans, sexuality and sexual activity are more directly influenced by social and psychological factors than by hormone levels. Females can be sexually receptive whenever they wish to be.

FIGURE 4.1 Changes in Hormone Cycle

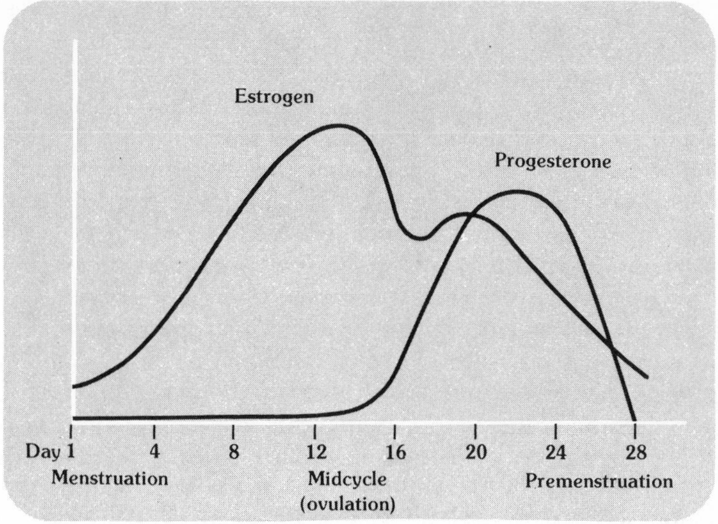

Source: from William D. Odell and Dean L. Moyer, *Physiology of Reproduction* (St. Louis: The C. V. Mosby Company; 1971) Used by permission of the publisher and the authors.

The hormone cycle does, however, play a part in the pattern of tension, confidence, and sociability generally experienced by women (see Figure 4.1). The menstrual cycle involves an average of 28 days. Very simply, it includes three phases that are characterized by changing patterns of hormones at different levels (McCary, 1978).

Destructive phase The uterine lining is discharged. The menstrual flow lasts from three to seven days. During this period progesterone, which was responsible for building up the lining of the uterus, drops to a minimal level.

Follicular phase After menstruation, follicles in the ovaries secrete estrogen which stimulates the development of the ova. One ovum reaches maturity and at about the 14th day of the cycle it is released. The concentration of estrogen increases throughout this phase, reaching its peak at ovulation.

Luteal phase Once the ovum is released the pituitary gland stimulates the remains of the ovarian follicle to produce progesterone, which builds up the lining of the uterus and provides sources of nourishment for the potential fertilized egg. High levels of estrogen and progesterone eventually signal the pituitary gland to stop production, and if fertilization has not occurred, the uterine lining is shed and the cycle starts again.

There is some evidence that the period of about three days before menstruation begins through the first three or four days of the menstrual flow is a time of irritability and tension for many women. According to Bardwick (1971), changes in the level of estrogen and progesterone are correlated with emotional changes at various phases of the menstrual cycle. The periods of high estrogen production at the beginning of the menstrual cycle when there has been a relative absence of estrogen and at ovulation when estrogen is at a peak are associated with feelings of self-acceptance, alertness, and well-being. Periods of low estrogen and low progesterone are associated with anxiety, shame, and fears of mutilation.

Consider the possibility that knowing the period is about to start may influence a woman's anxiety level. Perhaps the change in mood is a reflection of concern about menstruation rather than a product of hormone changes. Paige (1971, 1973) evaluated this hypothesis by comparing women who were not taking oral contraceptives, women who were on a combination birth-control pill that provided constant levels of progesterone and estrogen for 20 days, and women who were on a sequential pill that produced a more natural hormone cycle. Those on the combination pill had less premenstrual anxiety than those on the sequential pill or on no oral contraceptive. This finding supports the hormone-based concept of mood shifts. However, Paige also found that the amount of menstrual flow was directly related to premenstrual anxiety, regardless of the birth-control method. Women who had a heavy menstrual flow were more anxious than those who did not. Once again, this anxiety may be related to an underlying hormonal factor, or it may be related to the mess and unpleasantness of menstruation itself.

Is it possible that expectations about menstruation can increase one's perception of related symptoms? Ruble (1977) told women that it was possible through scientific tests to predict the date of the next menstruation. One group was told that their menstruation was due in a week to ten days. The second group was told that their menstruation was due in the next day or two. The women in the second group reported more menstrual symptoms even though both groups were equally unlikely to begin menstruation in the next few days. Just thinking that one's menstrual period is due can prompt the associated physical symptoms.

What are the consequences of these premenstrual mood shifts? Some accounts suggest that women are more aggressive, more likely to commit suicide, and more likely to perform poorly in tests of achievement during the premenstrual phase. The following data support this notion of a disruptive menstrual phase:

> During this 25 percent of each month, to cite but a few examples, occur 49 percent of all crimes committed by female prisoners, 45 percent of punishments meted out to school girls, 53 percent of [female] suicides, and 46 percent of [women's] admissions to mental hospitals. In advanced examinations, the pass rate of female students was 13 percent lower [during the menstrual period]. The British Road Research Laboratory reports that 60 percent of women's traffic accidents also occur during the same phase. (Gadpaille, 1975, p. 351)

Let us consider the possibility that intellectual ability is altered just before menstruation. Golub (1975) gave a number of personality tests and intelligence tests to a group of women during the four days before menstruation and once two weeks later. She did find evidence of premenstrual anxiety and depression. But on 11 of 13 tests of intellectual ability there were no differences related to the menstrual cycle.

Rodin (1976) found even more striking results. She compared three groups of women, those with severe menstrual symptoms, those with moderate menstrual symptoms, and those who were not menstruating. Half of each group was emotionally aroused by threat of a painful electric shock. Rodin hypothesized that group one would use their severe menstrual symptoms to explain their high level of arousal. She argued that they would be less distracted from task performance than the other two groups. The high-arousal high-symptom group did in fact perform better than the other two high-arousal groups. They also showed greater tolerance for frustration and less fear of the shock. These women were able to explain their nervousness by the fact that they were menstruating rather than by the fear that the task would be very difficult or that they might fail and be shocked.

The research suggests that mood changes may very well occur during the hormone cycle. Certainly these mood shifts vary in extremity for different women. The consequences of the mood shifts are less clear. Some women learn to "read" their cycle and appropriately attribute changes in mood to this biological explanation. Other women may actually be made anxious by the events of menstruation and its cultural significance rather than the hormonal changes. Still other women simply carry on during menstruation in their usual manner.

The Male Cycle

There is some evidence of a male hormonal cycle, although it is by no means conclusive. Ramey (1972) reported on the results of a 16–year study of Danish males. Males showed a rhythmic change in hormone levels on a 30–day cycle. This cycle was associated with changes in irritability, efficiency, and reaction to stress. Males did not perceive their behavior as subject to cyclical patterns, but their responses to psychological tests revealed patterned shifts in mood, sociability, and response to stress. Other studies have found relationships between testosterone level and depressed mood. The testosterone cycle was not necessarily rhythmic. In one study of 20 men, 12 had regular cycles ranging from 8 to 30 days. The others did not (Doering, Brodie, Kraemer, Moos, Becker, & Hamburg, 1975).

There is some fascinating, but speculative, work suggesting the possibility of couple synchrony in hormonal function. In one study, there was a trend for the man's level of testosterone to peak around seven days after his wife's ovulation. At this point, his wife's testosterone level reached its postovulation peak as well. No behavioral consequences of this hormonal coordination were described (Persky, Lief, O'Brien, Strauss, & Miller, 1977). Another study found a shift in the husband's body temperature during the same midcycle period when his wife's body temperature showed a preovulation dip and a postovulation rise (Henderson, 1976). The possibility that this kind of coordination is mediated through the sense of smell, especially the odor of pheromones, is currently being investigated.

Pregnancy and Childbirth

Most American babies are conceived within the context of a relationship between a man and woman in their twenties or thirties. In 1979, among married women age 18–24, the average number of births expected was 2.03. About 5.6 percent thought they would have no children and about 11 percent thought they would have four or more (U.S. Bureau of the Census, 1980, 1981). Thus for most married couples, pregnancy and childbirth experiences will be confined to a few years during the early or middle adulthood stages.

The decision to have a child usually reflects a strong commitment between the partners about their ability to provide care and love to someone in addition to themselves. The decision to have a child may also be influenced by pressures from parents or peers, by early sex-role identifications with one's own parents, or by a sense of delight in interacting with young children. We know, too, that for some mothers the fact of pregnancy results more from chance than from a deliberate decision. Among unwed adolescent mothers, pregnancy is usually not planned, but simply happens to some 30 percent of sexually active girls (Zelnik & Kantner, 1977).

In most families, the decision to have a child is a carefully planned, deliberate event. With the availability of effective contraceptive devices, parents can determine the number of children they will have and the approximate spacing of children. With only two children planned, each one becomes a focus for attention, planning, and ritualization. Today, parents expect to have normal, even perfect babies. Many couples are beginning to focus on the choice of sex of their child, using techniques that include the timing of intercourse, the use of particular vaginal lubricants, and even sperm screening and artificial insemination to increase the chances of a male or a female child.

The planning for childbirth extends to prenatal health care, attendance in childbirth class, selection of a particular setting for childbirth that permits the continuation of family intimacy, and the selection of an obstetrician or nurse-midwife who will permit the kind of parent participation in delivery that the couple desires. Increasing numbers of adults are choosing to have their children at or in homelike birth settings rather than going to a hospital (Norwood, 1978). Many obstetricians advise participation in Lamaze natural childbirth training or some other childbirth preparation. Parents are coming to the birth event with new views about their ability to actively contribute to this important life occasion. Hospitals are even courting expectant parents with special facilities to encourage adults to use their maternity units. These special facilities include sibling visitation units, special dining areas where the new parents can eat together before they go home, and inclusion of the father as an active participant during labor and delivery.

In the following sections three general topics are discussed. First, a description of the birth process clarifies some of the biological events surrounding this important life occasion. Second, the psychosocial factors associated with pregnancy and delivery are discussed. This section emphasizes the variety of factors, including culture, socioeconomic status, and emotional well-being, that can influence the experiences of pregnancy and childbirth. Finally we consider the impact of certain characteristics of mothers on their babies. This section is relevant not only because of the potential costs to infants that result from certain maternal conditions but because these sources of potential infant impairment result in new kinds of stresses on the parent-child relationship.

The Birth Process Birth is accomplished by the involuntary contractions of the uterine muscles referred to as labor. The length of time from the beginning of labor to the birth of the infant is highly variable. The average time for a first labor (primipara) is 14 hours and for a later labor (multipara) is 8 hours (Fitzpatrick, Reed, & Mastroianni, 1971). The uterine contractions serve two central functions: effacement and dilatation. Effacement refers to the shortening of the cervical canal. Dilatation refers to the gradual enlarging of the cervix from an opening only millimeters wide to a diameter of about 10 centimeters, large enough for the baby to pass through. Effacement and dilatation occur without deliberate effort by the mother. Once the cervix is fully enlarged, the mother can assist in the birth of the infant by exerting pressure on the abdominal walls around the uterus. In addition, the baby helps in the birth process by squirming, turning the head, and pushing against the birth canal.

The medical profession describes three stages of labor. Stage one begins with the onset of uterine contractions and ends with full dilatation of the cervix. This is the longest phase. Stage two involves the expulsion of the fetus. It begins at full dilatation and ends with delivery of the baby. The third stage begins with delivery of the baby and ends with the expulsion of the placenta. This phase usually takes about five to ten minutes.

These three stages of labor do not precisely parallel the personal experience of childbirth. For example, while the birth of the placenta is considered a unique stage of labor in the medical model, it is rarely mentioned in women's accounts of their birth experiences. On the other hand, many of the signs of impending labor that occur in the last weeks of pregnancy might well be viewed as the experiential beginning of labor. In

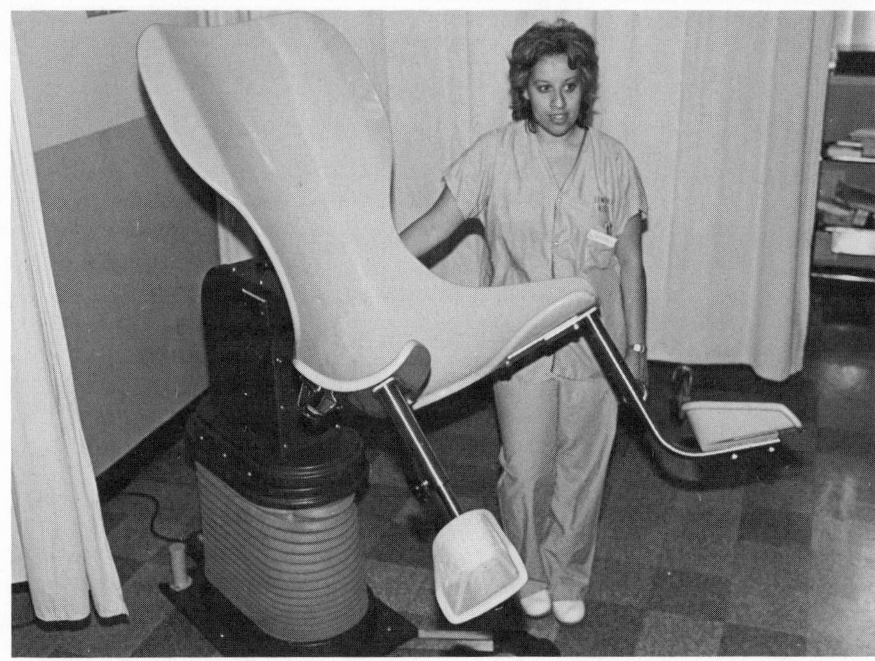

The birthing chair is considered an innovation in modern medical technology. It takes advantage of gravity to ease the birth process. The adjoining drawings show the obstetric chairs of the 16th, 18th, and 19th centuries.

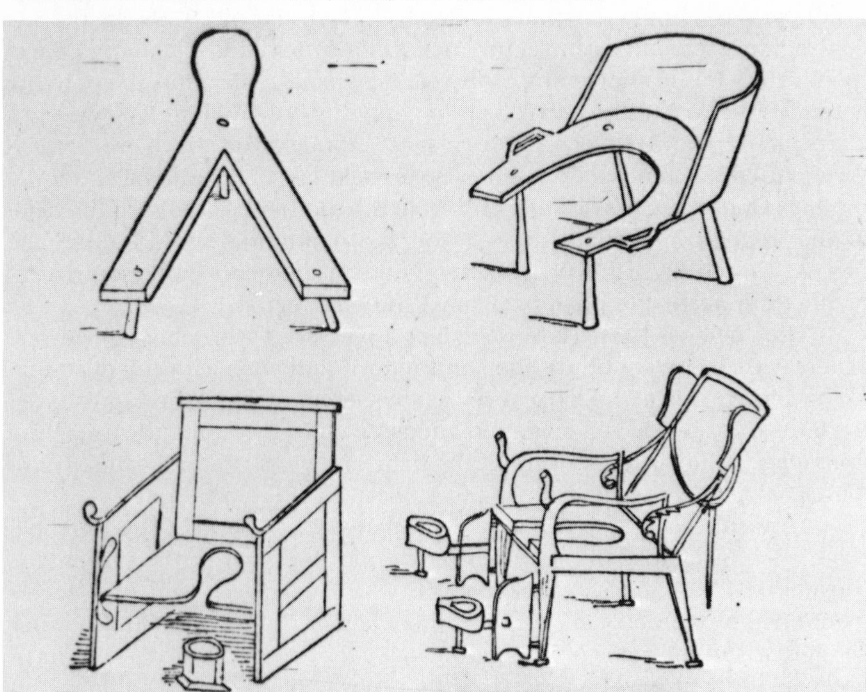

terms of the psychological adaptation to the birth process, labor can be viewed in five phases: (1) early signs that labor is approaching; (2) strong, regular uterine contractions signaling that labor has begun and generally accompanied by a move from the home to the hospital setting; (3) the transition phase, during which time contractions are strong, rest times in between contractions are short, and many women experience the greatest difficulty or discomfort; (4) the birth process, which allows for active participation of the mother in the delivery and which is generally accompanied by a move from the labor area to a more sterile delivery room; and (5) the postpartum period, which involves the initial interactions with the newborn, physiological changes that mark a return to the prepregnant stage, and a return to the home setting.

Ninety-one percent of mothers have visited a physician by the second trimester of pregnancy (U.S. Bureau of the Census, 1980). Women in metropolitan areas receive care earlier than rural mothers; women at lower socioeconomic levels come for a medical visit later in the pregnancy than do women at higher socioeconomic levels; and younger women (ages 12–19) come later in pregnancy than older women. In general, however, it is estimated that fewer than two percent of the population receive no medical care before birth. We can be fairly safe in assuming that the pregnant woman has, in the last trimester, been instructed about when to come to the hospital and what to expect when she arrives. We can also assume that when the pregnant woman arrives at the hospital, she is more fatigued, more anxious, and more alienated from her surroundings than would be ideal. A welling up of emotional concerns, including the desire to be recognized as an individual rather than being swallowed up in the anonymity of the institution, the desire to maintain competence and control, and the fear of loneliness and pain may interfere with the concentration and coping skills of even the most carefully trained expectant couples.

The difficulty of making the transition from home to hospital for the birth of a baby depends on several variables. First, some people are more familiar with the hospital setting and more trusting of health professionals than others. Second, some people arrive at the hospital with more training, experience, and self-confidence about the birth process than others. Third, some women are in better physical condition and are more rested than others as they begin the labor process. Finally, some hospitals are more sensitive to the individual parents' needs for information, privacy, and husband-wife intimacy during the labor than are others.

The physiological changes that occur after delivery are sizable and rapid. There is an enormous contrast between the state of arousal that is experienced during the birth phase and the fatigue that follows. Expulsion of the placenta signals a rapid alteration in the hormonal system, which brings the uterus from a weight of 2 pounds to its previous size of about 2 ounces in a five-to-six-week period. Hormones also stimulate lactation in nursing mothers. These dramatic changes are usually accompanied by a brief period of emotional lability that is commonly called postpartum depression or "blues." Mothers may cry for little reason, may feel extremely helpless and overawed by the responsibilities that await them, or may become withdrawn and irritable. Postpartum depression is usually a temporary expression that is probably most accurately explained as a consequence of hormonal changes, physical exhaustion, and the woman's emotional reactions to childbirth.

Psychosocial Factors Associated with Pregnancy and Delivery There are four categories of psychosocial variables that are associated with the ease or difficulty experienced during pregnancy and delivery. They are the mother's age, the emotional state of the mother, the mother's knowledge about the birth process, and the cultural patterns of responding to pregnancy and childbirth. These variables deserve attention, both for their impact on the mother as a developing adult as well as for their potential impact on the unborn child. As Grimm (1967) pointed out, much of the psychological research on factors associated with difficulties during pregnancy and delivery suffers from a variety of methodological maladies. The most striking problem is that women are not studied before they become pregnant in order to evaluate the degree to which the pregnancy itself contributes to their psychological state. Another limitation is the reliance on retrospective data, which may well be altered by the difficulties of labor and/or the health of the newborn. Finally, studies of the psychological factors associated with pregnancy tend to use small samples selected on the basis of who will volunteer for the research. Given these fair warnings, let us proceed.

Mother's Age The capacity for childbearing begins about one or one and a half years after the beginning of menarche and ends at the end of the climacteric. This provides about 35 years of potential fertility in a woman's life. Childbirth may occur at any or many points during this period (see Figure 4.2). The effects of childbirth on the physical and psychological well-being of the mother will differ greatly depending on her age and her emotional commitment to assuming the mother role. Similarly, the mother's age contributes significantly to the survival and well-being of her infant.

Women between the ages of 18 and 35 tend to provide a more ideal uterine environment and to give birth with fewer complications than do women under 18 or over 35. Particularly when it is their first pregnancy, women over 35 are likely to have longer labors and labor is more likely to result in death for either the infant or the mother than it is for younger mothers. The two groups of women who have the highest probability of giving birth to premature babies are those over 35 or between 15 and 19 (Illsley, 1967; LaBarre, 1969). The premature children of teenage mothers are more likely to have neurological defects that will influence their coping

FIGURE 4.2 Fertility Rates, by Age of Mother: 1940–1977

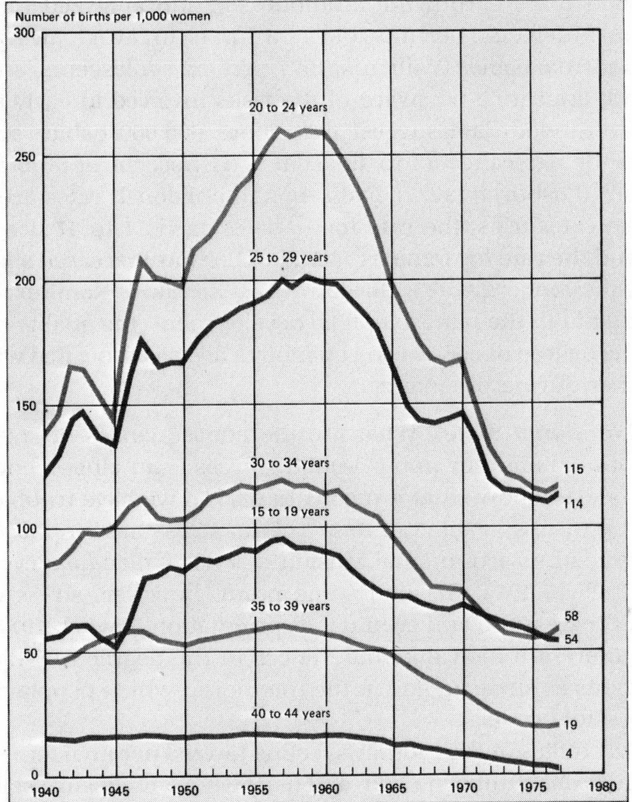

Source: *Social Indicators III,* by U. S. Bureau of the Census (Washington, D.C.: U.S. Government Printing Office), 1980, p. 16.

capacities than premature babies of older mothers. Young mothers (under 18) receive less adequate prenatal care and are less biologically mature than older mothers. Both of these factors make adolescent mothers more likely to experience complications during pregnancy that may endanger their infants as well as themselves (Menken, 1972).

One of the primary risks for infants of older mothers is the high incidence of Down's syndrome (often referred to as mongolism) among babies born to mothers who are over 40. Approximately one-third of all Down's syndrome babies are born to women over 40 (Reed, 1975). A woman's ova are present in a premature form from birth. The longer she lives, the older those cells become. It is hypothesized that some part of the high incidence of Down's syndrome among older women is the result of deteriorating ova.

Older women appear to be growing increasingly sensitive to the risk they take in having children after 35. The procedure of amniocentesis, in which fluid is drawn from the amniotic sac and analyzed for potential chromosomal defects, permits older women to avoid giving birth to severely abnormal babies (Williams, 1977). Young adolescents, on the other hand, do not appear to be aware of the risks involved in early childbirth. Planned Parenthood data suggest that about 600,000 babies are born to mothers in the age range 12 to 19. That is 21 percent of all births in the United States (Fosburgh, 1977). Even though childbirth rates are dropping in other age categories, the rate for females aged 14 to 17 has remained constant, and the rate for females 14 and under has increased slightly since the 1960s (Furstenberg, 1977; Gordon, 1973; Zelnik & Kantner, 1972). For the growing infant, the pattern of fetal development, the quality of prenatal care, and the degree of risk during childbirth are all associated with the age of the mother during pregnancy.

Mother's Emotional State What are the consequences of stress on the pregnant woman and her unborn child? Stress is an elusive concept, like happiness, we all know what it means to us, but we have trouble agreeing about what it means in general. Research on stress has emphasized that a certain degree of environmental tension can be challenging, even growth-producing (Selye, 1974). Beyond some point, however, stress can cause withdrawal, regression, and eventual disorientation (Paykel, 1974). We also know that there are individual differences in the degree to which people perceive events as stressful and in the manner in which people respond to similar stressful events.

Several studies of the mother's feeling toward her own femininity, her attitudes toward the unborn child, and her own psychological stability have demonstrated some association with difficulties experienced during pregnancy and delivery. Rosen (1955) found that of 54 women, those with more life stress experienced more vomiting and nausea. Hetzel, Bruer, and Poidevin (1961) compared 4 groups of women, 30 who experienced prolonged vomiting (hyperemisis), 40 who experienced toxemia (hypertension and swelling), 44 who had long labors, and 54 "normal" controls. Each of the three symptomatic groups had a significantly greater number of life stresses, particularly in the months preceding the symptoms, than did the control group. The more irritable, anxious, or depressed a woman is during pregnancy, the more medication she is likely to receive during delivery (Yang, Zweig, Douthitt, & Federman, 1976). The mother's orientation toward pregnancy and toward the child will be most directly expressed in her capacity to cope with the physical stress of labor. It may also be evidenced in more prolonged or complicated labor, but the psychological state of the mother can by no means be viewed as the single factor or even the strongest predictor in determining complications of labor. One study of particular interest found that women who viewed pregnancy as a "sick role" tended to have a longer labor and somewhat more complicated delivery than did those who viewed pregnancy as a "well role." Furthermore, when a woman viewed pregnancy in a role that was incongruent with the view held by her obstetrician, labor averaged more than seven hours longer than when patient and physician held congruent views (Rosengren, 1961). This kind of result suggests that psychological variables may be more directly related to cues surrounding the delivery itself rather than previously held attitudes or fears. Future research might consider such variables as the women's familiarity with the hospital setting and the degree of perceived support from health professionals as they influence the length and difficulty of labor.

Knowledge about the Birth Process The most obvious means of acquiring knowledge about the birth process is through having babies. Among women who have already delivered one child, the average length of labor is six hours shorter than labor among women who are having their first baby. While the discrepancy may be accounted for in part by the increased suppleness of the birth canal, it may also be possible that the woman who has already given birth is less tense, more capable of anticipating events in the labor, and more efficient both at relaxing when she can and exerting effort when it is required. It would be interesting to study women during more than one preganancy to evaluate the psychological differences in the birth process for women who are having their first child and women who have already experienced childbirth.

A number of training programs are available for parents to learn about the process of labor and delivery and to develop strategies for coping with the discomfort associated with the birth process. The programs, which are commonly referred to as "natural childbirth," are really coordinated techniques for managing birth. These programs are generally designed to allow the mother to participate actively in the delivery without the aid of anesthetics, which might interfere with her state of consciousness. The goals of childbirth instruction include teaching controlled relaxation, breathing, and exercise techniques to alleviate pressure on the contracting uterus, and providing emotional support during all phases of labor (Francoeur, 1982). The thrust of the various programs is to put the woman and her husband in a position of competence. Childbirth classes are designed to treat childbirth as a natural, healthy experience which will demand skill, concentration, and cooperation from husband and wife. When posed as an opportunity for active mastery, the events of childbirth lose many of their frightening connotations and become challenges to one's competence.

Studies to evaluate the impact of childbirth training provide mixed results. The most common finding is that women who have attended childbirth classes need less medication and anesthesia than those who do not attend (Earn, 1962; Roberts, Wootton, Kane, & Harnett, 1953). Two studies found that the length of labor is shorter for trained mothers (Thoms & Karlovsky, 1954; Van Auken & Tomlinson, 1953), but other studies report no difference in length of labor for prepared and untrained

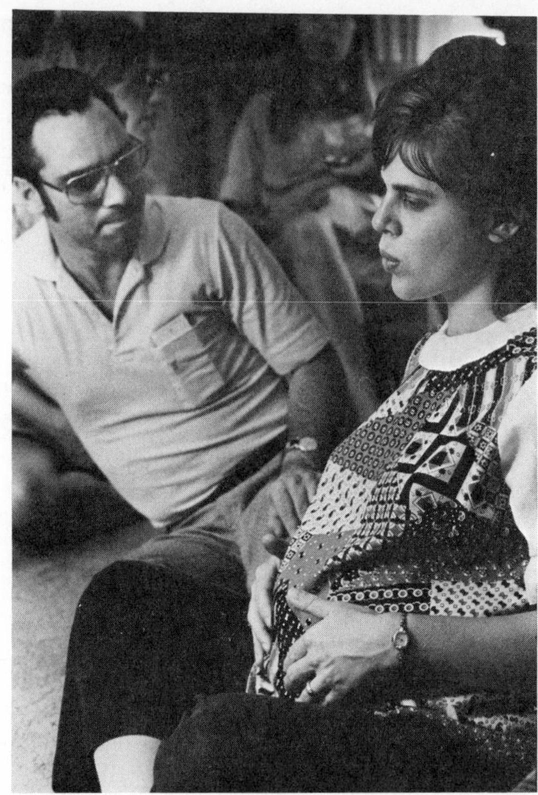

In the Lamaze method of preparation for childbirth the pregnant woman and her "coach" work together.

mothers (Davis & Marrone, 1962; Laird & Hogan, 1956). Newborns delivered to mothers who are trained in childbirth techniques are described as more alert and responsive than other babies. These results are most probably due to the diminished use of anesthetics.

Childbirth training teaches parents to take an active role in the birth of their child. Whether or not it speeds labor along, it certainly allows parents to feel more confident during the labor process and more immediately attached to their new child.

Cultural Patterns of Pregnancy and Childbirth A thorough appreciation of the events surrounding the birth of a child demands some perspective on the idiosyncrasies with which our culture approaches birth. The decision to have a child, the social experience of pregnancy, the particular style of help that is available for delivery of the child, and the care and attitudes toward mother, father, and baby after delivery can all be viewed as components of a cultural pattern, unique in some ways but part of a continuum of cultural orientations toward birth. Mead and Newton (1967) have collaborated on a paper that compares cultural patterns associated with pregnancy and childbirth. Much of the following discussion is derived from their paper.

Data on cross-cultural methods are drawn primarily from the Human Relations Areas Files and from Ford's (1945) comparison of reproductive behavior in 64 cultures. In many cultures men and nontribal women are not allowed to observe delivery. Furthermore, many of the events related to conception and delivery are considered too personal or private to discuss with "outsiders." Thus, the data on childbearing practices are not systematic. Comparisons across cultures can only serve to place the American system in a cultural context.

There is a strong assumption that the behavior of pregnant mothers and expectant fathers will influence the developing fetus and the ease or difficulty of childbirth. Among Ford's (1945) study, 42 of 64 cultures mentioned behaviors that either should or should not be performed by expectant parents. Many of the restrictions are dietary.

Among the Pomeroon Arawaks, though the killing and eating of a snake during the woman's pregnancy is forbidden to both father and mother, the husband is allowed to kill and eat any other animal. The cause assigned for the taboo of the snake is that the little infant might be similar, that is, able neither to talk nor walk (Roth, 1953, p. 122).

Attitudes toward pregnant women can be characterized along two dimensions: (1) solicitude versus shame and (2) adequacy versus vulnerability.

Solicitude toward the pregnant woman is shown in the care, interest, and help of others.

For example, it is said among Jordan villagers that "as people are careful of a chicken in the egg, all the more so should they be of a child in its mother's womb" (Granquist, 1950). As the Chagga in Africa say, "Pay attention to the pregnant woman! There is no one more important than she" (Guttmann, 1932).

Shame about pregnancy is shown in those cultures where pregnancy is kept a secret as long as possible. This may result from a fear that damage will come to the fetus through supernatural demons or because of shyness about the sexual implications of being pregnant. In either case, examples from the Ila of Africa, Ukrainian peasants, the Nahane of northern Canada, and from the peoples of the Punjab and Bulgaria demonstrate a desire to keep the fact of pregnancy hidden.

For many societies pregnancy brings feelings of adequacy and pride. It is a sign of sexual prowess and a means of entrance into social status. Some cultures do not arrange a wedding until after the woman has become pregnant. In a polygamous family the pregnant wife receives more of her husband's attention and may prevent her husband from taking an additional wife (Granquist, 1950). In some cultures women become more attractive after they have borne children.

"The Aymara widow of South America with many children is regarded as a desirable bride. Lepcha men consider that copulation with women who have borne more than one child is more enjoyable and less exhausting than with other adult women" (Mead & Newton, 1967, p. 158).

Vulnerability is expressed in the view that child-making is exhausting, that pregnant women are vulnerable, and that women grow more frail with each pregnancy. Among the Arapesh of New Guinea (Mead, 1935), pregnancy is tiring for both men and women. Once menstruation stops, the husband and wife must copulate repeatedly in order to provide the building materials for the fetus's semen and blood.

Taylor and Langer (1977) studied the reactions of others to pregnant women in American society. People were likely to stare at pregnant women or avoid them. Men acted as if the pregnant woman was a novel stimulus. They gaped or stared and were uneasy in interactions. Women were more likely to disapprove of the pregnant woman's functioning in an active, assertive role. There seems to be an expectation that pregnant women will withdraw from work settings as they enter their last months of pregnancy. Women who do not comply to this expectation are likely to receive a social message of rejection.

Childbirth in primitive cultures as well as in modern industrialized societies is an important event. The delivery is usually attended by two or more assistants who have specific roles to perform. Many cultures provide a special hut or site for delivery. In no primitive culture discussed by Mead and Newton is the delivering mother asked to move from one location to another in the midst of the birth. That appears to be a ritual reserved for modern industrial deliveries.

There appears to be a continuum of views about birth itself, from an extreme negative pole in which birth is dirty and defiling to an extreme positive pole in which birth is a personal achievement. The view that childbirth is a normal physical event would be the midpoint on this continuum.

When birth is viewed as dirty, as it is by the Arapesh of New Guinea and the Kadu Gollas of India, the woman must go to a separate area away from the village to deliver her child. Many cultures, including the ancient Hebrews, have extensive purification rituals which follow childbirth. In extreme cases, as in Vietnam, birth is seen as so defiling that the mother stays in for 30 to 100 days after delivery in order to avoid bringing bad luck to other people (Mead & Newton, 1967).

A slightly more positive orientation toward birth is to identify childbirth as a sickness. This view takes the pregnant Cuna Indian woman to her medicine man for daily medication. Although this view is changing among American parents (Lake, 1976), the delivery itself is usually treated as a medical crisis in much the same way as other surgical procedures.

The midpoint, what we might most appropriately describe as "natural childbirth," finds the mother delivering her baby in the presence of many members of the community, without much expression of pain, and without much magic or obstetrical mechanics.

Margaret Mead describes birth in Samoa (Mead, 1928):

> There is no privacy about a birth. Convention dictates that the mother should neither writhe, nor cry out, nor inveigh against the presence of twenty or thirty people in the house who sit up all night if need be, laughing, joking, and playing games. The midwife cuts the cord with a fresh bamboo knife and then all wait eagerly for the cord to fall off, the signal for a feast. . ..

At the most positive end of the scale, birth is seen as a proud achievement. Among the Ila of Northern Rhodesia:

> Women attending at birth were observed to shout praises of the woman who had had a baby. They all thanked her, saying "I give thanks to you today that you have given birth to a child." (Mead & Newton, 1967, p. 174)

A similar sentiment is expressed in Marjorie Karmel's description of the Lamaze method of childbirth:

> From the moment I began to push, the atmosphere of the delivery room underwent a radical transformation. Where previously everyone had spoken in soft and moderate tones in deference to my state of concentration, now there was a wild encouraging cheering section, dedicated to spurring me on. I felt like a football star, headed for a touchdown. (Karmel, 1959, pp. 93–94)

One consequence of the attitude held toward pregnancy is the degree of openness or secrecy practiced at the birth itself. The American culture

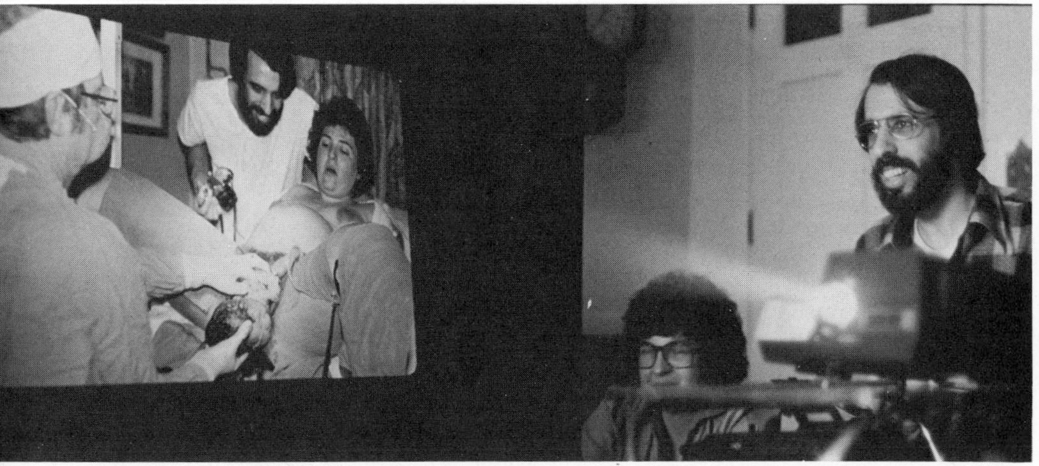

Today many couples are together during the birth of their child. Sharing this achievement may lead to increased intimacy.

places the birth in a comparatively private, closed context. Many men feel uncomfortable about viewing a delivery, and children rarely have an opportunity to watch a woman in labor. In contrast, the Navaho invite anyone who wishes to lend moral support into the hogan during a delivery.

Newton (1955) suggests that there are similarities between behavior during childbirth and behavior associated with sexual excitement. One might assume that the desire for modesty and privacy at childbirth, including prohibiting male observers, children, or strangers, is linked to the frank expression of sexual impulse at the time of delivery. Whether it is couched as modesty, protection against evil spirits, or protection against infectious disease, many societies attempt to isolate the delivering mother.

The Impact of Pregnancy and Childbirth on Fathers Even though pregnancy and childbirth bring important changes in the roles and status of fathers, little research has focused on fathers' reactions to these events. We know that in some cultures, as described earlier, the father's behavior is thought to have direct bearing on the infant's development. Often fathers reflect the general tone of the cultural orientation toward pregnancy. They may avoid, protect, or encourage their wives as the culture dictates. In some cultures the custom of *couvade* gives fathers a central role in childbirth. Even though the woman bears the child, it is the man who takes to bed, moans and groans, follows careful dietary restrictions, and receives guests. Couvade has been interpreted as a cultural means of claiming paternity.

In our own society, until recently men (with the exception of physicians) have been prevented from participating in childbirth and have had minimal opportunities to touch or hold their newborn infants during the hospital stay. Emerging from this imposed barrier between the father and the mother-infant dyad are a variety of doubts, fears, and resentments about the impact of the pregnancy and the impending new infant. The clinical literature has identified pregnancy and new fatherhood as a potential crisis point for men, leading to a variety of pathological conditions from psychosomatic symptoms to psychoses (Fein, 1976, 1978). There are those fathers who are simply uninterested in their newborns, uninvolved in the care of newborns, and doubtful about their own capacity to provide nurturance or to express love to this new infant (Parke & Sawin, 1976; Tavris, 1977).

Currently, there is a changing orientation toward a more positive, engaged prepaternal experience. Involvement in childbirth classes, the opportunity to attend the delivery, and the opportunity to hold and care for the newborn through a rooming-in arrangement have all been changes that have drawn fathers into the birth process. The childbirth classes place heavy emphasis on the father's role as "coach," providing fathers with a central function in a successful birth experience. In general, men have had

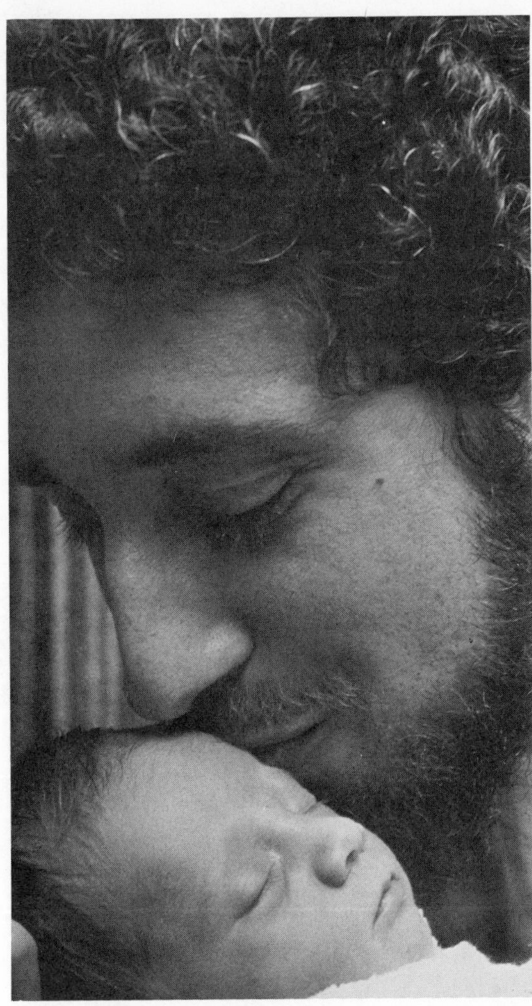

The birth of a child brings some fathers in contact with their own tender, nurturant feelings.

little prior training or encouragement for a nurturant child-care role. They come to fatherhood relying heavily on the image they had of their own parents as active or uninvolved, as warm and expressive or cold and distant.

There is some evidence that participation in childbirth classes and the opportunity to be present during labor and delivery lead to a more positive view of fathering (Cronenwett & Newmark, 1974). The facts that men are usually not given instructions in the care of the infant and that many new mothers do not involve their husbands in the infant's care may perpetuate the cycle of doubts about competence and disinterest. The more active the father's participation in all phases of childbirth the more likely fatherhood is to become a positive, central, and involving life role.

Abortion Abortion refers to the termination of pregnancy before the fetus is able to live outside the uterus, that is, before about 25 weeks from conception. Before 12 weeks, the pregnancy can be aborted by dilating the cervix and suctioning out the contents of the uterus with a vacuum aspirator or by dilating the cervix and scraping out the uterus. After 12 weeks, abortion can be induced, using injections of a saline solution or prostaglandin. The fetus can also be removed surgically using a procedure that is similar to that used in a cesarean section (Williams, 1977; Gordon, 1973; Kerenyi, 1973).

In 1920, after the Russian revolution, the USSR was one of the first countries to permit abortion at the mother's request (Van der Tak, 1974). While the legalization of abortion is a modern phenomenon, abortion itself is a strategy of birth control that has been practiced, along with infanticide, throughout history and across many cultures (Devereux, 1975). Both the Aranda of central Australia and the Hopi of Arizona, for example, have been noted to induce abortions by tying a belt very tightly around the mother's abdomen (Murdock, 1934).

The controversy over the legality of abortion stems from a conflict between those who value the woman's right to privacy and her absolute right to choose or reject motherhood (Prescott, 1975; Sarvis & Rodman, 1974) and those who seek to protect the rights of the unborn fetus, who is incapable of protecting its own interests (McCall, 1975). Those in the second group do not oppose abortions conducted for therapeutic reasons. They argue that once the fetus has become well differentiated it is entitled to protection and to life. One difficulty in the resolution of this conflict is the determination of a chronological point at which the embryo is fully individualized. In 1970, New York State passed a law that permitted women to request an abortion up to 24 weeks after conception. A more conservative view argues that after 12 weeks (the first trimester), the fetus is really a human being with all the potential for a full life.

The available evidence suggests that women do not tend to experience negative emotional reactions to abortions (Sarvis & Rodman, 1974). In studies of American women who had illegal abortions, few negative reactions were reported (Whittemore, 1970). In a study of 742 patients who used the abortion services of the State University Hospital in Syracuse, New York, 70 percent reported feeling very happy about the abortion and 76 percent were observed smiling. Only 5 percent reported feeling guilty and 12 percent said they were either sad or very sad (Osofsky, Osofsky, & Rajan, 1973). For most women an abortion represents a successful close to an undesired pregnancy (Burnell, Dworsky, & Harrington, 1972).

Abortions are usually less of an emotional strain than many professionals had expected (Fingerer, 1973; Smith, 1973). What is more, since the legalization of abortion, deaths associated with abortion have decreased by over 50 percent. Currently, maternal deaths associated with abortion are 2.6 per 100,000 as compared to 12.6 maternal deaths per 100,000 associated

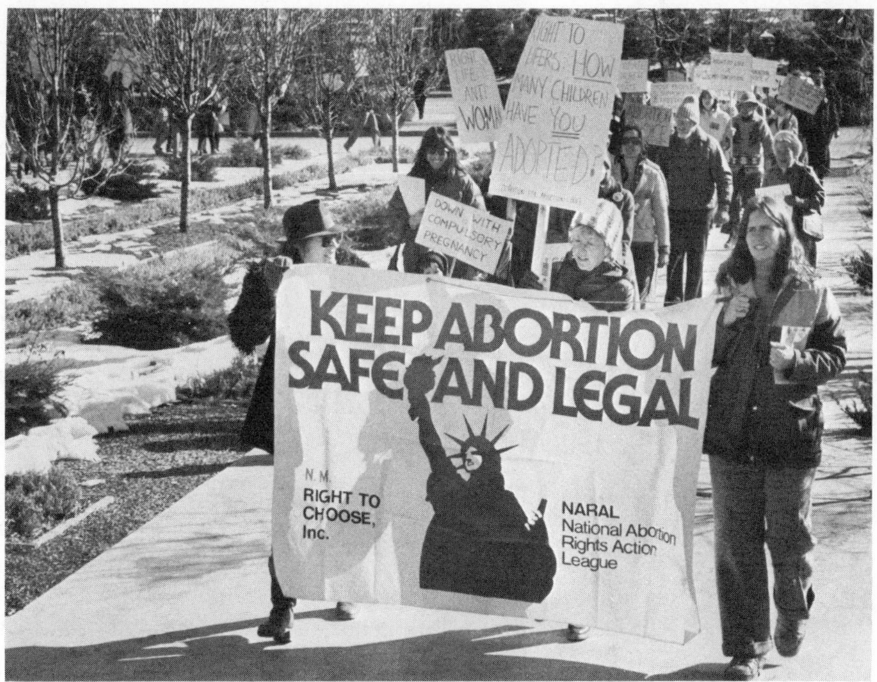

The legalization of abortion is still highly controversial in this country.

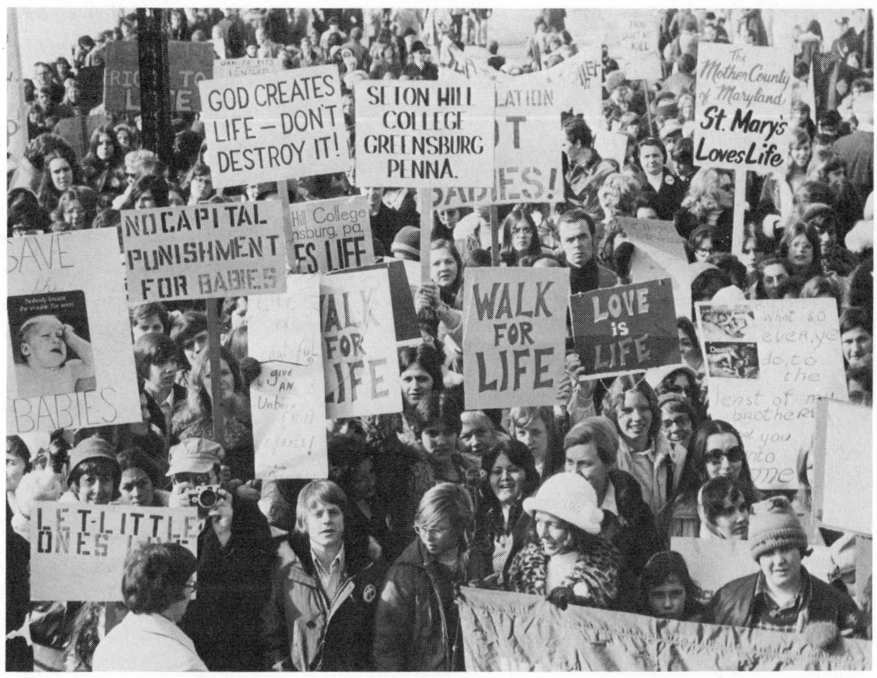

with childbirth (McCary, 1978; Tietze, Bongaarts, & Schearer, 1976). Abortion, especially before 12 weeks, is presently a much safer strategy for ending a pregnancy than carrying the baby to term.

In spite of the 1973 Supreme Court ruling prohibiting state intervention in the decision to abort during the first trimester, there is still considerable controversy about abortion in the United States (Blake, 1974; Jones & Westoff, 1973). In a 1976 national survey, 67 percent of the people sampled agreed that the decision to abort should be left up to the woman and her doctor. While many polls find agreement that legal abortions should be permitted when there is risk to the mother's health, on danger of birth defects, or when the infant was conceived because of rape or incest, a significant minority (about 20 to 25 percent) do not agree that abortion should be a legal strategy for women who feel they are too poor to have another child or who simply do not want to bear more children (Segers, 1977).

Two recent court decisions illustrate the continuing formulation of the government's position on abortion. In 1977, the Supreme Court ruled that no state was obligated to use public funds to pay for an abortion. The legal right to an abortion is thereby limited to those who can afford to pay for the medical services involved. This decision was made in the face of evidence that abortion is safer than childbirth and that the cost to the taxpayer of supporting a child for one year through the welfare system is almost 15 times greater than the cost of an abortion (Fraker, Howard, & Sciolino, 1977). The implication of this decision is that the state does not feel strongly enough about the woman's right to decide about childbearing to guarantee her access to the resources that would allow her to exercise this right.

In 1976, the Supreme Court ruled that a woman did not have to have the consent of her husband or the father of the child in order to have an abortion. This kind of requirement had been legislated in twelve states, including Missouri, Florida, Massachusetts, and Pennsylvania (Etzioni, 1976). While this ruling confirmed the 1973 decision not to interfere with the woman's authority in this matter, it has raised considerable question about the legal rights of fathers in the fate of their unborn children. This issue is clearly one that will continue to be debated as fathers become increasingly committed to their participation in parenting.

The Climacteric

The climacteric or involution and atrophy of the reproductive organs occurs gradually for the female during the years between the mid-thirties and the mid-fifties. There are many physiological changes that accompany this loss of fertility, including the cessation of menstruation (menopause), gradual reduction in the production of estrogen, atrophy of the breasts and genital tissues, and shrinking of the uterus (Sherman, 1971). There is some controversy about whether or not the menopause affects women at a psychological level, either because of its symbolic meaning or because of physiological changes.

Neugarten and Kraines (1965) administered a symptom checklist to 460 women in six age groups: 13–18, 20–29, 30–44, 45–54 (pre- or post-menopausal), 45–54 (menopausal), and 55–64. The two highest symptom groups were the adolescents and the menopausal subjects. The women in the 45–54 nonmenopausal group had lower symptom incidence than same-age women who were menopausal. These data suggest that dramatic endocrine changes, either increased production or decreased production of hormones, are likely to result in a high incidence of psychological and somatic symptoms. Neugarten and Kraines note that the younger group was more likely to report psychological symptoms, like crying and irritableness, while the menopausal group was more likely to report somatic symptoms, like hot flashes, pelvic or breast pain, and feelings of suffocation or shortness of breath.

The findings of this study of symptoms are in contradiction with the view that only neurotic women experience symptoms during menopause (Weiss & English, 1957). It is not known how many women experience menopausal symptoms. In a health screening program of Caucasian and Japanese women of Hawaii, 75 percent reported no menopausal symptoms (Goodman, Stewart, & Gilbert, 1977). Other studies have reported anywhere from 26 percent to 69 percent of women who had no symptoms (Greenhill, 1946; Crawford, & Hooper, 1973). The symptoms appear to be closely related to the drastic drop in the production of estrogen. Postmenopausal women produce only one-sixth the amount of estrogen of regularly menstruating women (Wilson & Wilson, 1963). Several studies on the use of estrogen treatment find that the administration of estrogen to menopausal women alleviates or even avoids many menopausal symptoms (Bardwick, 1971). However, prolonged use of estrogen therapy has been associated with increased risk of cancer of the lining of the uterus (Weg, 1978).

It is fairly well established, then, that the menopause brings about recognizable physical changes which may or may not be viewed by the adult woman as unpleasant. The severity of these changes may be determined in part by the attitude of the culture toward the infertile older woman. Flint (1976) has suggested that in cultures where women are rewarded for reaching the end of the fertile period, menopause is associated with few physiological symptoms. Similarly, a woman's own attitudes toward aging and her involvement in adult roles will influence the ease or difficulty with which menopause is encountered.

Neugarten and her associates (Neugarten, Wood, Kraines, & Loomis, 1963) sampled attitudes toward menopause from 100 women between the ages of 45 and 55. A variety of attitudes was revealed. Some women were fearful, particularly of having mental breakdowns or of losing their sexual attractiveness. Some women appeared to be anxious about menopause but were actively defending against their anxiety. They would repeat advice like: "If you keep busy, you won't think about it, and you'll be all right" (p. 141). A third group, particularly at the upper-middle-class level, felt that menopause had no social or psychological significance for them.

It might be suggested that the degree of anxiety about menopause depends on the individual woman's feelings about no longer being able to bear children, the amount of information she has about the nature of symptoms accompanying menopause, and the degree of anxiety she has about growing old. For example, Neugarten et al. found that attitudes toward menopause were more positive among their sample of women 45 years old and older who were postmenopausal than among younger women (see Table 4.5). The older group realized that the symptoms were temporary and that after menopause there was the potential for some gains in feelings of well-being and vigor. In contrast to the younger group, they were aware that menopause may bring an upsurge in sexual impulses and activity.

It appears that as a young woman views menopause she confuses the physiological phenomena with all the negative connotations of growing old. The importance of physical beauty may be heavily weighted in a woman's definition of femininity. Further, the younger woman may be still quite invested in her role as mother and fearful of a potential end to her years of childbearing. The older woman, on the other hand, is likely to be glad to have reached the end of the years of childbearing and may be eagerly awaiting a future of new roles and new freedoms.

In a paper on the awareness of middle age, Neugarten (1968) pointed out that women who are in the middle adulthood years feel a sense of new opportunities opening to them as they redirect energy from childrearing into other areas of skill development. This study of attitudes toward menopause is good evidence for the difference in psychosocial growth between the premenopausal and postmenopausal groups. The younger women, still working on the task of generativity and still heavily involved in developing the skills necessary to make a creative contribution to society, fear menopause as a symbol of the termination of this creative period. The older women, having gone through the experience and having developed a sense of personal competence in their maternal role, are less threatened by this event. In fact, to some, menopause may symbolize a new beginning—a release from obligations of motherhood and an overture to the years of contribution beyond the family circle.

Neugarten and Kraines (1965) suggest that in evolving a model for the understanding of adult development, care should be taken in using physiological changes as explanatory concepts. They report that menopausal status and severity of menopausal symptoms of 100 normal women between the ages of 43 and 53 were unrelated to an array of personality

TABLE 4.5 Attitudes toward Menopause: By Age

Illustrative Items	Percentage Who Agree* in Age Groups			
	A 21–30 (N–50)	B 31–44 (N–52)	C 45–55 (N–100)	D 56–65 (N–65)
Postmenopausal Recovery				
Women generally feel better after the menopause than they have for many years	32*	20*	68	67
A woman gets more confidence in herself after the change of life	12*	21*	52	42
After the change of life, a woman feels freer to do things for herself	16*	24*	74	65
Many women think menopause is the best thing that ever happened to them	14*	31	46	40
Extent of Continuity				
Many women think menopause really does not change a woman in any important way	58*	55*	74	83
Control of Symptoms				
Women who have trouble with the menopause are usually those who have nothing to do with their time	58	50*	71	70
Women who have trouble in the menopause are those who are expecting it	48*	56*	76	63
Sexuality				
If the truth were really known, most women would like to have themselves a fling at this time in their lives	8*	33	32	24
After the menopause, a woman is more interested in sex than she was before	14*	27	35	21

*Subjects who checked "agree strongly" or "agree to some extent" are grouped together.

*The difference between this percentage and the percentage of Group C is significant at the 05 level or above.

Source: Adapted from "Women's Attitudes toward the Menopause" by B. L. Neugarten, V. Wood, R. J. Kraines & B. Loomis, *Vita Humana, 6,* 1963, 140–151.

measures. They found that other events, such as serious illness or widowhood, were more significantly linked to personality changes. This finding is supported by a paper on depression in middle-aged women by Bart (1971), who identified the source of depression among a sample of women between the ages of 40 and 49 as the result of overinvolvement with their children and overidentification with the role of mother.

Thus, the hormonal events of menopause are not as significant as the woman's interpretation of her role and her degree of dependence on her children to fulfill that role. For overinvolved women, menopause may merely symbolize the finality of the end of motherhood and, in that way, may generate extended feelings of depression. Women who are already confused and depressed by the disintegration of a critical life role will be likely to find that the decline in estrogen production aggravates their condition. Here is an example of the interaction between a psychological condition and a physiological change. The reduced production of estrogen, which has been demonstrated to be associated with negative emotions (Bardwick, 1971), combined with a tendency toward depression caused by loss of role meaning, leads to a more serious psychological depression. The woman may, in fact, be unable to regain her earlier state of positive affect because of both the reduced hormonal production and the altered role relationship.

It would appear, then, that menopause may serve as a significant symbolic event for women at the end of the stage of middle adulthood. For those who have been successful in developing a sense of personal achievement in childrearing or in other work, menopause signifies the end of the childrearing years and the beginning of a period in which new energy can be directed to broader, community-oriented tasks. For the woman who has failed to develop a sense of generativity, who continues to view her children as a path for self-fulfillment, or who is frightened by the prospect of growing old, menopause may indeed highlight a sense of stagnation. Low mood, physical symptoms, and reduced muscle tone are likely to create a strong feeling of uselessness, emptiness, and unattractiveness which may permeate the woman's self-attitude as she enters later adulthood.

What about a climacteric for males? Is there any comparable decrease in reproductive capacity for adult men? There is no biological change comparable to the total involution of organs involved in menopause. Most adult males have the potential to fertilize ova throughout life. However, there is a gradual decline in the production of testosterone, resulting in a variety of changes in the sex organs and sexual activity. Sperm production is decreased. The testicular tubes become narrower, and there is less seminal fluid. Ejaculation therefore occurs with less force. Older males take longer to achieve an erection and require a longer rest interval before erection is possible again. Once the penis is erect, it can be maintained for quite a while, but orgasm itself is shorter (Weg, 1978).

For both males and females, some version of a climacteric alters the adult's hormone levels and modifies physiology. Even though these changes have consequences for the sexual response, they do not necessarily result in a loss of interest in sexual activity. Fortunately, there is complementarity in the changes that take place for men and women. Men require more time to achieve an erection and a longer period before ejaculation occurs. Women take longer to reach a plateau level where the vagina is adequately lubricated. Orgasm takes longer to reach. Thus, we can think of the climacteric as bringing a more leisurely approach to sex which may provide new opportunities for emotional intimacy.

Chapter Summary

Sexuality is a central component of the self-concept. In this chapter, we have described two different aspects of the sexual experience: sexuality as a source of physical pleasure and the reproductive career.

One's experiences with sexuality have important childhood origins. Each person's sexuality is built on the quality of care and comforting received from important caregivers. Through self-exploration and peer play, children learn about their bodies and the bodies of others. During childhood each culture imposes its own guidelines about the appropriateness of sexual exploration and its role in family life.

During adolescence three kinds of experiences contribute to the development of one's sexual nature. These include masturbation, sexual encounters with others, and the formation of strong emotional commitments. Conflicts around sexuality include uncertainty about what is normal behavior and difficulties in forming relationships that combine sexuality with emotional intimacy.

Recent research on adult sexuality has helped to clarify many misconceptions about the sexual needs and sexual behavior of men and women. Masters and Johnson have found that the experience of orgasm is quite similar for men and women. Men and women continue to have sexual fantasies and sexual urges throughout their life span. There is no evidence to support the belief that women are less sexually responsive than men.

Information about sexuality in marriage is limited and difficult to interpret because of a variety of methodological problems. It appears that sexual activity is more frequent in the early years of marriage and decreases as the partners age. Even in later adulthood, however, married couples continue to have intercourse about once a week. There is evidence that a larger number of married women experience orgasm through intercourse in modern marriages than was the case 30 years ago when Kinsey was reporting his research. In general, sexuality is both a product of marital satisfaction and a contributor to marital satisfaction.

With age the sexual drive appears to become less intense. However, there is no reason that older men and women cannot enjoy a satisfying sexual life. Some physical changes alter the aging man's capacity for erection and the aging woman's vaginal adaptability. The major barrier to sexuality in later life is the absence of a responsive partner.

From an evolutional perspective, the primary purpose of the sexual drive is reproduction. The reproductive career is much more clearly marked by discrete physical events for women than it is for men. We have described the reproductive career with respect to menstruation and the hormone cycle, pregnancy and childbirth, and the climacteric.

For females, sexual receptivity is not directly tied to the hormone cycle. There is evidence that changes in hormone level are associated with changes in mood. However, it is not clear that these mood shifts are in any way disruptive to daily functioning. Evidence of a male hormonal cycle is inconclusive. Males do show periods of high and low hormone level, but these periods are not necessarily rhythmic or cyclical.

Childbirth continues to be a normative experience of early and middle adulthood. Of married women aged 18 to 24, 94 percent expected to have at least one child in their lifetime. With the availability of effective contraceptives, families can be very deliberate in planning the number and spacing of their children. Most contemporary couples are highly involved in prenatal health care and preparation for childbirth. Both husband and wife have opportunities to contribute actively to the birth of their child.

Four psychosocial factors influence the experiences of pregnancy and childbirth. These include the mother's age, the emotional state of the mother, the mother's knowledge about the birth process, and cultural patterns of responding to pregnancy and childbirth. The way the pregnant woman is treated may have considerable influence on her willingness to seek prenatal care, her willingness to participate in the activities of her community, and her feelings of vulnerability.

The last phase of the reproductive career is the climacteric. Changes in the reproductive system appear gradually from the mid-thirties to the mid-fifties. For women, these changes bring a complete end to the reproductive potential. For men, there is a gradual reduction but not a complete close to reproductive capacity. The experience of menopause can be associated with a variety of physical symptoms that are tied to the drop in estrogen production. It is not known exactly how many women experience these menopausal symptoms.

The psychological consequences of menopause are varied. Some women respond with optimism and a sense of freedom from the obligations of motherhood. Other women who are very intensely involved in their childrearing role are more likely to experience depression with menopause. In general, the events of menopause appear to be more negative to younger women who have not experienced it than they are to women who have already passed through this phase of life.

References

Bardwick, J. M. *Psychology of women.* New York: Harper & Row, 1971.

Bart, P. B. Depression in middle-aged women. In V. Gornick and B. K. Moran (Eds.), *Woman in sexist society.* New York: Basic Books, 1971.

Bell, R. R. Changing aspects of marital sexuality. In S. Gordon and R. W. Libby (Eds.), *Sexuality today and tomorrow: Contemporary issues in human sexuality.* North Scituate, Mass.: Duxbury Press, 1976

Bell, R. R., & Bell, P. L. Sexual satisfaction among married women. *Medical Aspects of Human Sexuality,* March 1974, 10–31.

Blake, J. Elective abortion and our reluctant citizenry: Research on public opinion in the United States. In H. J. Osofsky and J. D. Osfosky, *The abortion experience.* Hagerstown, Md.: Harper & Row, 1973.

Burnell, G., Dworsky, W., and Harrington, R. Postabortion group therapy. *American Journal of Psychiatry,* 1972, *129,* 220–223.

Cameron, P., & Biber, H. Sexual thought throughout the life-span. *The Gerontologist,* 1973, *13,* 144–147.

Carns, D. E. Talking about sex: Notes on first coitus and the double sexual standard. *Journal of Marriage and the Family,* 1973, *35,* 677–688.

Crawford, M. P. & Hooper, D. Menopause, aging and family. *Social Science and Medicine,* 1973, *7,* 469–482.

Cronenwett, L. R., & Newmark, L. L. Fathers' responses to childbirth. *Nursing Research,* 1974, *23,* 210–217.

Davis, C. D., & Marrone, F. A. An objective evaluation of a prepared childbirth program. *American Journal of Obstetrics and Gynecology,* 1962, *84,* 1196.

Devereux, G. *A study of abortion in primitive societies* (rev. ed.). New York: International Universities Press, 1975.

Doering, C. H., Brodie, H. K. H., Kraemer, H. C. Moos, R. H., Becker, H. B., & Hamburg, D. A. Negative affect and plasma testosterone: A longitudinal human study. *Psychosomatic Medicine,* 1975, *37,* 484–491.

Earn, A. A. Mental concentration—a new and effective psychological tool for the abolition of suffering in childbirth. *American Journal of Obstetrics and Gynecology,* 1962, *83*(1), 29.

Etzioni, A. The husband's rights in abortion. *Trial Magazine,* November 1976.

Fein, R. A. Men's entrance to parenthood. *The Family Coordinator,* 1976, *25,* 341–350.

Fein, R.A. Research on fathering: Social policy and an emergent perspective. *Journal of Social Issues,* 1978, *34,*(1), p. 122–135.

Fingerer, M. E. Psychological sequelae of abortion: Anxiety and depression. *Journal of Community Psychology,* 1973, *1,* 221–225.

Fitzpatrick, E., Reed, S. R., & Mastroianni, L. *Maternity nursing* (12th ed.). Philadelphia: Lippincott, 1971.

Flint, M. Cross-cultural factors that affect age of menopause. In P.A. Van Keep, R. B. Greenblatt, & M. Albeaux-Fernet (Eds.), *Consensus on menopause research.* Baltimore: University Park Press, 1976.

Ford, C. S. *A comparative study of human reproduction.* Yale University Publications in Anthropology, No. 32. New Haven: Yale University Press, 1945.

Ford, C. S., & Beach, F. A. *Patterns of sexual behavior.* New York: Harper, 1951.

Fosburgh, L. The make-believe world of teen-age maternity. *The New York Times Magazine,* 7, 1977, pp. 29–34.

Fraker, S., Howard, L., & Sciolino, E. Abortion: Who pays? *Newsweek,* July 4, 1977.

Francoeur, R. T. *Becoming a sexual person.* New York: Wiley, 1982.

Freud, S. *Three essays on sexuality* (standard ed., Vol. VII). London: Hogarth, 1953.

Furstenberg, F. F. *Unplanned parenthood: The social consequences of teenage childbearing.* New York: Free Press, 1977.

Gadpaille, W. J. *The cycles of sex.* Ed. by L. Freeman. New York: Scribner's, 1975.

Gagnon, J. H. The creation of the sexual in early adolescence. In J. Kagan and R. Coles (Eds.), *Twelve to sixteen: Early adolescence.* New York: Norton, 1972.

Gagnon, J. H., & Simon, W. *Sexual conduct: The social sources of human sexuality.* Chicago: Aldine, 1973.

Gagnon, J. H., Simon, W., & Berger, A. J. Some aspects of sexual adjustment in early and late adolescence. In J. Zubin & A. N. Freedman (Eds.), *Psychopathology of adolescence.* New York: Grune and Stratton, 1970.

Gebhard, P. H. Factors in marital orgasm. *Journal of Social Issues,* 1966, *22*(2), 88–95.

Golub, S. The effect of premenstrual anxiety and depression on cognitive function. Paper presented at the 83rd annual convention of the American Psychological Association, Chicago, 1975.

Goodman, M., Stewart, C. J., & Gilbert, F. Patterns of menopause. *Journal of Gerontology,* 1977, *32,* 291–298.

Gordon, S. *The sexual adolescent: Communicating with teenagers about sex.* North Scituate, Mass.: Duxbury Press, 1973.

Gorer, G. *Himalyan village: An account of the Lepchas of Silskim.* London: Michael Joseph, 1938.

Granquist, H. *Child problems among the Arabs.* Helsingfas: Soderstrom, 1950.

Greenhill, M. H. A psychosomatic evaluation of the psychiatric and endocrinological factors in the menopause. *Southern Medical Journal,* 1946, *39,* 786–794.

Grimm, E. R. Psychological and social factors in pregnancy, delivery and outcome. In S. A. Richardson & A. F. Guttmacher (eds.), *Childbearing—Its social and psychological consequences.* Baltimore: Williams & Wilkins, 1967.

Guttmann, B. *Die stammeslèhvender dschagga* (Vol. 1). Munich: C. H. Beck, 1932.

Haas, A. *Teenage sexuality: A survey of teenage sexual behavior.* New York: Macmillan, 1979.

Henderson, M. E. Evidence for a male menstrual/temperature cycle and synchrony with the female menstrual cycle. *New Zealand Medical Journal,* 1976, *84,* 164.

Hetzel, B.S., Bruer, B., & Poidevin, L. O. S. A survey of the relationship between certain common antenatal complications in primiparae and stressful life situations during pregnancy. *Journal of Psychosomatic Research,* 1961, *5,* 1975.

Hite, S. *The Hite report.* New York: Macmillan, 1976.

Hunt, M. *Sexual behavior in the seventies.* Chicago: Playboy Press, 1974.

Illsley, R. The sociological study of reproduction and its outcome. In S. A. Richardson and A. F. Guttmacher (Eds.), *Childbearing—its social and psychological aspects.* Baltimore: Williams and Wilkins, 1967,

Jones, E. F., & Westoff, C. F. Changes in attitudes toward abortion: With emphasis upon the national fertility study data. In H. J. Osofsky and J. D. Osofsky (Eds.), *The abortion experience: Psychological and medical impact.* Harper & Row, 1973.

Juhasz, A. M. A cognitive approach to sex education. In J. F. Adams (Ed.), *Understanding adolescence: Current developments in adolescent psychology* (3rd ed.). Boston: Allyn and Bacon, 1976.

Karmel, M. *Thank you Dr. Lamaze.* Philadelphia: Lippincott, 1959.

Kerenyi, T.D. Midtrimester abortion. In H. J. Osofsky and J. D. Osofsky (Eds.), *The abortion experience: Psychological and medical impact.* New York: Harper & Row, 1973.

Kinsey, A. C., Pomeroy, W. B., & Martin, C. E. *Sexual behavior in the human male.* Philadelphia: Saunders, 1948.

LaBarre, M. The triple crisis: Adolescence, early marriage and parenthood. In *The double jeopardy, the triple crisis: illegitimacy today.* New York: National Council on Illegitimacy, 1969.

Laird, M. D., & Hogan, M. An elective program of preparation for childbirth at the Sloan Hospital for Women. *American Journal of Obstetrics and Gynecology,* 1956, *72,* 647.

Lake, A. Childbirth in America. *McCall's Magazine,* January 1976.

Larson, D. L., Spreitzer, E. A., & Snyder, E. E. Social factors in the frequency of romantic involvement among adolescents. *Adolescence,* 1976, *11,* 7–12.

Masters, W. H., & Johnson, V. E. *Human sexual response.* Boston: Little, Brown, 1966.

Masters, W. H., & Johnson, V. E. *Human sexual inadequacy.* Boston: Little, Brown, 1970.

McCall, R. J. Abortion: Another look at the issue. *APA Monitor,* 6(11), 1972, 20.

McCary, J. L. *McCary's human sexuality.* (3rd ed.). New York: D. Van Nostrand, 1978.

Mead, M. *Coming of age in Samoa.* New York: Morrow, 1928.

Mead, M. *Sex and temperament in three primitive societies.* New York: Morrow, 1935.

Mead, M. & Newton, N. Cultural patterning of perinatal behavior. In S. A. Richardson and A. F. Guttmacher (Eds.), *Childbearing—its social and psychological aspects.* Baltimore: Williams and Wilkins, 1967.

Menken, J. The health and social consequences of teenage childbearing. *Family Planning Perspectives,* IV, 1972, *3,* 49.

Micklin, M., Thomson, E., & Gardner, J. S. *Adolescent socialization and heterosexual behavior.* Seattle: Battelle Human Affairs Research Center, 1977.

Money, J. *Love and love sickness.* Baltimore, Md.: Johns Hopkins University Press, 1980.

Murdock, G. P. *Our primitive contemporaries.* New York: Macmillan, 1934.

Neugarten, B. The awareness of middle age. In B. Neugarten (Ed.), *Middle age and aging.* Chicago: University of Chicago Press, 1968.

Neugarten, B. L., & Kraines, R. L. Menopausal symptoms in women of various ages. *Psychosomatic Medicine,* 1965, *27,* 266–273.

Neugarten, B. L., Wood, V., Kraines, R. J., & Loomis, B. Women's attitudes toward the menopause. *Vita Humana,* 1963, *6,* 140–151.

Newton, N., *Maternal emotions.* New York: Paul B. Hoeber, 1955.

Norwood, C. A humanizing way to have a baby. *Ms Magazine,* May 1978.

Osofsky, J. D., Osofsky, H. J., & Rajan, R. Psychological effects of abortion: With emphasis upon immediate reactions and follow up. In H. J. Osofsky and J. D. Osofsky (Eds.), *The abortion experience: Psychological and medical impact.* Harper & Row, 1973.

Paige, K. E. The effects of oral contraceptives on affective fluctuations associated with the menstrual cycle. *Psychosomatic Medicine,* 1971, *33,* 515–537.

Paige, K. E. Women learn to sing the menstrual blues. *Psychology Today,* September, 1973, *7,* 41–43.

Parke, R. D., & Sawin, D. B. The father's role in infancy: A re-evaluation. *The Family Coordinator,* 1976, *25,* 365–372.

Paykel, E. S. Life stress and psychiatric disorder: Applications of the clinical approach. In B. S. Dohrenwend and B. P. Dohrenwend (Eds.), *Stressful life events: Their nature and effects.* New York: Wiley, 1974.

Persky, H., Lief, H. I., O'Brien, C. P., Strauss, D., & Miller, W. Reproductive hormone levels and sexual behavior of young couples during the menstrual cycle. In R. Gemme & C. C. Wheeler (Eds.), *Progress in sexology: Selected papers from the proceedings of the 1976 International Congress of Sexology.* New York: Plenum, 1977.

Pfeiffer, E. Sexuality in the aging individual. In R. L. Solnick (Ed.), *Sexuality and aging.* Los Angeles: University of Southern California, 1978.

Prescott, J. Abortion: The controversy continued. *APA Monitor,* September/October 1975, 6(9 and 10), p 17+.

Ramey, E. Men's cycles (they have them too, you know). *Ms.*, Spring 1972, pp. 8–14.

Reed, E. Genetic anomalies in development. In F. D. Horowitz (Ed.), *Review of child development research* (Vol. 5). Chicago: University of Chicago Press, 1975.

Reiss, I. L. *Family systems in America* (3rd ed.). New York: Holt, Rinehart and Winston, 1980.

Roberts, H., Wootton, I. D. P., Kane, K. M., & Harnett, W. E. The value of antenatal preparation. *Journal of Obstetrics and Gynecology*, British Emp., 1953, *60*, 404.

Robinson, I. E., & Jedlicka, D. Change in sexual attitudes and behavior of college students from 1965 to 1980: A research note. *Journal of Marriage and the Family*, 1982, *44*, 237–240.

Rodin, J. Menstruation, reattribution, and competence. *Journal of Personality and Social Psychology*, 1976, *33*, 345–353.

Rosen, S. Emotional factors in nausea and vomiting of pregnancy. *Psychiatric Quarterly*, 1955, *29*, 621.

Rosengren, W. R. Social sources of pregnancy as illness or normality. *Social Forces*, 1961, *39*, 260–267.

Roth, W. E. Precautions during pregnancy in New Guinea. In M. Mead and N. Calas (Eds.), *Primitive heritage*. New York: Random House, 1953.

Ruble, D. N. Premenstrual symptoms: A reinterpretation. *Science*, 1977.

Sarvis, B. & Rodman, H. *The abortion controversy* (2nd ed.). New York: Columbia University Press, 1974.

Schneider, H. K. Romantic love among the Tura. In D. Marshall and R. Suggs (Eds.), *Human sexual behavior*. New York: Basic Books, 1971.

Segers, M. C. Abortion and the Supreme Court: Some are more equal than others. *Hastings Center Report*, August 1977.

Selye, H. *Stress without distress*. Philadelphia: Lippincott, 1974.

Sherman, J. A. *On the psychology of women: A survey of empirical studies*. Springfield, Ill.: Charles C. Thomas, 1971.

Simon, W., & Gagnon, J. H. The pedagogy of sex. *Saturday Review*, 1967, *50*, 74–91.

Smith, E. M. A follow-up study of women who request abortion. *American Journal of Ortho-Psychiatry*, 1973, *43*, 575–85.

Sorenson, R. C. *Adolescent sexuality in contemporary America*. New York: World, 1973.

Spanier, G. B. Sexualization and premarital sexual behavior. *Family Coordinator*, 1975, *24*(1), 33–41.

Sullivan, H. S. *The collected works of Harry Stack Sullivan* (Vols. 1 and 2). New York: Norton, 1949.

Tavris, C. Men and women report their views on masculinity. *Psychology Today*, 1977, *10*, 34–43.

Tavris, C., & Sadd, S. *The Redbook report on female sexuality*. New York: Delacorte, 1977.

Taylor, S. E., & Langer, E. J. Pregnancy: A social stigma? *Sex Roles*, 1977, *3*, 27–35.

Thoms, H., & Karlovsky, E. D. Two thousand deliveries under a training for childbirth program: A statistical survey and commentary. *American Journal of Obstetrics and Gynecology*, 1954, *68*, 279.

Tichauer, R. The Aymara children of Bolivia. *Journal of Pediatrics*, 1963, *62*, 399–412.

Tietze, C., Bongaarts, J., and Schearer, B. Mortality associated with the control of fertility. *Family Planning Perspective*, 1976, *8*, 6–13.

U.S. Bureau of the Census. *Social Indicators III*. Washington, D.C.: U.S. Government Printing Office, 1980.

U.S. Bureau of the Census. Current Population Reports, Series P–20, No. 363. *Population profile of the United States: 1980.* Washington, D.C.: U. S. Government Printing Office, 1981.

Van Auken, W. B. D., & Tomlinson, D. R. An appraisal of patient training for childbirth. *American Journal of Obstetrics and Gynecology,* 1953, *66,* 100.

van der Tak, J. *Abortion, fertility, and changing legislation: An international review.* Lexington, Mass.: Heath, 1974.

Wax, J. Sex and the single grandparent. *New York Times,* September 19, 1975, pp. 43–47.

Weg, R. B. The physiology of sexuality in aging. In R. L. Solnick (Ed.), *Sexuality and aging.* Los Angeles: University of Southern California Press, 1978, 48–65.

Weiss, E., & English, O. S. *Psychomatic medicine.* Philadelphia: Saunders, 1957.

Westoff, C. F. Coital frequency and contraception. *Family Planning Perspectives,* Summer 1974, *3,* 136–141.

Whittemore, K. The availability of nonhospital abortions. In R. Hall (Ed.), *Abortion in a changing world.* New York: Columbia University Press, 1970.

Williams, J. H. *Psychology of women: Behavior in a biosocial context.* New York: Norton, 1977.

Wilson, R., & Wilson, T. The non-treated postmenopausal woman. *American Geriatrics Society,* 1963, *11,* 347.

Yang, R. K., Zweig, A. R., Douthitt, T. C., & Federman, E. J. Successive relationships between maternal attitudes during pregnancy, analgesic medication during labor and delivery, and newborn behavior. *Developmental Psychology,* 1976, *12*(1), 6–14.

Zelnik, M., & Kantner, J. F. Sexual experience of young unmarried women in the United States. *Family Planning Perspectives 4,* no. 4, October 1972.

Zelnik, M., & Kantner, J. F. Sexual and contraceptive experience of young unmarried women in the United States, 1976 and 1971. *Family Planning Perspectives,* March-April 1977, *9,* 55–71.

5 Cognition

It is a fact that the totality of sense experiences is so constituted as to permit putting them in order by means of thinking—a fact which can only leave us astonished, but which we shall never comprehend. One can say: the eternally incomprehensible thing about the world is its comprehensibility.

Albert Einstein, *Ideas and Opinions*, 1954.

Humans think about the events and objects that exist in their immediate environment. They think about past and future events. They create concepts where none had existed. Through thought they begin to invent new objects, create institutions, and discover the elements of the universe. People not only think about things, people, and relationships but they think about their own thoughts. Self-consciousness, introspection, and self-analysis are types of reflection about mental activity itself. The scope of thought is remarkable. It can be directed outward toward a future which has not yet been experienced and it can be directed inward to produce an increasingly detailed understanding of the mechanisms underlying

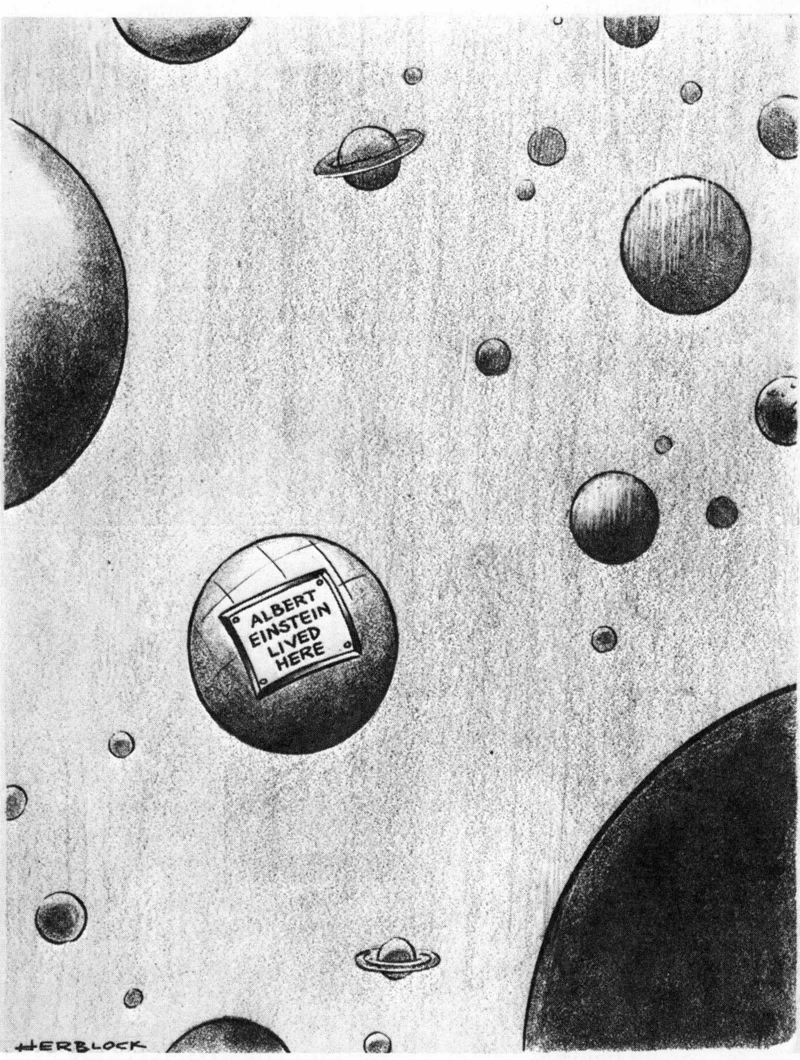

From *Herblock's Here And Now* (Simon & Schuster, 1955).

thought processes. There can be tremendous breadth and depth to the range of an individual's thinking. If we look over our college curriculum categories, we find course after course, discipline after discipline where the finest thinking in the field has been done by an adult.

Einstein provided the unquestionable answer to the historical debate among scientists about whether individuals can develop an intellectual understanding of something they have never experienced. He made up beautiful theories which worked remarkably well to explain aspects of the physical universe. Once he had demonstrated this skill, other physicists began to develop it in themselves. Einstein's talent was drawn upon during his early adulthood. In the fields of science, arts, and humanities the most advanced thinking has almost always been done by adults—sometimes young adults, sometimes middle adults, sometimes later adults. In this chapter we will explore aspects of thinking which develop during the adult years.

It is extremely important that the topic of mental functioning be placed in the proper perspective. If it is the great key to human dominance and control of the environment, it is also the creator of terrible monsters and spirits from whom adults as well as children cringe. We must learn to understand intellectual functioning by identifying properly what is reality and what is fantasy.

We are involved in a process of evolution which occurs at an extremely slow pace. We humans, because of the mental and interpersonal aspects of our behavior, have generated a field in the scientific study of evolution of species called *psychosocial evolution.* Julian Huxley (1942), a British scientist, discussed psychosocial evolution as his primary life's work. One of Huxley's most important contributions was his realization that through the development of writing and education we developed ways to train ourselves to be effective early in life. This left the current group of adults free to apply the principles of logic, the flexibility of associative thought, the integration of memory, and the creativity of fantasy to create new concepts which continue to allow increasing human control over the environment and increasing attention to the needs of all members of a society.

In adulthood, the individual makes a complicated set of life choices about marriage, career, life-style, and parenting. These choices have important implications for the quality of the environment that provides the context for cognitive functioning. In other words, individuals contribute to their own cognitive growth or stagnation by the relationships in which they choose to participate. People structure their lives in different ways. Some people are highly organized. They seek to limit uncertainty by defining their life activities and carefully scheduling the time and investment devoted to each. Other people are less concerned about organization and more committed to a search for diverse and invigorating experiences. In that case, productivity is related to the continued interaction with new ideas and new challenges. Other people seem to be both unorganized and uninterested. They let outside forces draw them from one activity to another, never really exerting or integrating force on the course of life events. Each style has consequences for the possibility of new cognitive growth in the adult years as well as for the specific areas that are most likely to be enhanced in each pattern.

In the following sections we focus on the specific characteristics of thought during adulthood. Descriptions of adult cognition and adult memory are followed by sections on the factors that stimulate change in adult thought, cognition and moral thought, and patterns of stability and change in measured mental abilities.

The Nature of Adult Cognition

Adult thought has many dimensions to it. Thought can vary in how fanciful it is, how much the person actually directs the train of thought, and how much the thought is related to objects or events in the immediate environment (Klinger, 1978). We can experience thought as playful imagining, where we do not deliberately focus on a particular reality-bound problem or task. Of course, sometimes these thoughts can be useful for problem solving without having been intended for that purpose. We can experience thought as a product of our own attention and will, as in specific problem solving. Thought may also be experienced as a random association of images, as it often is during the period before we fall asleep. Finally, thought can be focused on the content of our immediate environment or thought can be about memories, about the relationship among concepts, or about the process of thought itself.

Imagery and Fantasy

Mental images are central to the process of thinking. Mental images are mental representations that people often describe as pictures in the mind. Some people have more vivid mental images than others, but we can all produce them if we are prompted to. For example, if you are asked to draw a picture of your bedroom, you will most likely proceed by trying to match the mental image you hold of that room with a drawn map, where the size, shape, and contents of the room as they are encoded in your mental image are represented by symbols or actual replication. If you drew the map while you were in the room, you would not need the mental image, but if you drew the map while you were someplace else, the mental image would be your primary guide.

Mental images are most often associated with fantasy thought. Dreams, daydreams, and mind wandering are usually composed of sequences of images accompanied by feelings and sometimes by voices or other sense experiences. In adulthood, however, we have examples of mental images being used as a deliberate tool for problem solving (Pylyshyn, 1981). Perhaps the most famous of the problem solvers who used mental images was Einstein. Einstein (1954) depended on visualization of relationships as a primary means of experimenting with abstract variables. One of the most significant events in the history of physics took place during one of Einstein's "thinking experiments." As he visualized himself traveling alongside a light beam at a speed of 186,000 miles per second, a mental image occurred which identified to Einstein a characteristic of the physical universe which had previously been unknown. This vision of an undiscovered quality of nature led to a reformulation of electromagnetic theory.

Another example of the contribution of mental imagery to problem solving is Friedrich Kekule's work on chemical bonds and molecular structure. Kekule deliberately generated fantasies about the problems that he was studying. He frequently found that visualization helped him to understand the nature of the bonding of atoms in specific compounds. In one important visual experience Kekule "saw" a snakelike chain of molecules turn on itself as if biting its own tail. This image became the solution to the puzzle about the molecular structure of benzene and unlocked the door to modern organic chemistry.

Mental images have special qualities that make them valuable for certain types of problem solving (Shepard, 1978). Mental images permit the simultaneous integration of several variables. They can preserve three-dimensional space in a way that the written word or the drawn representation may not. Even though the mental image is usually based on dimensions of reality, it is not constrained by those dimensions. For example, one can begin with an image of an animal, let us say a cow, and systematically alter aspects of the animal, giving it another body shape, a different kind of coloration or coat, or even a different size. Mental images can permit movement through space, the unification of several characters or factors into one image, and the simultaneous existence of opposing or contradictory forces. One can, for example, imagine watching one's own funeral. One value of mental imagery, then, is its modifiability, permitting the systematic modification of objects or relationships without being limited by the constraints of the immediate environment. For these reasons, mental imagery may be especially useful in the solution to problems involving social relationships.

Mental images can also be used as a method for coping with stress. One can anticipate a stressful event, for example, surgery or separation, by imagining the event beforehand. Through imagination one can cull up various scenarios, from the most painful, vulnerable, and helpless state to the most resilient and composed. These images can help to reduce anxiety associated with stress by training one to retain a confident, calm emotional state even under the most stressful imagined conditions.

This technique, which is sometimes referred to as desensitization, does in fact help adults gain greater control over areas of intense fear (Wolpe, 1973). In real life, part of the difficulty of stressful events is the fact that we have so little chance to prepare or to develop skilled responses. Desensitization makes use of the vividness of mental imagery and its similarity to real experience to help provide practice in encountering stress. With each imagined encounter, the person learns to approach the feared event with an attitude of confidence.

As in childhood, the amount of mental imagery and fantasy thought people are likely to use will vary from person to person. People have different degrees of a predisposition to fantasy (Singer, 1973). In addition to this individual factor, settings differ in the extent to which they encourage fantasy, and cultures differ in the extent to which they value or place credence in fantasy.

Reasoning and Problem Solving

The events of adult life pose continuous challenges to our capacities for reasoning and problem solving. In every sphere of adult experience, including management of a household, parenting, maintaining meaningful interpersonal relationships, and work, uncertainties and conflicts call for decision-making, careful reasoning, and effective problem solving. These challenges of adulthood are not quite the same as the problems we were asked to solve in school. The problems we face are not usually defined by someone else. Rather, it is up to each adult to recognize problems as they arise and to identify the essential components of those problems. Adults also have to determine for themselves what the goals or desired outcomes of a conflict or problem might be.

Many problems of adult life do not have a single correct solution. In fact, for some problems of adult life, like the decision to choose a particular career, to end a marriage relationship, or to move to a new town, it is hard to say in advance that one choice is correct and another is wrong. One can imagine successful adaptation or maladaptation resulting from several choices. A great deal depends on the adult's capacity to assess his or her own resources as well as on the adult's attitude toward the problem being faced.

Problems of adult life tend to be more complex and long term than the problems of earlier stages. This calls for a new time perspective on problem solving. One may be asked to project forward toward the adolescence or adulthood of your own children. One may have a five- or ten-year plan for one's business organization. One may in fact be trying to solve problems about retirement which is forty or fifty years away. Realizing the complex and repeated nature of these challenges, individuals are drawn toward the need for a guiding philosophy or life plan that gives direction, emphasis, and style to the problem-solving orientation. Problems become more than discrete disruptions, inconveniences, or stumbling blocks. They become the patterned, propelling energy source for continued life growth.

Problem solving involves six components (Adams, 1980). Although we could see these six components as steps or stages, one following the next, people seem to differ in which step marks the beginning of their own problem-solving process. The components are:

1. Identification and definition of the problem
2. Collection of information about the problem
3. Production of alternative solutions
4. Deciding among alternatives
5. Taking action to solve the problem
6. Evaluation of action taken

This list suggests that problem solving is primarily a rational process. One begins with a careful understanding of the nature of the problem. Some would argue that once the problem has been properly defined, the path toward a solution is already indicated. The steps also rely on the capacity for logical thought. One must be able to consider a solution and mentally evaluate the consequences of that solution. Here is where the problem solver relies on the capacity for information-processing and mental imagery. There is also a need for objectivity in evaluating the solution one has chosen. One may find that the preferred solution is not actually solving the problem. In that case the rational problem solver must return to step 3 and produce new solutions. Many of us may be tempted to abandon the problem if our first solution does not work out. Others continue to apply their first solution repeatedly in the face of failure.

When a life problem is confronted in an active, directed way, cognitive growth is stimulated in several ways. First, in identifying the problem, one experiences some discrepancy between what one wishes were true of reality and what one assesses to be true. This discrepancy itself is energizing, stimulating the person to a new level of arousal and attention. Alert and attentive, the whole mental system is roused from a more "automatic" level of functioning. In this state, there is the opportunity to benefit from heightened sensitivity to sensation, increased vividness of imagery, a more lively sense of humor, or greater levels of concentration. Being in a problem-solving state can be mentally stimulating.

Second, the search for solutions can be stimulating. When problems are complex, the problem-solving search usually involves generating many solutions and pursuing the consequences of each solution mentally. This is similar to Einstein's *Gedanken* ("thinking") experiments. In the mental pursuit of solutions there is the opportunity to play with reality, modifying conditions so that they suit one's own goals more satisfactorily. During this process, there is the possibility of stumbling across refreshing new conceptualizations. One can discover solutions to the problem that evoked the search, but one can also identify solutions to unrelated problems. Consider the following situation. In trying to decide how to lose some weight, Jennifer reviewed the reasons she was likely to gain weight. She thought about various aspects of her life, including time she spent alone, time she spent preparing and eating meals, and people who influenced the kinds of food she was likely to eat. In thinking about her eating habits, she realized that many of her life choices were determined by her husband's preferences. The solution to losing weight led to a new analysis of her marital relationship.

During the implementation and evaluation of a solution, a person has a chance to learn how closely his or her own problem-solving skills anticipated reality. Having tried to identify relevant variables, plan for a reasonable time period, and anticipate consequences of the choices involved, the voice of reality provides new opportunities to improve one's problem solving. In each implementation, aspects of the solution that succeed confirm the strategy and the logic employed. Aspects of the solution that do not succeed generate new discrepancies, new uncertainties, and the need for new conceptualizations. It is possible to become aware of new aspects of reality or to reevaluate one's own resources in light of the consequences that any particular problem-solving strategy produces.

By young adulthood, we expect the development of cognition to have reached the point where abstractions, hypothesis testing, logic, and a capacity for the manipulation of several variables simultaneously have all had a full opportunity to emerge. Yet there is some evidence that the quality of reasoning and problem solving changes during adult life. Two examples serve to illustrate possible variations in thinking through adulthood. Kastenbaum (1966) has described changes in time perspective. In adolescence, young people become increasingly aware of the uncertainty of the future as well as the reality of future events. Adolescents tended to have rich and complex expectations for the immediate future, but gave almost no thought to life after about age 25. Older adults were able to consider both past and future in an integrated time perspective when the situation was not related to their own personal life events. In relation to a personal history, however, the elderly were unwilling to consider future life events. It was as if the cognitive skills were subordinated by the uncertainty about and unpreparedness for their personal futures that they experienced.

A number of studies have reported that the elderly perform a variety of cognitive tasks at a less complex level than middle-aged subjects (Denney & Wright, 1978). An example is the game of 20 questions. Adolescents and middle adults generally approach that game by asking questions that eliminate large groups of possibilities (Is it alive?). The elderly, like young children, ask specific questions to test specific hypotheses (Is it my shoe?). The supposition is that the elderly are still capable of using the abstract problem-solving strategy, but they are not inclined to approach tasks from that orientation. When older adults are reminded of the more global strategy they quickly begin to use it (Denney & Denney, 1974). One might hypothesize that as adults narrow the focus of their attention more and more to immediate needs and immediate obstacles to the gratification of needs, they stop using the multifaceted, flexible problem-solving strategies that were called forth by the continuous uncertainties of early adult challenges.

Monitoring One's Thoughts

Not only do adults think and direct their thinking toward the solution of problems, but they direct their thinking toward thought itself. At a personal level, this kind of monitoring of thought includes a variety of administrative activities that psychologists refer to as metacognition (Flavell, 1978). For example, we review a set of concepts that has recently been learned and make an assessment, we might reread some sections, try to find additional information, or feeling confident, move on to something new.

Monitoring one's thoughts provides a means of detecting errors in logic or misunderstandings. When a decision has been reached, it is possible to stop and check the lines of reasoning that have led to a particular decision. Adults often enroll in seminars and workshops that provide training in just this kind of decision analysis. Adults are capable of imposing or removing constraints on their thoughts, thereby solving the same problem under varied conditions. The technique of "blockbusting" is designed to stimulate creative thought by encouraging the problem and to relinquish certain "sets" of orientations that might interfere with the generation of new solutions. Under these "no holds barred" conditions the mind operates at two levels simultaneously, at one level generating ideas and at another level keeping the usual constraints from interfering. In adult life, many levels of consciousness can exist simultaneously, each offering a unique contribution to knowing.

Metacognition includes one of the early tools of psychological study, introspection. In Wundt's early experiments, subjects were trained through 10,000 trials of introspection before they were asked to participate in an experiment (Lieberman, 1979). All this training led to the development of a capacity for detailed, systematic observation of one's own mental activities. At a more casual level, introspection is focused attention on one's personal thoughts. It might include evaluating the logic used in the solution of a problem, searching for the explanation of a strong emotional reaction, or comparing your perspective with the perspective of another person.

During adulthood the realm of thought devoted to metacognition expands. Greater amounts of time are spent in planning, evaluating, reminiscing, and predicting. Having encountered a variety of people and a variety of situations during adult life, one becomes increasingly aware that successful adaptation depends heavily upon the accuracy of two kinds of information: information about the environment and information about the self. The metacognitive functions are not those involved in the direct experience of the environment or in determining a response to an experience. Rather, they are the functions of analysis, interpretation, and integration that bring a broader perspective to life's experiences. Insofar as the challenges of adulthood become more philosophical, these functions become the cornerstones of adaptation. They permit the formulation of a philosophy of life and provide a basis for determining one's personal meaning. As the reality of one's own mortality becomes evident, adults spend energy evaluating their beliefs, assessing their life choices, and searching for the obstacles in their own life that may explain their current feelings of despair (Erikson, 1963). The more physical activity, meaningful work, and intimate relationships diminish in the life of the aging adult, the more introspection and reminiscence serve as a central context for continued psychosocial growth. Here we think of the importance of the life review as a vehicle for selecting and reinterpreting the past so that one can face death with a sense of completion (Butler, 1963).

Memory

Without memory much of what we have described as cognitive capacities of adulthood would be impossible. Only imagery would remain, and that only triggered by the immediate environment or complete fabrication. Every the concept we use is built upon the capacity to remember the word, its referrent, some previous encounters with concept, and the instances where the concept does or does not apply. Without memory, you would not be able to read, understand, or retain any of what you are now reading. In the following sections we will describe what is known about the memory process, discuss the special form of remembering called reminiscence, and consider some of the problems of memory experienced by the elderly.

The Memory Process

Memory is commonly viewed as a three-stage process including encoding, storage, and retrieval (Klatzky, 1975). Each of these elements is essential if an event or a piece of information continues to be useful in subsequent learning (see Figure 5.1). At each stage, errors can interfere with memory.

FIGURE 5.1 The Three Components of the Memory Process

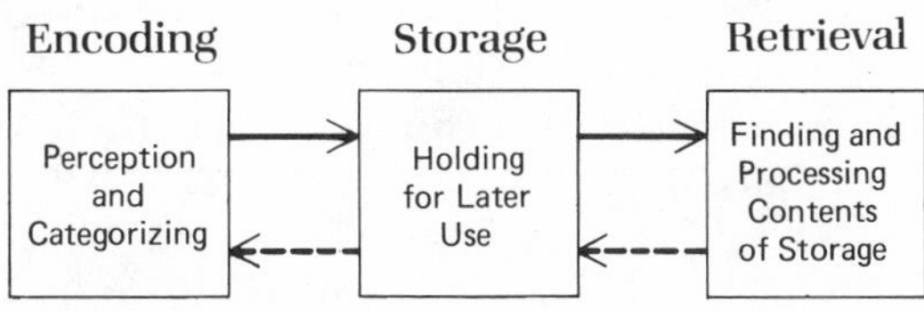

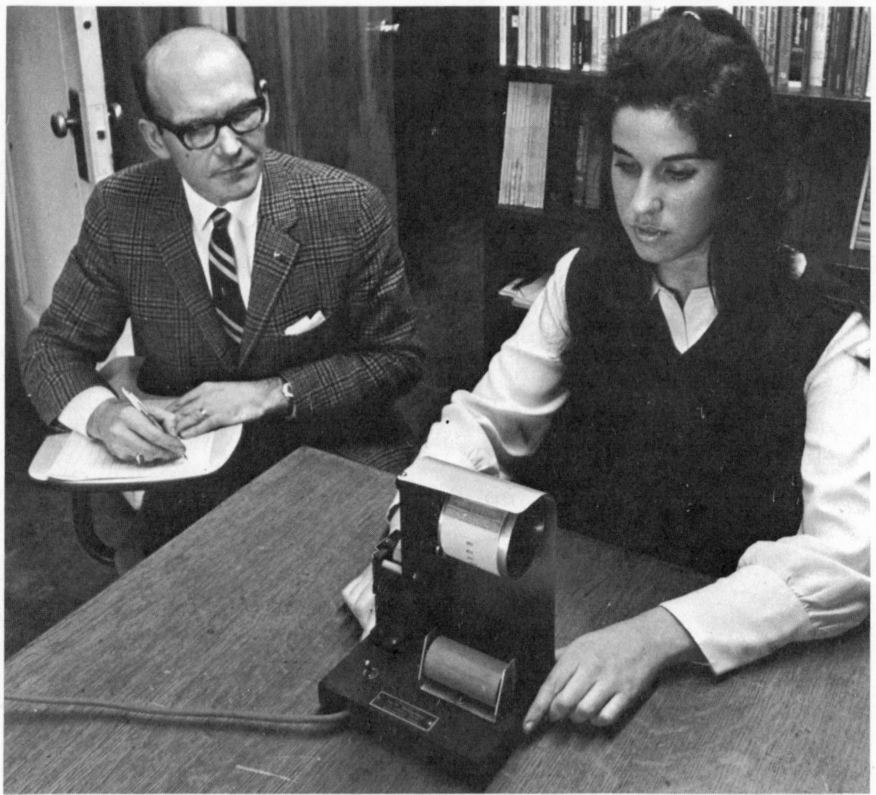

Memory is often studied in a highly structured laboratory setting where subjects try to recall lists of words or syllables.

In thinking about memory, a distinction is commonly made between short-term memory or events in the most immediate past, and long-term memory or the seeming unending pool of past events. There is strong evidence to suggest that the stages of encoding, storage, and retrieval operate differently for these two memories. Certainly the short-term and long-term memories are related, but different processes are involved when one is explaining memory over the past few minutes and memory over many years.

Encoding Encoding involves transferring some event, perhaps a phone number or a person's name, into a form that can be held in memory. In order to encode, the person has to pay attention to the information. If you take a ride in the country, you will probably not remember the number of speed limit signs you passed unless you were specifically focusing on that aspect of the trip. Encoding can occur by retaining the sound of the information or the visual pattern of the information (Martindale, 1981). In adulthood, so much of the information we are trying to remember is verbal that sound tends to be the strongest mode for immediate encoding. For long-term memory, the level of meaning in the information seems to be the factor that most directly influences the ease of encoding. The more completely the meaning is understood and the more richly elaborated the meaning is, the more likely it is that the information will be encoded in long-term memory. For long-term memory, repeated encounters with similar concepts or information will strengthen the earlier memory.

Storage The storage capacity of short-term memory is limited to approximately 7 ± 2 units of information. In memorizing words, numbers, names, or letters of the alphabet, only this range of from 5 to 9 separate items can be retained. This limited storage capacity means that once the number of items exceeds 9, each new item will displace earlier items. The more events take place between the initial event and the time for recall, the less likely it is that the item will be retained in storage. There are some strategies for increasing short-term storage capacity. These include rehearsal and "chunking," or collapsing separate units into meaningful groups. The more associations the adult can generate to new information, the more likely some kind of chunking process will succeed in adding information to short-term storage.

For long-term memory, the storage capacity would appear to be almost limitless. Of course, some past experiences may be dropped from memory, and some experiences are never fully encoded. However, we have learned from research on hypnosis and reports of psychoanalytic therapies that the storage system retains an enormous pool of information even though it may be difficult to retrieve.

Retrieval Stored information is not of much use unless we can call it up to consciousness when we need it. Otherwise, memory would be like our garage. It is jammed with all kinds of things, but you can never find anything in there. The retrieval process includes all those strategies that are involved in finding information that was experienced or learned at an earlier time. Any effort at retrieval depends on the *cues* that are present about the inforamtion we seek. Cues can be any aspects of the situation that help connect the desired information with its location in long-term memory. Cues can be auditory, visual, or semantic. They can refer to the time, the setting, or the emotional tone that was present when the information was learned. The more cues that are present, the easier it will be to retrieve the information.

In short-term memory, where there are only a limited number of items stored, retrieval appears to take place by scanning the contents of the memory. For example, if a person is asked to remember a set of numbers, say 5, 7, and 9, and then is asked whether 9 was in the list, the person reviews each item and answers yes or no. For each item added to the memorized list, it takes a slightly longer time to reach a yes or no answer about any specific item (Sternberg, 1966). Since short-term meory is very limited in capacity, its contents are continuously changing. Every new focus of attention displaces information that may have been presented earlier. Thus, one can only seek to retrieve the most immediate new information from this memory function.

Other information, if it remains in one's memory, must be found in long-term memory, and the retrieval process for that is quite different. Imagine if one had to scan every item in long-term memory to identify a piece of information. It would take a week just to remember your mother's name.

The process of retrieval from long-term memory is not fully understood. We do not know exactly how long-term memory retrieval works, but three characteristics seem to be important. First, the more fully understood and the broader the range of associations one has to the item, the more readily it will be retrieved. Second, information that is organized by some overarching category like social policy, family birthdays, or phone numbers of friends is more readily retrieved than items with no clear categorization. Third, the context and the emotional context seem to be cues for retrieval. It is easier to remember something when you are in a context similar to that which existed during encoding (Wickelgren, 1981).

Three retrieval strategies described here are recognition, recall, and reconstruction. Each one involves a different approach to the recovery of stored information (see Table 5.1).

Recognition Long-term memory is a highly organized system. This organization seems to make *recognition* easy. We can tell in a matter of seconds whether or not we are familiar with something. If someone asks you what the capital of Florida is, you may not be able to answer. If, however, you are then told it is Tallahassee, you would recognize the name. The process of recognition is central to performance on multiple-choice tests. The correct answer must be recognized and matched with a memory of that idea.

The amazing ability of humans to recognize large amounts of material was demonstrated in an experiment performed by Shepard (1967). Subjects were asked to look at three sets of 540 items or stimuli. The first set of stimuli was sentences, the second set was words, and the third set was pictures. On 60 test cards, the subjects were asked to indicate which of the two stimuli was familiar and which was unfamiliar. The subjects were

TABLE 5.1 Three Retrieval Strategies

Recognition	Judging whether a stimulus event is familiar or not Example: A multiple-choice test item
Recall	Searching memory to bring information into consciousness. Example: A fill-in-the-blank test item.
Reconstruction	Integrating stored information and inference to create a memory Example: Recognizing an absurd statement

88 percent accurate when the stimuli were sentences, 90 percent accurate when the stimuli were words, and 98 percent accurate when the stimuli were pictures. The high percentage scores of recognition of sentences and words along with the almost perfect percentage score when the stimuli were pictures shows the incredible capacity for humans to recognize familiar information.

Recall Fill-in-the-blank tests require another memory ability, *recall.* Recall involves searching through the organized categories of long-term memory and bringing the required memory to the conscious state. Recall is a more difficult retrieval task because there are fewer retrieval cues. The two retrieval strategies, recognition and recall, both require familiarity with the material and the ability to retrieve it from a specific category. That is, one can make a judgment about whether an event is "old" or "new," familiar or novel, and another judgment about the exact name, information, or timing of the event in the past.

Reconstruction When did you first learn about the planets? Can you draw a map of your hometown? As you approach these questions, you reconstruct a memory of what may have happened or how things must look based on what you know and what you can remember. Much of our reconstructive memory relies on inferences. You may not remember when you first learned about planets, but you can figure out when the topic might have first been introduced in your school curriculum. As you draw a map of your hometown, you probably cannot reproduce every street. You will reconstruct a representation of the town that combines your memory for specific landmarks with your knowledge of directions.

We can make a distinction between knowledge that is stored and knowledge that is inferred. For example, some specific properties of an animal must be stored directly. A cardinal is red, a canary is yellow. But some properties can be inferred by knowing that both cardinals and canaries are animals. Because they are animals we infer that they eat, sleep, have blood, move about, and reproduce. These kinds of information do not need to be stored for every animal we learn about. They can be reconstructed from our knowledge that the specific species is an animal and therefore must share the properties of animals.

Collins and Quillian (1969) were able to show that some information is reconstructed from inferred knowledge. They asked people to answer true or false as quickly as possible to specific statements. Consider these three statements:

1. A canary is yellow.
2. A canary can fly.
3. A canary has skin.

The correct response was given most quickly for statements like number 1 which are directly stored attributes. Responses were somewhat longer for statements like number 2 which involve one step of inference (a canary is a bird, birds have wings). Responses to statements like number three took longest because they involve two steps of inference (a canary is a bird, a bird is an animal, animals have skin).

Other evidence for our capacity to reconstruct memories from general information comes from our ability to detect false statements, contradictions, or ridiculous assertions. It doesn't take long to recognize that the statement "All horses are cows" is false or that "All fish are bicycles" is ridiculous. Yet we cannot possibly have a memory for everything that is *not* a specific feature of each concept. When we focus on a concept, it is likely that the related associational network is temporarily activated. We can scan the network to identify whether "Horse" and "Cow" are two examples of a larger subset or whether "horse" is a subset of "cow" (Glass & Holyoak, 1975). We use the capacity for inference to test relationships among stored information bundles.

Retrieval of long-term memory is a somewhat hazardous business. We can search for information at one time and simply be unable to recall it. Then at a later moment, the information is available. We can remember events or information incorrectly or only partially. Through psychoanalysis we discover that events may be blocked from retrieval because of emotional barriers but that they do in fact have a place in memory and can be recalled. Of course, we also assume that some information was either never encoded at all or never adequately transferred from short-term to long-term storage.

Metamemory

In adulthood, we become increasingly sensitive to the need for access to past events. The longer one lives and the greater variety of roles one performs, the more ideas, information, and people one encounters. It becomes essential to develop systems for keeping track of the accumulation of data that may be necessary for some future decision. The term *meta* in "metamemory" refers to those administrative functions that help evaluate and improve memory (Lachman, Lachman, & Thronesberg, 1979). Metamemory includes a sense of how well or how accurately a specific event is remembered, strategies for encoding or retrieval that help adults improve their capacity for remembering, and the creation of memory systems for encoding, storing, and retrieving vast amounts of information. File drawers, card catalogs, telephone books, encyclopedias, libraries, and computerized information-processing systems are all examples of the application of metamemory skills to the problems of remembering.

In a study of metamemory, young, middle, and later adults all showed equal accuracy in their feeling of knowing information (Lachman, Lachman, & Thronesberg, 1979). Subjects were shown a series of slides with topical questions such as "What was the former name of Muhammad Ali?" After trying to answer each question, the questions that the subject could

Copyright, 1982 Sidney Harris.

not answer were shown again. Subjects were then asked to judge whether they knew the answer or might be able to retrieve it. They could answer: (a) definitely do not know, (b) maybe do not know, (c) could recognize the answer if told, (d) could recall the answer given some hints and more time. On a later multiple-choice test, subjects actually did answer more questions that they rated *c* correctly than those rated *a* or *b*. Subjects were also accurate in the degree of confidence they had about whether an answer was correct. If they were certain of the answer, the answer was more likely to be correct. If they were unsure about the answer, the answer was more likely to be wrong.

In an era of what has been called the information explosion, it sometimes seems hopeless to try to keep track of all the data that one encounters. The tasks of adult life impose memory priorities so that some information is rehearsed, noted in written form, and/or shared with others to make it readily retrievable. Other information may be saved in some systematic way so that it is accessible to mechanical retrieval as in a filing system, but not part of one's personal memory. Still other information enters the "circular file." A decision is made that this event or data is simply not worth saving. Of course, sometimes that decision is incorrect. One learns to revise one's priorities after having mentally or physically discarded information that turns out to be important.

Memory Problems of the Elderly

Most people will agree that older people have trouble remembering some things. However, the exact nature of memory deficits is something of a controversy. In this section we will consider some of the areas of memory deficit that have been suggested and try to evaluate the validity of these claims.

One area that has been suggested is that the elderly have a more limited storage capacity in short-term memory than younger people. In this view, forgetfulness is simply a result of an inability to store as many items as younger adults or children can (Inglis, Ankus, & Sykes, 1968). However, there is increasing evidence that primary, short-term memory storage capacity does not decrease with age. When subjects were asked to recall items from lists of words up to seven items long, no age differences were observed (Arenberg, 1973). When subjects were exposed to two lists, one item to the right ear and then one to the left, there were no age differences in the ability to recall the first list of items to the right ear. These findings support the view that immediate recall does not decline with age.

Another observation has been that with age more time is required to respond to memory tasks. This finding is another example of behavioral slowing discussed in Chapter 3. Studies do tend to confirm this observation. Items are less well recalled by older adults when they are presented in rapid succession than when they are presented more slowly. As lists of items increase in length, the middle-aged and elderly take increasingly longer to determine whether a particular item has been presented (Treat & Reese, 1976). Some part of this increase in time to retrieve an item from memory has been attributed to a lack of confidence about the memory capacity (Reese, 1976). Older subjects are increasingly uncertain about the accuracy of their memory. When confronted with the task of having to say whether a particular item was presented on an earlier list or not, they are prey to feelings of doubt that interfere with the task itself. Once again, we see the role of cautiousness in cognitive functioning.

The elderly use less efficient retrieval strategies (Walsh, 1975). This observation refers to the self-initiated use of memory aids and poor organization of new items. Age differences in tasks involving recognition are minimal. However, in tasks requiring free recall where the retrieval cues are minimal, older subjects perform less well than young adults. During childhood, young children move through four stages in the use of memory strategies (Reese, 1976). First, they approach tasks without any memory strategy at all. Information is either recalled or it is not. Second, memory strategies can be taught but they are used inefficiently. Third, the strategy is used efficiently but needs to be prompted. Finally, children impose the memory strategies without having to be reminded. From this point, strategies merely become more complex, evolving, as we have suggested earlier, toward the ultimate in memory strategies, the computer.

A number of studies have provided evidence that older adults do not continue to use the complex memory strategies that became so automatic by the end of childhood (Reese, 1976). They do not draw upon imagery, verbal elaboration, or categorization strategies either in the encoding of information or to improve their recall. When these strategies are explained or modeled, the elderly can improve their performance (Denney, 1979).

Hultsch (1969) presented a free-recall task to three age groups of adults. When no special instructions were given, the two older groups performed less well than the youngest group in recalling a list of words. However, when subjects were told "to organize the words based on the alphabetical position of their first letter," free recall was equally high among all the age groups. The implication is that it is not the potential for recall that declines with age but the use of systematic memory strategies.

It is not that these memory strategies were never learned, but that they have fallen into disuse over the course of adulthood. Most likely, memory strategies are supported by the specific demands of school, particular kinds of work, and certain aspects of parenting activities. As the dominance of these settings diminishes, adults depend more and more on the recall of thematic characteristics of past events and less on the recall of specific elements or episodes (Horn, 1979).

In fact, we have very little evidence on what might be called the ecologically valid memory tasks of adult life (Schaie, 1978). We do not know what kinds of memory are required to function effectively during adulthood. Few studies consider the actions adults take in order to ensure that they will remember something at a future time. Clearly, the culture itself makes dramatic efforts to preserve the memory of special events or people. Monuments, holidays, and memorials ensure that some elements of our past are remembered by many at all ages.

A final aspect of memory that poses problems for the elderly is the blurring or confusion about past events. As one ages and accumulates a greater store of memories, it may become difficult to place events clearly in sequence or to accurately recall which events occurred together. An analysis of the interviews of centenarians conducted by the Social Security Administration in 1963 provides some insight into the nature of time perspective of older adults (Costa & Kastenbaum, 1967). Subjects were asked specific questions about their earliest memory, the most exciting event of their lives, and the most salient historical event. They were also asked about future ambitions. For each of the past memories, there was an attempt to establish during which period of life the event occurred. Subjects differed in whether they were able to offer a memory for each of the three categories. They also differed in whether or not they were able to specify the life stage when the event occurred. Subjects were divided into four groups depending on how many of the three memories they were able to recall. Of 268 subjects, 30.8 percent recalled all three events, 34.4 percent recalled two of the three, 22.1 percent recalled only one event, and 12.7 percent recalled none of the three. This last group had the least differentiated sense of past, whereas the first group had the most highly differentiated sense of the past. Costa and Kastenbaum then asked about the relationship between a differentiated sense of past and responses to the question about future ambitions. Those centenarians who had the most vivid sense of past were the most likely to also have ambitions for the future. Those who had limited recall of the past also had minimal future orientation.

We infer from these observations that older adults differ markedly in their sense of time. Rather than attributing confusion about the past to the aging process, we might more accurately begin to assess time perspective as a dimension of cognitive style. Most likely we will find that at every life stage there are individual differences in the degree to which past, present, and future time are categorized and differentiated. In fact, we may begin to appreciate the role that time perspective plays in coping behavior throughout adulthood by clarifying some of the ways that individuals conceptualize their own personal histories.

In reviewing the evidence about memory problems of the elderly, it appears that there are some areas where older adults perform less well than younger adults. If we can assume that older learners are motivated to remember new information, then the research we have reviewed suggests some ways to improve their performance.

1. Modify the pace in the presentation of new information so that the speed of presentation does not deter from learning.
2. Minimize the penalty for errors and encourage risk-taking so that the tendency toward cautiousness is less likely to interfere with learning
3. Provide ideas for organizing information and for elaboration of categorization of new material.
4. Tie new material to ideas or events that are relevant to the learner to help integrate that material and to give it distinctiveness.

The Process of Change in Adult Thought

Thought, including the content of thoughts, the pattern of associations, the complexity of thought, and the monitoring of one's thoughts, can undergo change throughout adulthood. Thought, as Piaget (1978) described it, is a product of actions. Actions upon the physical environment, social interactions, sensorimotor experiences, or actions upon thoughts themselves constitute the basic elements of thought. Throughout adulthood, changing interactions with people and settings continue to produce changing

Assimilation.
Copyright, 1982 Sidney Harris.

Accommodation.
Copyright, 1982 Sidney Harris.

thoughts. As adults perceive other people in a new perspective they are likely to encounter new forms of interaction. Similarly, as adults are involved in new kinds of interactions, their thoughts about relationships change. Such shifts in social relationships as marriage, parenting, job promotion to a new level of responsibility, and becoming an employer rather than an employee are all examples of new interactions that prompt changes in the content and complexity of thought.

Cognitive change occurs through a process of adaptation. Adaptation involves two reciprocal elements: assimilation and accommodation (Piaget & Inhelder, 1969). In each experience a person recognizes the similarity between the object or event and some concept that is already formulated. This is assimilation. We seek to understand a new experience as an example of a concept we already have available in our memory. However, with each new experience there is likely to be some novelty. When we meet a new person, we realize that he or she is not exactly like anyone else we know. When we taste a new food, we perceive it to be unique in some respects. The existing concepts must be modified to take into account the new properties of the experience. This is accommodation. It permits the necessary alterations of our thoughts so that novelty can have an impact. The process suggests that encounters with diversity will prompt adaptation and cognitive change. This process continues throughout adult life.

Factors That Contribute to Cognitive Change

In the following sections we consider three factors that contribute to the divergence of cognitive orientations across the life span: (1) the impact of the environment; (2) the impact of life experiences; and (3) the impact of one's life stage. This is a speculative analysis that suggests some characteristics of thought that become more prominent during adulthood.

The Environment and Cognitive Change In adulthood, people have the physical, intellectual, and social skills to exert considerable impact on their surroundings. Adults not only react to but create elements of their environment. To the extent that the environment influences thought, the world that each adult creates will influence the quality of thought. Adults can seek diversity of interactions or settings (for example, through travel) in order to maintain diversity and flexibility of thought. A person might impose a high degree of organization and order in the home or business setting to help support organized and logical problem solving. A person may select a particular physical location or develop a pattern of landscaping that stimulates creativity or fosters a desired mood. In the extreme, adults make use of drugs that depress certain mental activities or increase others. In all of these and other ways, the quality of thought itself comes more under the adult's direct control.

Over the course of adult life, thinking moves away from its intimate involvement with the immediate environment. Adults use inquiry, set-breaking, and introspection to assess their reactions and their plans. Thoughts become less commanding as adults appreciate their representational quality. In this process there is a greater freedom to reconceptualize ideas, to generate new interpretations, or to create new hypotheses. As adults become less physically resilient and encounter more and more physical barriers to activities, the value of thought itself increases. Thinking about actions may replace the actions themselves. Through thought, especially logical reasoning, insight and theory can be considerably more powerful than action.

Thinking in adulthood often takes place within a group context. Marriage partners work together to solve problems about finances, to plan their time, or to evaluate their separate experiences. Workers may help each other to solve a problem, to plan a new activity, or to evaluate ongoing practices. In these group contexts, thoughts are modified through interaction with others who hold a different perspective. One's own hypotheses can be enhanced through collaboration with another thoughtful adult.

Diversity of opinion serves to bring one's own point of view into question. In the face of opposing positions, one must begin to evaluate, question, and reconceptualize. In some cases, the opinions of others turn out to be incorrect. Adults come to respect their own judgment and to anticipate areas where they are best off holding to their own views. Likewise, adults discover areas where their judgment is likely to be inadequate. In some extreme cases, adults discover that the opinions of others are consistently incorrect or unhelpful. For example, as Thomas Edison worked on the light bulb he was frequently confronted with opinions about how to proceed. Through years of experimentation, Edison learned to rely on his own capacity for invention and to ignore or distrust the opinions of others. This lesson, which was formulated as a result of his struggle with the light bulb, cost him dearly as he persisted in a later scheme to mine iron ore with an enormous electromagnet, a scheme that never succeeded (Conot, 1979).

Life Experiences and Cognitive Change Why do we say "wait until you're older" to young children? Obviously, we believe intuitively in the notion that some things simply are not readily understandable until they have been experienced. In adolescence, we observe the emergence of the capacities for logical thought that characterize the best or most complex capacities of adulthood. Often, however, adolescents lack the information or experience to translate their hypothetical formulations into workable practices. This is one of the important changes in adulthood. Adults can blend the principles of logic with the limitations of reality. They know how to present ideas so that they are more likely to be accepted. They plan change so that the potential objections or resistances can be avoided or handled. They recognize the difference between plans that have a chance to succeed and those that will be very difficult to achieve. Experience wears away some of the rough edges of idealism. It encourages negotiation and compromise rather than rebellion or rejection. In that sense, experience tends to strengthen the conservatism of adulthood (Labouvie-Vief, 1980). As Robert Frost wrote: "I never dared be radical when young for fear it would make me conservative when old."

Part of learning from experience involves greater tolerance for ambiguity or even open contradiction. In childhood, we tend to believe that the world operates by rules or principles that have an inherent meaning or good. Judges are honest and make their judgments on the merit of the case. Students are admitted to college on the basis of their competences. Workers are hired or given raises because of their skills. In adulthood, we appreciate that rules of fair play live side by side with rules of politics and power. Competence may be rewarded, but so may social status, wealth, or assertiveness. Teachers may evaluate some students on the basis of performance and others on the basis of race, family background, or physical attractiveness. Adults realize that contradictory factors do exist, neither canceling the other out, but both directing the course of events. In fact, there is an argument that opposite factors are necessary for the existence of the total dimension. Opposites like good and evil, or love and hatred, are both necessary in order for either to exist. Through conflict with its opposite, each pole is clarified (Riegel, 1976).

In adult life, the tension among opposites poses continuous challenges to adult thought. Especially when life choices require a reconciliation of these opposite forces, a new level of thinking is stimulated that permits the integration of opposing factors. Parents must respond to their children's simultaneous needs for dependence and independence. Employers struggle to create working conditions that create allegiance to the goals of the organization and also exact maximum productivity. Religions teach about a loving God who also punishes and takes vengeance. As parents become old and ill, adult children wish for their parents' recovery and also for their death. In all of these examples, the seeming conflict of opposites stimulates a new conceptualization of values, meaning, and life goals.

As experiences accumulate, adults have the opportunity to observe the patterns of regularities of events as well as to experience the unpredictable. Part of learning from experience is learning to anticipate future events. In this respect, adult thought changes in the direction of becoming more attuned to prediction and preparation for the future than is the case in childhood. Although adults recognize that the future is uncertain, they can draw on an expanding store of past experiences to try to prepare themselves for upcoming events.

Parenting, perhaps more than any other adult role, draws on the capacity for anticipation. At first, when infants are not able to speak, parents must learn to anticipate infant needs from changes in behavior, increases in irritability, or expressions of alertness and interest. In prepar-

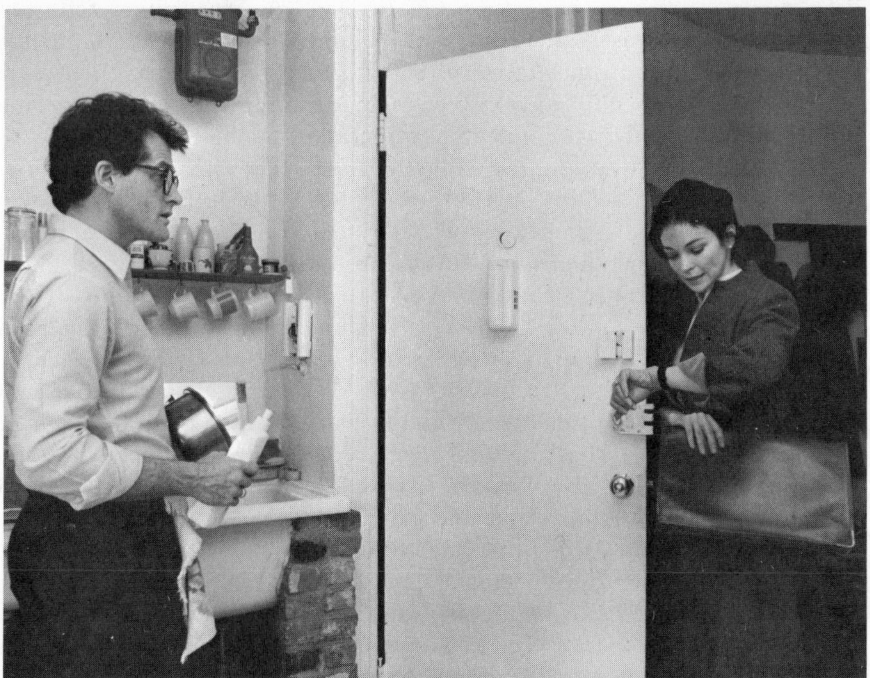

The tension between conflicting forces is a constant stimulus to adult thought.

ing a safe and stimulating environment for young children, parents have to anticipate potential dangers, and remove or minimize them. In the selection of clothing, toys, or food, parents anticipate the child's changing needs as maturation takes place. At subsequent stages, children foster greater anticipation of future life stages. Parents may make decisions about their child's education, begin saving for a college education, begin preparing the social network that they envision as most supportive or enhancing for their child's future. Parents may even begin to anticipate changes in the parent-child relationship as children mature. This process leads to a new view of one's personal future as well as the future of one's children. As we face an adulthood where parents and children can expect to participate in a continued relationship well into adulthood, anticipation of the future should lead to a more careful crafting of the formative period of parenting. We can see a time when decisions about parenting will be reached with some serious thought to how those decisions will effect the ability to maintain a meaningful, reciprocal relationship during the child's adulthood.

Life Stage and Cognitive Change There is a good reason to believe that one's stage in life stimulates new thoughts and a new perspective. For example, during middle adulthood people recognize that they have already lived more years than they have yet to live. This realization tends to motivate an active assessment of achievements and goals. Adults at this period feel an urgency to set priorities about their life choices. They begin to articulate the specific meaning of their lives and to evolve a personal philosophy that provides conceptual integration to the many roles, relationships, and activities that consume their daily life. This kind of conceptual work is motivated by a more concrete recognition of one's own mortality. The death of one's own parents, the maturation of one's children, and the crystallization of career achievements all push adults toward a more active search for personal meaning.

At a later phase, after about age 70, adults begin to turn away from their own personal future to an assessment of their past. The uncertainty of death and the fear of becoming feeble or dependent are unpleasant associations to future time. Anxiety and fear are likely to push thoughts of the future out of awareness. In their place, older adults may focus more on past achievements in light of earlier life goals. Through reminiscence and introspection, older adults experience a dynamic process of life evaluation. Butler (1963) describes this process as the life review.

The life review is both engrossing and complexing. It may involve revising old memories to fit life aspirations or revising aspirations to fit with past memories. Thoughts of the past may be fleeting or a constant obsession. They emerge at various levels of consciousness—including dreams, fleeting images, or dominant preoccupations. A 76-year-old man described his experience: "My life is in the background of my mind much of the time; it cannot be any other way. Thoughts of the past play upon me; sometimes I play with them; encourage and savor them; at other times I dismiss them" (Butler, 1963).

Depending on the outcome of the review, adults can emerge with a strong sense of confidence and pride in the pattern of life choices and life outcomes. Adults can also emerge with a sense of depression, worthlessness, or despair. Although we do not fully understand the factors that contribute to a sense of integrity, we do expect that some adults do achieve this remarkable state of integration and acceptance during later adulthood.

The final achievement of a sense of integrity results from an ability to introspect about the gradual evolution of life events and to appreciate the significance of each event in the formation of the adult personality. This state can only be reached through individual effort. One may even have to isolate oneself temporarily, shutting out the influences of potentially competitive or resentful associates.

One of the major modes of engaging in self-evaluation involves a kind of remembering called reminiscence. This process of nostalgic remembering allows adults to recapture some of the memorable events in the life history. Reminiscence usually serves to increase the adult's feeling of youth, competence, attractiveness, and closeness to others (Fallot, 1977). On the other hand, some adults tend to dwell on sad events and allow earlier disappointments to preoccupy their current thoughts.

The process of reminiscence appears to lend continuity to older adults' self-concepts. They can trace the path of their own development through time and identify moments which are of central importance to the crystallization of their personal philosophy. We see reminiscence as an integrating process which has positive value for an eventual attainment of integrity. In excess, however, reminiscence can dominate reality. In that case, the adult's past life takes precedence over current circumstances. No new events can compete with past memories in engaging the adult's attention and energy. Under these conditions, a realistic acceptance of one's total life history is not possible.

Of course, the process of self-evaluation will be affected by selectivity of memory, the dominant value orientation, and the general quality of supportiveness or destructiveness in the social milieu. Given these contaminants to a purely objective self-assessment, individuals must engage in repeated soul-searching efforts to sort out their lives and to come to terms with some of the discordant events which will inevitably be a part of their history. They must determine whether the essential nature of their personal identity has survived through time. They must evaluate the quality of their close relationships and determine the degree to which they are able to meet the needs of others. They must identify those contributions that represented a serious effort to improve the quality of life for others. Finally, they must determine the extent to which their philosophy of life has been accurately translated into a pattern of significant actions.

Ultimately, the attainment of integrity is a result of thought. Adults' thoughts about their lives will generate a predominant stance toward their feelings of personal contentment and worth. The final outcome of this process of introspection is not a direct translation of the number of positive or negative events in one's life or the number of successes and failures in one's efforts to achieve. There are some adults who have experienced grave, lifelong trauma or have serious physical handicaps and can still maintain an attitude of contentment with their lot in life. On the other hand, there are adults whose life has been comparatively conflict-free who still view their past with great dissatisfaction and resentment. Resolving the conflict of integrity versus despair is a process of achieving an attitude of self-acceptance through private introspection.

Evidence of Cognitive Change in Adulthood

For a long time psychologists have painted a picture of declining intellectual ability that begins in early adulthood and continues until the end of life (Birren, 1964). This approach is based on an analysis of intelligence-test scores which show a pattern of decline from age 30 on. But as Birren points out, the definition of intelligence that is used in the design and appli cation of these intelligence tests refers to capacities that are predictive of school-related success. The criteria for assessing adult intelligence are necessarily more heterogeneous than the ability to succeed in the school curriculum.

A more complete picture is achieved by looking at issues of work-related productivity, health, and problem solving as well as the more traditional intelligence-test data.

Changes in Work-Related Productivity In attempting to define intelligence in a slightly different way, several researchers have looked at the pattern of productivity in the work setting (Dennis, 1966; Lehman, 1953; Simonton, 1977). Lehman, in examining high-quality production, reported that the decade of the thirties is the peak for productivity of a very high quality. Work that is rated as "worthy" was observed to peak somewhat later and decline gradually. Dennis, in considering total work productivity, identified the decade of the forties as the most productive period. He differentiates patterns of productivity among a variety of professions. Among those he studied, productivity of scholars in the humanities continued at a high level until the seventies, while for those in the creative arts the decline after 40 was comparatively rapid. These data may reflect a pattern of expectations about productivity as well as indication of intellectual capacity. Those adults who anticipate retirement at age 65 would not be likely to invest a great amount of energy in their work as they approach that age.

Margaret Mead remained productive and challenged the status quo throughout her adult life.

Mental Decline as a Predictor of Death A new trend has been to consider the relationship between health and cognitive capacities during adulthood. Riegel and Riegel (1972) have presented the notion that the older adult group really consists of two distinct subgroups, those who are healthy and will survive and those who are sick and will soon die. In reviewing data from longitudinal studies of mental abilities, the Riegels found a decline in intellectual performance among people who were nearing death. Those subjects who showed this sudden drop were no longer alive at the next data-collection period. The Riegels found that they were able to predict who in their sample was likely to die before the next testing point by examining the pattern of change in intellectual abilities. The data also suggest that a cross-sectional study of intellectual capacity is contaminated by the inclusion in a single group of those who will soon die and those who will survive. Intellectual functioning appears to remain at a constant level until shortly before the person is going to die, at which point there is a rapid deterioration.

Different Kinds of Abilities and Different Developmental Patterns Another approach to the study of adult intelligence looks at the various abilities that contribute to intellectual functioning. Declining competence with age has been identified in a number of areas including reaction time, visual-motor flexibility (translating visual information into new motor responses), and memory. Older subjects tend to respond more slowly in reaction-time tasks (Birren, 1974; Botwinick, 1970, 1973; Waugh, Fozard, Talland, & Erwin, 1973). This observation has been qualified somewhat by looking at the phases of the task. When college-age subjects and adults between the ages of 60 and 87 were compared, the older subjects took longer to decide what the stimulus was. They did not take significantly longer to press the button once the stimulus was presented (Simon & Pouraghabagher, 1977).

With regard to memory, Botwinick (1967) has described a gradual increase in the number of people whose memories decline at each age level. Botwinick (1970) also suggests that short-term memory is more seriously affected by aging than long-term memory is. Thus, an older person may find it more difficult to store newly acquired information and then retrieve it than younger subjects would (Fozard & Poon, 1976; Reese, 1976). In studies of long-term memory, older subjects seem to lose information in the short period right after learning, but then to retain a high level of recall for the remaining material for up to 130 weeks later (Fozard and Poon, 1976).

In Chapter 2, we described some of the unique features of formal operational thought. Piaget (1967) had assumed that some modification of this level of abstract, logical, hypothetical reasoning was the dominant characteristic of adult cognition. Research on formal thought in adulthood raises questions about this assumption.

The change to formal operational thought does not occur uniformly across all problem-solving dimensions. What is more, not all people seem to function at a formal operational level. Dulit (1972) compared formal reasoning among four groups: adolescents aged 14 of average intelligence; adolescents aged 16 and 17 of average intelligence; gifted adolescents aged 16 and 17; and adults aged 20–55 of average intelligence. The group with the highest percentage of subjects using formal operational thought across many problem areas was the gifted adolescents. In this group, 75 percent used abstract, systematic problem-solving strategies. Among the older adolescents and the adults of average intelligence, 50 percent of males and 15 percent of females used formal operational problem-solving strategies.

Denney (1979) reviewed studies of adult performance on Piaget-type tasks in the areas of formal operations, classification, egocentrism, and moral reasoning. Elderly adults performed less well on many of these tasks than middle-aged adults. On tasks of conservation, the evidence is mixed. Papalia, Salverson, and True (1973) found that older adults aged 64 to 85 had increasingly more difficulty the more abstract the conservation problems became. Other studies have found that older adults perform just as well as middle-aged adults on conservation problems (Selzer & Denney, 1977). There does seem to be a positive relationship between educational level and performance on these tasks, regardless of age.

Building on the work of others, John Horn (1979) has proposed that the course of mental abilities across the life span is not uniform. Some areas are strengthened while others decline. He argues that primary mental abilities can be grouped together into six factors: crystallized intelligence (Gc), fluid intelligence (Gf), general visualization (Gv), general auditory organization (Ga), short-term acquisition and retrieval (SAR), and tertiary storage and retrieval (TSR). The abilities that are related to each of these factors are listed in Table 5.1.

In the fullest use of human intelligence, both Gf, the ability to impose organization on information and to generate new hypotheses, and Gc, the ability to bring to bear the knowledge and information that has been accumulated in past learning, are called into play. Some primary abilities like formal reasoning or associative memory are involved in maintaining both factors. However, the two factors appear to draw differentially on neurological and experiential underpinnings. Crystallized intelligence reflects the consequences of life experiences within a society. Socialization in the family, exposure to media, and participation in school, work, and community settings all emphasize the use and improvement of these valued abilities. The abilities included in crystallized intelligence are overrepresented in their experiential base and in their neurological foundation. These abilities increase with age, experience, and physical maturation. They remain at a high level of functioning throughout adulthood.

Fluid intelligence seems to be more characteristic of what we mean when we say someone has "a good head on their shoulders." The ability to

TABLE 5.1 Six Second-Order Mental Abilities

Second-Order Abilities	*Examples of Primary Abilities*
1. Crystallized intelligence	*Verbal comprehension.* Reading and generally understanding the content.
	Experiental evaluation. Having a good sense of what is diplomatic or acceptable in a social situation.
2. Fluid intelligence	*Induction.* Finding a general relationship and applying it.
	General reasoning. Being able to approach problems logically.
3. General visualization	*Visualization.* Imagining what a spatial configuration might look like.
	Spatial orientation. Determining the way objects appear in space.
4. General auditory organization	*Speech perception under distraction/distortion.* Identifying and understanding one sound among many.
	Temporal tracking. Memory for the order of sounds.
5. Short-term acquisition and retrieval	*Memory span.* The number of units and retrieval recalled.
	Discrimination among sound patterns. Being able to remember sound patterns.
6. Tertiary storage and retrieval	*Associational fluency.* Having retrieval access to certain associations.
	Ideational fluency. The ability to generate ideas when given a stimulus.

Source: Adapted from "The Rise and Fall of Human Abilities" by J. L. Horn, *Journal of Research and Development in Education,* 1979, *12*(2), 59–78.

figure out a correct answer without knowing the information or without having been trained in the skills is evidence of fluid intelligence. Older adults do not spontaneously impose organization on new information. They are less likely to attend to the incidental information or process level learning that contributes to Gf. Horn also suggests that Gf is more dependent on the specific number of neurons available for its functioning than Gc. As neurological loss accumulates, it influences those components of intelligence that are not overrepresented in the mass of neurons.

In conclusion, the interaction among the factors of experience, physiological change, and maturation influence the course of crystallized and fluid intelligence differently (see Figure 5.2). Crystallized intelligence becomes increasingly effective as the benefits of socialization and experience accumulate. Fluid intelligence declines as the specific neurological support for this kind of functioning decreases. If overall intelligence is a product of both Gf and Gc, then if Gf declines and Gc increases the overall IQ ought to remain about the same.

The pattern of cognitive change over the life course is confounded by the methods of research that are used. Most studies use a cross-sectional design (Denney, 1982; Baltes, Reese & Nesselroade, 1977). This means that they compare young adults, middle adults, and older adults who are living at a given time. This strategy does not control for educational differences across the three age groups. Since the oldest group is likely to have had fewer years of formal education, they may be at a distinct disadvantage that

FIGURE 5.2 Cumulative Influences and Developmental Outcomes over the Life Span

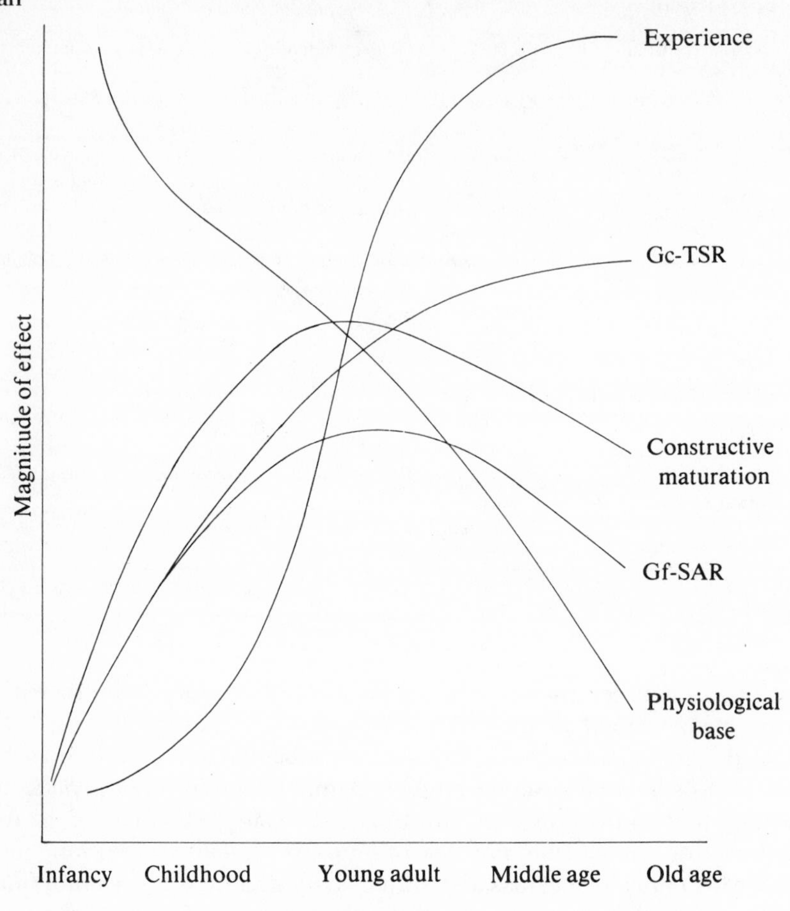

Source: "Cognitive Development in Adulthood" by J. L. Horn, in O. G. Brim, Jr., and J. Kagan (Eds.), *Constancy and Change in Human Development* (Cambridge, Mass.: Harvard University Press, 1980), p. 492.

is not related to aging but to cultural and historical opportunities. Many of the studies also compare an older-adult group that has been hospitalized or resides in a nursing home with healthy, highly autonomous college students. Thus the health status and environment of the groups are not comparable. These group differences make it difficult to interpret performance decrements in adulthood as a necessary product of aging. Even longitudinal studies of change do not usually permit us to separate cohort differences from age. The group being studied has been exposed to a certain array of educational demands and resources that are unique to its era. The emphasis on achievement may differ from one historical period to another. Today's adults are much more likely to engage in continuous learning in educational settings than were the adults who were subjects of research in the 1950s and '60s. The impact of television on the generation who were children in the 1950s and '60s may make them different as adult learners than previous cohorts. The introduction of electronic games may create an even more distinct cohort of the children of the 1980s.

Another problem in understanding cognitive changes in adulthood is related to the theoretical expectations we hold. Our stage theories direct us to expect one higher level of functioning that will sit atop the pyramid of cognition and characterize adult thought. However, in adulthood an increasing number of settings, decisions, and life events can contribute to one's cognitive orientation. The demands of work, family life, or religious commitments will increase emphasis on some types of problem-solving strategies and not others. The reinforcement contingencies of a hospital or nursing home may require very concrete adaptations. The result is a diversity of responses that take into account setting and relational demands. This view has been described as contextualism. In this perspective, the reality of specific adaptations to specific contexts is the product of adult cognitive maturity. "Contextualism suggests the identification of multilinear developmental paths leading to pluralistic goals" (Labouvie-Vief & Chandler, 1978).

Cognition and Social Life

Much of adult thought focuses on social relationships and social situations. Adults are frequently involved in solving problems that center around the interpersonal rather than the physical demands of their surroundings. Where the child struggles to reach a doorknob or ride a two-wheeled bicycle, the adult struggles to achieve intimacy with a marriage partner or to have a productive collaboration with a colleague.

As Simon (1975) argues, many of the same principles of thought that apply to solving mathematical or scientific problems apply to understanding social relationships. "Information is extracted from a complex stimulus situation; it is subjected to the kinds of information processes we call thinking, judging, problem solving, or inferring; during the course of that processing, there is brought to bear upon it a wide range and variety of information already stored in memory. We neither need nor want separate theories of social thinking and other (anti-social?) thinking. We simply need a theory of thinking" (p. 3).

With this orientation in mind we focus on the way thinking is used in social relations as a means of clarifying the quality of adult thought as well as describing the cognitive bases of certain social relationships.

Social thinking, although very complex, is more subjective than thinking about how to solve a mathematics problem or finding the solution to a chemistry problem where there is one clear, correct solution. One way that thinking is used in adulthood is in the creation of a view of the world that is supportive of the person and where the importance of the person is preserved to a greater extent than it might be in anyone else's analysis. Social thought, then, is more than an analysis of the objective social reality. It is a creation of an image, an outlook, and/or a mythology about the meaning of life that orients decision-making. This outlook guides one's attention toward certain social realities and away from others. It functions to interpret social events so that the person's own life goals are viewed as appropriate. What is more, social thought generally uses personal experience as the basis for interpretation.

It is important to bear in mind that the capacity for imposing reason and logic in social relations is influenced by a variety of motives that blend into the person's thinking, just as memory contributes a rendering of past experiences to thought. Needs for affiliation, power, or intimacy, or fears of rejection, failure, helplessness, or isolation may influence the way a person perceives the dynamics of a situation or the possibilities for action. What a person wants will in part determine his or her behavior. In the following sections, we will discuss the individual in face-to-face relations and internal thought systems for behavioral guidance.

The Individual in Face-to-Face Relations

Most people have six categories of face-to-face relations (see Figure 5.3). These categories are:

1. Single Encounters. Over the course of a year, people have a certain number of first-impression relations. A traveling salesperson may have many of these, including potential customers, hotel clerks, seat mates on airplanes, and waitresses in restaurants. An academic recluse will have comparatively few. Every person has some new encounters that do not go beyond a single interaction.
2. Associational relations. Because of group membership, residence in a particular apartment building or neighborhood, or regular attendance at particular settings, people have repeated encounters with certain people over the course of time. These associational relations generally do not lead to a high degree of intimacy, although it is possible for an associational relation to take on greater intensity. One's public image is known through these relationships, and in that sense they can be very important for establishing an adult's reputation in a community.
3. Business or colleaguial relations. All workers have interactions with others because of their work. These relations may involve long hours, close quarters, a high degree of interdependence, and, in some cases, intense emotional involvement. Work relations usually are defined by norms that govern the quality of interaction and limit the degree of personal investment. We know that these relations can be terminated because of promotion to a new position, transfers, firings, or a decision to look for a new job. In this sense, work relations have the peculiar quality of calling forth distancing mechanisms and engagement simultaneously.
4. Friendship relations. For most people, a small number of others are categorized

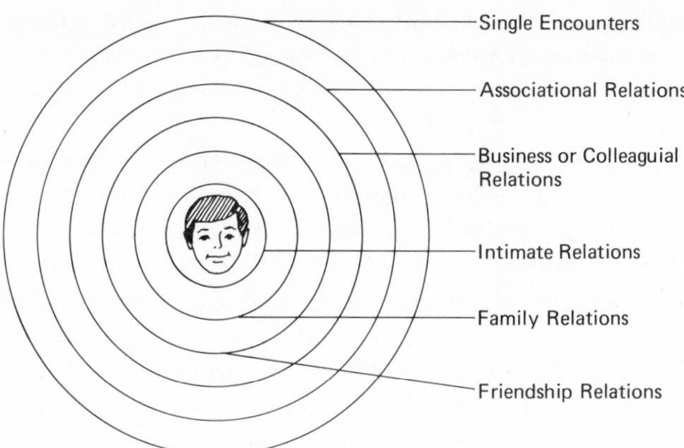

FIGURE 5.3 Six Categories of Face-to-Face Relations

as friends. These people like each other, feel warmly toward each other, and provide an important source of personal support.

5. Family relations. Family bonds encompass a whole network of relationships from parents, spouse, and children to aunts, uncles, cousins, and in-laws. Even though some of these associations provide only occasional interactions, people usually feel a special way toward family members that distinguishes these relations from those of any other type. The concept of family, in other words, frequently overrides other dimensions that govern relationships, including frequency of interaction, similarity of interests and values, physical attractiveness and likability. Some people have frequent and involving interactions with family members while others have few family encounters.
6. Intimate relations. A special subset of relations can be categorized as intimate. These relations, which may exist between husband and wife, between parent and child, or between lovers, are characterized by deep understanding and intense emotional commitment to the well-being and continued development of the other.

For any particular person, there will be a different pattern of regular, face-to-face relationships. People differ in how much emphasis or energy they give to any single category of relationships. A good part of daily thought is devoted to these daily personal relationships. Depending on the pattern of emphasis, adults will be preoccupied with problems of a particular type. For example, the business relations will impose certain limits on interaction, certain demands for leadership or collaboration, or certain problems in managing the performance of others. If a large part of thought is devoted to these problems, the direction of thought about self-other social systems will evolve in a different direction than if the majority of thoughts is focused on family, associational, or intimate relations.

The demands of each of these interpersonal systems for thinking is considerable. It may be that these relations are the most compelling life stimuli for thought. Each system requires an analysis of the demands of that system, an evaluation of one's effectiveness in each sphere, monitoring any single person's movement from one kind of relationship to another, and maintaining continuity even when relations place contradictory demands.

The challenge in adulthood is to impose some integration on one's involvement at these various levels. Priorities must be set, a sense of self-awareness must be established, and conflicts among levels for allegiance or trust must be resolved.

The complexity of social thought and the demands placed by others makes the process responsive as well as initiatory. In order to limit the potential vastness of demands of others, individuals create strategies to permit themselves to be most effective. The predominant arena for intellectual activity for adults is devising plans for social interaction that meet personal needs and at the same time conform to the perceived societal norms for responsive, ethical relationships.

Thought Systems for Behavioral Guidance

In order to cope with the many levels of social relations and the various kinds of responsibility involved at each level, people develop systematic rules to govern social behavior. These rules, which we refer to as morality, political ideology, and personal philosophy, impose organization, limits, and meaning on interpersonal experience.

Moral Thought Several theorists have offered analyses of morality in adulthood. Freud identified morality as a mental structure that first emerged as a result of the resolution of the Oedipal or Electra complex at about age 7. At this age, the conscience, or superego, was strict, punitive, and dominated by a fear of retribution. Because the superego developed during a time of limited ego development, its contents focused on a narrow range of concerns and its organization was highly authoritarian. In adulthood, Freud argued, the superego matures. The strength of impulse weakens, people have more highly developed avenues for sublimation, and there are acceptable outlets for direct expression through love and work. Moral life, then, had its origin in sexual and aggressive impulses, especially impulses toward one's parents. Out of a need to maintain parental love and a fear of parental anger, the child restrains these impulses and incorporates the moral values of the parents. Morality, from generation to generation, is viewed as emerging from the inborn conflict between parental hate and parental love. The child's superego is formed as a product of efforts to resolve that conflict in a context of parental support or parental punitiveness.

The cognitive theorists, especially Piaget and Kohlberg, emphasize changing cognitive capacities that underlie changes in moral thought. In early childhood, moral judgments are based on observable consequences of actions. Intentions, principles, and motives are less relevant than the actual outcome of an act. Breaking ten cups by accident is viewed as worse than breaking one cup as part of an intentional violation. At the intermediate level, moral judgments reflect the desire to maintain the status quo. Rules are respected because they reflect the views of respected authorities. At the highest level, moral judgments reflect one of two positions: (1) The culture establishes moral contracts among individuals, we maintain certain moral commitments in order to ensure that others will maintain their commitments to us. (2) In adulthood it is possible to take an overview of the moral code and appreciate it in relation to moral systems in other societies. Under these conditions of awareness, the adult imposes moral judgments that reflect their own, internal code regardless of the norms of the culture.

It is these last two stages of moral thought that are most likely to emerge during the adult years. Of course, many adults continue to function at an intermediate level. Some may believe that the cultural code is really an expression of their own moral position. In these cases, socialization has worked to create a highly responsive, norm-sensitive adult. However, it is possible to recognize morality as the human construction that it is. The compelling nature of a moral precept is its shared acceptance by many other adults. Only by encountering diverse moral systems can the relativity of morality be fully appreciated. Once adults recognize that it is up to them to determine the content of their own morality, the opportunity for generating new and creative systems for guiding moral behavior becomes possible.

Political Thought Political thought is that system that governs a person's relationship with community, county, state, or federal levels of organization. For many adults, political thought is not highly developed. At some point, perhaps in early adolescence, these adults make an allegiance to the general orientation of the government. After that point, they do their part by paying their taxes but do not become actively involved in political decision-making. This approach is an acceptable adult stance in the United States insofar as the government functions through a system of representation. Those who are elected as representatives can assume the active role in the political process while those who elected the representatives are free to devote their time and energy to work, family, or personal development. The generally low percentage of voters who participate in state and local elections suggests that the vast majority of adults do not feel compelled to exercise their political conceptualizations by trying to change the direction of government.

We assume that these politically inactive adults are aware of the nature and organization of the political system that operates in this country. Based on what they learned about American government and American history in elementary school, high school, and perhaps college, these adults take the stance that they are satisfied with the overall pattern of government. They cannot be viewed as lacking a political conceptualization. Rather, they can be seen as living a life that is in harmony with the system. Successful political socialization has created a pool of adults who feel highly identified with the United States, who support its government, and who do not feel the need to actively influence the political system.

Of course, some adults have a much more active, highly compelling conceptualization of the political system. Political scientists, politicians, political activists, community-change agents, and federal, state, county, or city employees are examples of groups of people who are likely to be more aware of political controversies and who experience more demands to clarify their own political conceptualization. We would expect these groups to be more aware of the process of political decision-making, more sensitive to the origins of social policy and legislation, and more realistic about the range of influence of the political system on individual lives. These adults may in fact have a political ideology that actively directs their decision-making. Concepts about the public good, individual rights, the system of checks and balances, executive power, and the relationship between state and federal levels of decision-making are all examples of political conceptualizations that may be directly translated into action.

With the widespread use of television, it is becoming increasingly difficult to avoid the influence of the political system in daily thought. Political events of all kinds, from gasoline shortages to riverboat cruises, from papal visits to terrorist kidnappings, are part of the public awareness. Given the publicity that the political arena receives, today's adults are continuously challenged to adapt their political ideology to the reality of political life. One might argue that we have an adult population that is more fully informed about political events than any other previous generation. Unfortunately, many adults do not have a conceptualization that is adequate to integrate the information that is continuously presented. In today's society there is some uneasiness among many adults who realize the gap between the hugeness of the political system and their own capacity to understand, interpret, or predict the pattern of political events.

Personal Philosophy Moral thought governs the quality of relationships among individuals. Political thought governs the quality of relationships between people and political units. Personal philosophy governs the quality of relations between individuals and their experience. One's philosophy is a guide to the meaning and purpose in experience.

A personal philosophy is the creation of a mature mind. Generally, the philosophy is forged from the analysis of past experiences and anticipation of future possibilities. The philosophy is based on interactions at every level of relationship. It includes some content from one's political, moral, and/or religious orientation, but generally it is a broader and more abstract formulation than any of these. It includes the answers to basic questions that are first asked in the childhood years. These questions include: How did the world begin? Why was I born? Why do I have to die? What makes me happy? Will I always be loved? Why do I experience pain? In adulthood, the answers to these questions are gradually formulated. Important factors in the maturation of a personal philosophy include one's work, one's relationship with a spouse, parenting, and one's encounters with political and/or historical events. In addition to the contribution of real-life events and real relationships, adults bring insight, a sense of aesthetics, and creativity to bear in order to find meaning in what is bound to be an accumulation of contradictions, accidents, irrelevancies, and redundancies as well as planned or predictable events. In this respect, a personal philosophy is a creative reduction of enormous amounts of data into a few convincing principles. Although it is possible for this personal philosophy to change, once established it is more likely to be the lens through which events are interpreted than to be the object of interpretation itself.

Chapter Summary

Through adult cognition we realize some of the most outstanding achievements of our species. We recognize that not all of adult thought has the power to alter the thought of subsequent generations. Periodically, however, such thoughts do emerge that set us on a new road. Thoughts about one God, thoughts about evolution, or thoughts about relativity are some examples of the most remarkable achievements of the capacity to know.

Adult thought encompasses imagery and fantasy, reasoning and problem-solving, and monitoring of one's own thoughts. Each of these capacities permits a process of integration between internal states and external realities. During adulthood, the area of metacognition or monitoring of thought expands to provide the critical capacity for analysis and interpretation of thought.

Memory is a separate mental activity that permits thoughts to expand on previous experience and learning. Memory involves three processes, including encoding, storage, and retrieval. For short-term and long-term memory these processes appear to operate slightly differently. Each aspect of the memory system is influenced by the cognitive capacities of adult thought. Similarly, changes in memory strategies or memory efficiency will influence the flexibility and richness of thought.

Reminiscence is a special memory activity that has central importance during later adulthood. In order to achieve a sense of life acceptance and a feeling of preparation for death, older adults spend time reviewing, rehearsing, and reconstructing the past. Through reminiscence, adults achieve a sense of continuity with the past and recognition of important life events.

The memory process undergoes some changes with age. Older adults seem to need more time to accomplish memory tasks. They have less confidence in the accuracy of their memory. They use less efficient retrieval systems and less complex memory strategies for categorizing or retrieving information. Among very old people (100 years and more), considerable variability was observed in the clarity with which past events were remembered and the degree of differentiation of past, present, and future time.

Adult thought continues to undergo change and modification during early, middle, and later adulthood. New roles, increased control over the environment, and a greater capacity to distance oneself from experience all serve to modify the quality of adult thought. Adults think about things differently at different phases of the life course. One's chronological age, health, and stage of family or career development all contribute to the preoccupations with meaning, with death, and with past, present, and future. As experiences accumulate, adults can appreciate the regularities of life. The capacity to hold opposing views and tolerate the tension of that seeming contradiction is an important consequence of having lived through a variety of life events.

A major focus of concern about cognition in adulthood is the question of declining mental abilities in later adulthood. Although we have emphasized the strides in cognitive maturity that can be achieved during adulthood, there seems to be some evidence of patterned decline in some of the specific elements of thought. The interpretation of these findings is difficult. One hypothesis is that the physical decline that precedes death often is accompanied by deficits in thinking and problem-solving. Each new group of older adults reflects a different array of educational opportunities and information. Abilities that reflect education and socialization are retained at a high level throughout adulthood. Abilities that can be thought of as evidence of "raw intelligence" seem to decline with age. In general, we recognize ill health, past education, individual differences in cognitive style, some slowing of responsiveness, and a reduction in motivation as factors that might influence adult performance on tests of mental ability.

A central arena for adult thought is social relations and social behavior. Social thought involves understanding, planning, and resolving conflicts in face-to-face relations. It also involves the formulation of systematic conceptualizations that govern behavior in the areas of morality, political ideology, and personal philosophy. In all these areas, adulthood brings the potential for the creative generation of ideology that redefines the nature of social relations and social responsibility.

References

Adams, J. L. *Conceptual blockbusting: A guide to better ideas* (Rev. ed.). San Francisco: Freeman, 1980.

Arenberg, D. Cognition and aging: Verbal learning, memory, and problem solving. In

C. Eisdorfer and M. P. Lawton (Eds.), *The psychology of adult development and aging.* Washington, D.C.: American Psychological Association, 1973.

Baltes, P. B., & Labouvie, G. V. Adult development of intellectual performance: Description, explanation and modification. In C. Eisdorfer and M. P. Lawton (Eds.), *The psychology of adult development and aging.* Washington, D. C.: American Psychological Association, 1973.

Baltes, P. B., Reese, H. W., & Nesselroade, J. R. *Life-span developmental psychology: Introduction to research methods.* Monterey, Calif.: Brooks/Cole, 1977.

Baltes, P. B., & Schaie, K. W. The myth of the twilight years. *Psychology Today,* 1974, *7,* 35–39.

Baltes, P. B., & Schaie, K. W. On the plasticity of intelligence in adulthood and old age: Where Horn and Donaldson fail. *American Psychologist,* 1976, *31*(10), 720–725.

Bayley, N. Cognition and aging. In K. W. Schaie (Ed.), *Current topics in the psychology of aging: Perception, learning, cognition and personality.* Morgantown: West Virginia University Library, 1968.

Bayley, N., & Oden, M. The maintenance of intellectual ability in gifted adults. *Journal of Gerontology,* 1955, *10,* 91–107.

Birren, J. E. *The psychology of aging.* New York: Prentice-Hall, 1964.

Birren, J. E. Translations in gerontology-From lab to life. Psychophysiology and speed of response. *American Psychologist,* 1974, *29,* 808–815.

Botwinick, J. *Cognitive processes in maturity and old age.* New York: Springer, 1967.

Botwinick, J. Geropsychology. *Annual Review of Psychology,* 1970, *21,* 239–272.

Botwinick, J. Geropsychology. In P. H. Mussen and M. R. Rosenzweig (Eds.), *Annual Review of Psychology,* 1971, *119,* 241–249.

Botwinick, J. *Aging and behavior.* New York: Springer, 1973.

Butler, R. N. The life review: An interpretation of reminiscence in the aged. *Psychiatry,* Feb., 1963.

Canestrari, R. E., Jr. Paced and self-paced learning in young and elderly adults. *Journal of Gerontology,* 1963, *18,* 165–168.

Collins, A. M., & Quillian, M. R. Retrieval time from semantic memory. *Journal of Verbal Learning and Verbal Behavior,* 1969, *8,* 240–247.

Conot, R. *A streak of luck: The life and legend of Thomas Alva Edison.* New York: Seaview, 1979.

Costa, P., & Kastenbaum, R. Some aspects of memories and ambitions in centenarians. *Journal of Genetic Psychology,* 1967, *110,* 3–16.

Denney, N. W. Aging and cognitive changes. In B. B. Wolman (Ed.) *Handbook of Developmental Psychology.* Englewood Cliffs, N. J.: Prentice-Hall, 1982, 807–827.

Denney, N. W. Problem solving in later adulthood: Intervention research. In P. B. Baltes & O. G. Brim, Jr. (Eds.), *Life span development and behavior* (Vol. 2). New York: Academic Press, 1979.

Denney, N. W., & Denney, D. R. Modeling effects on the questioning strategies of the elderly. *Developmental Psychology,* 1974, *10,* 458.

Denney, N. W. & Wright, J. C. *Cognitive changes during the adult years: Implications for developmental theory and research.* Paper presented at the American Psychological Association Meetings, Toronto, 1978.

Dennis, W. Creative productivity between the ages of twenty and eighty years. *Journal of Gerontology,* 1966, *21,* 1–8.

Dulit, E. Adolescent thinking a la Piaget: The formal stage. *Journal of Youth and Adolescence,* 1972, *1,* 281–301.

Einstein, A. Physics and reality. In A. Einstein, *Ideas and opinions.* New York: Dell, 1954(a).

Einstein, A. Remarks on Bertrand Russell's theory of knowledge. In A. Einstein, *Ideas and opinions,* New York: Dell, 1954(b).

Erikson, E. H. *Childhood and society* (2nd ed.). New York: Norton, 1963.

Fallot, R. A. *The impact on mood of verbal reminiscing in later adulthood.* Paper presented at the American Psychological Association Meetings, San Francisco, 1977.

Flavell, J. H. *Metacognition.* Paper presented at the American Psychological Association Meetings, Toronto, 1978.

Fozard, J. L., & Poon, L. W. *Research and training activities of the mental performance and aging laboratory (1973–1976).* Technical report 76–02. Boston: Veterans Administration Outpatient Clinic, 1976.

Glass, A. L., & Holyoak, K. J. Alternative conceptions of semantic memory. *Cognition,* 1975, *3,* 313–339.

Horn, J. L. Organization of data on life-span development of human abilities. In L. R. Goulet and P. B. Baltes (Eds.), *Life-span developmental psychology: Research and theory.* New York: Academic Press, 1970.

Horn, J. L. Human ability systems. In P. B. Baltes (Ed.), *Life-span development and behavior* (Vol. 1). New York: Academic Press, 1978.

Horn, J. L. The rise and fall of human abilities. *Journal of Research and Development in Education,* 1979, *12*(2), 59–78.

Hultsch, D. Adult age differences in the organization of free recall. *Developmental Psychology,* 1969, *1,* 673–678.

Huxley, J. *Evolution: The magic synthesis.* New York: Harper and Beros, 1942.

Inglis, J., Ankus, M. N., & Sykes, D. H. Age-related differences in learning and short term memory from childhood to the senium. *Human Development,* 1968, *11,* 42–52.

Jones, H. E. Intelligence and problem solving. In J. E. Birren (Ed.), *Handbook of aging and the individual.* Chicago: University of Chicago Press, 1959.

Kastenbaum, R. On the meaning of time in later life. *Journal of Genetic Psychology,* 1966, *109,* 9–25.

Klatzky, R. L. *Human memory: Structures and processes.* San Francisco: Freeman, 1975.

Klinger, E. Dimensions of thought and imagery in normal waking states. *Journal of Altered States of Consciousness,* 1978, *4,* 97–114.

Labouvie-Vief, G. Beyond formal operations: Uses and limits of pure logic in life-span development. *Human Development,* 1980, *23,* 141–161.

Labouvie-Vief, G., & Chandler, M. J. Cognitive development and life-span developmental theory: Idealistic versus contextual perspectives. In P. B. Baltes (Ed.), *Life-span development and behavior* (Vol. 1). New York: Academic Press, 1978.

Lachman, J. L., Lachman, R., & Thronesberg, C. Metamemory through the adult life span. *Developmental Psychology,* 1979, *15,* 5, 543–561.

Lehman, H. C. *Age and achievement.* Princeton, N. J.: Princeton University Press, 1953.

Lieberman, D. A. Behaviorism and the mind: A (limited) call for a return to introspection. *American Psychologist,* 1979, *34,* 4, 319–333.

Luria, A. R. *The mind of a mnemonist.* New York: Avon, 1968.

Martindale, C. *Cognition and consciousness.* Homewood, Ill.: Dorsey, 1981.

Nesselroade, J. R., Schaie, K. W., & Baltes, P.B. Ontogenetic and cognitive behavior. *Journal of Gerontology,* 1972, *27,* 222–228.

Papalia, D. E., Salverson, S. M., & True, M. An evaluation of the quantity conservation performance during old age. *Aging and Human Development,* 1973, *4,* 103–109.

Piaget, J. *Six psychological studies.* New York: Random House, 1967.

Piaget, J. *Behavior and evolution.* New York: Pantheon, 1978.

Piaget, J., & Inhelder, B. *The psychology of the child.* New York: Basic Books, 1969 (originally published in French in 1966).

Pylyshyn, Z. W. The imagery debate: Analogue media versus tacit knowledge. *Psychological Review,* 1981, *88,* 16–45.

Reese, H. W. The development of memory: Life-span perspectives. In H. W. Reese (Ed.), *Advances in child development and behavior* (Vol. 11). New York: Academic Press, 1976.

Riegel, K. F. The dialectics of human development. *American Psychologist,* 1976, *31,* 679–700.

Riegel, K. F., & Riegel, R. M. Development, drop, and death. *Developmental Psychology,* 1972, *6,* 306–319.

Schaie, K. W. A general model for the study of developmental problems. *Psychological Bulletin,* 1965, *64,* 92–107.

Schaie, K. W. Age changes and age differences. *The Gerontologist,* 7(2,) pt. 1. Philadelphia: Gerontological Society, 1967.

Schaie, K. W. A reinterpretation of age-related changes in cognitive structure and functioning. In L. R. Goulet and P. B. Baltes (Eds.), *Life-span developmental psychology: Research and theory.* New York: Academic Press, 1970.

Schaie, K. W. Can the longitudinal method be applied to psychosocial studies of human development? In F. J. Monks, W. W. Hartup, & J. deWit (Eds.), *Determinants of behavioral development.* New York: Academic Press, 1972.

Schaie, K. W. Methodological problems in descriptive developmental research on adulthood and aging. In J. R. Nesselroade & H. W. Reese (Eds.), *Life-span developmental psychology: Methodological issues.* New York: Academic Press, 1973.

Schaie, K. W. External validity in the assessment of intellectual functioning in adulthood. *Journal of Gerontology,* 1978, *33,* 695–701.

Schaie, K. W., & Labouvie-Vief, G. Generational versus ontogenetic components of change in adult cognitive behavior: A fourteen-year cross-sequential study. *Developmental Psychology,* 1974, *10*(4), 305–320.

Selzer, S. C., & Denney, N. W. Conservation abilities among middle aged and elderly adults. Paper presented at the biennial meeting of the Society for Research in Child Development, March 1977, New Orleans.

Shepard, R. N. Recognition memory for words, sentences, and pictures. *Journal of Verbal Learning and Verbal Behavior,* 1967, *6,* 156–163.

Shepard, R. N. The mental image. *American Psychologist,* 1978, *33*(2), 125–137.

Simon, H. A. Discussion: Cognition and social behavior. C.I.P. Working Paper No. 298, mimeo, 1975.

Simon, J. R., & Pouraghabagher, A. R. *The effect of aging on the stages of processing in a choice reaction time task.* Paper presented at the American Psychological Association Meetings, San Francisco, 1977.

Simonton, D. K. Creative productivity, age and stress: A biographical time-series analysis of 10 classical composers. *Journal of Personality and Social Psychology,* 1977, *35,* 791–804.

Singer, J. L. *The child's world of make believe: Experimental studies of imaginative play.* New York: Academic Press, 1973

Sternberg, S. High speed scanning in human memory. *Science,* 1966, *153,* 652–654.

Treat, N. J., & Reese, H. W. Age, imagery, and pacing in paired-associate learning. *Developmental Psychology,* 1976, *12,* 119–124.

Walsh, D. Age differences in learning and memory. In D. S. Woodruff & J. E. Birren (Eds.), *Aging: Scientific perspectives and social issues.* New York: D. Van Nostrand, 1975.

Waugh, N. C., Fozard, J. L., Talland, G. A., & Erwin, D. E. Effects of age and stimulus repetition on two-choice reaction time. *Journal of Gerontology,* 1973, *28,* 466–470.

Wickelgren, W. A. Human learning and memory. In M. R. Rosenzweig & L. W. Porter (Eds.), *Annual review of psychology,* Palo Alto: Annual Reviews, 1981.

Wolpe, J. *The practice of behavior therapy* (2nd ed.). New York: Pergamon, 1973.

6 Personality and Coping

Heaven knows we are never allowed to forget that the "personality" doesn't exist any more. That is the theme of half the novels written, the theme of the sociologists and the other -ologists. We're told so often that human personality has disintegrated into nothing under pressure of all our knowledge that I've even been believing it. Yet when I look back to that group under the trees, and re-create them in my memory, suddenly I know it's nonsense. Suppose I were to meet Maryrose now, all these years later, she'd make some gesture, or turn her eyes in such a way, and there she'd be. Maryrose, and indestructible.

Doris Lessing, *The Golden Notebook,* 1962

Personality is the relatively consistent set of thoughts, feelings, and behavior patterns that guide the organization of experience and the direction of new growth. One of the important issues raised by the study of personality "development" is how to consider stability and change. The term development implies change. We assume that the potential exists for growth, redefinition, and reorientation of personality throughout life. However, our definition of personality also includes the concept of consistency. If people responded in a thoroughly unpredictable, random manner to each new event, the concept of personality would never have evolved. If all people responded in the same way, defined themselves and others in the same terms, and shared the same array of feelings, the study of personality would probably be much nearer completion than it is. Both variability and predictability are part of the reality of studying personality.

Walter Emmerich (1964) has provided a useful distinction for thinking about stability and change in personality. The dimension of stability or instability refers to the consistency of personality. Stability would be reflected if a person retained the same position on a personality dimension in comparision to his or her age cohort over time. Thus, a stable characteristic would be relatively high, moderate, or low at school age, adolescence, and adulthood. Another sign of stability would be certain characteristics remaining in the same configuration or hierarchy over time. If a person had stronger motives for nurturance than for power at school age, adolescence, and adulthood, the motivational profile would be described as stable.

The dimension of continuity or discontinuity is a reflection of personality change. Continuity refers to whether the meaning of a behavior and its function for the person remain the same at different times in life. The evidence for change is a bit more difficult to identify. In part, the conceptualization of change depends on one's theoretical perspective. Some theories, like Erikson's psychosocial theory or Piaget's cognitive theory, propose an invariant sequence of stages that can be expected to occur during the life span. Other theories, such as Brim's social-role theory or Neugarten's theory of the "social clock," propose that role acquisition or social adaptation causes change.

Looking across the life span, it is sometimes difficult to know whether a behavior pattern that is observed in adulthood is really a new personality structure or a new, socially acceptable expression of a continuing personality dimension. For example, Freud would propose that most adult behaviors are sublimations of childhood sexual or aggressive needs that remain unsatisfied. Behaviors themselves may look very different in childhood, adolescence, and adulthood, but the symbolic meaning of these behaviors remains the same. In contrast, Erikson would propose that the psychosocial crises of each stage introduce new dimensions of personality that had not been present in earlier stages. The need to achieve intimacy, for example, does not reach its period of peak relevance until adulthood. At this time, new levels of competence, new capacities for social understanding, and a new view of oneself produce a shift in the focus and organization of personality. The attainment of intimacy is not simply an adult replication of childhood needs to receive and give love. It is a unique accomplishment that fulfills adult needs.

In considering adult personality we have reasons to expect stability and reasons to expect change. Stability may be a result of personal characteristics that have an enduring nature across settings. Some people are outgoing, some people are shy. Some people are very active and others are calm. These qualities may persist regardless of the roles, the life events, or the socialization pressures of adult life. Another source of stability is the achievement of a personal identity. This concept suggests that toward the end of adolescence or early adulthood people form an integrated view of their traits, their personal history, and their goals for the future. Identity then serves as a focal point for directing life choices.

There is also reason to expect change in personality during adult life. Adulthood brings a number of new roles and new life events. The expectations for role performance and the challenges of these events call for new skills. Adults engage in new forms of relationships, including marriage, parenting, sexual intimacy, and expert or teacher roles, to name a few. These roles could prompt a reorganization of thoughts and behavior that had not been observed during childhood. Adulthood also provides many opportunities to face serious challenges. There are repeated demands to overcome threat or loss. In such times, new strengths may emerge or vulnerabilities may be uncovered.

In the remainder of this chapter, five themes that have captured the focus of research on personality development in adulthood will be discussed. The first theme is the examination of stability of traits from childhood or adolescence to adulthood. Does an irritable child become an irritable adult? Or do adults become irritable because of the lives they lead? This research generally seeks evidence for consistency in personality across the life span.

The second theme is the formation of identity. Is there evidence that adolescents achieve identity as Erikson has proposed? Does identity formation have implications for subsequent adult development? This research seeks evidence for a central core of commitments, stable values, and goals around which adult life is structured.

The third theme is life transitions. Here we expect to see evidence for discontinuity or change. As adults enter new roles or experience unpredictable life events, do they undergo a restructuring of personality? Are there discoveries about the self that only become evident in the process of enacting the parent role, becoming an administrator, or having the responsibility of caring for one's aging parents?

The fourth theme is social participation. How do adults engage their social environment? Does the pattern of social involvement or life-style remain consistent during adulthood, or are there systematic changes in social participation at different periods of life?

The fifth theme is coping and adaptation. What resources do adults bring to meet the challenges and demands of adult life? Can we describe stable coping styles, or is coping highly dependent on situational demands?

Two topics that must be considered in each theme are sex roles and sex differences in adulthood. Many of the studies that address the themes listed above also comment on distinctions between men and women. In our society at the present time, the patterns of personality development for men and for women are not identical. There are biological differences that initiate distinct temperamental patterns. There are childrearing practices that emphasize different patterns of behavior for boys and girls. There are cultural stereotypes about men and women that preserve distinctions about interests and abilities. Finally, there are differences in the range and pattern of role acquisition and role loss for men and women. All these factors contribute to distinct socialization experiences for men and women. They may also restrict the opportunities to fully express or develop one's potential array of personality characteristics.

Traits

One of the oldest and most persistent directions in the study of personality has been the effort to identify stable characteristics of the person that endure through time and across situations. The concepts of "trait," "type," "temperament," and "disposition" all reflect such an approach. This view of personality emphasizes that there are meaningful categories that can be applied in order to highlight the similarities among some people and their differences from others. For example, we might say that some people are more "outgoing" and others are more "reserved." This is not to say that all outgoing people are alike on all other traits. Rather, the use of the trait points out the similarities among people with respect to social encounters and at the same time contrasts them with people who have quite a different social orientation.

The most stable variables have a direct physiological basis, such as heart rate or activity level. We are somewhat less likely to find stability in measures of intelligence, and least likely to find it in more global personality characteristics, such as dependency or self-confidence (Macfarlane, 1963). For example, Sontag (1966) reported on the stability of the heart rate during the fetal period and in adolescence. Subjects who showed high variability in heart rate during the fetal period were also likely to have a variable heart rate at age 18. To the extent that heart-rate variability is linked to differences in levels of arousal or emotionality, we can begin to see the foundation for a physiologically based view of temperamental stability.

Traits from Childhood to Adulthood

In an effort to study the stability of temperament across the life span, Lerner, Patermo, Spiro, and Nesselroade (1982) have identified five trait dimensions. These dimensions can be observed by mothers who are rating their 3- and 4-year old children, by elementary-school-age children (mean age = 11) who are rating themselves, and by college-age students (mean age = 21) who are rating themselves. The five dimensions include activity level, attention span/distractibility, adaptability/approach-withdrawal, rhythmicity, and reactivity. These traits have a physiological component. They reflect the patterning of physical activity, sensitivity to the environment, and irritability or comfort in response to internal states or external demands. The importance of these variables is that they serve as gatekeepers to interactions with the environment.

Other work has focused on social or interpersonal traits. Bronson (1967) reported on a sample of subjects who had been studied from infancy until about age 30. The dimension of expressive/outgoing versus reserved/withdrawn was especially consistent for males from adolescence through adulthood. Expressive adolescent males were described as warm, self-accepting, and productive adults. Thus, expressiveness was not only a stable personal quality for males but a good predictor of other positive adult outcomes. For females, a consistent pattern of expressiveness was observed for one group but not for others. In this group, expressiveness was associated with adult ratings of assertiveness.

Another dimension, placid/controlled versus reactive/ explosive, showed a very different pattern. For females, the rating of reactivity or control in the period from 11 to 13 was a consistent, stable predictor of adult style. This dimension was a good predictor of adult adjustment, especially characteristics of warmth, stability, openness, and responsibility. For males, there were three patterns: some males were consistent, some showed an increase in control during the adolescent and adult years, and some became less controlled from early childhood to adolescence. Remaining consistently controlled was related to adult productivity, some degree of constriction, and lack of a sense of humor. A decline in control was associated with disruptive impulsiveness in adulthood.

Kagan and Moss (1962) reported on the results of a longitudinal study of children who were observed during infancy, preschool age, middle childhood, early adolescence, and adulthood. Some of the major traits that were described in this study included passivity, dependency, aggressiveness, achievement, heterosexual behavior, sex-role interests, and social-interaction anxiety. The goal of the study was to document stability or instability in personality characteristics. Another goal was to determine whether certain childhood characteristics could be viewed as forerunners of related adult characteristics (Moss & Susman, 1980).

Passivity and dependency were stable characteristics for both boys and girls during childhood. Among the female subjects, dependency on

The trait of expressiveness may be woven in to a personal and professional identity in adulthood.

female adults in childhood was associated with a dependent, passive relationship with males in adulthood. Among the male subjects, dependency in adolescence was associated with emotional dependency on friends in adulthood. There was no consistent relationship for males between dependent relationships with adults in childhood and their relationships with loved ones in adulthood.

Aggression from childhood to adulthood was more stable for males than for females. Boys who were aggressive toward their mothers and dominant in peer relations showed retaliative behavior as adults. For girls, a high degree of physical aggressiveness during childhood was associated with minimal aggressiveness during adulthood. There was some evidence that childhood conflicts over aggression were expressed in adulthood. Children who inhibited aggression to parents and other adults and who showed a high level of conformity were likely to show anger, repression, and conflict over expressing anger in adulthood.

Achievement-related behaviors were quite stable during childhood, expecially intellectual achievement and fear of failure. Achievement at age 10 and concern with intellectual competence during adolescence were both associated with concern for intellectual competence in adulthood. This variable did not show the same divergence of paths for men and women as was observed for passivity, dependence, and aggression.

Tuddenham (1959) reported on the stability of 53 personality characteristics from adolescence to adulthood in a longitudinal sample. The variables included traits such as introspection, creativity, animation, and social assurance. For the male sample, 10 variables showed stability. The strongest of these was aggression. For the female sample, 9 variables were stable. The strongest was social prestige. Variables showing little stability included physical attractiveness, self-confidence, and, for men, leadership and popularity.

Tuddenham makes two important observations about his findings. First, a fairly large group of variables showed a positive correlation across the long interval from adolescence to adulthood. We can infer from this that the notion of long-term stability of personal characteristics is a valid concept. The second observation, however, is that the magnitude of these correlations was low. In other words, on every variable measured it would be difficult to predict whether a particular person was more likely to remain the same or to change.

Traits during Adulthood

The question of stability in personality during the adulthood years was studied in the Normative Aging Study (Costa and McCrae, 1978). Their evidence is based on a ten-year longitudinal study of men in three age groups: 25–34, 35–54, and 55–82. There was a high degree of stability for most of 16 personality factors that were measured. Over the ten years, each age group showed significant increases in brightness and independence. Other than these two variables the primary evidence is for continuity during adulthood.

Norma Haan (1981) described dimensions of personality in four subsamples at four periods of life: early and late adolescence and early and middle adulthood. At each period, subjects were asked to describe themselves using a set of 86 adjectives. From their descriptions, six factors emerged that Haan labeled as follows:

1. Cognitively invested. Ease and interest in dealing with intellectual matters; interest in personal achievement.
2. Emotionally under/overcontrolled. Aggressive, dramatic, and rebellious or calm, dependable, and sympathetic.
3. Open/closed to self. Self-expressive and open to one's own thoughts or defensive and uncomfortable with uncertainty.
4. Nurturant/hostile. Considerate and warm or suspicious and hostile.
5. Under/overcontrolled, heterosexual. Sexualized and gregarious or suspicious of the opposite sex and vulnerable.
6. Self-confident. Assertive and effective in interpersonal relations.

In general Haan found developmental trends for all but factor 2. The pattern for factors 1 and 3 are shown in Figure 6.1. Cognitive investment increases over the life span. Gains are made especially during adolescence

FIGURE 6.1 Developmental Trends in Major Personality Dimensions from Adolescence to Adulthood
Note: Initials refer to 4 subsamples:
OGS = Oakland Growth Study born 1920–21
GS = Guidance Study born 1928–29
♀ = Female
♂ = Male

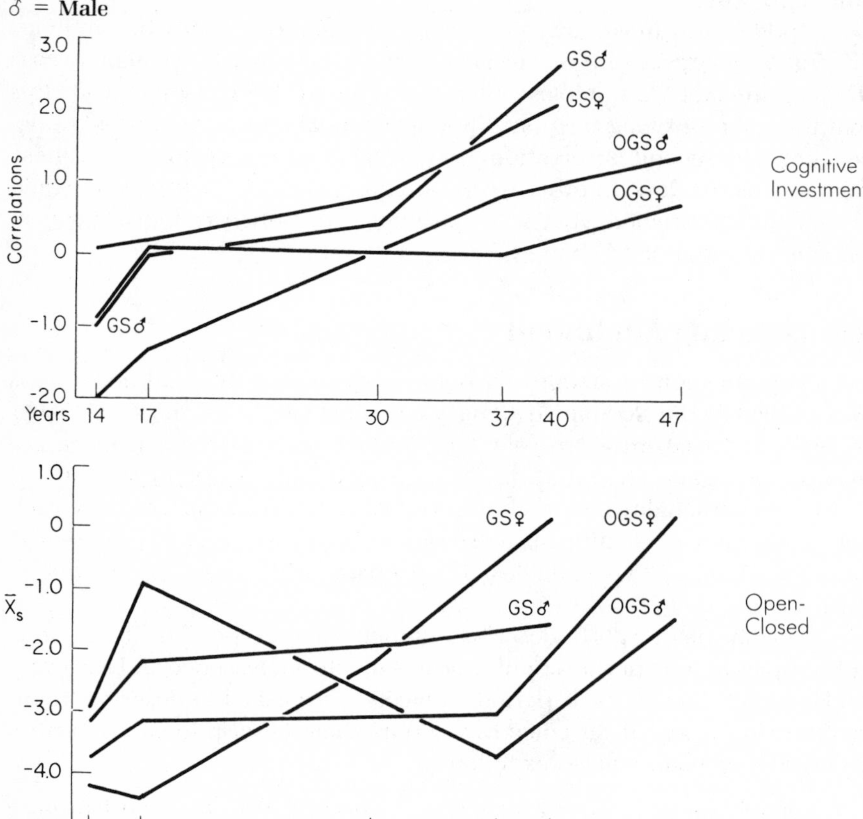

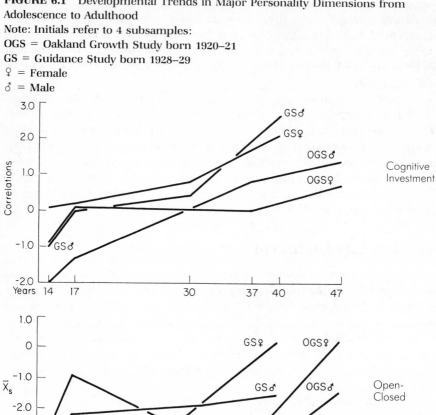

Source: "Common Dimensions of Personality Development: Early Adolescence to Middle Life" by N. Haan, in D. H. Eichorn, J. A. Clausen, N. Haan, M. P. Honzik, & P. H. Mussen, *Present and Past in Middle Life* (New York: Academic Press, 1981), p. 132.

(14 to 17) and during adulthood (30 to 47). The open/closed dimension shows movement toward greater openness. During adolescence both male groups were more open than the females; however, women end up being more open than men by midlife. Over the periods of the life span that were studied, three of the samples became more varied in their degree of openness. In this way, Haan was able to show that responses to life events, both successes and failures, contributed to significant variability in the

degree to which personality reflected openess and self-understanding or a more closed, defensive posture.

Differences between Changers and Nonchangers

Block (1971) has added to our understanding of the relevance of continuity or change in personality traits through his analysis of longitudinal data from the Oakland Growth Study and the Berkeley Guidance Study. Both studies were developed through the Institute of Human Development at the University of California at Berkeley. The consistency of personality dimensions across three periods of life was examined. The periods were junior high, senior high, and adulthood. For both males and females, from junior to senior high, there was a strong consistency in personality dimensions. From senior high to adulthood, the consistency in personality dimensions decreased slightly. These findings once again suggest some basic continuities across life stages, with decreasing consistency across longer periods. The findings disguise the various patterns of change experienced by individuals in the sample. Among the males, for example, 13 subjects showed almost no similarity between ratings in senior high school and adulthood. Among the females, 4 subjects showed a tendency toward a negative relation between ratings in senior high and adulthood.

In order to understand the question of stability and change more fully, Block separated those subjects who showed a stable pattern from one period to another from those who changed from one period to another. Table 6.1 illustrates some of the differences observed between those who changed and those who did not. Data are presented separately for males and females, and for the periods from junior to senior high and senior high to adulthood.

The findings are summarized as follows:

> The Changers appear less adjusted during the adolescent years and particularly during the senior high school period displayed a marked neuroticism. However, they then manifested appreciable maturation and by the adult years the earlier differences . . . appear to have vanished. There are certain strengths and certain weaknesses in the Changers as adults and there are different strengths and different weaknesses in the Nonchangers in the most recent interval during which they were assessed. On the average, they cannot now be distinguished but the qualities underlying these averages are still clearly visible. (Block, 1971, p. 106)

From this analysis we realize that some people have a personality structure that crystallizes earlier than others. This leads to greater continuity across life stages for some than others. What is more, the tempo of growth or change is associated with different degrees of complexity, flexibility, and self-insight.

The pattern of change appears to have different consequences for males and females. In general, for males, stability of personality is

TABLE 6.1 Characteristics of Changers and Nonchangers

Period of Change	Changers		Nonchangers	
	Males	Females	Males	Females
Junior to senior high school	thin-skinned, fearful, brittle, self-defensive, overconcerned with own adequacy, compares self with others, uncomfortable with uncertainty, complicating of simple situations, reluctant to act, aloof, condescending, deceitful.	Productive, turned to for advice, ethically consistent, physically attractive.	Intellectual capacity, values intellectual matters, rapid tempo, insightful, introspective, arouses liking, socially poised, straightforward, gregarious, giving, physically attractive, interested in opposite sex.	Moody, self-pitying, self-deceiving.
Senior high school to adulthood	self-defensive, extra punitive, projective, undercontrolled, self-indulgent, irritable, bothered by demands, deceitful, fluctuating moods.	Fantasizing, thinks unconventionally, initiates humor, sensuous, rebellious, married, contacts parents frequently, politically conservative, involved in politics, high family income, felt parents urged to high standards of conduct, would not consider financial security in evaluation of job possibility.	Wide interests, verbally fluent, values intellectual matters, socially perceptive, incisive, ethically consistent, philosophically concerned, introspective, warm, calm, overcontrolled.	Conservative, moralistic, conventional, self-defensive, high aspiration level.

Source: Adapted from J. Block, in collaboration with N. Haan, *Lives through Time* (Berkeley, Calif: Bancroft, 1971).

associated with greater social and moral maturity. For females, the consequences of personality change are more varied. Females who are observed to change from junior to senior high appear to be following what might be described as a normal pattern of personal maturation. In other words, for females, changes during the years from 11 or 12 to 15 or 16 reflect the normative pattern of personal development. Change from senior high to adulthood is more complex. Females who continue to modify basic elements of their personality after their high school years can be seen as moving in a less traditional, more highly differentiated direction. More than likely many of these women begin to test out the limits of the female sex role in an effort to achieve a life-style more congruent with their unconventional orientation.

Summary

The trait studies cover different periods of time from childhood through adolescence and into adulthood. In general there is greater stability across short time periods than across longer periods. We would have to conclude that the evidence for stability of traits over the life span is impressive considering the many factors that might be expected to influence their expression. Evidence has been given for stability in such dimensions as expressiveness, achievement orientation, activity level, and social anxiety. These and other dimensions are central to the person's adaptation to social relationships as well as to personal values and goals.

The picture of trait stability in adulthood is complicated by three factors. First, there are differences in the kinds of traits that show stability for men and women. One explanation for this is that the socialization environment is differentially accepting of certain characteristics for men and women. For example, if aggressiveness is accepted in men, men would be under less pressure to inhibit this characteristic than women. Second, stability itself may be more characteristic of some people than others. Third, the expression of traits in behavior is likely to vary from one life stage to another. We cannot always take the same behavior as evidence of the same underlying trait.

Identity

In Erikson's psychosocial theory, the concept of personal identity plays a pivotal role. Identity achievement refers to a creative integration of past identifications and personality characteristics with a commitment to future aspirations. In their efforts to define themselves, later adolescents must take into account the bonds that have been built between themselves and others in the past, as well as the direction that they hope to be able to take in the future. Identity serves as an anchor that allows the person an essential experience of continuity in social relationships. Erikson states:

> The young individual must learn to be most himself where he means the most to others—those others, to be sure, who have come to mean most to him. The term identity expresses such a mutual relation in that it connotes both a persistent sameness within oneself (self-sameness) and a persistent sharing of some kind of essential character with others. (1959b, p. 102)

The concept of identity has two implications for personality development in adulthood. First, identity achievement should serve as a basis for value continuity in adult life. Commitments to values and goals that are made in the process of formulating a sense of personal identity should provide a strong conceptual and emotional guide to subsequent life choices. Second, in Erikson's theory identity formation is a necessary prerequisite to later growth in adult personality. The capacity for intimacy, generativity, and integrity follow from the critical examination of one's self and one's life goals during the period of later adolescence.

The Assessment of Identity Status

James Marcia (1966) has devised a questionnaire to assess the status of identity resolution. Using Erikson's conceptualization (1963, 1959b), he determined identity status on the basis of two criteria: crisis and commitment. Crisis is conceived of as including a period of role experimentation and active decision-making among alternative choices. Commitment includes the expression of personal values and the demonstration of personal involvement in the areas of occupational choice, sexuality, religion, and political ideology. Table 6.2 shows the criteria for classification in four identity statuses. People who are classified as *identity-achieved* have already experienced a crisis time and have made personal commitments. People who are classified as *identity-foreclosed* have not experienced a crisis but demonstrate strong personal commitments. Their occupational and ideological beliefs appear to be very close to the beliefs of their parents. People who are classified as being in a state of *psychosocial moratorium* are involved in ongoing crisis. Their commitments are diffuse. People who are classified as *role-diffused* may or may not have experienced a crisis and demonstrate a complete lack of commitment. Marcia mentions that the identity-diffused group has a rather cavalier, playboy quality, which allows members to cope with the college environment. He suggests that the more seriously diffused person (such as those described by Erikson, 1959b) may not appear in his sample because they are unable to cope with college.

Marcia gave the identity-status questionnaire and a group of other test instruments to 86 male college students. He found that the identity-achieved group demonstrated somewhat greater ego strength than any of the other three groups. He also found that the identity-foreclosed group had a strong commitment to obedience, strong leadership, and respect for authority. Of all the groups they demonstrated the most vulnerable self-esteem and weakest ego strength.

It must be noted here that the group that Marcia has identified as identity-diffused is probably made up of immature adolescents who have

TABLE 6.2 The Relationship between Identity Status, Crisis, and Commitment to Values

	Crisis	Commitment
Identity achievement	X	X
Identity foreclosure	—	X
Moratorium	X	Partial
Identity diffusion	X	—

not yet begun the work in identity that is represented in the other groups. It is unlikely that out of a sample of 86 subjects one would find a group of 21 subjects characterized by role diffusion, as Marcia does; his instrument does not measure a condition of anxiety about identity which is characteristic of truly identity-diffused subjects. What Marcia has demonstrated is that for males, identity achievement produces the strongest personality; identity foreclosure is a somewhat brittle and vulnerable resolution; and the psychosocial moratorium is a period of transition and flux between childhood and adulthood.

Marcia and Friedman (1970) repeated the identity-status research with women. They found that the identity-achieved women and the identity-foreclosed women were most similar on dependent measures of ego strength. This was in contrast to the findings with males, in which identity-achieved and moratorium subjects were most similar. Marcia and Friedman proposed that while the status groupings for males were based on approximation to mature achievement, the status groupings for females reflected an underlying dimension of stability versus instability.

A later study by Schenkel and Marcia (1972) found that identity formation among women was more related to issues of sexuality and religion, as compared to the males' concern with occupation and politics. The similarity between identity-achieved and identity-foreclosed women was validated in a study relating identity status to conformity (Toder & Marcia, 1973). Women who had been identified as having either an achieved or foreclosed status conformed to peer pressure significantly less than women who had been identified as of either moratorium or diffuse status. The identity-achieved and identity-foreclosed groups also were similar in indicating less negative affect than the other two groups. These studies suggest that while identity achievement is clearly the most mature resolution of the crisis for both men and women, identity foreclosure (possibly existing as temporary foreclosure) is also a positive adaptation to reality for women (Donovan, 1975; Marcia & Friedman, 1970).

Changes in Identity Status

The process of identity formation appears to be a dynamic, changing integration of competences and aspirations rather than a fixed typology or clear progression through stages. In looking at changes in identity status across age ranges, several of Erikson's notions about identity have been confirmed. In a cross-sectional comparison between 13- and 14-year-olds and 19- to 24-year-olds, older subjects scored higher on all aspects of ego identity (Protinsky, 1975). Longitudinal studies of college students have found increases in identity achievement from the freshman to the senior year (Constantinople, 1969; Waterman, Geary, & Waterman, 1974). In the Waterman et al. study, which was done at an Eastern engineering school, there was a general shift away from moratorium status and toward achievement. Surprisingly, about 30 percent of the seniors remained in a diffused state with regard to either occupation or ideology.

Marcia (1975) has provided an even longer time perspective in a six-year followup of 30 men who were first interviewed during college. All the moratorium-status subjects had changed their status. What is more surprising, four subjects who had been described earlier as identity-achieved and two who were in moratorium were described as foreclosed during young adulthood. These six subjects seemed to have abandoned the search and experimentation that had been part of their college orientation for a more conservative, restricted life-style. One of the subects who changed from achievement to foreclosure was described as follows:

> "interviewed at his insurance office after hours, (he) was pin-neat in a gray sharkskin suit. He, like several other Foreclosures, had also married his high school sweetheart. About the "revolution," he said, "It's safe to say that I didn't get too involved." He questioned the value of his college education; he would rather have been in a work-study program "where you get hooked into a company right from the beginning." Of his future, he said, "I believe that family and professional life are the basis for personal happiness. We're satisfied, although we feel that we should be making more money." (p. 10)

In the follow-up study, Marcia also looked at the relationship between identity and intimacy. Both previous and current identity status were associated with successful achievement of an intimate relationship. Subjects who had changed to an achieved identity also experienced intimacy. Those who had changed to a foreclosed or diffuse status had stereotyped relationships, or were experiencing isolation. In other words, work on identity continued to play a part in the young adult's ability to participate in a mutually satisfying personal relationship.

Whitbourne and Waterman (1979) studied the course of psychosocial development during the 10 years from age 20 to age 30 (see Figure 6.2). Subjects were studied as college students in 1966 and again in 1976. Another group of college students were studied in 1976 to provide a cohort comparison group for the 20-year-olds. (Those who were 20 in 1966 and those who were 20 in 1976). The subjects were asked to respond to a 60-item questionnaire that measured 6 of Erikson's psychosocial crises from trust versus mistrust to intimacy versus isolation. Psychosocial development was observed in three areas: industry versus inferiority, identity versus identity diffusion, and intimacy versus isolation. The other three

FIGURE 6.2 Psychosocial Development from Age 20 to 30

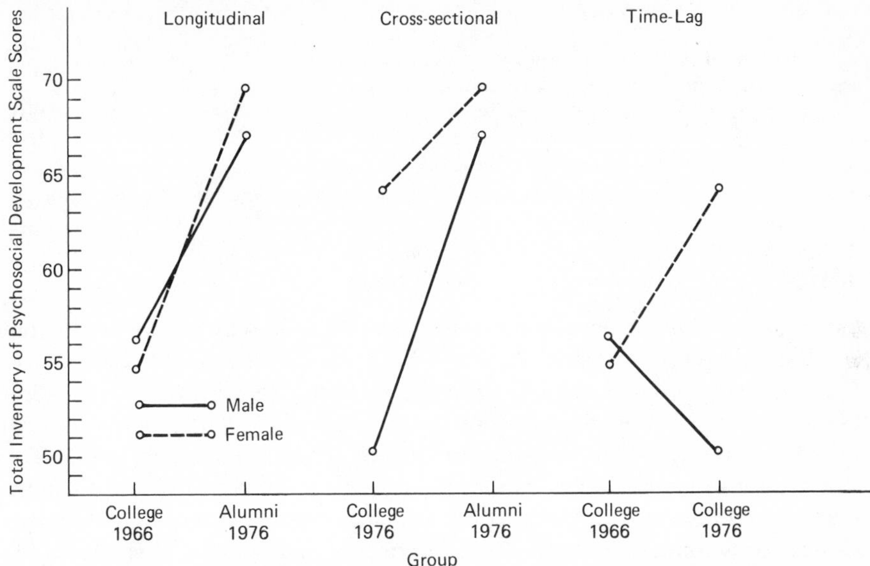

Source: "Psychosocial Development during the Adult Years: Age and Cohort Comparisons" by S. K. Whitbourne and A. S. Waterman, *Developmental Psychology,* 1979, *15,* p. 376.

stages were stable across the 10-year period. Both the longitudinal and cross-sectional comparisons indicated psychosocial development. In 1976, the college-age women were significantly more mature with respect to industry and intimacy than their 1966 comparison group had been when they were 20. These historical differences make it difficult to determine whether the longitudinal changes seen in the 1966 women were primarily a result of psychosocial development or a result of a changing historical climate.

Summary

The study of identity has revealed at least four potential resolutions to the crisis of identity versus role diffusion. These are identity achievement, identity foreclosure, moratorium, and identity diffusion. Each status reflects a somewhat different level of ego strength, self-esteem, and reliance on authorities. The experince of experimentation and questioning serves to be more central to personal growth for men than for women.

The hypothesis of a well-formulated identity that provides a basis for further growth is left in question. Some studies show continued work on identity at least into middle adulthood. On the other hand, identity achievement does seem to permit further work on mutually satisfying intimate relationships.

Sequence of Life Events and Life Transitions

The study of adulthood brings us face to face with the diversity and interdependence of the many roles we play. The patterning of adult life must be viewed along four dimensions (Neugarten, 1977):

1. Life time—chronological age.
2. Social time—age periods structured by society with specific expectations and opportunities.
3. Historical time—the period in history when the individual life events occur.
4. Psychological time—the person's perceptions of their place in the life course.

The process of adult development may be influenced by events on any one or all of these dimensions.

We can think of stressful life events along three dimensions. First, some events are linked to chronological time periods and are therefore somewhat predictable. Entering first grade at age 6, having a first child in the twenties or early thirties, and losing one's spouse in the late sixties or early seventies are examples of events that are likely enough that they deserve anticipatory thought. Other events, such as a flood, early death of a parent, or death of a child, are less likely and highly unpredictable. Second, life events can produce chronic or temporary stress. Some families repeatedly experience unemployment, whereas for other families job loss is a sudden and shocking occurrence that is quickly followed by a new job search and continued employment. Third, crisis can be the consequence of personal incompetence, or it can be the consequence of fate, environmental disaster, or deliberate manipulation by others. Of course this last dimension depends heavily on the person's point of view. One woman might blame herself for the dissolution of her marriage, feeling that she had not been attractive or clever or devoted enough to keep her husband. Another woman might blame the husband, the secretary, the community, or the weather for her husband's lack of affection. In fact, the perception of any set of events as a crisis depends heavily on the perceiver. Feelings of helplessness, vulnerability, or guilt may contribute to the interpretation of the self as responsible for the crisis. In contrast, feelings of high self-esteem, efficacy, and pride all contribute to a belief that crisis is not of one's own making and certainly not insurmountable.

Measuring the Intensity of Life Events

To study the impact of stress, it is necessary to have some yardstick to measure the intensity of life events. Meyer (1948) argued that both positive and negative life events could produce stress. He found that there were temporal links between major life events and physical and mental disorders. Building on this idea, Holmes and Rahe (1967) developed the Social Readjustment Rating Scale to measure the perceived stressfulness of 43 life events. Subjects were given the list of events and told that the event of marriage had a value of 50 Life Change Units. They were then asked to score all the other events on a scale from 1 to 100, using the value of 50 for marriage as a point of reference. Table 6.3 shows the average ratings by over 5,000 subjects in Europe, the United States, Central America, Oceania, and Japan. Interestingly, only six life events were viewed as requiring greater adjustment than marriage. This suggests that marriage may not have been a true midpoint in the list of life events. Stated another way, marriage may be one of the more stressful events encountered in many people's lives.

Individual Differences in Response to Stress

An important observation in the assessment of stress is that both positive and negative events can create stress. In part, the degree of stress may be related to the way the event is perceived (Lazarus, 1974). One person may perceive a life change to be threatening while another person perceives the same change as exhilarating. Young adults going away to college offer a good illustration of how the same life changes may be perceived differently. Two young men from a small rural community are going to the same college at the end of the summer. It is the first time either has been away from his family and friends. One of the young men is quite worried that the college, which is located in a big city, will be an unfriendly, lonely, and threatening place. The other is excited about the many new people and experiences such a college and city offer. However, any life change that requires a reorganization of life activities or a reconceptualization of selfhood will absorb a great amount of energy and personal resources. From this point of view, joyous events have the same stress potential as tragic events.

People differ in what they perceive as stressful and in how their bodies react to stress. The amount of control people think they have over a situation (perceived control) is an important factor in determining whether a situation is experienced as stressful (Baum, Singer, & Baum, 1981). When people have information about an impending stressor, such as how long it might last or why it is necessary, the stress is reduced. In the case of physical pain, when people believe that they can control the frequency or intensity of the stressor, the pain is experienced as less severe (Staub, Tursky, & Schwartz, 1971).

Some people interpret stressful events as a threat to their control. Friedman and Rosenman (1974) described these people as Type A personalities. For them, any loss of control is stressful. Their reaction to stress is to become more hostile, more competitive, and more anxious about "wasting" time to resolve the stress. In contrast to Type A's, Type B's are not plagued with a sense of urgency. They can relax fully without feeling guilty about not being at work. The B's are more confident of their abilities and less preoccupied by having to prove themselves to others.

The Type A person runs a high risk for stress-related diseases,

TABLE 6.3 Social Readjustment Rating Scale

Rank	Life Event	LCU value
1.	Death of spouse	100
2.	Divorce	73
3.	Marital separation	65
4.	Jail term	63
5.	Death of close family member	63
6.	Personal injury or illness	53
7.	Marriage	50
8.	Fired from job	47
9.	Marital reconciliation	45
10.	Retirement	45
11.	Change in health of family member	44
12.	Pregnancy	49
13.	Sex difficulties	39
14.	Gain of new family member	39
15.	Business readjustment	39
16.	Change in financial state	38
17.	Death of close friend	37
18.	Change to different line of work	36
19.	Change in number of arguments with spouse	35
20.	Mortgage over $10,000	31
21.	Foreclosure of mortgage or loan	30
22.	Change in responsibilities at work	29
23.	Son or daughter leaving home	29
24.	Trouble with in-laws	29
25.	Outstanding personal achievement	28
26.	Wife begins or stops work	26
27.	Begin or end school	26
28.	Change in living conditions	25
29.	Revision of personal habits	24
30.	Trouble with boss	23
31.	Change in work hours or conditions	20
32.	Change in residence	20
33.	Change in schools	20
34.	Change in recreation	19
35.	Change in church activities	29
36.	Change in social activities	18
37.	Mortgage or loan less than $10,000	17
38.	Change in sleeping habits	16
39.	Change in number of family get-togethers	15
40.	Change in eating habits	15
41.	Vacation	13
42.	Christmas	12
43.	Minor violations of the law	11

Source: "The Social Readjustment Rating Scale" by T. H. Holmes and R. H. Rahe, *Journal of Psychosomatic Research*, 1967, *11*, 213–218. Reprinted with permission, Pergamon Press, Ltd.

especially coronary heart disease. Type A people show a greater increase in blood pressure and pulse rate in response to challenging tasks than Type B's. However, despite this increased effort, Type A's do not actually perform better than Type B's.

Type A's are more likely than Type B's to deny the threat of a stressful situation. They cope by minimizing or making light of their difficulties. The result is that they endure a stressful situation longer, exert a higher level of physical effort, and report less fatigue than Type B's (Pittner & Houston, 1980). Because Type A people minimize the seriousness of the threat and minimize how much effort they are using to meet the stress, they remain in a stressful situation longer than Type B people. They are more likely to reach the exhaustion phase of the G.A.S. than the Type B's. This research on Type A and Type B personalities highlights individual differences in how people respond to stress.

Asynchrony as a Source of Stress

Every stress event requires adaptation. The extent to which the event is disruptive may depend on the kind of preparation the person has made in anticipation of the event. Stress events also tend to be more difficult when several occur simultaneously. For example, Riegel (1975) described the possibility of crisis emerging from the *asynchrony* of life events. Crisis occurs when there are strong, competing claims for limited resources or when heightened uncertainty in one role leads to deficient performance in other roles. For example, starting a new job and having a baby at the same time may be viewed as a crisis of asynchrony. The simultaneous occurrence of retirement and widowhood would be a potential source of crisis. Although many of life's events appear to move in harmony with new skills building neatly on earlier achievements, a normal life can also be seen as replete with discord and contradiction. One may be hired for a job for which one is not qualified. One may marry a person who does not share one's personal aspirations. One may live in a community where one is a victim of racial or ethnic prejudice. Examples of potential life conflicts are numerous. The important point is that people are not necessarily devastated by these conflicts. In fact, some seek conflict as a more desirable alternative to the boredom of predictability. The existence of asynchrony in people's lives promotes a need for new resources, skills, and aspirations that is likely to stimulate personal growth.

Perceptions of Life Events at Four Stages of Life

Two rather different approaches to the analysis of life events and life crises help us appreciate the importance of this concept for the study of personality. Research by Lowenthal, Thurnher, and Chiriboga (1975) has focused on the exposure to life events and changes in self-image that characterize life at four key periods: high school seniors, newlyweds, middle-adult parents, and adults about to retire. Research by Elder (1979) focused on the impact of a major historical event, the Great Depression, on the subsequent development of two cohorts of children.

In the four stages of life study (Lowenthal, et al., 1975), adolescents and newlyweds reported more frequent encounters with life stressors than did middle adults or preretirees. For the younger groups, stressors included some very positive life challenges, including dating and marriage, as well as negative stressors related to moving, health, or death. For the younger group the most frequent stressor was education. For the older groups the most frequent stressors were health and work.

The impact of life events on the self concept differed for men and women at each of the four life stages. Table 6.4 shows how men and women described themselves. A plus sign means that characteristic was applied more at that stage than the average for all ratings by others of the same sex. A minus sign means that characteristic was applied less often at that stage than the average for all ratings. For men we see a period of uncertainty and confusion in adolescence giving way to self-expression and interpersonal experimentation in early adulthood. At middle age men appear to settle on a comfortable, strong self-image that is preserved into the preretirement period. This pattern is quite similar to the progression that Daniel Levinson described in his retrospective study of adult development (see Chapter 2). For men, the sequence of life events in adulthood seems to foster an active process of analysis and reorganization that is resolved during the decade of the forties.

The pattern for women is somewhat different. Young women are not only uncertain but critical of their own competence. They view themselves as lazy, helpless, and not intelligent. Early adulthood brings a high level of involvement with the intimacy of marriage with little energy for other directions. Unlike the case with middle-adult men, no clear sense of self-confidence emerges in middle adulthood. Even though later adulthood is a period of a number of negative stresses it is this time that brings the clearest expression of a positive self-concept for the women. Since this study is based on a cross-sectional comparison of four age groups, one cannot be certain whether the age comparisons are a product of cohort differences or developmental changes. In other words, we do not know if the oldest women would have been more positive about themselves during their high school years than the current high school students. The developmental perspective would suggest that they became more confident as a consequence of the competent enactment of life roles. The cohort explanation would be that they were always a more confident group.

The Impact of the Great Depression on Personality Development

Elder's (1979) study considered the impact of an historical change on the life patterns and personality of two groups. The Oakland cohort was born in 1920 and 1921. This group was entering early adolescence in 1933 at the time of the greatest economic loss to their families. The Berkeley cohort was born between 1928 and 1929. They were still in the period of early childhood in 1933.

TABLE 6.4 Changes in Self-Description with Age

Listed are adjectives that men and women used significantly more frequently (indicated by plus signs) or less frequently (minus signs) than the average of others of the same sex.

High School Men	Newlywed Men	Middle-Aged Men	Preretirement Men
Dissatisfied +	Cautious −	Cautious +	Ambitious −
Frank −	Cruel −	Disorderly −	Dissatisfied −
Friendly −	Dramatic +	Frank +	Hostile −
Persevering −	Hostile +	Lazy −	Reasonable +
Timid +	Impulsive +	Masculine +	Restless −
Unhappy +	Poised −	Sarcastic −	Unhappy −
	Reserved −	Self-pitying −	Uninterested −
	Restless +		
	Sarcastic +		
	Self-controlled −		
	Unconventional +		
	Versatile +		

High School Women	Newlywed Women	Middle-Aged Women	Preretirement Women
Dependent +	Energetic −	Absentminded +	Absentminded −
Guileful +	Jealous +	Unhappy +	Assertive +
Helpless +	Warm +		Dependent −
Idealistic −			Disorderly −
Intelligent −			Dramatic −
Lazy +			Easily embarrassed −
Restless +			Guileful −
Sentimental +			Intelligent +
Suspicious +			Lazy −
Undecided +			Self-indulgent −
			Stubborn −
			Suspicious −
			Undecided −

Source: From M. F. Lowenthal, M. Thurnher, and D. Chiriboga, *Four Stages of Life* (San Francisco, Calif.: Jossey-Bass, 1975), p.68.

Looking at the development of the two groups at adolescence, the economic deprivation had the most disruptive consequences for the younger Berkeley cohort, especially the boys. They experienced a disruptive loosening of their ties with their fathers. They felt victimized, self-defeated, and helpless. In contrast, the Oakland boys, who experienced severe deprivation, expressed a strong sense of optimism. They took on jobs, became more responsible, and generally advanced their entry into adult roles. The Berkeley girls appeared to be buffered from the disruptions of economic loss by the strengthening of the mother-daughter bond. Mothers became more central figures of strength and influence when fathers became unable to support the family. In families where there was a strong, positive relationship between the husband and wife, economic loss

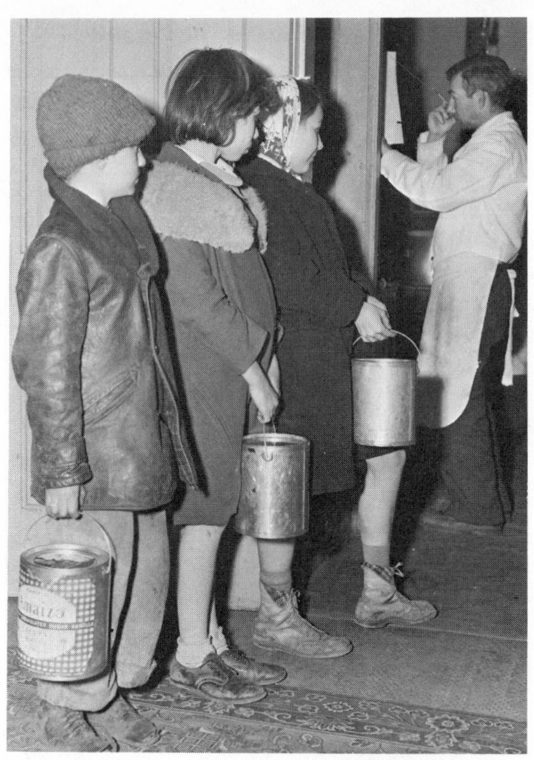

The Great Depression reached into the daily lives of young children as they lined up at the soup kitchens.

seemed to enhance feelings of closeness between all the family members. However, where there was marital discord, the father became quite estranged from his children. This had the most serious consequences for the young boys.

Elder also looked at the two groups as they adapted to adult life. In middle adulthood the seriousness of deprivation or the age at which deprivation occurred did not predict psychological health or occupational achievement. The remnants of depression-related disruption during childhood were seen in the greater likelihood of the Berkeley cohort to drink heavily, to complain about a loss of energy, and to worry. Sometime during the decade from 30 to 40, even the most sorely stressed managed to overcome the disadvantages of their childhood experiences. A combination of military service, education, marriage, successful work experiences, and parenting contributed to a sense of self-acceptance and a mature orientation toward others. The main residue of their childhood deprivation was in their evaluation of the past. Adults from economically deprived homes look back on childhood as a time of fear and insecurity. In contrast, adulthood is the best time of life. Especially for the Berkeley males who experienced economic loss, adolescence was viewed as the very worst time of life.

Summary

The life-events perspective permits a detailed look at the ways adults encounter major changes in resources, roles, or settings. Each person's life history brings encounters with a varied array of life events. Both positive and negative events may challenge existing competences and produce a sense of uncertainty. The pattern of developmental transitions is complicated by the overlay of unpredictable historical events that may occur. The timing of those events in the person's life is a critical factor. What is more, vulnerability to disruption is mediated by the quality of the family support system and by one's own interpretation of the events themselves.

Social Participation

A fourth theme in the study of personality in adulthood is the concern with the pattern of social participation and psychological investment in meaningful relationships. If we take Erikson's theory as a guide, we would expect to see heightened focus on dyadic, intimate relationships in early adulthood in an effort to resolve the crisis of intimacy versus isolation. This would be followed by a more generalized social involvement with children, students, co-workers, community organizations, and religious organizations in efforts to achieve a sense of generativity. In the last life stage, Erikson's theory predicts a greater degree of inward-turning. The crisis of integrity versus despair brings renewed focus to personal values and accomplishments rather than to broadening or even deepening relationships with others.

Disengagement Theory

Somewhat in line with this view, Cumming and Henry (1961) introduced a view of adaptation to aging which they called *disengagement theory*. They argued that because death is an inevitable end, it is to the benefit of both the individual and the society to gradually disengage from social roles and withdraw from social interaction in order to accept this eventuality more easily. From the perspective of disengagement theory, older people who are less invested in their social community, their social relationships, and their social responsibilities will experience higher morale than those who continue to remain involved with their social milieu. Several factors contribute to the gradual diminution of the life space, including retirement, widowhood, the departure of children from the home, and the death of peers. These events stimulate a perception of a limited social context. One response to this loss of relationship is a gradual reduction of involvement in these and other social encounters. Cumming and Henry describe the aging process as one of increased egocentrism, including a dominance of personal motives, increased expressivity and declining concern with reality. What is more, the disengagement theory proposes that these changes are desireable strategies for adapting to aging and death.

A contrasting theory, *activity theory,* suggests that full participation in adult life roles is desired by aging adults. In this view, older adults resist distancing themselves from their social environment. There is no question that role loss occurs during later life. However, activity theory suggests that the adaptive response to role loss is to replace previous relationships with new meaningful alternatives (Streib, 1977).

Research on the issue of social participation and emotional investment of the elderly has helped resolve this conflict.

There is evidence that disengagement is not a new adaptation during later life. It is a continuation of a life-style. In a discussion of activity level and life satisfaction among the elderly, Maddox (1968) has suggested that individuals who are high or low in activity generally maintain that ranking through repeated observations. People who displayed the disengagement pattern, that is, high satisfaction and low activity, were the very oldest ones. Maddox points out that they may have arrived at this pattern through several paths, not just as a new adaptation to old age.

Havighurst, Neugarten, and Tobin (1968) have reported an analysis of the Cumming and Henry sample after seven years. This sample consisted of one cohort between the ages of 50 and 70 in 1956, when the first interviews were conducted, and another cohort between the ages of 70 and 90 in 1958, when they joined the study. Havighurst et al. attempted to differentiate between social engagement and psychological engagement. *Social engagement* refers to activity in daily interactions and in life roles. *Psychological engagement* refers to a personal investment in these relationships and a readiness to engage the complexities of social reality. Both of these dimensions were found to decrease with age. This supports the disengagement process. On the other hand, measures of life satisfaction and emotional attitudes toward social activity showed that those who were most active were most satisfied with life. Those who were least active were least satisfied with life. There was no decrease in life satisfaction with age. But many older subjects expressed regret at the loss of role activity. Older subjects were able to accept their current loss of activity, albeit with some dissatisfaction, and still maintain their overall sense of self-esteem. These data point out the strong value that is placed upon social interaction and role activity among older adults. The fact that they can adapt to a decrease in activity does not support the notion that they wish it, but rather indicates that they can be resigned to it.

In reviewing the relationship between social role activity and life satisfaction in their longitudinal sample, Havighurst, Neugarten, and Tobin emphasized the importance of personality. The central needs and values of the person direct behavior toward meaningful choices. If the environment permits the person some freedom of choice, the person will select or reject involvements in order to achieve personal values. This process seems even more intense in later adulthood as people strive to achieve consistency between their needs and their actions.

> People as they grow old, seem to be neither at the mercy of the social environment nor at the mercy of some set of intrinsic processes—in either instance, inexorable changes that they cannot influence. On the contrary, the individual seems to continue to make his own "impress" upon the wide range of social and biological changes. He continues to exercise choice and to select from the environment in accordance with his own long-established needs. (Neugarten, Havighurst, & Tobin, 1968, pp. 176–177)

Stability and Change of Adult Life-Styles

The question about stability of social involvement from early to later adulthood was addressed directly in a study by Maas and Kuypers (1975). Parents of the children who participated in the Oakland Growth Study and the Berkeley Guidance Study were the subjects. They were first interviewed in the 1920s as their children entered the study. They were interviewed periodically over a 40-year span until their children reached the age of 40. Parents ranged in age from 60 to 82.

From interview data on major roles and life contexts, four father life-style patterns and six mother life-style patterns were described.

Family-centered father Highly involved and satisfied with marriage; sees children and grandchildren often; participates in clubs or informal groups, but is not too involved with religious or political organizations; relationship with child has improved over time.

Hobbyist father Many recreational interests, mostly pursued alone; more involved in social and recreational activities than in the past; infrequent interactions with grandchildren; relationship with child is a source of satisfaction; relationship with wife is based quite heavily on helping one another.

Remotely social father Marital relationship is not close and not very satisfying; not very close to child; perceives relationship with child as having grown more distant over time; has become more involved in political volunteer work over time.

Unwell-disengaged father Dissatisfied with relationship with children and grandchildren; preoccupied with illness and the sick role; marital relationship is changing for the worse; involvement with close friendships has declined.

Husband-centered mother Highly involved and satisfied with the marriage; perceives the marriage as changed for the better; minimal interactions with children, grandchildren, or siblings; no special involvement with groups or formal organizations.

Uncentered mother Interacts with children and grandchildren often; high involvement as a guest or visitor (for example, playing bridge); low involvement with work or clubs; dissatisfied with finances, health, and life since retirement.

Visiting mother Often has visitors and is involved as a hostess; marriage is changing for the worse; retains close friendships and close relations with siblings; very satisfied and involved as a group member; low involvement in politics and a discouraged view of the world in general.

Employed mother High involvement and satisfaction with work; close relationship with child; many not still married.

Disabled-disengaging mother Minimal social interactions as visitor or hostess; few interactions with children or grandchildren; low group involvement; close relationship with marriage partner; sees marriage as improving; concerned about health.

Group-centered mother High involvement with clubs, church, and community; positive interactions with children and grandchildren; involved and satisfied in the retiree role.

These life-style patterns suggest that there is enormous variety in the focus and pattern of life during later adulthood. Ill health seems to be associated with a tendency toward disengagement. Many of the other life-styles go well beyond involvement in work and family relationships.

The patterns of life-style changes from young adulthood to later adulthood are different for the fathers and the mothers. Fathers show a high degree of stability. The hobbyists were activity- and leisure-centered in

The "visiting mother" builds a lifestyle around her friendships and her role as hostess.

their early adulthood. Likewise the unwell-disengaged were preoccupied with health and somewhat disengaged in their early adult years. The remotely social fathers change in one significant area. They show a decline in involvement with parenting. Family-centered fathers become increasingly family-centered with age but do not show a reorganization of priorities.

The mothers seem to show much greater variability in life-style over the adult years. Changes in health, income, marital status, and work all contribute to these changes. Of the six groups, only the visiting mothers and the husband-centered mothers show continuity of style. Aging seems to improve the life satisfaction of the employed mothers. They show more energy and involvement as older adults than they showed in their early adulthood. The group-centered mothers also show greater satisfaction and compatability with their club and community leadership roles than they expressed as young wives and mothers.

In contrast to these two groups who seem to have found more enhancing life-styles in later adulthood, two other groups suffered a loss of involvement. The uncentered mothers changed from satisfied and involved wives and mothers to an unfocused life. Their later adult years are troubled by economic problems, loss of spouse, and no activity-based replacement for their earlier adult roles. The disabled-disengagement mothers were not socially withdrawn in early adulthood but became so in later life. A poor relationship with children remains unimproved in later life, but an earlier conflictual relationship with the spouse actually improves over time.

Summary

The question of social involvement in adulthood has emerged to be a complex question. There are a variety of life choices and life-styles available to older adults. In some respects, stable personality traits direct life choices that retain their essential qualities across the life span. This seems especially true for men. For women, the discontinuities between early and later adulthood in role involvement, health, and economic factors may produce greater reorganization of social involvements.

In general, there does appear to be some overall decline in activity and psychological involvement with age. For some adults, this deline is a regrettable but inevitable consequence of role loss and ill health. For others it is a life-style choice that reflects a desire for more intimate involvement with spouse or children.

Coping and Adaptation

Coping refers to a person's active efforts to reduce stress and to create new solutions to the challenges of life events (Erikson, 1959). The idea emphasizes the personal resources and competences that are brought to bear on each new environmental challenge. Coping is often contrasted with defense as a mechanism for responding to stress (Kroeber, 1963). Defense generally has as its goal protecting the integrity of the ego. It is an instinctive reponse to internal and/or external threats (A. Freud, 1936). Usually, the protection requires some distortion of reality. The extent of the distortion varies. For example, in rationalization there is minimal distortion. In the process of rationalization, the real reason for doing something is replaced with an acceptable reason. The unacceptable wishes or events are recognized and explained away through a series of arguments or explanations that appear logical to the person but may be highly subjective to an outside observer. In contrast, a defense such as repression is a global distortion of reality. In the process of repression, the stressful event or thought is simply removed from conscious awareness. All normal people use both coping strategies and defense mechanisms in their efforts to maintin control over their emotions in stressful situations.

Coping emphasizes mastery of the situation rather than protection of the self. This is not to imply that there is no concern for self-protection. In fact, the coping process affirms the commitment to a strong, competent, effective self that insists on confronting each life challenge. White (1974) offers three components of the coping process that emphasize the orientation toward growth. First, coping requires the ability to gain and process new information. New information is required if the person is to redefine the situation or establish some new position in the face of threat. Second, coping requires the ability to maintain control over one's emotional state. This does not mean that one eliminates emotional responses. Rather, it suggests the importance of a capacity to correctly interpret emotions, to express them when necessary, and to limit their expression when necessary. Third, coping requires the ability to move freely in one's environment. This third criterion suggests that at times flight may be a legitimate coping strategy.

Coping Strategies

People use different strategies for coping with stress. At this point there is no comprehensive, widely accepted model for categorizing consistent personality differences in coping styles. Rather, there are separate observations of responses to specific kinds of stress. These observations alert us to the contribution of personality to the coping process. One of the repeated themes in these studies of coping is the role of denial in response to stress. People differ in how seriously they treat the stress, how fully they are willing to accept the severity of the situation, or how vulnerable they will allow themselves to be to environmental conflict.

Janis (1962) observed that people responded in two quite different ways to a "near miss," or close brush with danger. Some felt a heightened anxiety about their own mortality. They had never realized how vulnerable they were. Others saw the same situation as evidence for their resilience. Having come so close to death, they interpreted their survival as evidence that they were meant to continue living. A similar distinction has been observed among combat pilots, civilians who survived an air raid, and survivors of a tornado. The narrow escape made some people increasingly anxious about the threat of potential disasters, while others were confirmed in their belief of invulnerability (Janis, 1974).

Wolff, Friedman, Hofer, and Mason (1964) observed the bereavement process in parents whose children were dying of leukemia. Some parents relied heavily on denial to minimize the stress. They felt sure that the child would not die and that some cure would be found. Other parents, who did not deny the seriousness of the child's illness, showed far greater emotional and physical signs of stress. They were not able to use denial to buffer the pain of the crisis. During the prolonged illness, the parents who could deny the seriousness of the child's condition were able to protect themselves from the stress and continued to have a hopeful, optimistic outlook. The study does not tell us what happened after the children died. One might expect that parents who had denied the seriousness and hopelessness of the illness would be much more devastated by the child's death than those who had begun to grieve while the child was still alive.

The capacity to buffer oneself against the emotional intensity of a situation can protect some people from the stresses that generate illness, anxiety, and fatigue. In an experimental test of this concept, subjects were shown films of woodshop accidents in which serious injuries were depicted. They saw two films without any viewing instructions. Then, half the subjects were instructed to detach themselves from the third film and then to try to totally involve themselves in the fourth film. The other subjects were given the opposite instructions, involvement preceding detachment. Despite the pain and serious consequences of the accidents, subjects were able to control their feelings. Measures of heart rate and subjective reports of emotional experiences indicated that cognitive strategies, such as reminding oneself that the film participants were actors, were effective in minimizing the impact of stress (Koriat, Melkman, Averill, & Lazarus, 1972). As discussed above, in real situations, without the benefit of coaching or instructions, people seem to differ in their natural capacity to resist stress. Whether the crisis is the stress of the work setting, separation, or death, the ability to minimize its impact is associated with better physical health and greater self-acceptance (Tanner, 1976).

However, coping does not always involve minimizing the impact of environmental events. Consider quite the opposite coping strategy, which Janis, Mahl, Kagan, and Holt (1969) have described as "the work of worrying," or "emotional inoculation." This concept was based primarily on observations of patients who were undergoing major surgery. In one study, three groups of patients were identified. The first group showed intense preoperative fear and continued anxiety after surgery. Their feelings of vulnerability produced a constant state of emotionality and fear. The second group had little anticipatory anxiety. They were cheerful and calm before surgery, but afterward they were angry and bitter about their treatment, and felt highly vulnerable. The third group was described as showing moderate anticipatory fear. They were concerned about particular aspects of the operation and tried to find out as much as they could about it. They were somewhat anxious before surgery but tried to remain calm by distracting themselves with other activities. After surgery this group showed the least emotional distress. They were described as cooperative and generally confident about their recovery.

Janis et al. explained the differences among these groups as due to differences in the ability to work through some of the feelings of threat and pain before they actually occurred. Some amount of worrying beforehand allowed the moderate group to feel reassured after surgery that things were going much as they had expected. Their recovery process was, in fact, confirmation of their own competence to test reality and therefore evidence that they were not really helpless or vulnerable to whims of the medical staff or the hospital environment.

A further test of this concept involved giving additional information about postoperative pain to one group of surgical patients and omitting this information for the control group (Egbert, Battit, Welch, and Bartlett, 1964). The information included a description of the pain, reassurance that the pain was normal, techniques for relaxation that could relieve some of the pain, and information that medication for pain would be available as the patient needed it. After surgery the group that had been informed required significantly less pain medication. They were released from the hospital an average of 2.7 days earlier than the control group. During their hospital stay, they were rated by "blind" observation as in better emotional and physical condition than the controls. (In this kind of observation the observer does not know which patients are in the treatment group and which in the control group.) Janis et al. offer this conclusion about the work of worrying: "A person will be better able to tolerate suffering and deprivation if he worries about it beforehand rather than remaining free from anticipatory fear by maintaining expectations of personal invulnerability" (1969, p. 105).

The research we have discussed above emphasizes individual differences in the use of repression as a mechanism for minimizing stress. Repression is customarily defined as a defense mechanism in which anxiety-producing thoughts or wishes are lost to conscious awareness. An assumption is usually made that these thoughts are stored in the preconscious and continue to influence behavior without the person's knowledge. The effectiveness of repression as a strategy for minimizing stress depends both on the person's ability to block out information and on the nature of the stressful situation. We might suggest that when the stressful situation includes opportunities to recover or to modify the conditions of stress, repression interferes with coping. When the stress is sudden and inalterable, then repression may in fact be adaptive.

A Longitudinal Study of Coping and Adaptation

Another approach to the study of coping was Vaillant's (1977) longitudinal work on coping and adaptation. The Grant Study began about 40 years ago in an attempt to understand the adaptive capacities of healthy, competent adults. Young men at a major Eastern university were selected according to the following criteria: (1) they met the requirements for college graduation; (2) they had no record of physical or psychological illness in their health-service record; (3) they were identified by the college deans as independent and "sound." From the 268 subjects in the original sample, Vaillant selected 95 for intensive interviews 30 years later. These men were in the classes 1942 to 1944.

During the college years, about 20 hours were required of each subject. Data came from eight psychiatric interviews, a social history, a session at the home of each subject's parents, a two-hour physical exam, psychological tests, an electroencephalogram, and a somatotyping session by a physical anthropolotist. Until 1955, the men were sent questionnaires annually. After that, questionnaires were sent every two years. These instruments focused on employment, family, health, habits, and political views. The men were all interviewed once in the period 1950–1952, and the subsample of 95 were interviewed again in the early 1970s. From this pool of data, Vaillant addresses the course of adaptation. He describes the maturation of ego functions and the success or failure of negotiating the Eriksonian life crises of identity, intimacy, and generativity.

Perhaps the most significant contribution was Vaillant's developmental analysis of defensive styles. Figure 6.3 shows the percentage of vignettes (observed episodes of behavior) showing evidence of 15 defensive styles. The width of each band shows the percentage of episodes that gave evidence of each defense at each age. Vaillant described a maturing of defensive styles in middle adulthood that is characterized by more frequent use of sublimation, altruism, and suppression and declines in hypochondriasis, acting out, and fantasy. This maturity of defensive style results in a more productive, dependable life orientation. The pattern of maturation is even stronger if one separates the subjects who in adulthood achieved a sense of generativity, the capacity to contribute to the quality of life for future generations, from those who remained "perpetual boys." The latter group showed fewer immature defenses in adolescence. They took few risks and maintained an image of steady equilibrium. In adulthood, however, these steady adolescents appeared to be rocked by the greater intensity of adult challenges. The men who as adolescents appeared to be confused, impulsive, or angry were more likely to emerge in adulthood with a flexible, warm, and vigorous adaptive style.

Vaillant identified factors within the person and factors in the

FIGURE 6.3 Proportion of Vignettes That Give Evidence Of Immature, Neurotic, and Mature Defenses at Three Age Periods.

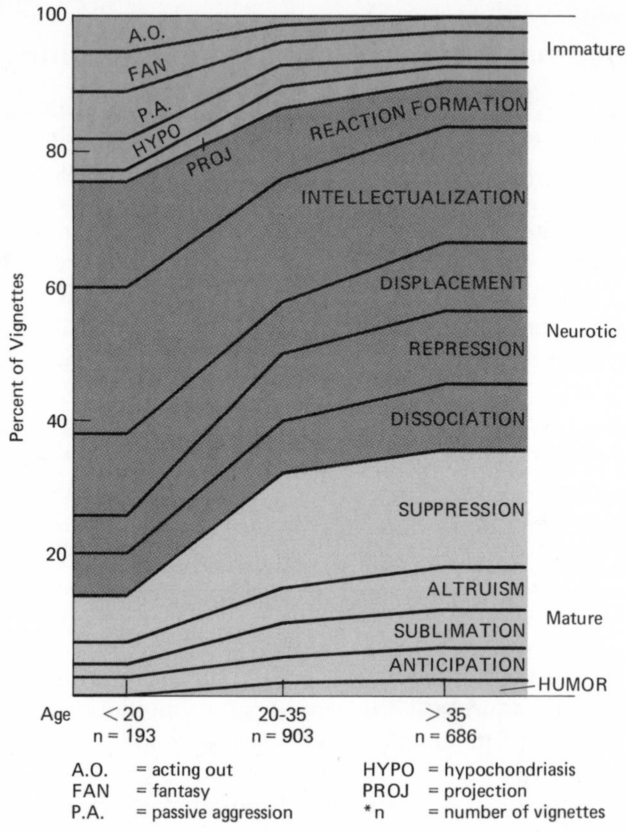

Source: G. E. Vaillant, *Adaptation to Life* (Boston: Little, Brown, and Co., 1977), p. 331.

environment that combine to support development toward a mature adaptive style in adulthood. Three inner factors contribute to adaptation. First, biological injury may result in temporary regression to a less mature adaptive style. The injury may call for greater distortion of one's view of reality, more impulsiveness, or greater dependency in relationships. Vaillant sees this regression as a potentially transitory shift that can be abandoned for a mature style once the injury is passed.

Second, adaptation reflects continued intellectual growth. Through experience, more complex analyses of events and a greater capacity to entertain multiple explanations of the same event emerge. Intellectual and ethical growth are fostered by participation in a variety of role relationships and by the demand to chart a life course using one's own problem-solving skills.

The third inner resource is the capacity to be involved in meaningful, loving relationships. Some part of this capacity depends on environmental supports; another element stems from the social competences and capacity for intimacy that the person brings into adult life. Over the life course, involvement in loving relationships and the need to experience intimacy increase. A deep investment in human relationships appears to be a component of health.

Among the Grant Study men, three environmental factors contributed to adaptation. First, early experiences of loving relationships helped the children to bear pain, anticipate positive outcomes, and feel themselves worthy of love. Second, the array of adults, children, and heroic figures in the child's world provided the content for identification. Through this process, the values and strengths of significant others became internalized. People acquired new adaptive capacities by taking in some of the admired qualities of the target of identification. The defenses themselves were modeled by adults to whom the young men in the study felt very close.

Third, the stresses and opportunities of the environment promoted or inhibited adaptation. The untimely death of a parent, rejection from a job, and participation in military maneuvers involving the destruction of life are all examples of life events that brought intense stress. When a person is under stress, susceptibility to environmental influence is greater. The capacity to cope is directly influenced by the amount of environmental support available during stressful periods. It is much easier to appear to be coping in a mature manner when others express admiration and support one's personal growth. If the social environment is competitive or hostile, then periods of vulnerability may provoke additional attacks in order to demonstrate one's limitations.

Vaillant argued that there is significant change during adulthood, both in the inner mechanisms of adaptation and in the observable behaviors defined as adjustment. Some adults emerge from a background of resources, opportunities, and parental encouragement to become restrained, depressed, and angry at others for their own failures. Others with

TABLE 6.5 Three Inner Factors and Three Environmental Factors that Contribute to Adaptation

Inner Factors	
1. Biological injury	may lead to temporary regression
2. Intellectual growth	permits more complex analysis and capacity to generate multiple explanations
3. Capacity for intimacy	contributes to feelings of meaning and joy in life
External Factors	
1. Early loving relationships	helps children bear pain, take optimistic outlook
2. The array of targets for identification	contributes content to internalization process determines aspects of the adaptive or defensive style
3. Stresses and opportunities	stress increases vulnerability to environmental pressures

Source: Based on *Adaptation to Life* by G. E. Vaillants. (Boston: Little Brown, 1977).

far less support in childhood grab hold of opportunities and squeeze satisfaction out of each encounter. In general, the healthy members of the group became more involved with appreciating others and contributing to the lives of others. They showed a maturing religious commitment that integrated formal religious teaching with a caring, active moral orientation. There was continued redefinition of the parent/child relationship. The men rediscovered the strengths and weaknesses of their parents. They moved past the idolization of early adolescence or the critical distance of their young adulthood to a more complete appreciation of their parents as persons. Finally, healthy adaptation resulted in a vigorous engagement in life. In contrast to the self-absorption of adolescence or the guilt and depression of the thirties, after 45 the most successful Grant Study men showed a "celebration" of life.

Summary

In the study of coping and adaptation we find evidence of individual differences as well as growth. The pattern of mature adaptation is in the direction of greater flexibility, creative sublimation, and the deliberate use of cognitive of strategies to reduce stress. Adults can learn to modify their coping strategies through the use of strategies including deliberate relaxation, self-statements that reduce anxiety, and anticipation. Personality structure does contribute to a natural orientation toward life stresses. There appears to be some evidence for discontinuity from adolescence to adulthood in this regard. Vaillant has argued that early stability may leave one less confident in coping with the uncertainties of adult life.

Chapter Summary

In the study of personality during adulthood, five themes have been emphasized. Traits are stable characteristics that endure across time and across settings. Longitudinal research finds evidence for the stability of certain physiological characteristics from infancy into young adulthood. Social characteristics like expressiveness, aggressiveness, and achievement orientation also show stability from childhood to adulthood. The fate of some childhood traits seems to depend on sex role socialization and the differential acceptability of certain qualities for males and females. During adult life, the evidence supports a relatively high degree of stability. Individual differences in the extent of stability or instability of traits make it difficult to predict patterns for individuals. Some people show more of a constant pattern from childhood through adulthood while others show greater evidence of change.

Identity refers to a creative integration of past identifications, personality characteristics, and future aspirations. Four identity statuses have been described: achieved identity, foreclosed identity, moratorium, and identity diffusion. The two primary components in the process of identity formation are crisis and commitment. Not all young adults achieve a personal identity. However, there does appear to be progress in this direction during the later adolescent and young adult years. Identity does serve as an anchor point for values that persist through adulthood. Identity is not as permanent as the theory has suggested. There may be revisions and even regression to a less mature identity resolution during young adulthood.

The sequence of life events and life transitions is a major source of potential change in adult personality. Lives are punctuated by varying stress events. People also differ in the ways they perceive and cope with stress. One way of describing this is the distinction between Type A's, who fear loss of control and approach life with a sense of great urgency, and Type B's, who seem more confident and willing to accept their limitations.

One way to appreciate the impact of life events is to compare the frequency and type of life stressors at different periods of adult life. Adolescence and early adulthood seem to be the most stress filled. In contrast, later adulthood has the greatest proportion of negative life stressors. Adaptation seems to take a different path for men and women. Men come to an earlier sense of self-confidence and focus than women.

The study of the Great Depression illustrates the overlap of historical time on personal and social time. It appears that this event was most difficult for young boys whose families experienced serious economic loss, and whose parents were already experiencing marital conflict. The disruptive effects of this event were modified by later successes and self-initiated coping strategies.

The theme of social involvement reflects a concern with the patterning of social relationships and social activity during adulthood. Personality and life events seem to interact to produce a life-style pattern. Overall, adults seem to have fewer social activities and less psychological investment in relationships with age. However, there are many different life-style patterns observed in adulthood. Some people continue a pattern of high activity, some continue a pattern of disengagement, some (especially women) become more disengaged over time, and some become more active over time.

The final theme of coping and adaptation refers to the solutions people create to meet life demands and to reduce threat. While one would expect that coping might depend heavily on the kinds of stresses that are encountered, there is evidence for some stability in coping strategies. Some people use denial to minimize threat. Some people use the work of worrying to anticipate and think through stressful situations before they occur. In Vaillant's longitudinal study, evidence was found to support a gradual maturing of coping and defensive styles. The characteristics of mature adult coping included the use of sublimation, altruism, and suppression. The most mature men expressed a warm, optimistic orientation toward life. The less mature men showed a more fearful, discouraged outlook.

In adulthood, there are many difficult challenges to one's optimism and sense of worth. There are also many opportunities to experience competence and to have an impact on others. Adults have the resources to make midcourse corrections or self-initiated improvements. The study of personality suggests that some people experience greater stability and others experience more discontinuity. Stability may result in a pattern of lifelong satisfaction or lifelong despair. Discontinuity may lead to growth and a greater sense of self-awareness. It may also lead to a sense of vulnerability and loss. We are impressed by the fact that the structure of personality seems to permit some people to modify their behavior and to find new meaning in life experiences. For others the personality structure itself seems to prohibit the acquisition of new coping skills or the openness to enjoy others.

References

Baum, A., Singer, J. E., & Baum, C. S. Stress and the environment. *Journal of Social Issues,* 1981, *37,* 4–35.

Block, J. *Lives through time.* Berkeley, Calif.: Bancroft, 1971.

Bronson, W. C. Adult derivations of emotional expressiveness and reactivity-control: Developmental continuities from childhood to adulthood. *Child Development,* 1967, *38,* 801–817.

Constantinople, A. An Eriksonian measure of personality development in college students. *Developmental Psychology,* 1969, *1,* 357–372.

Costa, P. T., & McCrae, R. R. Objective personality assessment. In M. Storandt, I. C. Siegler, & M. F. Elias (Eds.), *The clinical psychology of aging.* New York: Plenum, 1978.

Cumming, E., & Henry, W. E. *Growing old: The process of disengagement.* New York: Basic Books, 1961.

Donovan, J. M. Identity status: Its relationship to Rorschach performance and to daily life pattern. *Adolescence,* 1975, *10*(37), 29–44.

Egbert, L., Battit, G., Welch, C., & Bartlett, M. Reduction of postoperative pain by encouragement and instruction of patients. *New England Journal of Medicine,* 1964, *270,* 825–827.

Elder, G. H., Jr. Historical change in life patterns and personality. In P. B. Baltes and O. G. Brim, Jr. (Eds.), *Life-span development and behavior* (Vol. 2). New York: Academic Press, 1979.

Emmerich, W. Continuity and stability in early social development. *Child Development,* 1964, *35,* 311–332.

Erikson, E. H. *Childhood and society* (2nd ed.). New York: Norton, 1963.

Erikson, E. H. Growth and crisis of the healthy personality. *Psychological Issues,* 1959, *1*(1), Monograph 1, 50–100(a).

Erikson, E. H. The problem of ego identity. *Psychological Issues,* 1959, *1*(1), 101–164(b).

Friedman, M., & Rosenman, R. H. *Type A behavior and your heart.* New York: Knopf, 1974.

Freud, A. *The ego and the mechanisms of defense.* New York: International Universities Press, 1936.

Haan, N. Common dimensions of personality development: Early adolescence to middle life. In D. H. Eichorn, J. A. Clausen, N. Haan, M. P. Honzik, & P. H. Mussen *Present and past in middle life.* New York: Academic Press, 1981.

Havighurst, R. J., Neugarten, B., & Tobin, S. S. Disengagement and patterns of aging. In B. Neugarten (Ed.), *Middle age and aging.* Chicago: University of Chicago Press, 1968.

Holmes, T. H., & Rahe, R. H. The social readjustment rating scale. *Journal of Psychosomatic Research,* 1967, *11,* 213–218.

Janis, I. Psychological effects of warnings. In G. W. Baker and D. W. Chapman (Eds.), *Man and society in disaster.* New York: Basic Books, 1962.

Janis, I. Vigilance and decision making in personal crises. In G. V. Coellio, D.A. Hamburg, & J. E. Adams (Eds.), *Coping and adaptation.* New York: Basic Books, 1974.

Janis, I. L., Mahl, G. F., Kagan, J., & Holt, R. R. *Personality: Dynamics, development, and assessment.* New York: Harcourt Brace Jovanovich, 1969.

Kagan, J., & Moss, H. A. *Birth to maturity.* New York: Wiley, 1962.

Kelly, E. L. Consistency of the adult personality. *American Psychologist,* 1955, *10,* 659–681.

Koriat, A., Melkman, R., Averill, J. R., & Lazarus, R. S. The self-control of emotional reactions to a stressful film. *Journal of Personality,* 1972, *40,* 601–619.

Kroeber, T. C. The coping functions of the ego mechanisms. In R. W. White (Ed.), *The study of lives.* New York: Atherton, 1963.

Lazarus, R. S. Cognitive and coping processes in emotion. In. B. Weiner (Ed.), *Cognitive views of human motivation.* New York: Academic Press, 1974.

Lerner, R. M., Palermo, M., Spiro, A., & Nesselroade, J. R. Assessing the dimensions of temperamental individuality across the life span: The dimensions of temperament survey (DOTS). *Child Development,* 1982, *53,* 149–159.

Lessing, D. *The golden notebook.* New York: Simon & Schuster, 1962.

Lowenthal, M. F., Thurnher, M., & Chiriboga, D. *Four stages of life.* San Francisco: Jossey-Bass, 1975.

Maas, H. S., & Kuypers, J. A. *From thirty to seventy.* San Francisco: Jossey-Bass, 1975.

Macfarlane, J. W. From infancy to adulthood. *Childhood Education,* 1963, *39,* 336–342.

Maddox, G. L. Persistence of life among the elderly: A longitudinal study of patterns of social activity in relation to life satisfaction. In B. Neugarten (Ed.), *Middle age and aging.* Chicago: University of Chicago Press, 1968.

Marcia, J. E. Development and validation of ego identity status. *Journal of Personality and Social Psychology,* 1966, *3,* 551–558.

Marcia, J. E. Identity six years after: A follow-up study. Mimeographed report, 1975.

Marcia, J. E., & Friedman, M. L. Ego identity status in college women. *Journal of Personality,* 1970, *2,* 249–263.

Meyer, A. *The commonsense psychiatry of Dr. Adolf Meyer* (A. Lief, Ed.). New York: McGraw-Hill, 1948.

Moss, H. A., & Susman, E. J. Longitudinal study of personality development. In O. G. Brim, Jr., & J. Kagan (Eds.), *Constancy and change in human development.* Cambridge, Mass.: Harvard University Press, 1980.

Neugarten, B. L. Personality and aging. In J. E. Birren and K. W. Schaie (Eds.), *Handbook of the psychology of aging.* New York: Van Nostrand-Reinhold, 1977.

Neugarten, B. L., Havighurst, R. J., & Tobin, S. S. Personality and patterns of aging. In B. L. Neugarten (Ed.), *Middle age and aging: A reader in social psychology,* Chicago: University of Chicago Press, 1968, 173–177.

Pittner, M. S., & Houston, B. K. Response to stress, cognitive coping strategies, and the type A behavior pattern. *Journal of Personality and Social Psychology,* 1980, *39,* 147–157.

Protinsky, H. O. Eriksonian ego identity in adolescents. *Adolescence,* 1975, *10,* 428–432.

Riegel, K. F. Adult life crises: A dialectic interpretation of development. In. N. Datan and L. H. Ginsberg (Eds.), *Life-span developmental psychology: Normative life crises.* New York: Academic Press, 1975.

Schenkel, S., & Marcia, J. E. Attitudes toward premarital intercourse in determining ego identity status in college women. *Journal of Personality,* 1972, *3,* 472–482.

Sontag, L. W. Implications of fetal behavior and environment for adult personalities. *Annals of the New York Academy of Sciences,* 1966, *132*(2), 782–786.

Staub, E., Tursky, B., & Schwartz, G. Self-control and predictability: The effects on reactions to aversive stimulation. *Journal of Personality and Social Psychology,* 1971, *18,* 157–162.

Streib, G. F. Changing roles in the later years. In R. A. Kalish (Ed.) *The later years: Social applications of gerontology,* Monterey Calif.: Brooks/Cole, 1977.

Tanner, O. *Stress.* New York: Time-Life Books, 1976

Toder, N. L., & Marcia, J. E. Ego identity status and response to conformity pressure in college women. *Journal of Personality and Social Psychology,* 1973, *26,* 287–294.

Tuddenham, R. D. The constancy of personality ratings over two decades. *Genetic Psychology Monographs,* 1959, *60,* 3–29.

Vaillant, G. E. *Adaptation to life.* Boston: Little, Brown, 1977.

Whitbourne, S. K., & Waterman, A. S. Psychosocial development during the adult years: Age and cohort comparisons. *Developmental Psychology,* 1979, *15,* 373–378.

Waterman, A. S., Geary, P. S., & Waterman, C. K. A longitudinal study of changes in ego identity status from the freshman to the senior year at college. *Developmental Psychology,* 1974, *10,* 387–392.

White, R. W. Strategies of adaptation: An attempt at systematic description. In G. V. Coelheo, D. A. Hamburg, & J. E. Adams (Eds.), *Coping and adaptation.* New York: Basic Books, 1974.

Wolff, C. T., Friedman, S. B., Hofer, M. A., & Mason, J. W. Relationship between psychological defenses and mean urinary 17–hydrorycorticosteroid excretion rates: I. A predictive study of parents of fatally ill children. *Psychosomatic Medicine,* 1964, 26, 576–591.

Intimacy and Love

To love and to be loved is as necessary to the organism as the breathing of air. Insofar as the organism fails in loving, it fails in living, for to live and love, is for a human being, the equivalent of healthy living. To live as if to live and love were one is not simply an ideal to be achieved, but a potentiality to be realized, a destiny to be fulfilled.

Ashley Montagu, *The Meaning of Love,* 1953, p.19

Much of adult thought is about social relationships. In the next three chapters we will discuss some of the ways that the content of those thoughts is translated into social behavior. We begin with a search for the origins and expressions of the most powerful of social sentiments, intimacy. In the following chapters, we will consider family and work as two other domains where inner motives, ideas, and aspirations are expressed in complex patterns of social behavior.

In Chapter 5 we defined intimate relations as those relations that are characterized by deep understanding and intense emotional commitment. To expand on this definition, we would say that intimacy includes the ability to experience an open, supportive, tender relationship with another person without fear of losing one's own identity in the process of growing close. The possibility of achieving intimacy depends on the confidence one has in oneself as a valuable, competent, and meaningful person. In this sense, we see the achievement of adult intimacy as dependent upon establishment of a clearly defined personal identity. Once a sense of identity is formed and the person can move toward commitments with confidence, the capacity for deep bonds with others can be fully developed. Perhaps the most important quality of an intimate relationship is the experience of giving and receiving intense pleasure with another person. This pleasure, based on many dimensions including sensory, sexual, intellectual, and aesthetic, places the intimate relationship in a cherished position among all other social interactions.

Developmental Antecedents of a Capacity for Intimacy

Despite the fact that intimacy is a characteristic of adult relationships, the capacity for intimacy does not emerge suddenly in adulthood. It is the product of an integration of many earlier experiences, each of which shares something of the intensity, closeness, and sense of pleasure that dominate adult intimate relationships. Several kinds of relationships in childhood give children opportunities to experience mutuality and closeness as well as opportunities to observe mutuality and closeness in others. The four relationships that seem most influential are those with caregivers, siblings, extended family members, and peers.

Infant-Caregiver Relations

The first building block for a sense of intimacy is the formation of an attachment to a caregiver. Attachment signals several important qualities in the early relationship: (1) the infant differentiates the object of attachment from others; (2) the infant prefers interactions with the object of attachment over interactions with others; (3) the infant is more readily

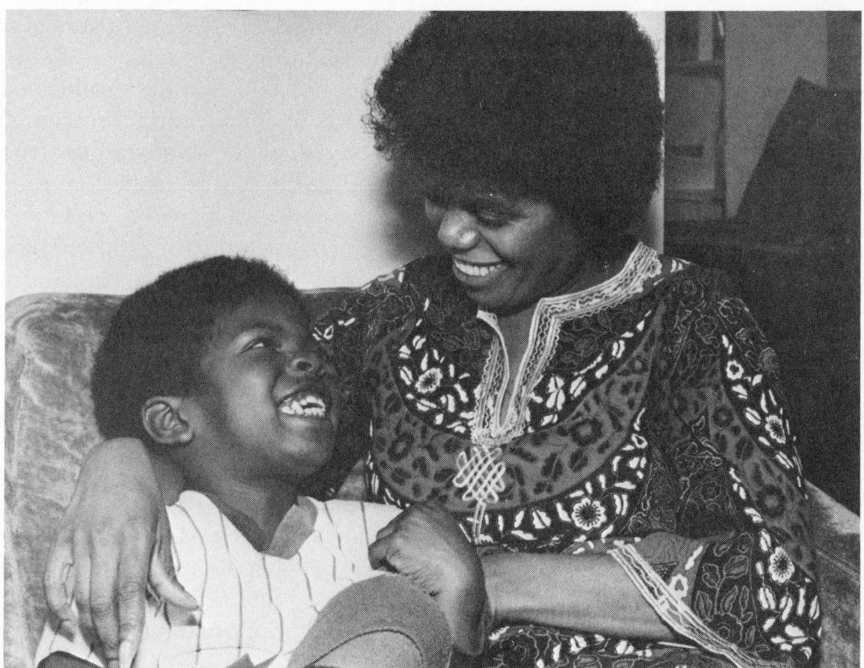

The child's early feelings of trust and delight in interactions with a loving parent provide a basis for the adult capacity for intimacy.

soothed by the object of attachment than by others; and (4) the infant actively tries to maintain contact with the object of attachment, at first by clinging or gazing, and later by following, talking, and playing with the object of attachment. Attachment, more commonly thought of as a baby's love, has in it many elements that continue to characterize later loving relationsips. Each of the characteristics listed above could also be applied to adult loving relationships. The focus on a small group of others who are the object of intense preferences and whose responses are more meaningful than the responses of others seems to be a very basic component of intimacy.

An infant's love can be nurtured or stifled by the quality of caregiving. Responsiveness, that is, the ability to meet the baby's needs relatively quickly and accurately, builds a sense for the infant that the world is predictable and that at least some people understand his or her needs. Warmth, that is, tender, soothing, kind interactions, communicates that the baby is lovable and valued. The combination of responsiveness and warmth permits babies to experience a sense of basic trust in their own bodies, feelings of love for themselves and for others, and a willingness to begin to control their own needs or impulses in order to share loving feelings with others.

The process of establishing love between infants and caregivers is so natural and so basic to human life that we might not even notice it if there were not cases where this early bond was not successfully established. Instances of parent-child separation through hospitalization, divorce, or death provide some evidence of the grief, anger, withdrawal, and mistrust that can result when attachments are disrupted. Probably the most profound failure of the formation of attachment is observed in childhood autism. Here, the child seems unable to form meaningful relationships. Interactions with caregivers are experienced as frightening or painful. Autistic children shut out adults by looking away, refusing to talk, curling into a ball, or stimulating themselves so that no other stimuli can intervene.

For most adults, however, the first glimpse of intimacy occurs in infancy through the sense of trust that is a product of a warm, responsive caregiver in interaction with an expressive, responsive infant who is fully capable of participating in social interactions. We hypothesize that an infant's early attachment experiences provide a prototype for later intimate relationships. Infants are active in their participation in these early attachments. They learn to anticipate the possibility of engaging in other mutually satisfying relationships based on early opportunities to give and receive love (Kahn & Antonucci, 1980).

Sibling Relationships

Much of what we hear about sibling relations refers to the rivalry or jealousy that is experienced. This orientation has a theoretical basis in Alfred Adler's (1964) work on siblings. Adler argued that the first child feels dethroned by the birth of the next child and that much of the firstborn's character is influenced by trying to compensate for this feeling of having been displaced. Similarly, later-born children always view their family position as inferior since they were not firstborn. Much of their childhood adaptation, Adler argued, was focused on compensating for being later-born.

Obviously, parents can strengthen this orientation among siblings by expecting hostility, showing preferences for some children over others, and encouraging rivalry for their attention and affection. Parents can also encourage a loving orientation among siblings by valuing each child's uniqueness, encouraging frequent sibling interaction, and openly expressing love to one another as well as to their children.

There are several characteristics of sibling interactions that can provide a basis for intimacy in adulthood. First, there can be no doubt that sibling interactions are usually more intense than other peer interactions. Siblings, whether they are playing or fighting, angry or compassionate, are often engaged in interactions that are more serious and more focused than relations with other peers. This intensity is often demonstrated when siblings strike out to protect or defend a sibling under attack. It may be shown in intense feelings of empathy or guilt when a sibling is experiencing pain. It is most clearly shown in the convergence of joy, pride, and envy that siblings feel in one another's successes.

Second, siblings share the same home environment just as many adults who have intimate relationships do. Siblings may eat together, use the same bathroom, see each other dressing, see each other when they are sick, sleep in the same room or even the same bed, and wear each other's clothing. In all of these ways they share the details of everyday life. The relative lack of physical boundaries and privacy between siblings is a part of the quality of intimate relationships.

The third characteristic is a vital component of intimacy. Siblings often confide in each other. When children anticipate that parents or teachers or even peers will not understand, they may still be willing to talk to their brothers or sisters about their concerns. Frequently parents use the confidence that exists between siblings to try to obtain information about a child's behavior or to send a message of concern to a rebellious child. Since siblings are often confronting a similar social reality, they may be closer to the concerns and conflicts of each other's lives than parents are.

Finally, siblings experience a sense of bondedness because of their family ties that has its counterpart in other intimate relations. Siblings know that no matter what happens, they will always be connected. Even when they are separated by a great distance, by diverse interests, or by antagonistic families, siblings recognize the irrefutable tie that exists between them. A sense of being bound to the existence of another person is an experiential element of intimacy. Even if the relationship eventually ends, the power of the intimate context continues to bind the participants to the intensity of their shared reality.

The likelihood of siblings actually experiencing intimacy with one another in childhood or adult life depends on the nature of the family context. If there is constant competition for resources, reciprocity of relationship may be unlikely. If parents support a pattern of interaction where they are the focus and interactions among the children are unimportant, children may not seek out each other. If children learn to mistrust or devalue one another because of the orientation that is modeled by parents, the incentive to establish intimacy will be minimal.

If siblings do achieve intimacy with each other they will have laid the foundation for building intimate relations in adulthood. Throughout adulthood, siblings can provide a source of support, understanding, and reassurance for each other (Cicirelli, 1980). At each phase of adulthood, it becomes more and more difficult to share the significant events of one's past life with new acquaintances. Siblings are among the few social contacts who know and who do not need to be educated about one's family history. The deepening of sibling relationships in adulthood adds a unique historical dimension to the intimate bond.

The Extended Family

The extended family is composed of all of an individual's relatives beyond parents and siblings. Normally these family members do not live in the same household. The importance of this group of people in someone's life varies a great deal from one person to the next. A great deal depends on the frequency of interactions among family members. For some people the nuclear family provides all the familial relationships. For others, grandparents, aunts, uncles, cousins, nieces, and nephews provide important relationships in a variety of patterns. When extended family members are prominent in a person's life, they provide opportunities for learning about intimate relationships. The relations with extended family members are almost unique in a person's life. They provide the opportunity for extensive private relationships as individuals grow older.

Several patterns of relationship with extended family members are especially relevant as childhood antecedents of a capacity for intimacy in adulthood. First, children have access to observations of the quality of adult relationships in the interactions they observe between parents and grandparents, grandparents with each other, and aunts and uncles. The styles of interaction include ways of expressing affection, power relations, and communication of support or understanding. As observers, children begin to develop a picture of what adult intimacy might be like by watching extended family members interact.

Second, children are likely to experience some intense involvement with an aunt, an uncle, or an older cousin that in itself is a loving relationship. In these kinds of relationships children discover that it is possible to have close ties with people outside the immediate nuclear family. When the support of a close relative is strong, children are less vulnerable to the fluctuations in their parents' expressions of affection or support. Even when parents are angry or preoccupied, children who have close relationships in the extended family can preserve the sense of being valued and loved.

A third and somewhat special contribution of the extended family to a capacity for intimacy involves the grandparent-grandchild relationship. We know that grandparents have different ways of defining their role (Neugarten & Weinstein, 1964; Mead, 1974). Some adults are distant and even critical in their interactions as grandparents. Some see themselves as teachers or interpreters of the past. However, many grandparents see themselves as special advocates for their grandchildren. They indulge their grandchildren's desires and give them "ammunition" for conflicts with parents by discussing what their parents were like when they were children. Some grandparent-grandchild relationships come as close as

FIGURE 7.1 Patty knows her grandmother is old and hobbles, but that is inconsequential to her. To Patty "She can't walk too well," but "I like to snuggle into her and smell her . . . And she is the best back-rubber in the world."

Source: Excerpt from *Grandparents/Grandchildren: The Vital Connection* by Arthur Kornhaber and Kenneth C. Woodward. Copyright 1981 by Arthur Kornhaber and Kenneth C. Woodward. Reprinted by permission of Doubleday & Company, Inc.

possible to achieving a state of unconditional positive regard. Without the responsibility for discipline or for trying to socialize cooperative behaviors, grandparents are free to enjoy their grandchildren and to encourage their development. Grandchildren may experience a special sense of warmth and comfort with their grandparents, a comfort that comes from being loved and supported without a set of conditions attached. Being with grandparents, in these cases, is like being on vacation from the reality constraints of other adult-child relationships. In Figure 7.1, Patty expresses this warmth toward her grandmother. In a study of 300 grandchild-grandparent relationships only a small number of children (5 percent) felt adored by their grandparents in this "no strings attached" kind of affection (Kornhaber & Woodward, 1981). In adult intimate relationships, we continue to look for this kind of wholehearted support. In some cases, a grandparent-grandchild relationship, with a mutually accepting bond, may not be duplicated in any other life relationship. In this section we have described the quality of intimacy in the grandparent-grandchild relationship. In Chapter 8 we will explore the grandparent role in more detail.

False Intimacy There is a phenomenon that occurs in some extended family relationships that we describe as false intimacy. Children are told that family members are a close, supportive network. They are encouraged to express affection, to be respectful, and to give special consideration to the expectations or demands of aunts, uncles, and grandparents. In these families, however, the needs of children are viewed as unimportant in comparison to the needs and goals of adults. The love children are forced to express is not reciprocated. In fact, the image of closeness among adults may only be a disguise for competition and jealousy. Adults may even feel pleasure when the offspring of a son or daughter or a brother or sister fails. If one parent dies or a couple divorces, the children readily observe the disappearance of that parents' extended family members. When a child reaches the point of being unwilling to continue in an unreciprocated love relationship the illusion of intimacy in the extended family begins to dissolve.

Childhood Peer Friendships

As a result of repeated encounters in a positive context, children form strong emotional ties to one another. Children as young as preschool age come to feel deeply for a friend. They may tell secrets, make plans, sleep at each other's houses, collaborate on projects, and play together for hours. They actively seek each other out. Children will grieve at the loss of their friends and do what they can to protest separation or to maintain contact after separation.

The potential intensity of these childhood ties is illustrated in Freud and Dann's (1976) case study of a group of war orphans. Six children were raised together. All of them had lost their parents before they were two. They were grouped together and sent from one concentration camp to another during the war. The children became closely attached to one another. They protected each other from danger. They refused to be separated from one another. They shared anything that was given to one child. After the war, when these children were taken to England to be put in foster homes they fiercely resisted any attempts to separate them or to treat one differently from another.

Close peer friendships teach children about the possibility of intimacy with an age mate outside the nuclear family. The similarity of competences and resources that characterizes peer friendships provides an important element of equality in peer friendships. The bond of commitment is maintained because of affection and opportunities for interaction. Peers cannot threaten one another with disciplinary measures, or reduction of resources. Their differences must be resolved within the context of a currency of affection and social acceptance.

Peer interactions have a special quality. Peers are more comparable in their skills and their status, and their life experiences than are parents, other adults, or older or younger siblings. Generally, peer group friendships do not involve long-term responsibilities and commitments. One can play for hours with a friend without having to make promises for the future. There are at least four ways that peer play makes an impact on the developing child. Peer friendship provides opportunities for (1) new learning; (2) exploration; (3) experience with changing role relationships; and (4) understanding feelings.

Children learn from other children. They learn motor skills, games, information, language, and even misinformation. Children bring different skills, experiences, and beliefs to their play. Interactions with many different playmates can teach a young child about ideas, family styles, and information that might not be learned at home. Sometimes the things children learn from peers are not wholly accepted or desired by parents. In the following example, a four-year-old boy is very convinced about some information he secured from an older playmate.

Coming home from work a father engages in the following conversation with his four-year-old son (Lewis, Young, Brooks & Michalson).

> Son: Did you know God is a woman with many arms?
> Father: There is no such thing as God. Who told you such a story?
> Son: There is too a God. Linda told me. (Linda has been the child's best friend for the last two and a half years. They live next door to each other and are constantly together.)
> Father: Linda is wrong.
> Son: Linda is older than me and she knows better. (She is six years old.)
> Father: But I'm older than Linda, right? (long pause)
> Son: It doesn't matter—she told me.

Children learn about the world from each other. Friends spend time at one another's homes. They explore their neighborhood together. In the company of a peer, children are likely to be away from home longer and to wander farther than they might alone. Even at home, a visiting friend brings new life to a familiar environment. They see new uses for familiar toys, new hiding places, and new adventures.

Both symbolic play and games with rules involve multiple roles. As children play with peers, they have the experience of exchanging roles. One is the hider and then the seeker, the catcher and then the thrower, the statue maker and then the statue. Through peer play, children have an opportunity to experience the give and take of relationships. Many of a child's roles are fixed. In such roles as child, sibling, or student, there is no chance to take another part. In play with peers, children experience multiple perspectives of the same event (Lee, 1975).

In adulthood, we strive to blend friendship and sexuality in the formation of intimate relationships. Much of what we seek in a companion has its roots in childhood friendship. In those relationships, we discover the joy of intense closeness, mutual satisfaction, and adventure. All through life, the close companionship of an age-mate can be a great source of happiness.

Cultural Norms about Intimacy

It is a testimony to the power and pervasiveness of culture that we commonly do not recognize the many ways that the capacity for or the expression of intimacy is shaped by cultural norms. The ways people express love, the ideals they hold about loving relationships, and the people who are seen as acceptable partners are all influenced by cultural expectations. Four areas where cultural variability is likely to influence the experience of intimacy are male-female antagonisms, modes of expressing affection, norms for how people spend time together, and the range of acceptable partners. There may be other influences of culture on the establishment of intimacy. The ones we have selected to discuss relate most closely to the sentiments of affection and the experience of free choice in selecting an intimate companion. These are central to the patterns of romantic love in Western societies.

Male-Female Antagonism

In different societies there are different norms for male-female relationships. Sometimes antagonism is an expected and structured characteristic of the interactions between men and women. Several characteristics of the society appear to be related to the degree of hostility or distance in male-female relationships (West & Konner, 1976; Whiting & Whiting, 1975). First, the primary mode of subsistence is related to husband-wife intimacy and is reflected in other male-female relationships. Cultures that rely primarily on hunting, herding, and simple or advanced agriculture are more likely to show distance and even hostility between males and females. Distance may be evidenced in separate sleeping arrangements and prolonged periods of separation for married couples and in the extreme authority and power of men over women in general.

Second, in cultures where war is common, males are trained to be aggressive and authoritative. In warlike cultures, males are often isolated from their mothers at the end of childhood and inducted into the male culture through initiation ceremonies or puberty rites. From this time on, males are filled with a sense of their physical superiority and emotional fierceness.

The third factor that contributes to distance or antagonism between males and females is the practice of polygyny (having more than one wife at the same time). The practice of polygyny permits the male to demand allegiance from many wives and children. Frequently, wives are acquired through warfare, raiding, or bride theft. Once the brides are acquired, the

The practice of polygyny permits a man to expect allegiance from several wives and all their children.

sons and the father begin to form a small military band that functions to protect property and to add more wives. The irony of polygyny is that even though the wives are viewed as a valued addition, their value is primarily in their capacity to bear children. In cultures that practice polygyny the relations among men and women are often distant, suspicious, or openly hostile. An example of this cultural pattern is the Baganda, a group of over 1 million people who live in Uganda, a country of central Africa.

> Polygyny, the type of marriage in which the husband has plural wives, is not only the preferred but the dominant form of marriage for the Baganda. The king has hundreds of wives, chiefs, dozens, and commoners, two or three. Since wives are expensive, the commoner must work hard to acquire them. However, . . . each wife becomes a source of income and constitutes an economic investment. Polygyny is permissively sororal; the husband

may acquire as wives the sisters of his spouse or even the widows of his brothers.

> The Baganda woman at the time she enters her wifely duties is given a new hoe, water pot, cooking pot, and a basket in which to carry food. Her primary duty . . . is the cultivation of the family garden allotted her by the husband. A diligent wife who uses her hoe until through wear the handle breaks is usually given a goat by her husband as a present. Quite likely at the same time he also gives her a new hoe! It bears repeating that the value of a wife lies primarily in her ability to be economically and biologically productive. Her work begins at daybreak and continues until past dusk. For the male a few hours' work early in the morning and a few late in the day are considered appropriate to his status as a male, if not a provider. (Queen & Habenstein, 1974, p. 73, 74, & 86)

Male-female antagonism is not restricted to nonindustrial cultures. In our own society, the hostility and distance between the sexes is no longer built into readily observable cultural patterns but persists in the quality of interactions that characterize many relationships. Think a moment of the relationship characterized by Archie and Edith Bunker. Although clothed in humor, we see a continuous theme of Archie as a male in authority who is ridiculing and criticizing his wife's thoughts and activities. For her part, Edith battles back by going around Archie's back, by arranging interactions that he will not like, or by flatly refusing to be governed by his authority. Although we are often reminded of the loving bond that exists for this couple, the most persistent tone in their interactions is one of irritability and hostility.

The basis for male-female antagonism in our culture comes from at least two sources. First, there is the inner pressure to reject qualities that are characteristic of the opposite sex in order to assert one's own sex role identity. This pressure is especially strong for males who have learned to reject many female characteristics as weak or immature. Second is the competition generated by the increasing participation of women in all aspects of the world of work. Given a limited number of jobs, the entry of a large pool of competent and intelligent workers who had previously remained at home stimulates a new level of male-female antagonism. This hostility may be equally strong for females who perceive men as shutting them out of career opportunities and for men who perceive women as threatening to replace them.

Norms for Expressing Affection and Sexual Intimacy

Among humans, the female is continuously receptive to sexual intercourse even when she is not ovulating. There are no biologically controlled mating periods. Humans have developed cultural guidelines about the expression of affection and the appropriate conditions for engaging in sexually intimate behavior. These guidelines vary dramatically from one culture to another. We see differences in courtship behaviors, in values about romantic love, and in the degree of permissiveness about sexual relations. The contrast of four cultures helps us to understand the variety of cultural patterns that have developed to govern modes of expressing affection.

The Toda of Southern India The Toda are a handsome people. They are tall and have light-brown skin and long black hair. Marriages are arranged by a boy's father while the boy and his bride are children. After the arrangements are made, the father and son make a visit to the bride's family, bringing a loincloth with them as a gift. "The boy salutes the father of the child, the mother, and the brothers, kneeling forward to be touched upon the forehead with each of the other's feet" (Queen & Habenstein, 1974, p. 30).

The boy continues to visit the girl twice each year, bringing a loincloth as a gift at every visit. Just before the girl reaches puberty, she experiences a defloration ceremony. First a young man, not her husband, comes and lies down next to her for a few minutes, covering them both with a cloak. Two weeks later another young man comes for one night to have intercourse with the girl. Among the Toda, it is very important that this ceremony occur before the girl begins to menstruate. A year or so after this ceremony, the girl goes to live with her husband in his village.

The Hopi Indians of Arizona Hopi adolescents practice a custom called dumaiya. At night, boys put on disguises and visit the girls they find attractive. The boys stay all night but leave early in order to avoid meeting the girl's parents. Girls of marriageable age are usually visited by several lovers. When the girl becomes pregnant, she names her favorite lover and a marriage is arranged. Girls do have a way to signal their interest in a certain boy. At several ceremonies that are held in the men's house, girls generally bring a cake as part of the refreshments. On those occasions, if a girl prepares a sweet cornmeal bread instead of the usual cake and gives it to a particular boy, it is a sign that she would like him to be her husband.

Medieval England Two opposing views of sexuality existed side by side in medieval England. On the one hand the church taught that sexual desire was sinful. The sexual act was viewed as permissible only for the purpose of procreation. Even then it was not to be enjoyed. Marriage was a relationship bound by duty. Marriage was arranged by one's parents to preserve the lines of inheritance and to maintain the social status of the families involved. Pleasure, romance, and love were irrelevant.

On the other hand, the code of chivalry inherited from France glorified romantic love. Sexual pleasure was an important element in courtly love. These relationships were normally experienced between the knights and the ladies of the nobility. Wives entertained unmarried noblemen. Married noblemen sought the favor of other men's wives. A lady's love was viewed as a "free gift" unrestrained by the expectations of marriage (Queen & Habenstein, 1974).

Colonial New England Of course, much of the orientation toward courtship and marriage in the colonies was an outgrowth of English culture. However, practical considerations led to some modifications. Courtship in the colonies was a blend of structure imposed by law and individual autonomy. In several colonies, a young man was required by law to ask permission from a girl's father before beginning courtship. The father gave or refused permission depending on his assessment of the boy's economic resources. Boys looked for girls who promised to be accompanied by a large dowry. Boys could be tried and fined for beginning a courtship without having paternal consent.

Sexual behavior was scorned as frivolous and a violation of biblical teachings. Sexual offenses were punished publicly. These offenses included premarital intercourse, bearing a child too early in marriage or out of wedlock, adultery, and incest. In some colonies adultery was punishable by death. In 1639, a woman who was found guilty of adultery was sentenced to be "whipt at a cart tayle," "weare a badge upon her left sleeve," and if she went out without the badge to be "burned in the face with a hott iron" (Howard, 1904, p. 172). Other activities that were restricted included mixed dancing, men and women riding together to another town to drink and party, and May Pole dancing.

In contrast to these restrictions on sexual intimacy, the practice of "bundling" has been described. If a stranger was taken in for the night, he or she would share a bed with a family member, regardless of sex. When a young man went courting, he often "bundled" with his young girl under the covers to keep warm while they talked. There was a lot of gossip about sex, public interest in the punishment of sexual offenses, and frequent public confessions. The cultural efforts to minimize and restrict sexual intimacy resulted in a counterbalancing preoccupation with this theme (Queen & Habenstein, 1974).

The four cultures reflect very different views about the integration of sexuality, emotional intimacy, and the marriage relationship. Among the Toda, the young bride and groom become acquainted, but the experience of sexual intimacy is not part of that acquaintance. One has the sense that the marriage is an extension of each child's respect and devotion to his or her parent. For the Hopi, sexual intimacy is much more directly tied to love and marriage. Sexual intimacy is viewed as an appropriate prelude to marriage. In medieval England, sexuality was not a central element in marriage but romantic love had its expression in the code of chivalry among the nobility. Finally, in colonial New England, sex was viewed as sinful and almost all its expressions were banned. As among the Toda and in medieval England, marriage was arranged under the careful guidance of parents. Unlike among the Toda or the Hopi, young women were expected to enter marriage as virgins.

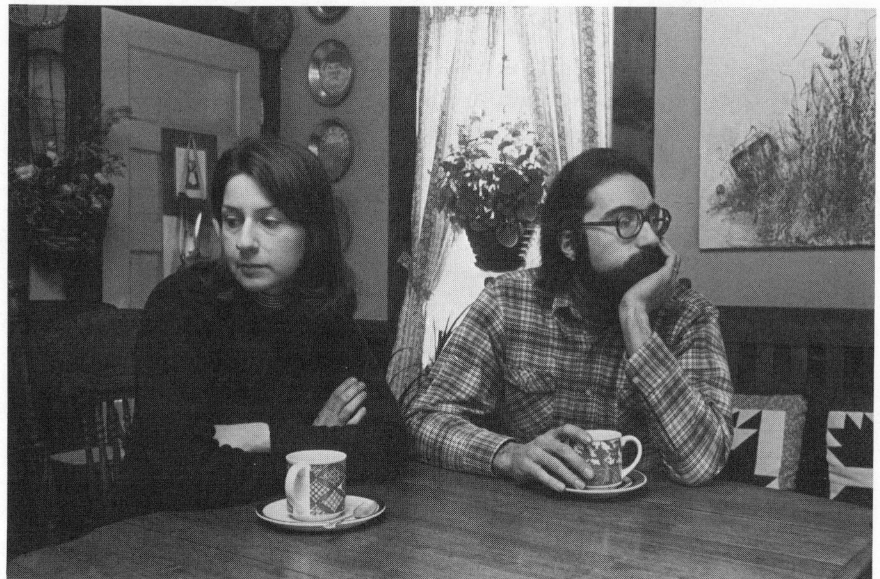

Sometimes when couples spend time together their minds are preoccupied by thoughts about work.

Norms for Time Together

Intimacy is built upon opportunities for interaction. Cultures differ in how much time they expect adults to spend together in the creation of an intimate bond. For example, in the !Kung San of Botswana men and women each work about half the week. There is a lot of leisure time, and much of it is devoted to the comfort, care, and entertainment of young children. Families are grouped together in bands of about 30 people. Among these groups, relationships are warm, supportive, and permissive.

Such factors as the length of time between marriage and the birth of the first child, who else besides the husband and wife live in the same dwelling, and the number of hours men and women are involved in separate work activities all effect the amount of time that can be shared by spouses. In our own society, for example, there is a trend toward delaying the birth of the first child and an expectation for having fewer children than 20 years ago. However, much of the time that might be devoted to the marriage partner when children are not present is devoted to the work setting instead. In about 50 percent of marriages, both partners work (U.S. Bureau of the Census, 1981). Young workers are expected to show their commitment to the work setting. Energy and thought that might be freed to focus on one's companion are focused on the skills, stresses, and authority relations of work. Time that might be spent together is spent with colleagues or clients.

The Range of Acceptable Partners

Even though we think that we are free to choose the people with whom we seek to achieve intimacy, culture directs our attention away from some choices and toward others. A very basic rule governing selection of an intimate partner is the taboo against incest. Incest can be narrowly defined to rule out sexual relations among members of the immediate nuclear family. It can also be rather far-reaching, setting all members of a totem, clan, or other kinship group out of bounds. Among the Hopi household, for example, groups are linked together through the female's ancestry. Groupings of families form phratries or kinship constellations. Marriage is not permitted between family groups within the same phratrie. Even though Hopi adolescents have considerable freedom to express preferences and initiate courtship, the culture directs their preference away from a large group of age mates as potential partners.

In our own culture, norms about the range of acceptable partners go beyond kinship limitations. One is not expected to seek intimate relations with someone either much older or much younger. Even though marriages across racial, religious, and socioeconomic groupings occur, they usually take place in the face of parental and peer opposition. Similarity of background is a characteristic that has been associated with stable marriages. Discrepancies in subcultural experiences are usually raised as a barrier to intimacy and as a source of continued conflict. Children are taught to perceive others who are like them as more attractive or more acceptable than those who do not share their ethnic heritage. Young people are encouraged to express their affection toward others who are as much like members of their own family as possible without actually being family members. In extreme cases, parents will threaten withdrawal of love, financial support, or communication if they see their children moving close to an "undesirable" choice of partner.

Efforts to Achieve Intimacy and Love

We have argued that the capacity for intimacy does not emerge fully developed in adulthood. Rather it is a product of participation in earlier loving relationships. A person's capacity for intimacy in adulthood is influenced by changing cognitive capacities that enrich relationships through the use of symbolism, the ability to take the perspective of the other, and the thoughtful analysis of interactions. The modes of expressing loving feelings, the norms about intimacy, and cultural prescriptions about acceptable partners also contribute to the experiences of intimacy in adult life.

Differences between Loving and Liking

Relationships can travel a variety of paths. Not every positive first impression leads to liking. Not every liking leads to friendship. Certainly not every friendship leads to love. In talking about friendship and love, we are talking about concepts that are difficult to define and even more difficult to operationalize in research.

Rubin (1973) views love as one type of interpersonal attraction and friendship as another. He attempted to demonstrate the separateness of these two kinds of relationships by devising two questionnaire scales—a love scale and a liking scale. An item from the loving scale is: I would forgive ______ for practically anything. An item from the liking scale is: I think that ______ is unusually well adjusted. Rubin asked couples to complete the scales, responding once about their partner and once about a same-sex friend. For women, the correlation between the loving and liking scales for their boyfriends was +.36. This level of correlation suggests that the two scales are measuring distinct concepts. For men, however, the correlation between the two scales for their girlfriends was +.56. Men do not seem to differentiate between liking and loving their opposite-sex partner as clearly as women do.

The liking and loving scales showed that the couples loved and liked their opposite-sex partner. In evaluating their feelings about a same-sex friend, the couples showed a high degree of liking and a lower score on loving. This was especially true for men. They made a very clear discrimination between *liking* a male friend (mean score = 78 out of 117) and *loving* a male friend (mean score = 54 out of 117).

Love is experienced as a powerful and mysterious feeling. Friendship may be viewed as positive, comforting, and rewarding. But love may be passionate, intense, and even conflictual. When we love in the passionate sense, there may be great pain and confusion as well as pleasure. Berscheid and Walster (1974) have stated that two conditions are necessary for a person to experience love: (1) the person must be intensely aroused; and (2) the cues in the situation must suggest that love is an appropriate label for those intense feelings. This analysis emphasizes the importance of the person's efforts to actively interpret the situation and to label the arousal state in a way that is congruent with the situation. Feelings of excitement and arousal might be labeled as feelings of passion in one situation and fear in another.

Couples have different expectations for a loving relationship. The more traditional men or women are about their sex-role definition, the more they base their relationships on infatuation and on romantic dependence on the other partner to complete their personality. The traditional view of sex roles portrays men and women as having rather opposite characteristics. Love relationships offer a completion of the missing parts through the blending of contrasting qualities. Men and women who have a more egalitarian view of sex roles emphasize trust and understanding as the basis for love. They do not see extreme differences between males and females. In a love relationship, they look for a friend who will offer support and compassion.

In our own society, efforts to achieve intimacy take many forms. There is a children's rhyme that says, "First comes love, then comes marriage, then comes baby in a baby carriage." Today, the elements can come in any order. Sexuality, love, and marriage are three separate expressions of intimacy. We see experimentation in the rules that govern intimate relationships, the sex and number of partners involved, and movement in and out of intimate relations.

Most people seek intimacy throughout the life span. They satisfy their needs through a number of relationships that vary in intensity. Despite active efforts to maintain some arrangement of intimate bonds, either with one intense relationship or through several different levels of relationship, people continue to suffer from periodic feelings of loneliness. These feelings attest to the depth and centrality of the need for the warmth and support of other people (Kieffer, 1977). Regardless of the mode through which intimacy is achieved, the search for intimacy directs much of social behavior during adolescence and adult life.

Adult Peer Friendships

Adult friendships are varied in nature. Some friendships survive over the years, despite few meetings and many life changes. It is as if the bond of understanding and mutual support lives in the minds of the two friends. Like a cactus that needs minimal watering, the friendship thrives on minimal interaction. Other friendships emerge out of the day-to-day life of the work setting or the neighborhood. These relationships develop because the people are near each other and see each other often (Gamer, Thomas, & Kendall, 1975). They may talk to each other daily, participate in the same social activities, and share contemporary problems. Yet if one or the other is transferred to a new location or buys a home in a new neighborhood the friendship may quickly dissolve. Adult relationships may continue for many years within a work setting and never extend to family or home life. Two physicians, for example, may serve on committees together, see each other frequently at conferences, and keep abreast of each other's research activities. These two consider one another good friends, and yet they may know nothing about each other's family or early history.

Some adult friendships have a more practical nature. Adult friends may support one another's business activities. They may look after one another's children, or check one another's homes during vacations. The friendship has meaning as a resource system that helps the adults meet their obligations.

Weiss and Lowenthal (1973) interviewed men and women at four stages of the life span: high school seniors, newlyweds, parents whose youngest child was about to leave home, and a group preparing for retirement. From the discussions of friendship, five dimensions of a friendship relation were identified:

1. Commonality—shared values, attitudes, and/or activities.
2. Reciprocity—understanding, mutual help.
3. Role-model—ideal qualities, admiration.
4. Compatability—ease and pleasure in companionship.
5. Continuity and proximity—physical closeness and length of relationship.

The most frequent basis for friendship was commonality, but reciprocity was seen as the most desirable basis for friendship. Adults described different friends as serving different functions.

In a survey of over 1,000 California residents, Fischer (1982) described the nature of nonkin networks. As you might expect, the quality of the relationship was related in part to the physical distance between the people involved. Social activities and hobbies are much more likely to be shared with a nearby friend. However, when it came to advice about a really serious matter or asking for a loan, people were just as likely to rely on a close friend who lived far away. Only when the cost of communicating with a distant friend is more than the person can afford or visiting a distant friend is physically more demanding than the person can manage does distance really reduce the possibility of physically remote intimate relationships. This is most likely to be the case for the poor or the elderly.

Men and women have been described as having different types of friendships. In childhood, boys tend to have more friends and friendship is "activity-oriented." Girls tend to have a few close friends, and the friendships focus more on sharing confidences. During adolescence, young women are more likely than young men to emphasize the importance of an intense, intimate friendship in their own personal development (Strommen, 1977). Many young adult men have never had a close male friend with whom they could express affection, doubt, or vulnerability without fearing ridicule (Komarovsky, 1976).

In a study of college seniors, Komarovsky (1976) found that 27 of the 62 men in the sample had their most open relationship with a female confidante. Usually, the young woman was the man's girlfriend. Young men spoke about their willingness to express feelings, fantasied aspirations, and doubts to the female confidante. They valued the fact that the female friend would not exploit their weaknesses or make fun of their wild dreams.

There were 17 males who had their closest relationship with a male friend. Of these 17, 12 were virgins. There was a general relation between sexual experience and the capacity for personal disclosure. Young men who were not sexually experienced also seemed to have less open communication with male and female peers.

Opposite-sex friendships can be both desirable and problematic. In a study of black college students, friendships between the sexes were more intimate than friendships between members of the same sex (Peretti, 1976). Opposite-sex friendships were characterized by more sharing of information about the self, more participation in shared activities, and stronger feelings of reciprocity than same-sex friendships. Male friends can be very important resources when they support the untraditional aspirations of females (Tangri, 1972). We also expect that males may benefit from close friendships with females. In these friendships it is possible for males to share some of their personal thoughts about doubts and weaknesses without being viewed as overly dependent or incompetent. Usually women are more comfortable than men about sharing private thoughts and feelings. Since this makes them more vulnerable to exploitation or rejection, they are likely to encourage male friends to make similar disclosures. If a male friend is able to collaborate with a female friend in the process, it is possible that the male will benefit by increasing his feelings of being understood (Derlega & Chaiken, 1977).

Although friendships between males and females may have some beneficial and satisfying consequences, there are some serious barriers to opposite-sex friendships. If we think of the facilitation of identity formation and value clarification as goals of friendship, then relationships that interfere with these components of personal growth are not in the best interests of the people involved. It is from this standpoint that male-female friendships are most likely to run into difficulties.

Men and women often do not share the same commitment to the equal participation of women in all spheres of cultural life (Roper & Labeff, 1977; Zey-Ferrell, Tolone, & Walsh, 1978). Furthermore, both men and women tend to agree with a stereotyped image of women as less competent, more submissive, and less independent than men (Broverman, Vogel, Broverman, Clarkson, & Rosenkrantz, 1972). Women who reject the traditional female sex role and strive for academic competence or innovative careers will find it difficult to find male friends who really share those values.

Both men and women have stereotypes about the opposite sex that may interfere with the development of a friendship. Women tend to expect that men will have fewer "feminine" characteristics than they actually have (Nicol & Bryson, 1977). Thus, women will expect men to be less supportive, empathic, dependent, or nurturant than the men feel they are. In this sense, women may not be ready to accept or support the interpersonal or emotional qualities that are part of a male friend's personality. In contrast, men have trouble accepting the intellectual challenge of a bright female friend. Despite the growing value in finding a life partner who will provide intellectual companionship, many men have difficulty with heterosexual relationships in which they do not feel superior (Komarovsky, 1973). Such men avoid heterosexual relationships that might threaten their feelings of intellectual competence or they try to turn their female companions into "good listeners." For their part, some women play into the male superiority stereotype by pretending to be less competent or by disguising their abilities. Although this kind of charade is becoming less acceptable among women, it continues to be an expectation that women encounter in academic and work settings. Obviously a productive friendship would not be easy to achieve in a relationship in which one partner had to disguise her intellectual abilities.

Ironically, despite these barriers, many men and women end up with their marriage partner as their closest friend. For men, this outcome results from an inability to achieve closeness among co-workers where competition and the masculine stereotype of stoicism prevent self-disclosure. For women, this outcome results from isolation from adult peers, especially during the childbearing years. Many women also hold a rather negative view of other women. Women often distrust one another, and view each other as uninteresting. These views result in a self-selected isolation among adult women.

With the increased involvement of women in the paid labor force, there are new opportunities for women to achieve friendships outside the family. This may have positive consequences in reducing young women's feelings of social isolation. It may have negative consequences in threatening the exclusiveness of the husband-wife relationship for providing adult confidantes.

Friendship remains a central source of life satisfaction in later adulthood. In a study of 280 adults aged 60 and older, Lowenthal and Haven (1968) reported that the ability to have and maintain a close relationship with a peer is significantly related to the maintenance of high morale, positive psychiatric status, and an absence of depression. Part of the satisfaction of such an intimate relationship probably comes from the values, experiences, and knowledge shared between the two intimates. Particularly when the adult encounters widowhood, friends become an essential component of life satisfaction (Flanagan, 1978). In the following description, we see how important friendship is to the vitality of a vigorous older woman.

> Currently at age 81, J. gives much of her time to her house and grounds. She is an impressive woman, only 5 feet 4 inches tall, but large in build and overweight; with strong features and becoming white hair. She talks endlessly in a loud, raucous voice (she is somewhat deaf) punctuated with occasional ear-splitting guffaws. It is difficult to get a word in edgewise, or to bring the conversation to an end and escape. She is overpowering but consistently good natured and likeable. She rides around on her power mower cutting the grass on her extensive grounds, or rolling the lawn. She drives her elderly friends places in her aged Cadillac (several are younger than she). She has many visitors; and knows hundreds of friends, former students, and business men. She plays bridge regularly. (Hamlin, 1977, p. 22)

The experience of being alone in the later years poses different challenges for men and women. As part of a study of consumer decision-making, Bikson and Goodchilds (1978) reported on the social and situational variables associated with living alone at three ages: young (25–35), young-old (65–74), and old-old (75 and older). Women living alone and both men and women who are still married are in better health and have more regular health care than do men living alone. Fewer single men than the people in the other groups eat their meals at home. This is especially true for the old-old males. In their leisure time, two-thirds of the older men are involved in activities by themselves, whereas two-thirds of the older women participate in social activities. On a three-point scale where one is "most of the time" and three is "hardly ever," men living alone are the most lonely. However, no groups describe themselves as lonely most of the time.

It is interesting to find that older married women were more likely to feel alone than older married men. Often the responsibilities for health care, meal preparation, and decision-making fall on the shoulders of the older married woman. These responsibilities create a more stressful living condition than living alone. For this group, the companionship of marriage is outweighed by the demands of caring for an aging partner. For men, living alone is more lonely and more demanding than being married. Many adult men are not prepared for assuming household tasks in later life. Only 33 percent of old-old males live with a spouse (Glick, 1977). A great majority of older males are struggling with the many challenges of living alone. These challenges include looking for companionship and help in meeting everyday needs.

Cohabitation

In an effort to achieve a satisfying emotional relationship with someone of the opposite sex, some people decide to live together. In Figure 7.2 the pattern of couples living together by age is shown for 1970, 1977, and 1980. In 1970, the largest groups of couples living together were in the two older age groups. Since that time, older couples make up a smaller percentage and the younger couples make up a considerably larger percentage. The age group 25–44 has shown the greatest increase in cohabitation as a life style. The college environment has been the context in which most of the data about living together or cohabitation has been accumulated. In a study at Cornell approximately 30 percent of the students had lived with someone for a period of three or more months and shared the same bed or bedroom (Macklin, 1974).

> Young adults living informally as unmarried couples of opposite sex are still a numerically small group but are increasing at a very rapid rate. Since 1970, the number has more than doubled, rising from 530,000 *couples* in 1970 to 1,137,000 in 1978; or from 1.1 million *adults* in 1970 to 2.3 million adults in 1978; the number rose 19 percent between 1977 and 1978. About two-thirds of these couples lived in the house of the man and one-third in the house of the woman. Three-fourths of the couples were under 45 years of age, but one-tenth included a man or woman who is 65 years old or older. Close to 4 percent of all unmarried adults and 8 percent of all divorced men under 35 were partners in an unmarried couple lifestyle. About 5 percent of all one-parent households, as defined in census reports, included

FIGURE 7.2 Unmarried Couples with No Children Present by Age: 1970, 1977, 1980

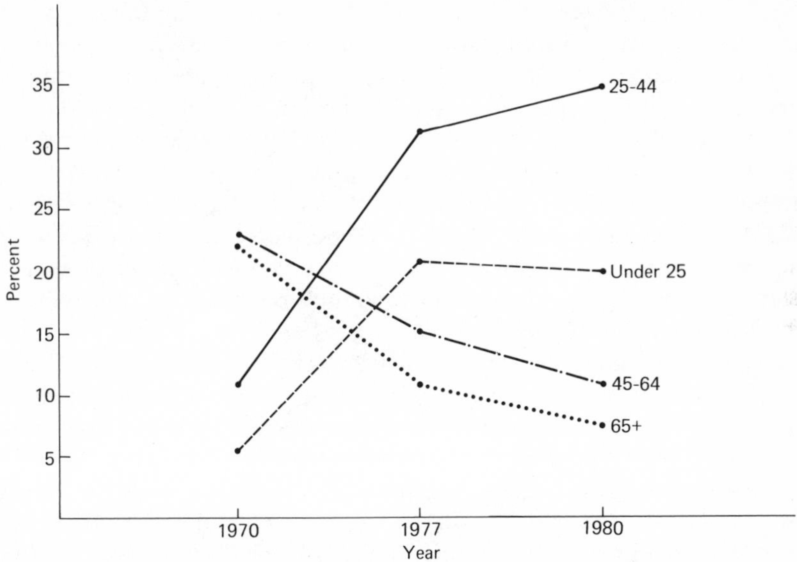

Source: U.S. Bureau of the Census, Current Population Reports, Series P–20, No. 363, *Population Profile of the United States: 1980* (Washington D.C.: U.S. Government Printing Office, 1981).

> an unmarried couple, but in fact some of these households actually included the two unmarried parents of the children who were involved. Among unmarried couples under 25 years of age, the man and woman were more likely to have had college education than their married counterparts. (Glick, 1979, p.5)

When students who had lived together were compared to those who had not, the similarities between groups were striking. Students who lived together and students who were not living together were from similar family backgrounds, showed similar levels of academic performance, and had similar views about marriage. Students who lived together had a general view that they were trying out this form of intimate living arrangement in order to extend a strong sense of emotional closeness they felt for one another. Only a small percentage saw the relationship as leading to marriage.

The experience of cohabitation is clarified somewhat by a national survey of young men born between 1944 and 1954 (Clayton & Voss, 1977). In this sample, 18 percent had lived with a woman for six months or more but only 5 percent were living with a woman at the time of the interview. Cohabitation was more frequent among men who were not in college or who had not attended college than among those who were currently enrolled in college. The youngest of these subjects was 20, so many of them were already past the college years and had attended college when cohabitation was viewed as a serious breach of campus ethics.

The interesting relationship in this national sample was the link between cohabitation and other forms of experimentation. In comparison to those who had never lived with a woman, men who had cohabited were more likely to have lived in a commune, meditated or explored an Eastern religion, tried an organic or vegetarian diet, participated in a political demonstration, studied astrology or ESP, and "bummed around" for a while. In other words, living together can be seen as another expression of the need to experiment with the traditional role expectations of American life. It represents an agreement between both partners to experiment with their capacity for intimacy.

People live together for a variety of reasons. Some people want to avoid the pressures of playing the field. They select a single relationship that offers companionship and sexual expression. They put their energy and thought into this relationship to the exclusion of others.

Some people live together in order to experiment with the complexities of an intimate relationship. They test the limits of physical, intellectual, emotional, and social intimacy. By living together for a period of time, they have the chance to learn about what is involved in close relationships and about their own capacity for intimacy.

Sometimes, men and women with similar interests and limited finances decide to pool their resources and live together. These roommates may not have a deep emotional commitment to one another. Their relationship may not involve sexual intimacy or any notion of social exclusivity. It is friendship and compatibility of life style that make this kind of arrangement practical and satisfying.

Cohabitation is possible at any point in the life span. Men and women enter into cohabiting arrangements after divorce, after widowhood, or as adult singles who do not plan to marry. Living together, whatever the original motive, cannot help but provide opportunities for increased depth and breadth of interactions. For those who are seeking emotional intimacy, cohabitation offers a setting for achieving a sense of closeness. For those who have not established confidence in their own autonomy, the demands of cohabitation may prove threatening. For most partners, cohabitation is a transitional arrangement. It is maintained as long as the sense of mutuality outweighs the demands or conflicts of the relationship.

Intimacy in Marriage

Marriage is the context within which most people work on intimacy and the development of mature social relationships. Glick (1977) provides a comparison of marriage and childbearing experiences of women in their forties over the past 80 years. Of women born in 1940 and 1950, well over 90 percent were married. In fact, fewer adult women remained single in the 1970s than during the period from 1900 through the 1920. The main change in the marriage pattern is that more young adults are postponing marriage until the end of their twenties. In 1960, 69.4 percent of women 20–24 years old were married. In 1978 only 48 percent of women in that age group were married (U.S. Bureau of the Census, 1980). There is, of course, the possibility that among this larger group of single men and women a larger proportion will remain single than has in the past. In this section, we discuss the decision to marry and the process of establishing intimacy in marriage.

The Decision To Marry

While dating, one meets potential marriage partners. What determines whether or not the dating relationship ends in matrimony? One important factor is the readiness of the two individuals for a long-term commitment. Work on identity must be far enough along so that the person does not feel threatened by the possibility of a deep emotional involvement. In a study of the relationship between identity status and the resolution of the crisis of intimacy versus isolation, Orlofsky, Marcia, and Lesser (1973) found that men who had acheived identity reported the most genuine intimate relationships. They also found that men whose identities were confused were the least intimate and most isolated.

In our culture, individuals have a great amount of freedom to determine both the time of marriage and the marriage partner. Given the reality that the expectations to marry are very strong, young adults can at least follow their own timetables. Once the person is ready to choose a marriage partner, the choice is usually guided by similarity in personal characteristics (Barry, 1970) and similarity of social class and cultural backgrounds (Brim, 1968; Rubin, 1973). Most people tend to seek others to populate their private worlds who share their beliefs, values, and life goals.

For some young adults, the possibility of closeness with another person seriously threatens the sense of self. They are unable to make the decision to marry. They imagine intimacy to be a blurring of the boundaries of their own identity, and they cannot let themselves engage in such relationships. People who experience isolation must continually erect barriers between themselves and others in order to keep their sense of self intact. A fragile sense of self results from accumulated experiences in childhood which foster the development of a sense of personal identity that is rigid and brittle or totally diffused. A weak sense of identity requires that individuals constantly remind themselves who they are. They may not allow their identity to stand on its own strength while they lose themselves, even momentarily, in a relationship with another. They are so busy maintaining their identity or struggling to make sense out of diffusion that they cannot attain a sense of intimacy.

Isolation may also be the result of situational factors. A young man who goes off to war and returns to find that the "eligible" women in his town are married and the young woman who rejects marriage in order to attend medical school may find themselves in situations where their desires for intimacy cannot be met. While we may say that the lonely person should try harder to meet new people or should develop new social skills, it is possible that the sense of being isolated interferes with more active coping strategies (Peplau, Russell, & Helm, 1979).

Establishing Intimacy in Marriage

During the early years of marriage, several factors are potentially disruptive to the establishment of intimacy. These include (1) the challenges of the early period of mutual adjustment, (2) the stress caused by the birth of the first child, and (3) the social expectations of members of the extended family.

Once the choice to marry has been made and the thrill of courtship has passed, the first few years of marriage involve a process of mutual adaptation. The young married couple may find it difficult to anticipate the strains that are to come. The partners may be quite distressed to find their "love nest" riddled with the tensions that are part of carving out a life together. Data suggest that the probability of divorce is highest during the first years of marriage and peaks somewhere between two to four years, (see Figure 7.3). After seven years of marriage, 50 percent of those marriages that will end in divorce have already been dissolved (U.S. Bureau of the Census, 1976).

There are many sources of tension early in a marriage. Perhaps the single factor that is most directly correlated with divorce is income. Lack of financial resources may prevent the couple from meeting their expectations for support and protection. Anxiety about meeting basic physical needs may interfere with the formation of a sense of mutuality and emotional security within the relationship (Cutright, 1971; Levinger, 1976). Preoccupation with survival needs makes it difficult for the couple to relax and to enjoy each other's company. If the couple does not share similar religious, educational, or social-class backgrounds, many value decisions will have to be made that involve compromise on the part of each person. Assuming a shared value orientation, certain life-style decisions still generate tension. The couple must establish a mutually satisfying sexual relationship. They must work out an agreement about the expenditure and saving of money. They must respond to each other's sleep patterns, food preferences, and toilet habits. Temperamental differences might generate tension. If one partner is very active and the other is more slow-going, they might have difficulty accommodating to one another's pace. The need to

FIGURE 7.3 Intervals between First Marriage, Divorce, and Remarriage for Men and Women under 75 Years Old in 1975

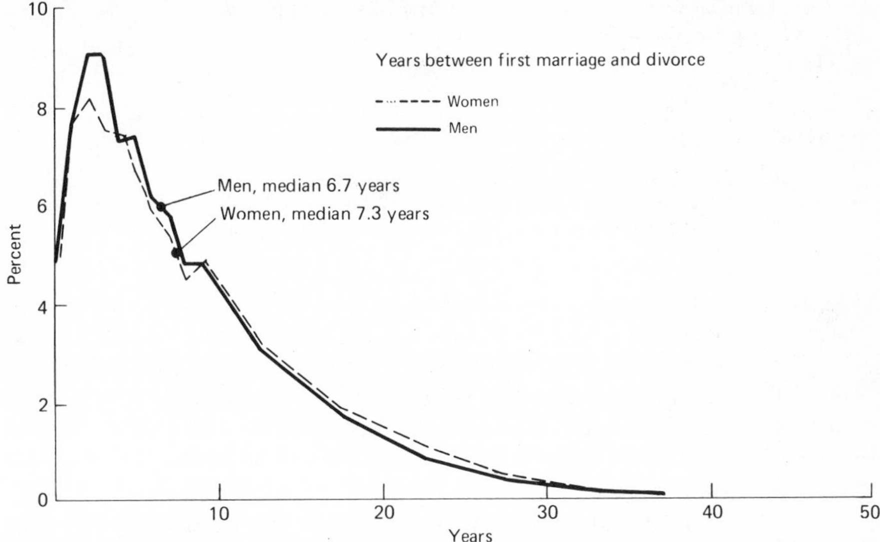

Source: U.S. Bureau of the Census Current Population Reports Series P–20, No. 297, *Number, Timing and Duration of Marriages and Divorces in the U.S.: June 1975* (Washington, D.C.: U.S. Government Printing Office, 1976).

adjust to so many aspects of life-style brings conflict and tension into marriage relationships.

In addition to the matters of behavioral adjustment, the process of psychological commitment also must take place. The marriage ceremony is intended to make that commitment public and binding. Yet the individuals concerned probably do not fully accept the reality of their marriage vows until they have tested the relationship. There is a period of testing during which each partner may put strain on the relationship just to see how strong it really is. The matter can be posed in this way: "Will you still love me even if I do. . . ?" Or "Am I still free to do what I did before we were married?" It is this see-saw between independence and loving that stimulates impulsive behavior during the early years. The marriage must be able to absorb these pressures from both partners in order to survive. Both people must feel that they still have some freedom. They must also feel that the limits on their freedom are worth the love they gain in return.

As each test is successfully passed, the partners grow closer. They trust each other more and they become increasingly sensitive to each other's feelings. The tests diminish as the question of trust is resolved. In a study of trust within an intimate relation (Larzelere & Huston, 1980), people in various kinds of relationships were asked to respond to an eight-item Dyadic Trust Scale (See Table 7.2). For both men and women, trust in

TABLE 7.2 Dyadic Trust Scale

1. My partner is primarily interested in his (her) own welfare.
2. There are times when my partner cannot be trusted.
3. My partner is perfectly honest and truthful with me.
4. I feel that I can trust my partner completely.
5. My partner is truly sincere in his (her) promises.
6. I feel that my partner does not show me enough consideration.
7. My partner treats me fairly and justly.
8. I feel that my partner can be counted on to help me.

Source: "The Dyadic Trust Scale: Toward Understanding Interpersonal Trust in Close Relationships" by R. E. Larzelere, & T. L. Huston, *Journal of Marriage and the Family,* 1980, *42,* 595–604.

the partner was strongly related to love for the partner. The degree of trust varied with the nature of the relationships. Separated and divorced adults expressed less trust for their ex-partners than married adults expressed for each other. Couples who were dating casually expressed less trust than couples who were engaged, newly married, or married for a period over 20 years.

The pattern of trust between married couples was especially high for newlyweds and those married less than 6 years. The trust scores dropped for couples married 6 to 20 years, but was the highest for couples married over 20 years. This curvilinear pattern of trust across the marriage has not been verified by longitudinal research. It may be that couples who do not experience a strong sense of trust do not remain in the marriage. Another possibility is that the group differences reflect cohort differences in the importance of trust in a marriage. A third explanation is that the middle period of marriage involves some active differentiation of the partners that is expressed in a decline in trust.

Studies of the early years of marriage find that the husband is a critical factor in the success of the marriage because of his comparative strength in the relationship. The woman is often the partner who has to adapt most to the new situation. Commonly the woman alters her life-style to suit the career orientation and living habits of her mate.

A study of verbal interaction between newlyweds provides some insight into the process of conflict resolution during the early stages of marriage. Raush and his coworkers (1974) asked couples to role-play conflict situations in which one member of the couple was trying to maintain distance, while the other member was trying to close the distance between them. Conflict was created by telling one partner, for example the husband, that he wants nothing at all to do with his wife that night, that he just wants to be left alone. The wife is told that her husband has been acting very cold and distant and that she has made up her mind to find out what is wrong and overcome this barrier. The partners take turns playing the distant role.

Six categories of verbal behavior were used in the final analysis of interaction: (1) rational arguments, (2) resolution, (3) interpersonal reconciliation, (4) appeals, (5) rejection, and (6) coercion. In couples whose marriages were in difficulty, the husbands were more coercive and rejecting. They were less conciliatory than husbands of happier couples. Wives in the troubled marriages differed little from other wives. In the happiest marriages, husbands were very conciliatory and supportive. Here we see the theme that marital adjustment is the result of the husband's ability to work cooperatively and to give support.

There appears to be a developmental pattern to the management of conflict between the marriage partners. Using the data from the role-playing interactions, patterns of conflict resolution were compared at three early stages of marriage: newlywed, pregnancy, and childbearing. At the initial stage, men were more likely to be rejecting and coercive in maintaining distance and more conciliatory in closing distance. During pregnancy, men were more conciliatory in both roles, while women increased in coerciveness to maintain distance and conciliatory behavior to close distance. Their behavior was like the behavior of their husbands when the couple was newlywed. In the third stage, both men and women increased their use of rational arguments to resolve conflict.

This research suggests that successful husbands must be able to use the "expressive" mode in family problem-solving. Both husband and wife also learn to apply a more logical problem-solving approach as they gain confidence in their relationship. Wives are more likely to be upset by distance during the early years of marriage. As women gain confidence in their personal identity, they can be more direct in engaging in conflict, but, we would assume, they can also be more effective in expressing support and reconciliation.

Reedy, Birren, and Schaie (1981) have studied the nature of the love relationship across the life span. They asked couples to rate 108 statements for the extent to which each statement was characteristic of their own love relationship. Couples were in three age groups, young adult (average age, 28 years) middle adult (average age, 45 years) and older adult (average age, 65 years). All the couples had been nominated by others as being happily married, very much in love, and having a very satisfying love relationship. Figure 7.4 shows the importance of each of six components of love. The components are defined in the table below.

The three groups valued the six components in the same rank order: emotional security, respect, communication, help and play, sexual intimacy, and loyalty. However, as Figure 7.4 shows, there were some differences in emphasis on four of the components. Older lovers valued emotional security and loyalty more and sexual intimacy less than young-adult or middle-adult lovers. Young-adult lovers valued communication more than middle-adult or later-adult lovers. These results confirm the importance of disclosure and communication early in the marriage. As the relationship endures, a sense of interdependence develops. The themes of loyalty and

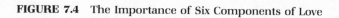

FIGURE 7.4 The Importance of Six Components of Love

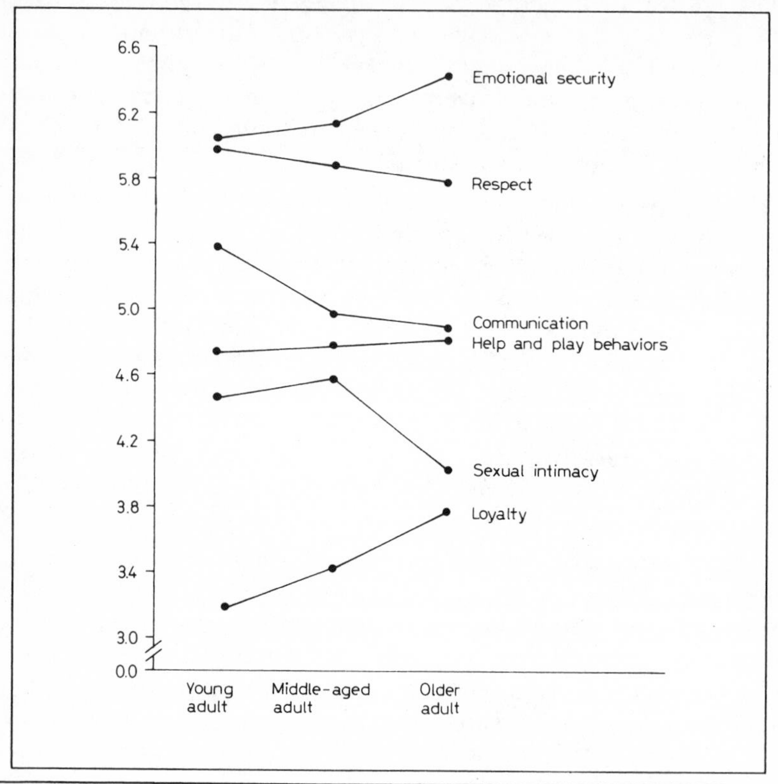

Component of love	Meaning	Sample statement
Communication	honest communication, self-disclosure, good listener	'He (she) finds it easy to confide in me.'
Sexual intimacy	physical and sexual intimacy, excitement, and/or tenderness	'We try to please each other physically.'
Respect	respect, understanding, patience, tolerance	'We share common goals for our lives.'
Help and play behaviors	common interests, shared activities, helpful, supportive	'We spend a great deal of time together.'
Emotional security	affection, trust, caring, concern, security	'I really feel I can trust him (her).'
Loyalty	commitment to the future of the relationship	'The future is sure to be perfect as long as we are together.'

Source: "Age and Sex Differences in Satisfying Love Relationships across the Adult Life Span" by M. N. Reedy, J. E. Birren, & K. W. Schaie, *Human Development,* 1981, *24,* 52–66.

security become more salient as the couple becomes more committed to the survival of their dyad.

Intimacy for Singles

Just as marriage does not guarantee intimacy, being single does not produce isolation. Being single can be a temporary or a permanent lifestyle. One can be single and isolated or single and fully involved in a complex social network.

Since 1970, the rate of first marriages has been declining. Both males and females are waiting longer to marry than they did eight or ten years ago. This is due to several reasons. More women are seeking advanced degrees and are entering the labor force. Males are concerned about being able to earn enough money to begin a family. There are about 5 to 10 percent more females in the age range 18 to 24 than males in the age range 20 to 26. This makes marriage less of an alternative for young women (Glick & Norton, 1977). In addition, current attitudes are more accepting of cohabitation. Couples are more likely to agree to the idea of testing a relationship before making a permanent commitment. There are also fewer limits on sexual involvement outside of marriage. Young adults do not feel the pressure to marry in order to have sexual relations.

Another group of singles are those who have been married and are currently divorced. The majority of people who are divorced remarry. There is, however, an increasing tendency to delay remarriage or to remain single after divorce. It is common for adults to wait three years between their first divorce and remarriage. Thus, some singles are in a transitional phase moving from one relationship to a new, and hopefully more fulfilling one.

The third major group of singles, and one we will discuss further in Chapter 8 are widows and widowers. In contrast to those whose marriage ended in divorce, many fewer adults remarry after having been widowed. In the age group 50 years and over, the people most likely to be living without a spouse are widowed women.

The last group of singles are the people who never marry. This group is small. It includes brothers and sisters who live together, children who continue to live with their parents, men or women who remain single and live independently, and members of certain religious orders. These groups probably have the most unusual lifestyle. They have never married. They are unlikely to have experienced the parenting role. They are a distinct minority.

The opportunities for intimacy among singles can include a wide variety of possible relationships. At one end of the continuum are the interactions among singles that lead to casual sex or "swinging." Roebuck and Spray (1967) studied 30 men and 30 women who were regular customers at a cocktail lounge. While all the women were single, most of the men were married. The women did not seek marriage nor did they want to disrupt the man's marriage. They really came to the lounge for social interaction and to meet someone for sexual pleasure. If they did get married, these women would stop coming to the lounge. The chance to have sexual contact without long lasting social bonds was satisfying for the males and the females. Singles bars, lounges, resorts, and "singles" housing units permit interactions with "ground rules" that limit entanglements. At the other end of the continuum is what Libby (1977) describes as "closed cohabitation." Some singles are intensely involved in a monogamous, exclusive relationship in which finances are shared, time is planned together, emotional needs, and sexual needs are met by the two partners.

Adjustment to being single depends on the needs of the person and on the point during the life span at which one experiences it. In Campbell's (1976) study of life satisfaction, he identified five points about the single lifestyle. First, people who were single were less satisfied with their lives than people who were married. Second, young single women felt that they were under more stress than did young single men. Third, single men over 30 were experiencing greater dissatisfaction than were single women over 30. Fourth, one of the two groups experiencing greatest life stress were divorced or separated women. This group of singles was adjusting to three sources of stress at the same time:

1. The loss of an intimate relationship.
2. The possible feeling that they might be a failure in the spouse role.
3. Sudden increased demands for self-sufficiency, independence, and competence.

Fifth, being widowed was less stressful than being divorced. In contrast to divorced women, widows are less likely to perceive themselves as having failed in the achievement of intimacy. Widows are also less likely to perceive social rejection in the responses of others.

Alternative Relationships

The desire for achieving intimacy remains vigorous throughout life. Just as adults need to find a good match between their competences and their work setting, they also need to find a good match between their capacities to give and receive love and an intimate relationship. Intimacy must be a reciprocal relationship. One cannot be intimate with someone if the person cannot return the intimacy. The many functions that intimate relationships are expected to serve make it unlikely that one form of intimacy will meet all people's needs. In the following sections on remarriage, group marriage, communes, and homosexual love we begin to see ways that adults modify the traditional relationships of friends and marriage partners to achieve their own desired blend of emotional, sexual, and social closeness.

Remarriage

Remarriage is certainly not a new phenomenon. In the early history of the United States it was not uncommon for women to die in childbirth. Men remarried in order to maintain their families and have a partner to help rear their children. Between about 1870 and 1970 the proportion of marriages ending in death or divorce was about the same. During the 1970s, the number of marriages ending in divorce exceeded those ended by death (Glick, 1981). It is estimated that 31 percent of men and 34 percent of women born between 1940 and 1944 will have their first marriage end in divorce. Of every 1,000 women widowed or divorced who are in the age range of 14 to 54, 134 will remarry (U.S. Bureau of the Census, 1980). Fewer adults who are widowed remarry than do those who are divorced.

Remarriage after divorce or widowhood has several challenges. The adults' children may interfere with a couple's efforts to achieve intimacy. In some cases, a parent is tempted to devote more attention to the children than to their new spouse. This is especially true if the parent feels the children have been deeply hurt by the divorce or death. Some children compete with the new spouse for the parent's affection. The new spouse may resent or dislike the children, generating new levels of hostility and competition.

Finances, especially after divorce, can disrupt a second marriage. If the husband is paying alimony, resources for the new marriage may be seriously strained. If the wife is supposed to be receiving child support and does not, her new husband may resent having to assume the expenses involved in the care of her children (Messinger, 1976). Even in marriages among two older adults, perhaps two who have been widowed, the reactions of children and the concerns about managing finances can create conflict. Children are alarmed by the introduction of a new older adult into their lives. Friends may resent a remarriage if it takes a friend away from the peer group. The most obvious benefits of these relationships are the opportunities they provide for companionship, sexual expression, and emotional support. The difficulties of maintaining a remarriage are evidenced in the fact that half the divorces that occur after remarriage occur within three years (Glick, 1979).

There appear to be two rather distinct paths for those adults who remarry after divorce. About 44 percent of second marriages will end in divorce. After a second marriage, remarriage is quite infrequent (Carter & Glick, 1976). For those who experience a second divorce we can surmise that there may be psychological limitations in the person's capacity for intimacy that prevent the appropriate choice of a partner or the effective establishment of a trusting, reciprocal relationship.

For many others who remarry, the second marriage leads to a positive intimate relationship. Following the conficts and stresses of divorce, many adults approach a second marriage with a more realistic, flexible orientation. Studies comparing remarried adults with appropriate comparison groups of first-married, single, or divorced adults find that remarried adults generally have high levels of well-being and self-acceptance, a high degree of satisfaction in their second marriage, and low levels of anxiety or worry (Kulka & Weingarten, 1979).

Group Marriage

In the United States, the most common family type is the monogamous nuclear family. In this kind of family one male and one female marry and live in the same household with their children. Any marriage between more than one member of either sex is called polygamy. While polygamy is unusual in our society, it does represent a kind of marital union that is viewed as normative in 419 of a sample of 554 societies studied by Murdock (1957). There are three varieties of polygamous marriages: (1) polygyny, in which one male has more than one wife, (2) polyandry, in which one female has more than one husband, and (3) group marriage, in which two or more males marry two or more females (Adams, 1975). In each pattern of marriage, there are different opportunities for interaction, children experience different patterns of care, and there are different norms for intimacy among partners. Patterns of interaction created by polygyny have been discussed earlier in this chapter.

Group marriages pose special challenges to intimacy. Since group marriage is contrary to basic social values in this society, people who enter a group marriage must overcome negative social evaluations. The compensating incentives for these relationships include diverse sexual encounters and opportunities to explore nontraditional sex roles. There is considerable pressure to resolve sexual orientations toward same-sex and opposite-sex partners. The ability to handle emotional intimacy with someone of the same sex poses serious problems, especially for men. Feelings of jealousy, competition, and lack of privacy are disruptive to intimacy in a group marriage. In fact, the group marriage appears to be a highly vulnerable form that tends to dissolve within a relatively short time (Constantine & Constantine, 1977).

Communes

The "commune" is a contemporary form of experimental community in which the emphasis is placed upon interpersonal relationships rather than on religious, environmental, national, or utopian goals. Although the atmosphere of the commune may vary, most American communes seem to be committed to experimentation with the definition of the family unit, with forms of education, and with possibilities for shared work endeavors that allow members greater opportunities for leisure time. Communes are usually relatively small in size, ranging from 5 to 25 people. They are located in urban, suburban, and rural settings. Some communes are engaged in re-creating a rather primitive, self-reliant life-style, while others take a more modernistic approach. The unifying theme for modern communes seems to be an attempt to escape interpersonal isolation through the mechanism of material interdependence. The members achieve feelings of closeness by attempting to reduce in-group competitiveness and by placing a high value on openness and acceptance in interpersonal relations (Whitehurst, 1972; Kanter, 1972, 1973).

One of the most striking conflicts that couples living in a commune must cope with is that traditional family boundaries and assumptions are open to other people. There is a dilution of the strength of intimacy and of the intensity of the family group (Jaffe, 1977). Other adults enter into a couple's arguments. Other people are available to meet sexual needs if one member of the couple is not willing. Adults do not always agree about how children should be treated, and parental authority may be challenged by other commune members. With others present, members of a couple are less dependent on one another, have less time alone, and have fewer decisions that they must make together.

Not all couples dissolve after joining a commune (Jaffe & Kantor, 1976). Some find that the reduced intensity and increased flexibility allow each member to grow and to develop a new conceptualization of their marriage. Some couples remain together, but leave the commune. Finally, some couples split up and one or both leave the commune. In some instances, the couple can separate but remain in the commune while they evaluate their own needs. In this sense the commune provides a context for maintaining intimacy with peers when the primary intimate relationship is not working.

Homosexual Love

Homosexuality is sexual attraction to someone of the same sex. We know that during childhood, most children are omnisexual. They express affection and seek pleasure in interactions with their own bodies, interactions with males and females, and interactions with older and younger people. During adolescence and adulthood, people begin to narrow the focus of their sexual and affectional relations to a more limited range of targets. It appears that strict homosexuality and strict heterosexuality emerge as two extremes of sexual expression during adult life. Kinsey, Pomeroy and Martin (1948) reported that 60 percent of men and 33 percent of women experienced at least one homosexual encounter involving sexual play by the age of 15. Approximately 37 percent of men and 13 percent of women reported achieving orgasm as part of a homosexual relationship. However, a much smaller group (only 4 percent of men and fewer women) were exclusively homosexual in adulthood.

It is difficult to know the exact proportion of adults who choose a predominantly homosexual orientation. The estimates range from 2.5

percent of the population to 10 percent of the population depending on the source (McCary, 1978). It is more likely for men to be exclusively homosexual and to begin their homosexual pattern at an early age. For women, bisexuality is more common. Women are likely to experience a sexual relationship with another woman as an extension of a strong friendship. Men are more likely to begin their homosexual relationship with a stranger (Blumstein & Schwartz, 1977).

Exclusive homosexuality and bisexuality are two different patterns that can evolve during adulthood. Exclusive homosexuality is a pattern that is more likely to be developed early in childhood. It can result from a combination of genetic predisposition, puritanical teachings against heterosexuality, and the absence of warm, competent models of the same sex. Once adolescents identify themselves as homosexual, they are likely to feel isolated and rejected. Their subsequent choices of partners will be influenced by their own preferences and by the sentiments of rejection that have come from heterosexual peers.

Bisexuals are more likely to discover their bisexuality during adulthood. This may happen when either a homosexual or a heterosexual person experiments with sexual involvement with a friend. It may result from sexual experimentation like group sex. It may also result as an extension of a liberal philosophy about the open expression of loving feelings. The encounter movement and the women's movement are examples of conceptual orientations that cause people to reexamine their assumptions about sexuality and intimacy.

Homosexuality is a more threatening and disruptive form of sexual expression for men than for women in our society. Although there appear to be two to three times as many male homosexuals as female homosexuals, males have more difficulty integrating their sexual needs in a warm, supportive relationship. Male homosexuals, just like male heterosexuals, are socialized to assume the competitive, assertive, sexually active role. This means that they are more likely than women to encounter conflict in their homosexual relationships (Burk, 1978). Add to this the strain on many men of trying to keep their homosexuality a secret, or trying to remain in a heterosexual marriage while acknowledging a homosexual preference, and the chance of achieving a relaxed, supportive relationship is even more dramatically reduced.

Barriers to Achieving Intimacy

The high rate of divorce, the pattern of increased experimentation with intimate life-styles, and the concerns with isolation, loneliness, and shyness all suggest that intimacy is difficult for adults to achieve. In this section we will consider some of the factors that interfere with intimacy. Our sense is that unless a person makes a strong commitment to nurture intimacy it will not flourish in this society.

Sexuality is a highly conflicted aspect of human functioning in our culture. Guilt about sex, feelings that sex is dirty or harmful, and shame about one's body all limit the openness and depth of a sexually intimate relationship. To the extent that either one or both partners are anxious or conflicted about sex, they will not be able to achieve mutually satisfying sexual interactions.

Intimacy may be limited by the negative experiences of past relationships. Hostility, sarcasm, or ridicule from parents, siblings, teachers, peers, or other important adults may make a person mistrustful of intimacy or lacking in feelings of self-worth. With a past history of shame, rejection, and hostility, it may be hard for a person to allow another to become close.

Even when past experiences are not extremely rejecting, adults may feel that aspects of their personality or thoughts are unacceptable. They feel that they have to hide some things from their closest friends, family, and loved ones. These secrets, whether they involve sexual fantasies or behaviors, illegal behaviors, hostile impulses, or immoral acts, impose limits to openness. They ensure that people can never feel totally understood or supported, since they do not accept these "secrets" themselves.

Life experiences lead adults to different levels of conceptualization. If loving partners encounter prolonged periods when their daily experiences are quite discrepant, they may find that they lose their intellectual intimacy. This happens when one partner travels extensively or becomes involved in complex organizational demands that cannot be shared with the other partner. It happens when one partner's work involves highly technical skill development that cannot be appreciated or explored with the other partner. All of these examples lead to discrepancies in sophistication, complexity, or interest that impose distance among intimates.

We know that the absence of adequate material resources is disruptive to intimacy. When there is not enough money to provide adequate food, shelter, and clothing, to say nothing of luxuries, tension increases. Potential intimates begin to compete with each other for scarce resources. They may squabble, belittle each other, or feel resentful. When there is not enough money, the time that might be spent with one another may be spent trying to make more money. In some cases, a family may feel that they will have access to more resources if the father leaves the family. In this way, the mother and children are eligible for public assistance. This strategy shows the willingness to sacrifice intimacy in order to more adequately meet survival needs.

Intimacy is not always supported by one's social network. At every life stage we see examples of social forces intruding on the formation of intimate bonds. In infancy, jealous fathers compete with babies for their wives' attention. In toddlerhood or early school age, a new sibling may impose physical and psychological needs on the exclusive parent-child relationship. In adolescence, parents set limits on the establishment of intimacy with peers. Peers for their part may compete or intrude on one another's special relationships. In early adulthood, the work setting is a major intrusion into the time and energy available for intimate relations. Add to this the birth of the first child, demands from relatives, and expectations for participation in a network of adult peers, and it is surprising that intimacy has any chance to develop. Even in later adulthood, disruptive social forces are at work. Older adults are self-conscious about their sexual needs. Older women find it difficult to meet suitable male partners since they so dramatically outnumber their male age mates. When couples do meet, peers and adult children often resent the movement toward intimacy and exert pressures to prevent new couplings.

The human species is characterized by diversity in physical appearance, intelligence, talents, temperament, and life history. It is unlikely that one will find a single other person with whom one can feel closeness in the dimensions of physical, intellectual, social, and emotional intimacy. In this sense it is most likely that even successful intimate relationships are deficient in some ways. The success of the relationship may depend on whether the partners can satisfy these needs in other ways without threatening one another or jeopardizing the intimate bond.

The Outcomes of Achieving Intimacy

If intimacy is so difficult to achieve, why do people strive for it? What are the promises that intimacy holds out? The answer is expressed in the songs, the poetry, the novels, and the plays of Western culture. It is both the great affliction and great cure. It is the state of perfect fulfillment.

Intimacy includes deep feelings of comfort and security. An intimate relationship provides a basis of social acceptance and social integration. From this basis, the person who has achieved intimacy can be free to take risks in thought, in communication, and in behavior without being constrained by the need for social approval from the wider group.

The capacity to experience intimacy and to act in a loving way toward others has implications for the total structure of one's social experiences. Vaillant (1977) carried out an in-depth longitudinal analysis of 95 men from their college years through their middle-adult years. Based on interview data, 27 men were described as *friendly.* They had achieved all of the following in their lives:

1. Getting married without later getting divorced.
2. Achieving at least 10 years of marriage that neither partner perceived as painful.
3. Fathering or adopting children.
4. Believing he had at least one close friend.
5. Appearing to others as if he had at least one close friend.
6. Enjoying recreation with nonfamily members.

Thirteen men were described as *lonely.* Only two or fewer of the six aspects of interpersonal involvement were true for them. The friendly and the lonely men were different in a great many other ways. Many of the lonely men had distant relations with their siblings as adults. They were less likely to parent and more likely to be described as distant fathers. Only one friendly man had a chronic illness by age 52. Half the lonely men had chronic illnesses. The lonely were much more likely to seek psychiatric help and medical treatment. The lonely men were likely to approach life with an underlying fear of their vulnerability and of the imagined threats of human closeness. The friendly men were likely to approach life with an underlying joie de vivre, a delight in the pleasures and mysteries of their lives.

Intimacy provides a sense of being understood. When thoughts, feelings, and actions are shared and accepted, the boundaries of the self are less painful. Intimacy protects people from feelings of isolation. It permits a deeper valuation of personal uniqueness because that uniqueness is cherished by another.

Intimacy is a deep emotional commitment. It is not bound by the logic of reason, of time, or of objectivity. People who share an intimate bond are devoted to one another. This means that in spite of failure, social ridicule, or physical disabilities, the intimate partners can expect to find comfort, support, and continued commitment from one another. Over time, those who share in an intimate relationship accumulate a history of mutual support that intensifies their relationship.

Through sharing both the breadth and depth of experience, partners in an intimate relationship have the opportunity to build on one another's ideas. The product of their combined problem-solving and planning are far greater than what each could achieve alone. Commitment in the relationship serves as a source of energy for new projects, for coping with stress, and for directing future life choices. People who care deeply for one another keep one another's needs in mind. They give more of themselves and bring more energy and concern to these relationships. Therefore, they can potentially accomplish more for one another than they might accomplish for an employer, for a neighbor, or even for a parent.

Chapter Summary

Intimacy is defined as the capacity to experience an open, supportive, tender relationship with another person without fear of losing one's own identity in the process. Intimacy produces a shared, subjective reality. It does not need to make sense to anyone else except to those involved. We can think of intimacy as developing along four dimensions: intellectual, physical, social, and emotional. At each level, the openness and breadth of shared experiences contribute to the intensity of the intimate bond.

The capacity for intimacy in adulthood is built on experiences in earlier relationships. These include attachment to a caregiver in infancy, sibling relationships, the feelings of closeness shared in the extended family, and peer friendships. Adult intimacy integrates these earlier experiences with the sexual desires, intellectual competences, and expanded social commitments of adult life. The earlier experiences provide information about how to express affection, whether or not one can expect love from others, and some of the benefits of experiencing closeness with others.

In addition to one's own life history, the capacity for intimacy is influenced by the culture. The ideals one holds about intimacy, the capacity for the expression of feelings, and the targets of affection are all guided by cultural norms. Some of the most salient aspects of culture that have an impact on intimacy include the extent of male-female antagonism, norms about sexual intimacy, norms for spending time with an intimate partner, and directives about who might be an acceptable partner.

The search for intimacy draws people into a variety of social relationships. Today, we see an increased frequency in experimentation in intimate life-styles. Current generations tend to hold greater expectations for satisfaction in all aspects of intimacy. People are willing to redefine sex roles, marriage relations, and family forms in order to achieve the high level of satisfaction they expect. Efforts to achieve intimacy can be seen in adult friendships, marriages and remarriages, cohabitations, group marriages, communes, and homosexual pairings. In each arrangement the quality of intimacy is influenced by the characteristics of each partner, the definitions they have of the relationship, and the support or interference that is provided by their social community. In all attempts to achieve intimacy, there are barriers and obstacles to overcome. These barriers may originate within the partners or from sources outside of the relationship. Regardless of their origins, the barriers to intimacy are not easy to surmount. For some adults, difficulties in achieving intimacy provide the stimuli for new coping and significant psychological growth. For others, barriers to intimacy are never overcome and adulthood is dominated by a pervasive sense of isolation.

References

Adams, B. N. *The family: A sociological interpretation.* New York: Rand McNally, 1975.

Adler, A. *Social interest: A challenge to mankind.* New York: Putnam, 1964.

Barry, W. A. Marriage research and conflict: An integrative review. *Psychological Bulletin,* 1970, *73* (1), 41–54.

Berscheid, E., & Walster, E. A little bit about love. In T. L. Huston (Ed.), *Foundations of interpersonal attraction.* New York: Academic Press, 1974.

Bikson, T. K., & Goodchilds, J. D. Old and alone. A paper for the Symposium on Family Patterns: Social myth and social policy. Presented at the American Psychological Association Meetings, Toronto,1978.

Blumstein, P. W., & Schwartz, P. Bisexuality: Some social psychological issues. *Journal of Social Issues,* 1977, *33,* 2, 30–45.

Brim, O. Adult socialization. In J. Clausen (Ed.), *Socialization and society.* Boston: Little, Brown, 1968.

Broverman, I. K., Vogel, S. R., Broverman, D. M., Clarkson, F. E., & Rosenkrantz, P. S. Sex role stereotypes: A current appraisal. *Journal of Social Issues,* 1972, *28,* 59–78.

Burk, M. P. Coming out: The gay identity process. In B. I. Murstein (Ed.), *Exploring intimate life styles.* New York: Springer, 1978.

Campbell, A. Subjective measures of well-being. *American Psychologist,* 1976, *31,* 117–125.

Carter, H., & Glick, P. C. *Marriage and divorce: A social and economic study* (Rev. ed.). Cambridge, Mass.: Harvard University Press, 1976.

Cicirelli, V. G. Sibling relationships in adulthood: A life span perspective. In L. W. Poon (Ed.), *Aging in the 1980's.* Washington, D.C.: American Psychological Association, 1980.

Clayton, R. R., & Voss, H. L. Shacking up: Cohabitation in the 1970s. *Journal of Marriage and the Family,* 1977, *39*(2), 273–283.

Constantine, L. L., & Constantine, J. J. Sexual aspects of group marriage. In R. W. Libby & R. N. Whitehurst (Eds.), *Marriage and alternatives: Exploring intimate relationships.* Glenview, Ill.: Scott, Foresman, 1977.

Cutright, P. Income and family events: Marital stability. *Journal of Marriage and the Family,* 1971, *33,* 291–306.

Derlaga, V. J., & Chaiken, A. L. Privacy and self disclosure in social relationships. Paper presented at the American Psychological Association Meetings, San Francisco, 1977.

Fischer, C. S. *To dwell among friends: Personal networks in town and city.* Chicago: University of Chicago Press, 1982.

Flanagan, J. C. A research approach to improving our quality of life. *American Psychologist,* 1978, *33,* 138–147.

Freud, A., & Dann, S. An experiment in group upbringing. In R. Eisler, A. Freud, H. Hartmann, & E. Kris (Eds.), *The psychoanalytic study of the child* (Vol. 6). New York: International Universities Press, 1976.

Gagnon, J. H., & Greenblat, C. S. *Life designs: Individuals, marriages, and families.* Glenview, Ill.: Scott, Foresman, 1978.

Gamer, E., Thomas, J., & Kendall, D. Determinants of friendship across the life span. In F. Rebelsky (Ed.), *Life: The continuous process.* New York: Knopf, 1975.

Glick, P. C. Updating the life cycle of the family. *Journal of Marriage and the Family,* 1977, *39,* 5–13.

Glick, P. C. Future American families. *The Washington COFO MEMO,* 1979, 2(3), 2–5.

Glick, P. C. Children from one-parent families: Recent data and projections. Paper presented at the Special Institute on Critical Issues in Education, the American University, Washington, D.C., 1981.

Glick, P. C. & Norton, A. J. Marrying, divorcing, and living together in the United States today. *Population Bulletin,* 1977, *32,* 3–39.

Hamlin, R. M. Restrictions on the competent aged. Paper presented at the American Psychological Association Meetings, San Francisco, 1977.

Howard, G. E. *A history of matrimonial institutions* (Vol. 2). Chicago: University of Chicago Press, 1904.

Jaffe, D. T. The first four long years of a family commune: A case study. In L. R. Allman and D. T. Jaffe (Eds.), *Readings in adult psychology: Contemporary perspectives.* New York: Harper and Row, 1977.

Jaffe, D. T., & Kantor, R. M. Couple strains in communal households: A four-factor model of the separation process. *The Journal of Social Issues,* 1976, *32,* 169–191.

Kahn, R. L., & Antonucci, T. C. Convoys over the life course: Attachment, roles, and social support. In P. B. Baltes and O. G. Brim, Jr. (Eds.), *Life span development and behavior* (Vol. 3). New York: Academic Press, 1980.

Kanter, R. M. *Commitment and community: Communes and utopias in sociological perspective.* Cambridge, Mass.: Harvard University Press, 1972.

Kanter, R. M. (Ed.). *Communes: Creating and managing the collective life.* New York: Harper and Row, 1973.

Kieffer, C. New depths in intimacy. In R. W. Libby and R. N. Whitehurst (Eds.), *Marriage and alternatives: Exploring intimate relationships.* Glenview, Ill.: Scott, Foresman, 1977.

Kinsey, A. C., Pomeroy, W. B., & Martin, C. E. *Sexual behavior in the human male.* Philadelphia: Saunders, 1948.

Komarovsky, M. *Dilemmas of masculinity: A study of college youth.* New York: Norton, 1976.

Kornhaber, A., & Woodward, K. L. *Grandparents/grandchildren: The vital connection.* New York: Anchor Press, 1981.

Kulka, R. A., & Weingarten, H. The long term effects of parental divorce in childhood on adult adjustment. *Journal of Social Issues,* 1979, *35,* 50–78.

Larzelere, R. E., & Huston, T. L. The dyadic trust scale: Toward understanding interpersonal trust in close relationships. *Journal of Marriage and the Family,* 1980, *82,* 595–604.

Lee, L. C. Toward a cognitive theory of interpersonal development: Importance of peers. In M. Lewis & L. A. Rosenblum (Eds.), *Friendship and peer relations.* New York: Wiley, 1975, 204–222.

Levinger, A. A social psychological perspective on marital dissolution. *Journal of Social Issues,* 1976, *32,* 21–47.

Lewis, M., Young, G., Brooks, J., & Michalson, L. The beginning of freindship. In M. Lewis & L. A. Rosenblum (Eds.), *Friendship and peer relations.* New York: Wiley, 1975, 27–66.

Libby, R. W. Creative singlehood as a sexual life-style: Beyond marriage as a rite of passage. In R. W. Libby & R. N. Whitehurst (Eds.), *Marriage and alternatives: Exploring intimate relationships.* Glenview, Ill.: Scott, Foresman, 1977, 37–61.

Lowenthal, M. J., & Haven, C. Interaction and adaptation: Intimacy as a ritual variable. *American Sociological Review,* 1968, *33,* 20–30.

Macklin, E. D. Cohabitation in college: Going very steady. *Psychology Today,* November 1974, *8,* 53–59.

McCary, J. L. *McCary's human sexuality,* (3rd ed.). New York: D. Van Nostrand, 1978.

Mead, M. Grandparents as educators. In H. J. Leichter (Ed.), *The family as educator.* New York: Teachers College Press, 1974.

Messinger, L. Remarriage between divorced people with children from previous marriages: A proposal for preparation for remarriage. *Journal of Marriage and Family Counseling,* 1976, *2*(2), 193–200.

Montagu, A. (Ed.). *The meaning of love.* New York: Julian Press, 1953.

Murdock, G. P. World ethnographic sample, *American Anthropologist,* 1957, *59.*

Neugarten, B., & Weinstein, R. The changing American grandparent. *Journal of Marriage and the Family,* 1964, *26,* 199–204.

Nicol, T. L., & Bryson, J. B. Intersex and intrasex stereotyping on the Bem Sex Role Inventory. Paper presented at the American Psychological Association Meetings, San Francisco, 1977.

Orlofsky, J. L., Marcia, J. E., & Lesser, I. M. Ego identity status and intimacy versus isolation crisis of young adulthood. *Journal of Personality and Social Psychology*. 1973, *27*(2), 211–219.

Peplau, L. A., Russell, D., & Helm, M. An attributional analysis of loneliness. In I. Frieze, D. Bartol and J. Carroll (Eds.), *New approaches to social problems.* San Francisco: Jossey-Bass, 1979.

Peretti, P. O. Closest friendships of black college students: Social intimacy. *Adolescence,* 1976, *11,* 395–403.

Queen, S. A. and Habenstein, R. W. *The family in various cultures* (4th ed.). Philadelphia: Lippincott, 1974.

Raush, H. L., Barry, W. A., Hertzel, R. K., & Swain, M. A. *Communication, conflict and marriage.* San Francisco: Jossey-Bass, 1974.

Reedy, M. N., Birren, J. E., & Schaie, K. W. Age and sex differences in satisfying love relationships across the adult life span. *Human Development,* 1981, *24,* 52–66.

Roebuck, J., & Spray, S. The cocktail lounge: A study of heterosexual relations in a public organization. *American Journal of Sociology,* 1967, *72,* 388–395.

Roper, B. X., & Labeff, E. Sex roles and feminism revisited. An intergenerational attitude comparison. *Journal of Marriage and the Family,* 1977, *39,* 113–119.

Rubin, Z. *Liking and loving: An invitation to social psychology.* New York: Holt, Rinehart and Winston, 1973.

Strommen, E. A. Friendship. In E. Donelson and J. Gullahorn (Eds.), *Women: A psychological perspective.* New York: Wiley, 1977.

Tangri, S. S. Determinants of occupational role innovation among college women. *Journal of Social Issues,* 1972, *28,* 177–199.

U.S. Bureau of the Census. Current Population Reports, Series P–20, No. 363, *Population Profile of the United States: 1980.* Washington, D. C.: U.S. Government Printing Office, 1981.

U.S. Bureau of the Census. *Social Indicators III.* Washington, D.C.: U.S. Government Printing Office, 1980.

U.S. Bureau of the Census. Current Population Reports, Series P–20, No. 297 (October) Number, Timing and Duration of Marriages and Divorces in the U.S.: June 1975. Washington, D.C.: U.S. Government Printing Office, 1976.

Valiant, G. E. *Adaptation to life.* Boston: Little, Brown, 1977.

Weiss, L., & Lowenthal, M. F. Perceptions and complexities of friendship in four stages of the adult life cycle. In *Proceedings of the 81st Annual Convention of the American Psychological Association* (Vol. 8). Montreal, Canada, 1973.

West, M. M., & Konner, M. J. The role of the father: An anthropological perspective. In M. E. Lamb (Ed.), *The role of the father in child development.* New York: Wiley, 1976.

Whitehurst, R. N. Some comparisons of conventional and counterculture families. *The Family Coordinator,* 1972, *21,* 395–401.

Whiting, B. B., & Whiting, J. W. M. *Children of six cultures: A psychocultural analysis.* Cambridge, Mass.: Harvard University Press, 1975.

Zey-Ferrell, M., Tolone, W. L., & Walsh, R. H. The intergenerational socialization of sex role attitudes: A gender or generation gap? *Adolescence,* 1978, *13,* 95–108.

8 The Family

The model of family behavior which emerges from the past is one of diversity and flexibility, a kind of controlled disorder that varied in accordance with pressing social and economic needs. The complexities, conflicts in roles, and variations imposed on individuals in modern society require an even greater diversity and malleability. If nothing else, history offers proof that families are able to display variety and diversity in their organization and timing and to contain conflicts between the needs of individuals and the collective demands of the family under changing historical conditions.

Tamara K. Hareven, 1978

There has been a lot of discussion in recent years about the family. Are American families dying, deteriorating, diversifying, or developing? Our concern reflects the realization that families are the basic social units of a society. In families, cultural norms are transmitted to the next generation. The desire to support and provide for family members is a central motive to maintain a productive work role. Commitment to loved family members leads to commitment to the community where those family members live and grow. Families are a consuming unit of major importance to industry. Families are the clients of elaborate mental health, social welfare, cooperative extension, and educational organizations. The needs of families for all varieties of services keeps large numbers of people employed. Families are the primary supporters of religious, recreational, and educational resources in a community. Through contributions of time and money, family members work to maintain the community's enthusiasm for family-oriented resources and activities.

The purpose of this chapter is to consider the family as a context for adult development. Since family groups differ so widely, we will consider a variety of family situations. The issues confronting families include pressures and demands from forces outside the family group. They also include changing views of family members themselves about what functions the family ought to serve and how best to accomplish those goals.

Definitions of the Family

In order to discuss the family as a context for development, we need to be in agreement about the definition of family. Several distinctions are helpful. First, a family can be defined broadly to include all people who share a common ancestry (Adams, 1975). This use of the term recognizes that a family member may feel bound to people who were never even living during his or her lifetime because of an ancestral tie. The status, reputation, material possessions, or ethnic origins of one's ancestors can influence an adult's own life choices as well as his or her personal definition of a family.

Second, a family is commonly defined as adults who share a household and participate in raising their children. Reiss (1980) stated that this definition of family captures a universal function of the family system. "The family institution is a small kinship-structured group with the key function of nurturant socialization of the newborn" (Reiss, 1980, p.29). Most people begin life in this kind of family. The exceptions are those babies who are raised in an institution. In some cultures, the biological parents do not actually participate in the total socialization process themselves. For example, in Murdock's (1957) sample of 554 societies, 125 societies are described as mother-child households in which the father lives in a separate house. In some of those societies, the father lives far away from the mother and child or may wander away for long periods of time. In two African societies, the Hehe and the Thonga, the grandmother keeps the child from the time it is weaned for a number of years and then returns the child to his or her parents (Stephens, 1963). In both of these examples, however, at least one of the biological parents is recognized as providing care in infancy and is required to supervise the transition phases from infancy to childhood or childhood to adolescence.

Family arrangements can be quite varied. They can include one, two, or more adults in the caregiving role. They can include two or more adults without children. They can include all male, all female, or male and female adults. They can include only the mother, father, and their children, or any arrangement of grandparents, grandchildren, aunts, uncles, cousins, or unrelated adults who participate in household tasks and child care. Within each of these constellations, whether or not the group is in fact a family depends on their own definition of their relationship. Deep emotional commitment, mutual protection, a willingness to provide for one another, and interdependence of the fates of the members are four characteristics that are essential to the psychological sense of family.

The family in which one participates as a child is called the *family of origin.* In the family of origin, we have our first lessons about how one enacts the adult roles of parent or spouse. Our ideas about these important adult relationships are first formed as we observe, listen, and interact with our own parents. Our parents may be models whom we seek to imitate. They may be models whom we overtly reject. They may be models who permit us to have a more realistic sense of our own talents and weaknesses. What is most important is that these early images of adult roles stay with us for a long time. They provide an intuitive basis for later decision-making. Some adults never do question the adequacy or appropriateness of their parents' example. They seek to reproduce their parents' qualities in their own enactment of the parent and spouse roles.

The third definition of family is the *family of procreation.* In the transition from childhood to adolescence to adulthood, we explore the possibility of intimate relations with people outside the family of origin. Eventually, most people make commitments to adult peers to form their own families. It is at this point that adults blend the identifications they have made with their parents with their own aspirations for family roles. Their definition of family will be influenced by their education, their peer group's attitudes about family, and the attitudes of their intimate partners.

In defining the family, adults must decide about the nature of the commitment between the adult partners. They hold views about the appropriate domain of responsibilities of the male and female partners. They usually include a commitment to childrearing and some definition of their parenting style. They have expectations about the relations between the immediate or nuclear family and the extended family. Each of these aspects of the family concept will influence the pattern of interactions, goals, and priorities that constitute the family context in adult life.

Family Styles

There is a great deal of diversity among American families today. In 1978, 44 percent of families fit the traditional expectations where the husband was the primary wage earner and the wife was not in the paid labor force (U.S. Bureau of the Census, 1980). In 38 percent of families, the wife was in the paid labor force. Fourteen percent of families were headed by a woman with no husband present, and almost 3 percent were headed by a man with no wife present. Figure 8.1 shows the change in the percent of family types from 1955 to 1978. In 1955, the traditional family was a clear majority (65 percent), but by 1978 the three other family types made up the majority of families (55.5 percent).

In the following sections four family styles will be discussed: traditional families; two-earner families; single-parent families; and voluntarily childless families. The issues raised about family life-styles over the past decade lead us all to examine our preconceived ideas about the concept of family. Creating a family requires continuous evaluation of personal expectations, attitudes, and goals. The creation of a unique social organization is dependent upon the effective use of resources including time, money, and people.

FIGURE 8.1 Families, by Type, Selected Years: 1955–1978

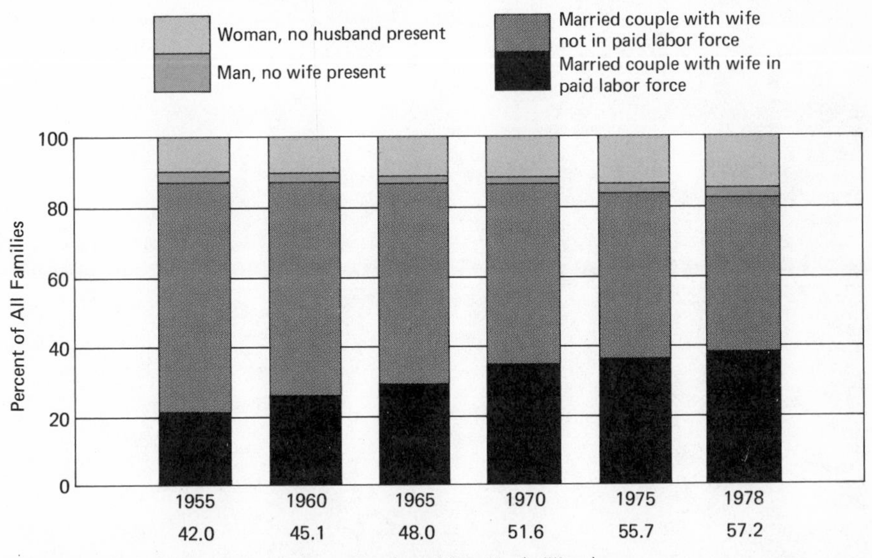

Source: U.S. Bureau of the Census, *Social Indicators III* (Washington, D. C.: U.S. Government Printing Office, 1980), p. 20.

The Traditional American Family

In the traditional family pattern, there has been a clear division of functions along sex lines. Husbands have been viewed as primarily responsible for providing the income to support the family's needs. This usually means that husbands are absent from the home for long periods each day. They may travel away from their hometown. Their success in the husband role is intimately tied to success as a provider. At home, husbands in the traditional family are minimally involved in child care. They may play with the children, teach them skills, or take them to special events like baseball games or on special outings like hunting or camping. Husbands in these families do not commonly assist in meal preparation, grocery shopping, laundry, household cleaning, or other routine chores. They are more likely to handle tasks that require some technical skill, like plumbing or electrical repairs, carpentry, and painting, or tasks that require physical strength, like mowing, snow-shoveling, or gardening.

Wives in traditional families are primarily responsible for caring for children and maintaining the household. Wives may keep the household budget and plan the daily and weekly family schedule. They may be involved in community activities, religious organizations, and their children's school-related activities. However, their primary investment of time

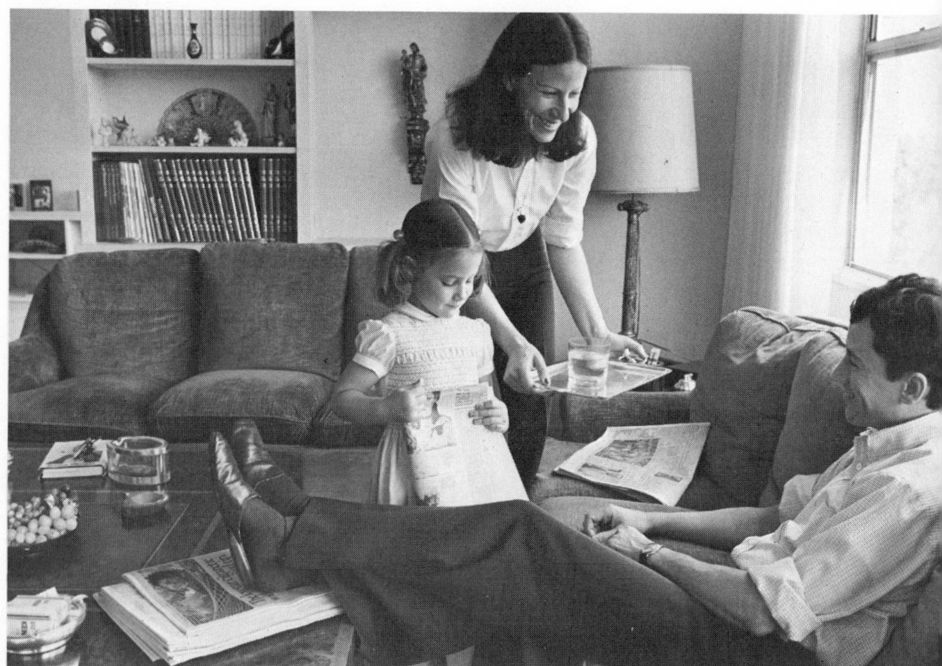

In the traditional family there is a clear division of labor between the sexes.

and effort is focused on the home. Many women also become highly invested in activities that will foster their husband's career (Papanek, 1973). This means providing social occasions for informal interaction with colleagues and being willing to adjust to job transfers, working hours, or special assignments.

Traditional families differ with respect to their pattern of decision-making and the allocation of power to various family members. Three patterns have been identified: the single executive, the adult executive, and the family executive (Newman & Newman, 1979). Each of these patterns will influence the kinds of responsibilities adults assume, the kinds of conflicts or stresses that are likely to arise, and the opportunities for creative family problem-solving. We have found this typology useful in guiding our thinking about family organization and family development. However as with any typology, some individual cases do not quite fit the model.

In the single-executive pattern, one adult assigns responsibility to all other family members. This person reserves the right of final approval on most decisions. The single executive is likely to be the primary source of rewards and punishments in the family, and is therefore likely to be the central figure for identification among the children. Demands upon the single executive are heavy and constant. This adult takes responsibility for family decisions with little or no assistance from others. The blame for poor decisions and family failure comes directly to the executive. If other family members resent the exeuctive's power, they may begin a pattern of criticism, belittling, or open resistance. Dissident family members may blame the executive for their own failures. The adequacy of the single executive rests on the degree to which other family members perceive this person as a legitimate authority and on the executive's ability to obtain accurate feedback from other family members about decisions.

The role of the other spouse in this pattern depends upon the activities that are assigned to that person by the executive. For some people this subordinate role may be quite agreeable, particularly if the single executive is successful in creating an effective home environment. For other people, the subordinate role may be forced upon them. It may lead to a limitation and misuse of their talents. If they are not able to influence the executive directly to redefine their roles, they may engage in subtler, less direct attempts to challenge the executive's authority, or they may leave their marriages. In the single-executive model, the family may be subjected to some of the idiosyncrasies of the executive. If for some reason the executive thinks that six o'clock is the time to eat dinner, then no matter what anyone else in the family is doing, dinner is served at six o'clock.

In the adult-executive pattern, the adults of the household assign responsibility for the tasks of the household. The children are subordinate and are not seen as capable of making decisions. In most cases the adult executive is really a husband-wife executive. In some cases, however, when a grandparent lives in the household, the adult-executive pattern may include more than the husband and wife. In either case, the process of assigning responsibilities and allocating resources becomes a group decision in which adults are involved. Group decisions require discussion, compromise, open conflict, consensus, and mutual respect. Occasionally decisions will be made that do not exactly reflect the opinion of one of the adult executives. The adults come to value the process of joint decision-making more than the individual feeling of being right every time. The adult-executive pattern is somewhat slower in its functioning than the single-executive pattern. Decisions are likely to be less impulsive and less idiosyncratic. More diverse opinions, suggestions, hypotheses, and courses of action are aired in the process of assigning responsibility. There is the opportunity for one of the decision makers to rest from time to time, without fear of the family's malfunctioning. The blame for misjudgments and incorrect decisions is shared. The exclusion of the children from the spheres of responsibility may bring some dissident response from them, including requests for participation. The psychological impact of these demands are shared, rather than resting upon a single individual.

The adult-executive pattern is probably the one most characteristic of the American family pattern (Adams, 1975). The nature of this "egalitarian" decision-making system is quite a bit more complex than one might assume. First, egalitarian attitudes do not always result in equal sharing of behaviors or responsibilities (Araji, 1977; Nye, 1976). For example, in many families the husband and wife believe that housework should be equally shared, but in fact the wife does most of it. Similarly, many couples feel that both the husband and wife should share the responsibility of providing income for the family, but men tend to be the primary providers. Second, in many families decision-making is tied to specific behaviors or activities. Thus even if the husband and wife share in decision-making, actual decisions are divided among the adults so that the wife has her domain and the husband has his (Douglas & Wind, 1978). Even in families where there is a high degree of joint decision-making, the male is likely to be more influential in decisions about purchasing liquor, tending the lawn, or choice and use of credit cards, while the wife is likely to have major involvement in shopping for food and doing the dishes.

In other words, attitudes about the value of shared decision-making and consensus are difficult to operationalize. Many factors, including traditional perceptions of sex-typed behaviors, discrepancies in the resources of the partners, and the number of people who are actually involved or influenced by the decision, will determine how a decision is reached and who ends up having primary responsibility for related behaviors. It is important to note, however, that even in families where men are the main income providers, the cultural norm operates to encourage them to share decision-making responsibilities. In this sense, power is not strictly tied to the person who brings in material resources. In the interest of maintaining an intimate relationship and for the benefit of an efficient home setting, husbands and wives commonly negotiate a sharing of family authority.

In the family-executive pattern, all members of the family share, as they are able, in the assignment of responsibility for family tasks. The problems are posed to the entire family, children included, and each person has an opportunity to offer opinions, suggestions, and solutions. When the children are very young they may be asked to participate in those decisions about which they are likely to have an opinion—where to go to dinner, whom to call for a baby-sitter, and what to do on a Sunday afternoon. While the adults may feel initially that they are extending executive responsibility to the children at their own discretion, the children quickly come to feel that they should be legitimate participants in all family decisions.

The family-executive decision-making process is probably the most cumbersome of all models because it requires consensus among people at varying levels of cognitive and emotional development and experience. However, such a process provides the family with the benefit of the child's unique point of view. Occasionally, a child's solution to a family problem or decision is better than any of the adults' solutions. In most cases, the family executive is highly influenced by the opinions of the adults, but the presence of the children in the executive group ensures that decisions are made with maximal attention to the needs of everyone. In this pattern the adults may need a great deal of patience and commitment to the format. The children have the advantage of learning about issues of decision-making, assigning and accepting responsibility, planning, goal-setting, and evaluation throughout their lives.

Each of these patterns provides the adult with significant areas of learning during the adult years. The single executive learns to make decisions, to shoulder the responsibility of those decisions, and to feel the personal satisfaction that comes from providing one's family with a good home. The adult-executive pattern calls for mutual decision-making and compromise. It makes equal use of the skills of both partners in the marriage. Success in the adult-executive pattern of decision-making strengthens the bond between the marriage partners as they grow more confident in their efforts. Satisfactions and responsibilities are shared in this arrangement. The family-executive pattern requires that the adults learn to be teachers as well as decision makers. They must learn to think out loud so that the children can begin to appreciate the complexity of the decisions as they are being made. Adults must also be ready for unexpected solutions to problems and be able to admit when these solutions are better than their own. The family-executive model probably has some short-term costs in efficiency, but it also provides the greatest long-term gains in group cooperation and mutual enhancement.

The Two-Earner Family

An estimated 38 percent of American couples participate in a dual-worker life-style. This includes adults who are involved in occupations that require special training, graduate degrees, and continuous career development. These couples are sometimes referred to as dual-career families (Bryson & Bryson, 1978). It also includes adults who are involved in semiskilled or unskilled jobs. These couples are sometimes referred to as dual-worker families (Rapoport, Rapoport, & Bumstead, 1978). The difference between dual-career and dual-worker families is primarily one of earned income and job opportunities. Low-income families have been living the dual-worker life-style for a long time. During the 1950s and '60s the cultural norm was to admire the unemployed wife as a sign of status. If a woman did not work it was evidence that her spouse could afford to support her. Today, more well-educated women have chosen to enter the paid labor force. They see occupational involvement as an expression of their personal identity. What is more, the economic pressures of inflation have made the single-earner life-style less possible even for those in higher-paying white-collar and professional careers.

The dual-worker pattern may be permanent or temporary. It may emerge later in the marriage after a period when the wife had not been employed. Couples manage the patterns of work and home life in various ways. Some couples are away from home during the same period of the day. If the couple have children they rely on baby-sitters or day-care services to care for the children in their absence. Of course, this means that some significant amount of the adults' income may have to be used to pay for child care. Other adults alternate working hours, one working day shifts and the other working evening or night shifts. This strategy avoids the need for child-care arrangements but gives the couple fewer opportunities for interaction. Another strategy is to share a single position (Arkin & Dobrofsky, 1978). In academic settings this would mean dividing the work load for one faculty member between the two adults. This strategy permits each one more leisure time or more time to pursue personal work activities. A third arrangement is the commuter couple (Gross, 1980). Some adults have full-time work commitments in separate locations. They come together only during vacations or nonworking days.

In the face of rising inflation, the dual-income family has become an increasingly common option. Many young people anticipate that they will enter a marriage in which both partners work full-time. Many young women deliberately delay marriage until they are established in their own careers. Especially those women with a college education are likely to plan to remain single longer in order to develop a strong foundation for a life-long career (Cherlin, 1980). In fact, for couples who begin their marriage while both are working, the decision to give up one income in order to have a child or for one partner to return to school becomes more and more difficult as the cost of living continues to rise. In a recent interview with 25–

year-olds who were in the business world, *Fortune* magazine found that the dual-wage couple was heartily enjoying its affluence and looking forward to greater rather than fewer monetary resources. "Dennis Eshleman, an associate product manager with General Foods, and his wife Kathy, a paralegal, earn about $45,000. Eshleman calculates they would have to sell the two-bedroom house they just bought in Eastchester, New York, if she quit work now to raise children. 'That would be a big adjustment,' he says. 'I'm willing not to have a family if it disrupts my wife's career' " (Kinkead, 1980).

The effects of the dual-worker pattern on marriage, family life, and adult development depend on two factors. First, what are the natures of the work settings where the two workers are involved? Handy (1978) has described some work settings as "greedy occupations." These occupations demand involvement that extends beyond the 40–hour work week. They may draw mental energy, involve whole families in a social network, and require travel or prolonged separation from the family. Most managerial positions are of this type. So are private businesses in which the success of the business can be directly related to the amount of time one devotes to its development. Certain service occupations have this "greedy" quality, reaching out beyond the office to the person's interactions in other parts of the community. Think of the life of a religious leader. Is there a single interaction that is not touched by the recognition on the part of others that this person is a rabbi, a priest, or a minister?

Greedy occupations become entwined with the worker's sense of self. It becomes impossible to separate the person who plays other roles as spouse, parent, or community member from identification with the worker role. Norms and goals of the work setting can become the norms the person holds for his or her own adult behavior. Success as an adult comes to mean success within the framework of the world of work.

In contrast, some work settings are not so greedy. Commitments are limited to the hours of employment. There is no expectation for the worker to represent the work setting in the community. The work setting does not demand allegiance from the family, and workers are free to be as involved or uninvolved with their co-workers as they wish. A worker may develop a sense of loyalty to the boss or the organization, but high commitment is not necessarily an expectation of the job. In these occupations the adult is free to establish his or her own norms about what it means to be a successful adult. The world of work does not cover a broad enough range of commitments to set the framework for adult maturity.

The second factor influencing the impact of work on the two-earner family is the nature of the individual worker, and the pattern of motives that dominate his or her work involvements. Individuals can be described as having needs for achievement, needs for companionship and support, needs for nurturance, needs to avoid failure, needs for power, and so on. The impact of the dual-worker experience depends on the extent to which certain needs have priority over others. Does the person have a stronger need for achievement than for nurturance? Can more motives or more important motives be satisfied by the work setting than by the family setting? We must understand not only the motives of one worker, but how the two workers' motives interact. It is possible that husband and wife both work, but that one is more focused on meeting achievement needs while the other is more concerned about companionship and support. For some couples, the work involvements of each are higher priority than the needs they have for support from one another. For still other couples, support and nurturance dominate achievement needs for both partners. Family and marriage take priority over work commitments.

BOX 8.1 CASE: Linda Francke: The Dual-Career Dilemma

Take *Newsweek* life-style editor Linda Francke: She recently took a nine-month leave of absence from the magazine because as a wife and mother she was heading for disaster. "I had been working for *Newsweek* for four years, and it was increasingly difficult to do cover story after cover story and keep any contact with the children [two girls, five and seven, and a boy, twelve]. The magazine comes out every week come hell or high water. . . . I realized I didn't even know if the children could swim. Someone else was nursing them. . . . We had a New York apartment and a weekend house which I loved and never saw."

The apartment was run on determination, courage, and vitamin C; there was a live-in, five-day-a-week nurse—at an outrageous salary—who took care of the kids and the wash, plus a cleaning woman. But at night, when Linda and her lawyer husband, Albert, would come home late, after the children had been fed, "there was rarely any food left. We would nibble leftovers because I had forgotten to defrost things or it was too late to cook." We even tried getting a Crock-pot, thinking it was the answer. We filled it with stew one morning and then never came home to eat that night. That was the last time we used it."

Her husband, she says, "was tolerant—to a point. Three times a week, it seems, we discussed who was more tired and harassed. I was burnt out. The household was my ship. My husband helped in many ways—whoever had the easier day took on more. Did I give up making beef Stroganoff? No, because I never made it. I was never Helen Housewife. Both of us really needed a wife."

Because of her workload, she says, she "just got more organized. One year I was so organized, I delivered the children to school 24 hours early."

What was Linda's solution? Not what former generations of mothers would have chosen. She didn't automatically drop out when the going got rough. She conceived a way to continue her career and be with her children, too. Francke got herself an advance of $20,000 from Random House for a book about abortion and happily withdrew to the country with kids and caboodle. "Now I live in the country and my husband stays in New York, and we get together on weekends. I love it out here. Today I got up at 6:30, the first time I've had breakfast with the children. I read in the paper today about a bash at Bloomingdale's. I was so happy I didn't have to go. . . ."

Linda Francke hasn't given up her career. She's just found a way-however temporary-of coping. The trade-off is less time with her husband.

Today more and more women are confronted with Linda Francke's problem. But they're not going back to the old solutions. It used to be there was a right way and a wrong way. But today there is no single way. Each couple has to work out its own solution. But as long as this society's support systems are inadequate—as long as there is no decent day-care system, no simple way of finding competent and trustworthy household help, and no backup from employers, women who want it all—marriage, career, and children—will have to fact facts; they've got to be superwomen.

Source: "The Dual-Career Dilemma" by J. Kron, *New York,* October 25, 1976, pp. 38–39.

The conflicts of the dual-worker experience are greatest when occupations are "greedy" and motives of the worker are not complementary. In the case of Linda Francke, the lack of complementarity began to lend a feeling of total family neglect. There are many complementary solutions. Both partners can place high priority on achievement, both can place high priority on companionship, or both can agree to allow one member to move outward in the areas of achievement and power while the other retains a more restrained work involvement. However, if one partner sees a greedy occupation as preventing his or her needs for support and companionship from being met, conflict will occur. Similarly, if one partner sees the other partner's needs for support and nurturance as preventing his or her needs for achievement and power from being satisfied, conflict will occur.

There has been some suggestion in the literature that women's increased participation in the labor force will result in marital disruption. Locksley (1980) examined this question using data from a large national study of perceptions of well-being carried out during 1976. Dual-worker families were compared to single-worker families with respect to marital adjustment and marital companionship. Table 8.1 shows the items that reflected adjustment and those that reflected companionship. Neither male nor female responses indicated that dual-earner marriages differed from single-earner marriages on these two general dimensions of adjustment and companionship. This finding was true regardless of the kind of work the woman did or her level of interest in the work.

A study of women who received high-level graduate degrees (Ph.D., Ed.D, M.D., D.V.M., D.D.S., and J.D.) during the period 1964 to 1974 confirmed the finding that employment status of women does not in itself account for marital adjustment (Houseknecht & Macke, 1981). This study looked at women's responses only. No significant differences in marital adjustment were found between the employed and not-employed women. Certain signs of support on the husband's part for the wife's educational and career goals do contribute to the woman's perceived marital adjustment. Women who have had to quit their jobs frequently for the husband's

TABLE 8.1 Indexes of Marital Adjustment and Companionship

A. Global Adjustment Indices
   1. Marital happiness
   2. Ever had a problem with marriage
   3. Ever felt inadequate as a spouse
   4. Ever felt inadequate as a parent
   5. Frequency felt irritated with spouse's behavior
   6. Frequency felt upset about sex
   7. Frequency felt tense from fighting
   8. Frequency work interfered with marriage

B. Companionship Indices
   1. Spend leisure time mainly with spouse
   2. Frequency chatted with spouse in last two weeks
   3. Frequency physically affectionate
   4. Frequency wished spouse talked more about thoughts and feelings
   5. Frequency wished spouse understood you better
   6. Marriage like two separate people or like couple

Source: "On the Effects of Wives' Employment on Marital Adjustment and Companionship" by A. Locksley, *Journal of Marriage and the Family,* 1980, *42,* 337–346. Copyrighted 1980 by the National Council on Family Relations. Reprinted by permission.

career show lower adjustment scores. Women whose husbands have moved to enhance their career show higher adjustment scores. One might wonder if men would show just the opposite pattern.

The challenge in the dual-worker family is to clarify each partner's commitments to the roles of spouse, parent, and worker. Adults have to claim their priorities and make decisions about time, involvement, and resources that reflect those priorities. Of course, the relative involvement in these roles will change during adulthood. There will be predictable periods that call for a realignment of commitments from both workers. However, if the experiences of the two workers are to add depth to the family there have to be some ground rules that promise to meet the needs of both partners.

Single-Parent Families

In 1978, one of every five families with children under 18 was headed by a single parent who had either been divorced, separated, widowed, or never married (Waldman, Grossman, Hayghe, & Johnson, 1979). Of these 5.7 million families, only 540,000 were headed by fathers. The number of one-parent families increased about 2 percent from 1960 to 1970 and about 8 percent from 1970 to 1978. There can be no question that one family style that will be with us over the coming decade is the single-parent family.

At the present time, the greatest stress on the single-parent family is the lack of financial resources. Twenty percent of all single-parent families and 40 percent of those headed by women are below the poverty line. The average income of one-parent families with working mothers was only 35 percent of that of two-parent families. Most single-parent families do not have a second wage earner. Since so many heads of single-parent families are women, they also suffer from the comparative wage inequities of all women workers.

In addition to the lack of financial resources, single parents suffer from social isolation and continuous pressure to meet the needs of their children. The conflict about leaving their children to go to work usually includes the concern about suitable child care or supervision and the fact that the money earned at work is not adequate to cover the costs of child care and family needs (Schlesinger, 1977). On the other hand, staying at home and relying on fluctuating, noncontrollable funds tends to erode the women's sense of efficacy and locks her into a cycle of helplessness (Bould, 1977; Feldman, & Feldman, 1973).

A study of decision-making in female-headed families described some of the difficulties that may arise in this family structure (Bleckman, 1977). First, in discussions about problems, the parent tended to focus on the task and the children tended to express more of the emotion. This was even more true in large than in small families. This means that there may be fewer opportunities to learn the skills of task-oriented decision-making in one-parent families. Second, when parents were task-oriented, children tended to be positive and friendly. When parents were less task-oriented, children expressed more hostility. This suggests that children have learned how to function cooperatively in a decision-making situation by acting supportive and not interfering with the task. However, when there is no clear decision at hand, hostility is likely to bubble out. Third, as families continued to talk over three sessions, the sessions grew more hostile and less task-oriented. In these families, the single parent who led most of the task-oriented conversation became the object of more and more angry feelings as the conflicts were repeatedly raised. Especially in the area of recurrent conflicts, the single parent becomes the brunt of angry feelings that no progress or understanding is being reached.

Despite the many difficulties encountered in single-parent families, this is a family style that is likely to persist. Some adults want to have the experience of caring for a child even if they have not found an adult with whom they wish to share an intimate relationship. Adolescent pregnancies continue at a high rate, and increasingly more young mothers are deciding to keep their babies. After a divorce, many parents report that they and their children are happier without the tension of a conflictual relationship. They may all prefer to prolong the calm and relative predictability of a one-parent family than to risk a new relationship.

Being a single parent is undoubtedly a tremendous challenge for any person. One must function in many roles, take on the full range of home and work responsibilities, and fight off the doubts that the child suffers from the parent's absence, the parent's presence, the absence of the parent's partner, or the presence of new partners. A lot depends on the

As the movie Kramer vs Kramer suggested, the single parent must cope with a number of role demands, some of which are in conflict.

adult's resources, especially educational background and job training. Under ideal circumstances one could find that the pressure to function as such a total person with few opportunities to relegate life tasks or responsibilities to someone else might produce a more fully human adult.

Voluntary Childlessness

A third variation on the traditional family constellation is voluntary childlessness. Some adults make a deliberate choice to remain childless. Among women who want to remain childless, there is greatest agreement about the view that childlessness has the advantage of freeing one from responsibilities that might interfere with self-fulfillment (Houseknecht, 1978). Other advantages of childlessness include fewer restrictions on career aspirations, freedom from economic costs, greater marital satisfaction, and freedom from the long-term problems associated with childrearing. Adults who do not wish to remain childless do not agree about the advantages of childlessness. In fact, there appears to be some overall consensus that childlessness is not an advantageous state; most people consider having children a factor that adds meaning to their lives, enhances a marriage, and offers some protection against loneliness in later adulthood (Blake, 1979). To express a strong commitment to childlessness, then, requires a high degree of personal autonomy. It also requires a social support system that promises to compensate for the sense of connectedness and meaning that are viewed by most adults as benefits of having children.

What do we know about the adjustment of adults who remain childless? Do they suffer from the negative consequences that those who desire children might anticipate? Evidence to date suggests that childlessness is a viable, personally satisfying option. When childless women were compared to a matched sample of women with children, childless women scored significantly higher in overall marital adjustment (Houseknecht, 1979). Childless husbands and wives were especially more likely to report that they shared outside interests with their spouses and that they had more frequent exchanges of stimulating ideas (Feldman, 1981). Childless women were more likely to discuss things with their husbands and to collaborate on projects with them. All these examples suggest that childless women may have a greater total investment in the lives of their spouses than do women with children.

Other studies have looked at the ego development or level of maturity of childless men and women. Brown and Magarick (1978) compared the level of adjustment of childless men who had been voluntarily vasectomized with fathers who had been vasectomized. No differences in adjustment or recollections of childhood happiness were found between the two groups. The childless men were more independent, less tied to tradition, and more flexible than the fathers. A similar comparison of childless women and mothers found the childless women to be more self-reliant, and assertive and to place a high value on personal freedom (Silka & Kiesler, 1977). Welds (1976) surveyed 590 professional women between the ages of 30 and 40 who had been in *Who's Who of American Women.* She found no differences between women who were mothers and those who were childless in the achievement of a sense of generativity or in overall ego development. She did find that women who were uncertain about their family size and who had not firmly resolved whether or not they would remain childless had higher anxiety and lower productivity than those who had decided one way or the other.

We have some evidence that parents and nonparents differ in how important parenthood is to achieving adult status. Parents frequently view parenthood as a life event that marks entry into adult status. Nonparents are more likely to see being self-supporting as marking the time when they felt most like an adult. For nonparents, there is clearly a different pattern of priorities and transition markers that guide progress through adult life.

No work we have seen on voluntary childlessness compares parents and nonparents on the dimensions that might be expected to be enhanced

Three systems of family life stages

Duvall (1971)	Hill (1965)	Spanier (1979)
I Married couple	I Establishment (newly married-childless)	I Couples married less than 6 years, with no children
II Childbearing families	II New parents (infant—3 yrs.)	II Oldest child less than 6
III Families with preschool children	III Preschool family (child 3–6 and possibly younger siblings)	III Oldest child between 6 and 12
IV Families with school children	IV School-age family (oldest child 6–12 and possibly younger siblings)	IV Oldest child between 13 and 20
V Families with teenagers	V Family with adolescent	V All others with at least 1 child present
VI Launching families	VI Family with young adult (oldest 20, until oldest leaves home)	VI All others with no child still present at home
VII Empty nest to retirement	VII Family as launching center (from departure of first to last child)	VII No children in home and husband 65 or over
VIII Retirement to death (aging families)	VIII Postparental family, The middle years (after children have left home until father retires)	
	IX Aging family (after retirement of father)	

through parenthood. For example, we have no evidence about the quality of nurturing behaviors, the capacity to provide a stimulating environment, the ability to interpret nonverbal behavior, or the ability to explain or help in problem-solving. We would expect that there is an array of competences that are stimulated by the demands of parenting that probably would not be developed to the same degree in nonparents.

Family Stages

The notion that families develop through an orderly sequence of stages has been an appealing and convenient approach to studying family systems. If families change over time, then these changes would most likely prompt changes in the competences of the family members. Of course, it could also be argued that changing adults create changes in families. As adults get older they bring different perspectives to the family group and have different needs that they try to satisfy. If families change over time, it is most likely a product of the reciprocity of influences among changing family members that promotes group development.

Several models of family stages have been proposed by students of family development. Three different schemes are presented in Table 8.2. They give a sample of the kinds of transitions that seem to make a difference in family functioning and family needs. As one compares these systems, it is clear that a central role in family stages is played by the maturation of the children. The implication, of course, is that it is the children's changing needs and competences rather than the adults' that stimulate changes in interaction, activity, and values. In each of these stage systems, at least three variables are confounded: length of marriage, age of adults, and presence of children. For families with children, it is simply not possible to disentangle these three components. However, it is possible that for some issues it makes more sense to consider adult age as a determining factor in understanding family change whereas in other matters the stage of the children is the key factor (Nock, 1979).

In the following analysis of changing family roles, the emphasis is placed on the impact of certain family transitions on adults. The sequence suggests a developmental framework. However, we know that individual adults may experience widowhood before grandparenthood, they may make a decision to marry after having had a child, or they may be a grandparent and also the parent of an adolescent. What follows, then, are some of the new challenges and potential opportunities for adult development in six significant family transitions: the decision to marry; childbirth; parenting adolescents; the departure of children from the home; grandparenthood; and widowhood.

The Decision To Marry

Of the many people we interact with over the course of time, what is it that draws two people into a relationship that leads to marriage? What factors account for this decision to make a major emotional commitment to a comparative stranger? We must look in two directions in order to understand this outcome. First, there are the factors that make a person feel ready to marry. Second, there are the factors that make another person attractive as a marriage partner.

For some young adults, readiness for marriage is a response to the "social clock." Within the social class, there are expectations about the best age for marriage. For working-class groups, the ideal age for marriage is between 18 and 22. Those who are dating seriously during high school are likely to marry soon after graduation. Once young working-class adults move past the age of 23 or 24, they find the pool of eligible partners significantly reduced, and their anxiety about finding a mate increases

(Gagnon & Greenblat, 1978). Young people who attend college tend to have a slightly later timetable for marriage. Men are expected to marry somewhat later than women. If a young woman is still single at 25, the family looks at her with questioning eyes. A male can remain single a bit longer, but by 30 the glances turn to him.

Readiness for marriage may be tied to achieving a specific goal such as finishing college, completing military service, or earning a certain income. Some cultures look at marriage as a major transition into adulthood. One marries in order to demonstrate to peers and to adults that one is ready to assume the adult role. Cross-cultural research has found a relation between social origins, educational level, and timing of the first marriage in many Asian societies (Smith & Karim, 1978). Women from rural settings marry earlier than urban women. Buddhist and Confucian women, whose religious teachings suggest a more traditional role for women, tend to marry earlier than Christian women. Finally, age at marriage is closely tied to educational attainment. Among Korean women, college-educated women married at an average of six years later than women with no formal postsecondary schooling (Kim & Stinner, 1980).

In Chapter 7 we suggested that work on identity is very closely tied to the decision to marry. For some, identity is so fragile and ill defined that an intense emotional commitment only threatens to dissolve it further. For others, marriage promises clarification of identity. A young girl may trade the uncertainty of her adolescence and the difficulty of trying to create an identity by stepping into the role of wife. Not so long ago women generally felt that it was ill advised to work too hard on personal identity until a marriage partner was selected. At that point, the man would provide the content and clarification that the woman lacked. Women would shape their own identities around the status and competences of their husbands (Douvan & Adelson, 1966).

The failure to establish a sense of personal identity is one reason why young marriages have so poor a chance of surviving. In addition to the lack of resources and the frequent addition of a young infant, there are strains caused by the fact that adolescents have not had the time nor the diversity of experiences to clarify their own sense of direction. Intimacy without identity threatens the integrity of the person's selfhood. Fears of being overwhelmed, disappointments at not being loved enough, and feelings of inadequacy eat away at the romantic ideals that may have motivated the decision. Any desire to change is perceived as a threat by the partner who has come to use the marriage itself as content for his or her identity.

Marriage also requires the availability of an appropriate partner who is equally desirous of marrying. Three factors are of major importance in selecting a marriage partner. First, partners are selected because they are available for interaction. One is more likely to feel that there is marriage potential in someone with whom one has interacted than in a total stranger. Second, partners are selected because they are "eligible." This term can be very broadly defined. For some, being eligible simply means the person must be human and not already married. For others, the criteria can include religious preference, race, educational background, or family's social class. Some adults would simply not consider a partner who did not share their religious background. For these people, then, only members of their own religious group are eligible partners.

The third dimension for selecting a partner is attractiveness. This is an elusive factor. The expression "Beauty is in the eye of the beholder" warns us that someone who is attractive to one person may not be attractive to another. Similarity seems to play an important part in attractiveness. For the most part, people do not find others attractive who hold opposing views, come from a dramatically different background, or have a temperament quite opposite to their own. We can understand this in that most people seek a marriage partner who will support and encourage them. They want to be understood, accepted, and perhaps even enhanced by the partner. It is unlikely that one would find this kind of emotional understanding and positive regard from someone who is quite different from oneself. However, this again is where identity plays such an important part. The decision to marry is made on the basis of understanding of the self as well as an understanding of the other. Sometimes the wishes for a relationship overshadow the guiding voice of one's own self-awareness. When work on identity has not been pursued, the person cannot accurately judge whether the qualities in the other that are viewed as attractive will actually be in harmony with his or her own personal goals.

Childbearing

During the years of young adulthood a decision is made between the husband and wife to have or not to have children. Often this is within the first few years of the marriage. Here again the notion of the social clock comes into play. Couples who wait too long to begin their families begin to be pressured by their parents, who are eager to enter the role of grandparenthood. The interdependence of generational roles is easily seen at this point.

The decision to have children is also an extension of the loving which is shared between the marriage partners. As an outcome of sexual intimacy, the conception of a child represents a feeling of expansiveness, of confidence in the future, of an ability to give love to more than one another. In fact, the prospect of childbearing is a highly romanticized time for most young people. It is a sign that one feels capable of taking care of others as well as taking care of oneself.

Decisions about having children are related to attitudes that are held about the value of children. Not all couples decide to have children; what is more, couples differ in the number of children they have. In a national sample of married women under 40 and their husbands, Hoffman and

Manis (1979) were able to describe the relationship between fertility and the value of children. Fertility was determined by the number of children the person had plus the number of additional children they desired. Women who had or desired the largest family (3.19 children) saw children as making one a more moral, less selfish person. Women who believed that having children promised a form of immortality had the smallest desired family size (2.68 children).

By far the most pervasive advantages for having children mentioned in this study were that children provide love, and companionship and help protect adults from loneliness. Men and women, blacks and whites, parents and nonparents were about equally likely to recognize this advantage. The implication is that for many adults the decision to bear children is related to needs for affection and social connectedness. The power of this need is very great throughout life. It pervades the child's attachment and later identification with parents, the adolescent's commitment to peers, the young adult's decision to marry, and the aging adult's search for companionship with family and friends.

When adults enter the parent role their own expectations as well as the expectations of others concerning the raising of a child are aroused. The daily demands that the child places on parents help them to define their own adult roles more realistically. Rather than wondering what parents should do, they are preoccupied by the concrete events of parenting. Through this experiential learning young adults actually formulate their own personal definitions of parental roles. At first, many parents feel inadequate to take care of the baby. They turn to their own parents, neighbors, pediatricians, and books for advice on how to parent. This lack of personal confidence creates tension between marriage partners. Feelings of jealousy, competition, and abandonment also can be raised in the first months after the child is born, as the exclusiveness of the husband-wife relationship is interrupted by the repeated demands of the new baby. Some of the high probability of divorce during the first few years of marriage may well be attributed to the stress placed upon the relationship by the newborn.

A variety of studies have documented a drop in marital adjustment for couples who have had their first child (Feldman, 1971; Ryder, 1973; Waldron, & Routh, 1981). The decrease in marital satisfaction is more notable for wives than for husbands.

In Figure 8.2 the results of three studies of marital satisfaction at each of eight stages of family life are shown. The stages include: (1) beginning families; (2) childbearing families; (3) families with preschool children; (4) families with school-age children; (5) families with teenage children; (6) families as launching centers; (7) families with adult children, and (8) aging families. All three studies show a steep drop in satisfaction from stage 1 to stage 3. Another drop is evident at stage 5 when the children are adolescents. It is important to note that over all stages the satisfaction scores

FIGURE 8.2 Pattern of Marital Satisfaction at Eight Stages of Family Life as Measured by Three Different Instruments

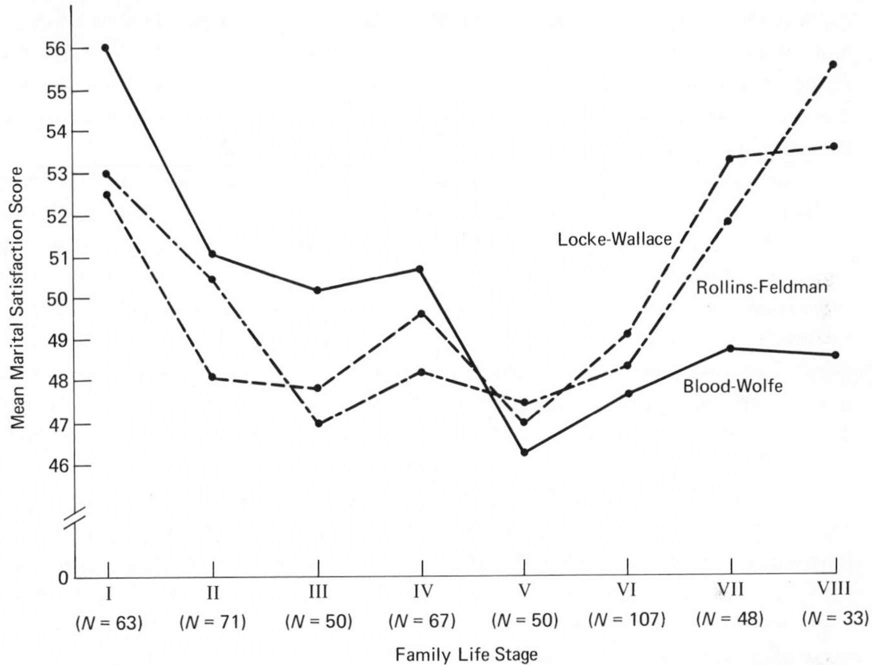

Note: Scores are standardized with a mean of 50 and standard deviation of 10 to facilitate visual comparisons of trends. Male and female scores are combined.

Source: "Marital Satisfaction over the Family Life Cycle: A Reevaluation" by B. C. Rollins, and K. L. Cannon. *Journal of Marriage and the Family,* 1974, *35,* 271–284. Copyrighted 1974 by the National Council on Family Relations. Reprinted by permission.

declined from 56 to 46 points. This is on a range from 14 (low satisfaction) to 70 (high satisfaction). At no point did family stage result in a pattern of scores that would reflect extreme marital dissatisfaction (Reiss, 1980).

Several explanations for this decrease in marital satisfaction have been offered. First, it may be that wives begin to feel that their husbands are not paying enough attention to them after the baby is born. Second, it may be that the couple has fewer opportunities for interaction after the child is born, especially interaction about topics that are not related to the child (Feldman, 1981). Third, it may be that couples who hold more traditional views of the male and female roles are more comfortable with the changes in roles that childbearing brings. However, those couples that hold more egalitarian views of the marriage relationship are seriously stressed by the separation of duties that childbearing commonly brings (Hobbs & Cole, 1976). Finally, it has been suggested that the presence of a child brings to light a whole array of questions that may create conflict between the parents. Issues of child care such as how much to let the baby cry, whether to allow the baby to sleep in the parents' bedroom, and whether to spank a baby are some examples of very specific child-care themes about which a husband and wife may disagree. These areas of conflict may not actually surface until the baby is born, at which point the need to act makes it impossible to ignore the differences between the partners.

Survival of these childbearing and childrearing years obviously serves to strengthen the bond between the man and woman. The couple begins to respect each other's competence in caring for their children. They also begin to conceptualize their roles as parents and to appreciate the increasing complexity of their family structure as a challenge rather than a burden.

Current research suggests that infants actively engage parents, evoke unique responses, and through their differential behaviors begin to shape the parenting behaviors of adults (Bell & Harper, 1977; Lamb, 1978). Mutuality is important in increasing the parents' capacity to experience intimacy. Successful child care results in the ability to anticipate children's needs, to stimulate their interest, and to delight their senses. The infant responds through shrieks of delight, elaborate smiles, and active pursuit of the loved one. Infants are unrestrained in their loving. They mouth, bite, grab, laugh, smile, squeal, and coo in response to pleasure. Through their open expressions of affection, they teach adults about the expression of love and increase the adults' ability to demonstrate love.

Adolescents and Parents

There are pressures on parents of adolescents to redefine and to clarify many aspects of the parent-child relationship. Adolescent children become physically and sexually mature. These changes prompt a new look at dominance relationships in the family. A parent simply cannot continue the same strategies of physical dominance with a child who may be taller, more muscular, or heavier than he or she is. Sexual maturation raises new cautions about physical intimacy in the family. Parents are forced to rethink the modes for expressing affection. Privacy becomes a theme of heightened concern. Parents also begin to think about their children's sexual encounters. The moral and practical concerns about adolescent sexuality force a rethinking about this aspect of social development.

Adolescents also press for behavioral independence. They spend more time away from home. They stay out late at night, drive a car, earn their own money, and make many decisions about their daily life. Parents are forced to identify the balance of rights and responsibilities that rest in the child's hands. There is a need to clarify the contributions that the child will be expected to make to the family. Parents may, in fact, depend on the adolescent to carry certain responsibilities in order for the family to function effectively. This increase in responsibility usually brings an increase in decision-making power. Adults struggle with the reality that they must take the adolescent child's views and desires into account as they make family decisions.

Cognitive growth makes the adolescent more of an equal to the parent with respect to logic and problem-solving. In fact, in some families it is during adolescence that children surpass the educational achievements of their parents. This can be viewed with pride or with envy. Parents can come to see their children as a critical resource for family problem-solving. However, some parents seem to belittle the child's educational progress in order to keep hold of some image of adult superiority.

Because they are cognitively more complex, adolescents will challenge the logic and validity of the rules and beliefs they encounter. These challenges may be directed at religious beliefs, political beliefs, the validity of school rules, or parental authority itself. Parents must begin to think through the system of values they have communicated and help clarify its meaning for their children. This process stimulates new thinking for parents who may have held on to certain views without giving them much thought. It also helps adolescents to understand the particular cultural orientation that has been transmitted in their own family.

To what extent are parents' values and adolescent peer values in harmony or conflict? Do peers have more influence over adolescents than their parents? One approach to these questions has been to survey the attitudes of adolescents and their parents on a range of issues, including sex, drugs, religion, war, law and law enforcement, racism, and politics. In surveys of this kind, attitudes of the two groups tend to be similar in most areas (Lerner & Weinstock, 1972; Weinstock & Lerner, 1972).

Another approach has been to pose hypothetical situations in which parents and peers offer opposing views of how to behave. Young people are then asked whether they would follow the advice of parents or peers. Early studies of this type suggested that adolescents turned to peers when the situation involved a current question about popularity or membership in a club but that they turned to parents in deciding about future plans or moral decisions with consequences for the future (Brittain, 1963, 1967–1968, 1969).

Later studies modified the method somewhat and came out with a rather different picture. In these studies (Larson, 1972) the subject was asked to tell what he or she would do in a given situation. The situation was described in two different ways, once so that the parents urged against some behavior that friends supported, and again so that friends urged against the behavior and the parents supported it. The majority of subjects (73.6 percent) were neither parent-oriented nor peer-oriented. They made their decision about the situation and did not modify it, regardless of who approved or disapproved. The next-largest group (15.7 percent) were parent-compliant. They went along with their parents' decisions in at least four of the six situations. In general, the group of adolescents tested in this situation were strongly parent-oriented. In other words, they felt that their parents understood them, supported them, and generally had good advice. Nonetheless, when the decision about how to behave in a particular situation had to be made, the adolescents made their judgments independent of their parents' wishes.

A third approach to the question of the respective impact of parents and peers on the values of adolescents is to simply ask adolescents directly how highly they regard parental advice. Curtis (1975) described the responses of over 18,000 adolescents in grades 7–12 to questions about the degree to which they valued the father's, the mother's, and friends' opinions. At every age, parents were more valued sources of advice and opinions than friends. However, the number of students who gave a high rating to parents declined rather steadily from 7th through 10th grade. At grade 11, the middle-class and working-class boys seemed to show an increased valuation of fathers. The value of friends' opinions and advice remained much more stable across ages. About 28 percent of boys and 50 percent of girls placed high value on their friends' opinions at every age. Although friends do not become more important, parents become somewhat less important, suggesting a gradual process of individuation and a strengthening of the individual's own value system.

We see a picture of adolescent friendship as providing companionship in activities, emotional support, and understanding. However, adolescents appear to realize that on some matters parental opinions are likely to be sounder, perhaps more protective of their well-being, and more likely to result in a positive outcome than the opinion of peers. In addition, personal judgment is emerging to provide a more autonomous basis for value decisions. Individual adolescents become increasingly capable of evaluating situations and making their own choices without guidance from parents or peers.

From the parent's point of view, having adolescent children is most likely to be the period of parenting that causes a lot of worry. In a national survey of the value of children to parents, parents of teenagers felt concerned that their children were more vulnerable to peer influence and out of their own sphere of influence. Concerns about drugs, sex, and being out late increased during this phase of parenting. Parents were also likely to sense a concern about whether there was adequate communication and understanding with their adolescent children. From the preschool to the adolescent years the focus of parental dissatisfactions shifted from feeling that young children disrupted their time together or their time alone to a concern about the well-being and vulnerabilities of their adolescent children (Hoffman & Manis, 1978).

Rossi (1980) asked mothers who were in the age range 36 to 51 to rate the difficulty of childrearing and the child's difficulty in growing up. As shown in Figure 8.3, the mothers confirmed the shift in focus described

FIGURE 8.3 Mean Ratings on Developmental and Childrearing Difficulty by Age of Child

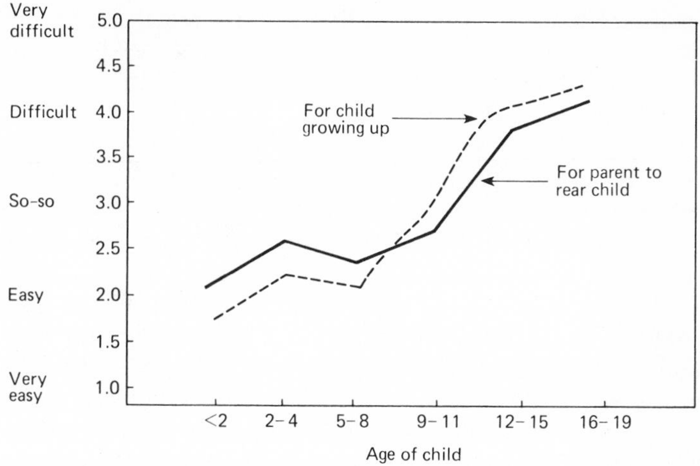

Source: "Aging and Parenthood in the Middle Years" by A. S. Rossi, in P. B. Baltes & O. G. Brim, Jr., *Life Span Development and Behavior* (Vol. 3). (New York: Academic Press, 1980), pp. 192.

above. They considered the task of parenting more difficult than the task of growing up in childhood, but the task of growing up more difficult in adolescence. However, these mothers perceive both growing up and parenting to be more difficult during the adolescent years.

Adolescent children are the front line of each new generation. The questions they raise and the choices they make reflect what they have learned, but also what they experience in the present and what they anticipate about the future. Parents of adolescents often feel that they have to absorb many influences that are beyond their control. Parents who respond in an active, open way to the changes their adolescents are experiencing can benefit by clarifying their own values and gaining insight into the overall process of psychosocial evolution.

The Period When Children Leave the Home

Sometime during the parents' late forties or early fifties in most families, children leave home in order to go to college, join the service, or form households of their own. In the 1970s the median age of mothers when the last child married was 52.3. The median age at the death of the spouse was 65.2. Thus, couples with children have an average of almost 13 years when they will remain together without active responsibilities for childrearing. This compares to approximately 1.5 years without children for couples in the 1900s (Glick, 1977).

The period when children leave the home has been called the "empty nest," the postparental period, retirement from parenthood, or the "launching" period. Basically, it is the time from when the oldest child leaves home to attend college, to marry, or to set up a household of his or her own until the youngest child leaves home. For families with few children, the transition may take only a few years. For families with three or four children or more, the transition may take 10 or 15 years. Duvall (1977) describes the challenge of this period of family life as follows: "The major family goal is the reorganization of the family into a continuing unity while releasing matured and maturing young people into lives of their own."

The transition to the "empty nest" requires readjustment by both parents (Lowenthal & Chiriboga, 1972). Several areas of adult development are directly affected by this critical change in roles. First, the relationship between the husband and wife is altered as the parental role diminishes. Second, both parents are likely to undergo some introspective evaluation of their performances as parents. Finally, each parent must recognize that energy and resources which have previously been directed to childrearing require new outlets.

Research on marital satisfaction across the life span suggests that satisfaction with the marriage relationship increases with age, and in particular after the children leave home. Once the children leave home, parents have more time for each other. There are fewer activities that are required for maintenance of the family, and adults feel somewhat more relaxed in general around the house. Some adults describe these years as bringing new intensity to their love relationship and new pleasure to their marriage (Deutscher, 1964). It is interesting to find that in one comparison of highly educated women, mothers whose children had left the home reported greater affection and cohesiveness in their marriage than women of the same age who had been childless (Houseknecht & Macke, 1981). The pattern of positive adjustment is most likely to take place when both marriage partners are already highly invested in their marriage relationship and in their family.

In some situations the husband may have an intense investment in work which he is not required to terminate at this time. In this home, the wife has a great deal of time freed by the children's departure, but the husband continues to direct his energy toward his work. This may result in some conflict as the wife seeks greater companionship from her husband and finds that he is unresponsive to her new needs.

As the children leave home, parents have more time available for new interests, new activities, or the reentry of earlier skills that may have been set aside as the children were growing. Parents may also find that they have extra financial resources, particularly as their children find work of their own. The new freedom and increased resources may bring some feelings of confusion as well as delight. Adults must decide what they wish to do with their time and how they can best express their newly acquired sense of generativity. Women may return to school, take a job, or become involved in politics or religious activities, or they may begin to volunteer their skills to any of a number of community charities or institutions. Men may engage in similar activities or develop more well-defined leisure-time pursuits. Some men find this time to be an opportunity to take some risks in their occupational roles. They may change jobs, begin a business of their own, or alter their occupational direction (Kelleher, 1973).

The emergence of new interests or new involvements may pose a threat to the satisfaction in the marriage. Partners may resist the idea of having their spouse engage in a broader range of activities or grow committed to a new career. On the other hand, these changes may be viewed as refreshing, bringing out new competences and skills in people who have grown uncomfortably predictable.

Once the children leave home, parents can no longer realistically view themselves as active socialization agents. They must accept the separateness of their children and view them with some greater degree of objectivity. As parents begin to see their children as adults who are confronting the challenges of the adult world, they have the opportunity to evaluate the outcomes of their socialization efforts. Some parents are undoubtedly extremely proud of the accomplishments and personal qualities they observe in their children. These children have attained goals that were of value and meaning to their parents, and thereby they contribute to their parents' overt feelings of accomplishment. Women whose children were adolescents during the late '60s and early '70s expressed great pleasure (and perhaps some relief) in seeing their children settle into a family and a career. "The women made such comments as: 'I am delighted with the girls my sons have married and happy to welcome each grandchild'; 'after a bad start, my son is straightened out and happily married'; 'it's great being a grandmother and having all the older children about settled down'" (Rossi, 1980). Some parents may find that their children are striving for goals that are quite different from their own hopes. Nonetheless, these parents may come to reassess their own aspirations and, out of love for their children, learn to accept the directions they have taken as meaningful. Other parents may view their children as inadequate or as failures. These parents are undoubtedly disappointed and suffer strong feelings of personal failure as well as outward disappointment. Given the great amount of energy, problem-solving, and worry that goes into the childrearing task, it is no wonder that one's evaluation of one's effectiveness as a parent would feed into one's overall sense of personal esteem. Since the parenting task is so clearly an opportunity for personal decision-making and creative problem-solving, it may in fact be an even greater source of self-esteem during adulthood than the work setting.

The gradual withdrawal from active parenthood poses a new challenge for creative adaptation during middle adulthood. The most important factor is to be able to adapt to this change in roles rather than denying that any change has occurred. Some adults who are highly identified with the parental role may find its termination to be extremely depressing. They may continue to call one another "father" and "mother." They lapse in their feelings of self-worth. As a result, they communicate feelings of guilt to their children and make any new relationship with their adult children impossible. Withdrawal from parenthood, coming as it does when the individual still has many years to live, requires some form of creative acceptance. Otherwise, the adult continues to function in a stagnant, meaningless role. For most adults, this transition signals the beginning of a new life stage marked by a sense of competence, freedom, and responsibility to social groups that are larger than the family. Most adults appear to approach this stage with eagerness and anticipation. They are happy to be finished with the tasks of childrearing and eager to enjoy the accomplishments that they and their children can achieve.

Let us add a caution about the idea of withdrawal from parenthood. Terms like "postparental period," "empty nest," and "retirement from parenthood" suggest that parenting ends and the parent role ceases to have any functions. As one man very firmly pointed out to us: "As long as my children are alive I am their parent." The parental bond changes in nature when the children leave the home and begin families of their own, but it does not end. In a study of three-generation families, Hill (1970) found an active exchange of helping interactions among grandparents, adult parents, and married children. Figures 8.4 and 8.5 show help received and help given by the three generations during a year's time. For each generation, the greatest source of help and the most frequent target for giving help was one of the other immediate family generations. Interdependence of the generations was reflected in problems related to illness, financial needs,

FIGURE 8.4 Sources of Help Received by Three Generations, over a Year's Time, by Percentages of Instances

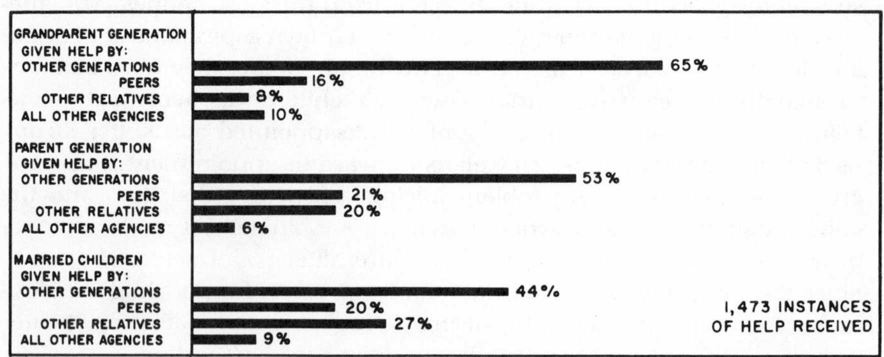

Source: Evelyn M. Duvall, *Family Development* (Philadelphia: J. B. Lippincott, 1971), p. 66. Based on data from *Family Development in Three Generations* (Cambridge, Mass.: Schenkman, 1970).

FIGURE 8.5 Help Given by Three Generations, over a Year's Time, by Percentages of Instances

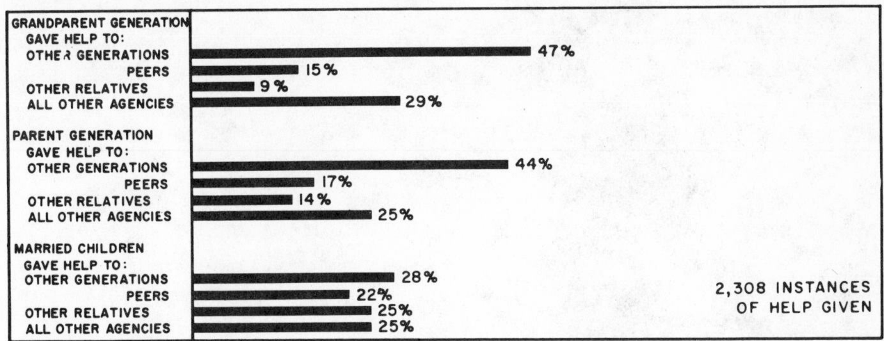

Source: Evelyn M. Duvall, *Family Development* (Philadelphia: J. B. Lippincott, 1971), p. 66. Based on data from *Family Development in Three Generations* (Cambridge, Mass.: Schenkman, 1970).

child care, emotional stress, and household management. This study clearly shows that the nurturant, caregiving role of parents does not end when children leave the home to start families of their own.

In some instances, for example after the birth of the first grandchild or at the death of one parent, the bond between adult child and adult parent may become even closer and more intimate than it had been during later adolescence or young adulthood. In some families, a child's divorce brings that adult child back to live with the parents for a while. The high cost of housing has increased the number of young adults who live with their parents during the early years of job search. Many college-age young adults continue to live at home, delaying the period when they leave the nest until they complete college. These changes in the economic and social climate may make the idea of a period when the nuclear family shrinks and parental responsibilities diminish less distinct than it was even 15 or 20 years ago.

Grandparenthood

Most older adults take great satisfaction and pride in their grandchildren. Grandchildren symbolize an extension of personal influence which will most assuredly persist well beyond one's own death. To this extent, grandchildren help older adults to feel more comfortable about their own death. They have concrete evidence that some thread of their life will persist into the future (Neugarten & Weinstein, 1964; Mead, 1975).

Grandchildren also stimulate older adults' thoughts about time, the changing of cultural norms across generations, and the patterning of history. In relating to grandchildren as they grow up, they discover elements of the culture that remain stable. Certain stories and songs retain

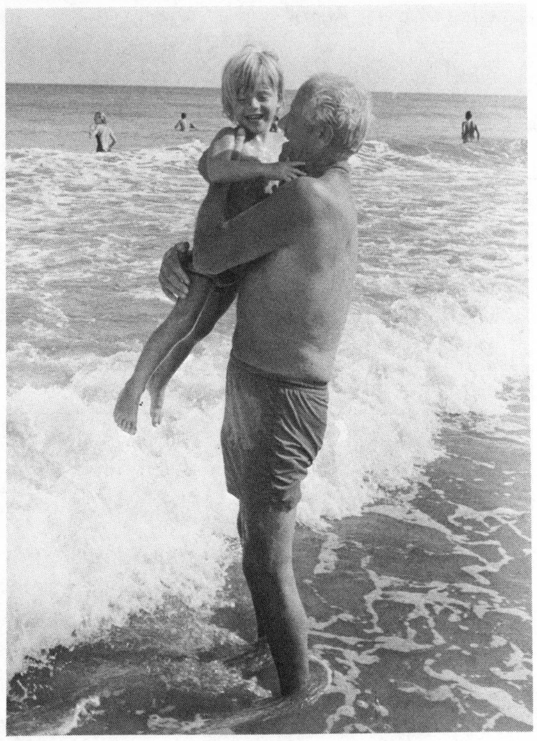

Grandparenting can provide opportunities for playful indulgence.

their appeal from generation to generation. Certain toys, games, and preoccupations of children of the current generation are remembered by grandparents from their own childhoods. On the other hand, grandparents become aware of changes in the culture which are reflected in new childrearing practices; new equipment, toys, and games designed for children; and new expectations for children's behavior at each life stage. The communication adults maintain with their grandchildren allows them to keep abreast of the continuities and changes in their culture as they are reflected in the experiences of childhood. Through their grandchildren adults can avoid a sense of alienation from the contemporary world (Kahana & Kahana, 1970).

Some adults interpret the role of grandparent as that of one who passes on the wisdom and cultural heritage of the family ancestry to the children. In the process of fulfilling this role older adults must attempt to find meaning in their experiences and to communicate this meaning to children in ways that they can understand. There are many avenues grandparents select in order to educate their grandchildren. Storytelling, special trips, long walks, attending religious services, and working on special projects are all activities that allow grandparents some moments of intimacy with their grandchildren. During these times grandparents can influence the thoughts and fantasies of their grandchildren. The process of educating one's grandchildren involves a deep sense of investment in those experiences and ideals that are believed to be central to a fruitful life.

Neugarten and Weinstein (1964) interviewed the grandmother and grandfather in 70 middle-class families. Five grandparenting styles were identified that described these adults' manner of enacting the grandparent role:

1. *Formal* These grandparents were interested in their grandchild but careful not to become involved in parenting of the child other than occasionally baby-sitting.
2. *Fun seeker* These grandparents had an informal, playful interaction with their grandchildren. They enjoyed mutually self-indulgent leisure-time fun together.
3. *Surrogate parent* This style is especially true for grandmothers who assume major child-care responsibilities when the mother works outside the home.
4. *Reservoir of family wisdom* An authoritarian relationship in which the grandparent, usually grandfather, dispenses skills and resources. Parents as well as grandchildren are subordinate to this older authority figure.
5. *Distant figure* A grandparent who emerges at birthdays or holidays but generally has little contact with the grandchildren.

In this sample, older grandparents (over 65) were more likely to be described as formal. Younger grandparents (under 65) were about equally divided among the formal, the fun-seeking, and the distant styles.

Grandparents and grandchildren influence one another's attitudes and life-style. Troll and Bengtson (1979) reported that political and religous orientations were transmitted from the grandparent to the grandchild generation. Specific behaviors might be very different between the older and younger groups, but the underlying attitudinal themes were often quite similar. In another study of dyads made up of grandparent and adult grandchild, at least 80 percent of each generation claimed to have tried to influence the other in issues like life-style, work, and ways of coping with life's challenges. In these dyads, there were also some areas that were clearly off limits. Grandparents and grandchildren seemed to have an unspoken agreement not to introduce certain conflictual topics into their discussions (Hagestad, 1978). This may suggest some fear about the vulnerability of the relationship. It may reflect the desire to preserve and protect the relationship because of the other symbolic and real benefits it provided (Troll, 1980).

Another kind of grandparent relationship is emerging in our culture as more adults are members of a four-generation family. In 1980, approximately 2,240,000 people, or about 1 percent of the population, were 85 years old or older. This reflects a 59 percent increase since 1970 (U.S. Bureau of the Census, 1981). Many older adults in their eighties and nineties are great-grandparents. These relationships can be joyful, but they can also be very conflictual (Shanas, 1980). For example, a woman of 65 just entering her role as grandparent may also be confronted with the responsibility of caring for a frail or ailing mother. The great-grandmother may resent the new great-grandchild as a competitor for her daughter's time and affection. The grandmother is caught in a painful conflict, wanting to become involved in the new life of her grandchild, but not wanting to abandon her own aged mother.

Shanas (1980) is optimistic about the resilience of kinship ties to accommodate these new and ill-defined family relationships.

> The future is uncharted for the old as it is for all of us. Family and kinship ties, however, have been amazingly resilient through the millennia. They may be different for old people in the future from what they are now, but they will continue to provide safe harbor for their members however long they may live. (p. 15)

Widowhood

In the course of a lifetime, one of the most difficult adjustments occurs when an adult loses a spouse through death. For many older people, this loss brings severe disruption, grief, and depression. The average woman is widowed at age 56 and has a life expectancy of 75. She has almost 20 years when she will be living in a new role status (Lopata, 1973; O'Leary, 1977). Because of differences in life expectancy, women are far more likely to experience widowhood than men. There are an estimated 10 million widows in the United States and only 2 million widowers (Lopata, 1978). What is more, almost 70 percent of men 75 years old or older are married whereas only 22 percent of women 75 years old or older are married (U. S. Bureau of the Census, 1977). We see that women are more likely to have to adjust to being a widow. Many women remain single from the time of the husband's death until their own.

Widowhood brings special challenges for those women who have placed strong emphasis on the wife and mother roles. They will be likely to have a decrease in financial resources. They may have no marketable skill and therefore feel uncertain about entering the labor market. They may be uninformed or uncomfortable about using social welfare services in the community. On the positive side, many widows become more involved in the lives of their children and grandchildren. Others establish their own households. For most women, the loss of the husband is felt most keenly as the loss of a vital emotional support. "He is most apt to be mentioned as the person the widow most enjoyed being with, who made her feel important and secure" (Lopata, 1978).

Widowhood is often the earliest time when adults are called upon to care for an aging parent. When widows were interviewed they reported that their children were the main sources of comfort in the early stages of their grieving (Lopata, 1978). Children give help, provide companionship, and give support. The adult children also benefit from this help-giving. It permits them to feel that they are returning some of the care and commitment that they received as children. It also allows identification with the dead parent. The children can feel closer to the lost father by filling some of the roles he may have performed.

The bereavement process may last a long time. Women may still be grieving and involved in bereavement a year, two years, or in some cases ten or more years after the death of the husband. The family, the adult children and their children, cannot sustain the intensity of help-giving for as long a period as the bereaved widow might require. Families therefore cannot be the total support system. The widowed parent needs other people to turn to, especially others who might understand the meaning of their loss.

It is important to recognize that as painful and confusing as widowhood is, most people cope with it effectively. Men and women seem to struggle with somewhat different aspects of this loss. Men usually are not prepared to maintain the household. They are unaccustomed to the tasks of meal preparation and housecleaning. They are also unlikely to want to join the family of a son or daughter, since they are accustomed to functioning as the head of a household. In many cases, widowers will remarry rather than live alone.

A greater number of widows live as a member of a child's family or live alone. Recall from Chapter 7 that older women who were living alone were in better health and felt less alone than older women who were married. Usually older widows' skills for coping with the demands of daily living are well developed. Widows more than widowers turn to children and to friends as sources of support and understanding. Widowhood brings some women into direct contact with the world of work for the first time in their adult lives. Without the support of a husband's income, adult women must try to evaluate their skills and seek some type of employment. This experience holds the promise of opening up a whole new world where skills can be learned and competence can be exercised. However, most women face this change with feelings of uncertainty, lack of a sense of worth, and little information about their "marketable" skills.

Despite the deep loss and potential feelings of anger and isolation experienced by widows, there is evidence of great potential growth in that loss. Widows may come to know themselves more intimately as a result of their deep unmet social needs. They may treat themselves with greater compassion and become more attuned to their own needs. Widows may become more sensitive to the grief and pain of others. Those widows who can transcend their loss can become more fully aware of the value of life and the need to live each moment to its fullest (Barrett, 1981). The following excerpt from a widow to her friends expresses this growth:

> To all of you, I would say (as I'm sure Mark would wish me to)—live out your love for one another now. Don't assume the future; don't assume all kinds of healing time for the bruised places in your relationships with others. Don't be afraid to touch and share deeply and openly all the tragic and joyful dimensions of life. (Cassem, 1975, p. 16)

FIGURE 8.6 Divorced Persons per 1,000 Married Persons with Spouse Present, by Sex: 1970, 1975, and 1980.

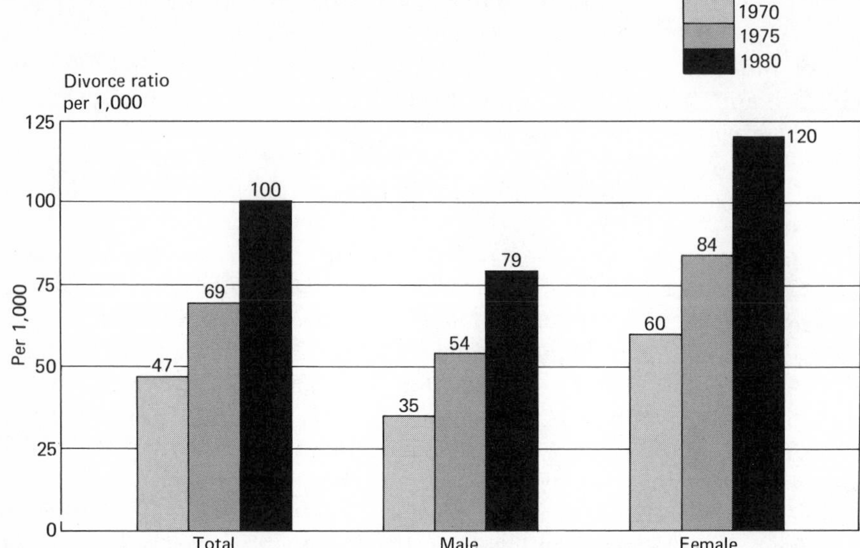

Source: U.S. Bureau of the Census, Current Population Reports, Series P–20, No. 363, *Population Profile of the United States: 1980* (Washington D.C.: U.S. Government Printing Office, 1981), p. 15.

Divorce

Americans have one of the highest rates of marriage among modern industrial societies. We like to get married and most everyone does. However, the divorce rate is also rising rapidly. You may have read that the divorce rate is one out of every three or one out of every two marriages. This rate is really not a very accurate way to describe the frequency of divorce. It is based on the number of divorces decreed and the number of marriages performed in one year. Most of the divorces are not an outcome of marriages performed in the same year. There are many more marriages that could end in a divorce during a single year than there are people planning to marry. This divorce to marriage ratio really inflates the picture we get of the frequency of divorce. One of the most stable indexes of the frequency of divorce is the number of divorced persons per 1,000 married persons. This ratio which is shown in Figure 8.6 increased by 113 percent from 1970 to 1980. The ratio is higher for women than for men and higher for blacks than whites (U.S. Bureau of the Census, 1981). It is projected that divorce rates will continue to increase over the next decade (Masnick and Bane, 1980).

Factors That Contribute to Divorce

Four variables that have been associated with the likelihood of divorce are age at marriage, income level, differences in socioemotional development, and the family history of divorce. In the United States the incidence of divorce is especially high for couples who marry under the age of twenty. These couples are about twice as likely to divorce as couples who are in their early or late twenties. Of course age at marriage is not a single explanatory dimension. Along with young marriages, we are more likely to find premarital pregnancy, dropping out of school, and lower paying jobs all of which contribute to the likelihood of divorce.

Despite the idea that divorce is a privilege of the wealthy, the divorce rate has tended to be higher among low income, semiskilled populations than among middle income college-educated groups. Many studies show a positive relationship between socioeconomic status and both length of marriage and marital satisfaction (Reiss, 1980). This relationship suggests that feelings of security about basic needs are critical to a sense of intimacy. Doubts about job security, difficulty paying the bills, and an inability to meet a partner's survival needs can undermine a couple's ability to meet other emotional needs.

One interesting exception to the relation of income and marital satisfaction is women who have continued on to post-graduate education. At this upper level of academic and occupational achievement, women are more likely to be divorced. Women who have a sense of financial independence are less likely to remain in a stressful or unfulfilling marriage (Levinger, 1976).

Socioemotional development is reflected in such dimensions as partner's self-acceptance, autonomy, and expressiveness. In the past women have experienced more stress and reported more problems in adjusting to marriage than men (Veroff, Douvan & Kulka, 1981). This is based on differences in competences and sense of self between men and women. Many women enter marriage having done less work on their identity than men. Women often have little or no preparation for childbearing and childrearing, which may be their main task. Women are often dependent on their husbands for financial security and social status. Because of the differences in power early in marriage, women often experience more emotional strain in the marriage than men. Mutual satisfaction in marriage depends heavily on the husband's qualities. Stability of the husband's masculine identity, the happiness of his own parents' marriage, his educational level, and his social status all affect marital happiness. "Husbands with strong identities can supply the security their wives need and can support them emotionally in the difficult years of married and parental life" (Barry, 1970, p. 50).

However, in many cases husbands come to a marriage with a deep need to be nurtured and to continue the pattern of care that they received in childhood. As we discussed in Chapter 7, the stability of a marriage depends on both partners achieving a sense of their own identities. This achievement will prevent the imbalance in power or respect that seems to interfere with a real emotional and intellectual intimacy.

The family's history of divorce is a fourth factor that contributes to marital instability. There is some evidence that children in families where divorce has occurred are more likely to experience divorce than children from intact marriages (Pope & Mueller, 1976; Kulka & Weingarten, 1978). One interpretation of this finding that has received some empirical support is that children of divorce hold more favorable attitudes toward divorce as a reasonable strategy for resolving marital conflict (Greenberg & Nay, 1982). It has not been demonstrated that children from divorced families are less committed to marriage as young adults or show any less adequate skills in their adult intimate relationships than children from intact families.

Coping with Divorce

It is an understatement to say that divorce is stressful. You may recall from the Holmes and Rahe Social Readjustment Rating Scale presented in Chapter 6 that of all the life events, divorce had the second most life change units after death of a spouse. Divorce may bring role loss, economic loss, and social isolation. Even when a divorce is viewed as a desireable solution, the period of time from when the divorce is suggested to the time it is concluded involves a variety of decisions and conflicts that may be very painful. Many people who experience divorce go through a time of intense self-analysis. They must try to integrate the failure of their marriage with their personal definition of masculinity or femininity, their competence as a loving person, and their long held aspirations to enact the roles of husband or wife, father or mother. When children are involved in a divorce there is the additional challenge of trying to work out the continuity of parental relationships even if the marital relationship dissolves.

The stress-related correlates of divorce are seen in the increased health problems of the divorced, the higher incidence of death of divorced, and the overrepresentation of divorced adults in all forms of psychiatric settings. More than 40 percent of divorced adults are in some form of psychotherapy or pastoral counseling (Bloom, Asher, & White, 1978). In one analysis of 80 divorced adults who had children, six specific stressors were identified: contacts with the former spouse; parent-child interactions; interpersonal relations; loneliness; practical problems like cooking or cleaning; and financial problems. Of these stressors, problems in interpersonal relations with peers was most closely tied to lower life satisfaction and a depressed, anxious mood (Berman & Turk, 1981).

One problematic area in coping with divorce is that many divorced people retain a strong attachment to their former spouse. The process of grief in divorce has been compared to bereavement in widowhood. In both cases, there is a loss and a need to adjust to that loss. While the loss due to death may be more intense, especially if death was sudden, the loss due to divorce may be more bitter. If an affectionate bond had been established, there is certain to be ambivalence about losing that bond even when the divorce is desired.

In a study of over 200 divorced persons, 42 percent expressed moderate or strong attachment to their former spouse. The feelings expressed in this continued attachment included wondering what the former spouse was doing, spending a lot of time thinking about the spouse, disbelief that the couple really divorced, and a feeling that the respondant will never get over the divorce. The attachment was stronger for people who had not initiated the divorce. The lingering feelings of attachment were associated with greater difficulties in adjustment to divorce, especially difficulties of loneliness and doubts about being able to cope with the single life (Kitson, 1982).

The fact that divorce is difficult and stressful does not mean that it is undesireable. Even among the attached spouses described by Kitson, many said they also felt a sense of relief about the divorce. Many single parents report that despite the difficulties of single parenting, life is more manageable than it was in the midst of continuing arguments and hostility. Bendo and Feldman (1974) compared four groups of low-income women: nonemployed, husband-absent; nonemployed, husband-present; employed, husband-absent; employed, husband-present. Both groups of women whose husbands were absent were less likely than the other women to see themselves as a second or submissive sex. They were more efficient, more ambitious, and better at managing their finances. The employed women whose husbands were absent had the greatest sense of productivity and the most optimism that their life could change for the better. The point is that ending a marriage can have very positive consequences for subsequent development.

Most people who experience divorce are also very determined to cope with the stresses it brings. Unfortunately, many adults may not anticipate the specific kinds of stressors they will encounter. Of course adults also have different coping strategies, some of which may not be effective for the special demands of divorce. Berman and Turk (1981) asked divorced adults to judge the perceived efficacy of 53 coping strategies for coping with their own stress. Six groups of coping strategies were identified: (1) *social activities* like dating or developing new friendships; (2) *learning,* including going back to school or talking to a counselor; (3) *personal understanding,* such as trying to understand what went wrong; (4) *expressing feelings;* (5) *autonomy,* such as becoming more independent or taking a job; and (6) *home and family activities,* especially taking care of the house or doing more things with the children. Of these six strategies, social activities, autonomy, and home and family activities were most strongly related to postdivorce life satisfaction. Expressing feelings was associated with lower life satisfaction. Social activities and autonomy were also linked to few perceived problems in the areas of loneliness and interpersonal relations.

We can begin to see that the process of coping with divorce involves devising strategies that are specific to the aspects of divorce that are perceived as most problematic. What is more, each of these coping strategies is an area that lends itself to intervention. It seems quite possible that human service professionals could be very effective in helping adults develop coping skills to resolve some of the interpersonal and pragmatic stresses of divorce.

Chapter Summary

The family context for adult development includes our sense of family ancestry, lessons learned as a child growing up in a family, and commitments made to others as adults in our own families. The diversity of family groups and family life-styles makes it difficult to generalize about the impact of the family on adult development. Some central questions involve the pattern of decision-making, definition of the male and female roles, the presence or absence of children and the philosophy of childrearing, and the number of adults present in the family group. If one compares the traditional family with the two-income family it is obvious that each pattern provides different demands for adult behavior. Personal growth is possible in each form. The direction of growth as well as the sources of stress vary in each family group. Some dimensions that contribute to personal adjustment in the family include emotional support from others, educational background, financial resources, and complementarity between personal needs and demands of the family.

The family context, no matter the family style, changes over time. Adults age. Children grow up. Work, community, and personal demands shift. Individuals look to the family for different kinds of satisfactions at different points in life. The significant transitions of the family that were discussed include the decision to marry, the decision to bear children, parenting adolescent children, the time when children leave the home, grandparenthood, and widowhood. Each transition brings the potential for modifying one's world view and for participating in new, meaningful relationships. With each change, values are clarified. Insight about one's self can increase as one examines the important qualities of one's most intimate relationships. The potential for growth is most likely to be fulfilled when adults are open to the demands for change. With each transition, being willing to entertain the possibility of new norms for behavior keeps the person and the family system dynamic and forward-moving.

References

Adams, B. *The American family: A sociological interpretation.* Chicago: Markham/Rand McNally, 1975.

Araji, S. K. Husbands' and wives' attitude-behavior congruence on family roles. *Journal of Marriage and the Family,* 1977, *39*(2), 309–320.

Arkin, W., & Dobrofsky, L. R. Job sharing. In R. Rapoport, R. N. Rapoport, & J. M. Bumstead (Eds.), *Working couples.* New York: Harper and Row, 1978.

Barrett, C. J. Intimacy in widowhood. *Psychology of Women Quarterly,* 1981, 5, 473–487.

Bell, R. Q., & Harper, L. V. *Child effects on adults.* Hillsdale, N. J.: Lawrence Erlbaum, 1977.

Bendo, A. A. & Feldman, H. A. Comparison of the self-concept of low-income women with and without husbands present. *Cornell Journal of Social Relations,* 1974, *9,* 53–85.

Berman, W. H. & Turk, D. C. Adaptation to divorce: Problems and coping strategies. *Journal of Marriage and the Family,* 1981, *43,* 179–189.

Blake, J. Is zero preferred? American attitudes toward childlessness in the 1970s. *Journal of Marriage and the Family,* 1979, *41,* 245–258.

Blechman, E. A. Behavior specialization and conflict in one-parent families. Paper presented at the American Psychological Association Meetings, San Francisco, 1977.

Bloom, B. L., Asher, S. J., & White, S. W. Marital disruption as a stressor: A review and analysis. *Psychological Bulletin,* 1978, *85,* 867–894.

Bould, S. Female-headed families: Personal control and the provider role. *Journal of Marriage and the Family,* 1977, *39,* 339–349.

Brittain, C. V. Adolescent choices and parent-peer cross pressures. *American Sociological Review,* 1963, *28,* 385–391.

Brittain, C. V. An exploration of the bases of peer-compliance and parent-compliance in adolescence. *Adolescence,* 1967–68, *2,* 445–458.

Brittain, C. V. A comparison of rural and urban adolescents with respect to peer vs. parent compliance. *Adolescence,* 1969, *3,* 59–68.

Brown, R. A. & Magarick, R. H. Social and emotional aspects of voluntary childlessness in vasectomized childless men. Paper presented at the American Psychological Association Meetings, Toronto, 1978.

Bryson, J. B., & Bryson, R. *Dual-career couples.* New York: Human Sciences Press, 1978.

Cassem, N. Bereavement as indispensable to growth. In B. Schoenberg et al. (Eds.), *Bereavement: Its psychosocial aspects.* New York: Columbia University Press, 1975.

Cherlin, A. Postponing marriage: The influence of young women's work expectations. *Journal of Marriage and the Family,* 1980, *42,* 355–365.

Curtis, R. L. Adolescent orientations toward parents and peers: Variations by sex, age and socioeconomic status. *Adolescence,* 1975, *10,* 483–494.

Deutscher, I. The quality of postparental life. *Journal of Marriage and the Family,* 1964, *26,* 26–36.

Douglas, S. P., & Wind, Y. Examining family role and authority patterns: Two methodological issues. *Journal of Marriage and the Family,* 1978, *40,* 35–47.

Douvan, E., & Adelson, J. *The adolescent experience.* New York: Wiley, 1966.

Duvall, E. M. *Family Development,* (5th ed.). Philadelphia: Lippincott, 1977.

Feldman, H. The effects of children on the family. In A. Michel (Ed.), *Family issues of employed women in Europe and America.* Leiden: Brill, 1971.

Feldman, H. A comparison of intentional parents and intentionally childless couples. *Journal of Marriage and the Family,* 1981, *43,* 593–600.

Feldman, M., & Feldman, H. The low-income liberated woman. *Human Ecology Forum,* 1973, 4.

Gagnon, J. H., & Greenblat, C. S. *Life designs: Individuals, marriages and families.* Glenview, Ill.: Scott, Foresman, 1978.

Glick, P. C. Updating the life cycle of the family. *Journal of Marriage and the Family,* 1977, *39,* 5–13.

Greenberg, E. F. & Nay, W. R. The intergenerational transmission of marital instability reconsidered. *Journal of Marriage and the Family,* 1982, *44,* 335–347.

Gross, H. E. Dual-career couples who live apart: Two types. *Journal of Marriage and the Family,* 1980, *42,* 567–576.

Hagestad, G. Patterns of communication and influence between grandparents and granchildren in a changing society. Paper pesented at the World Congress of Sociology, Sweden, 1978.

Handy, C. Going against the grain: Working couples and greedy occupations. In R. Rapoport, R. N. Rapoport, & J. M. Bumstead (Eds.), *Working couples.* New York: Harper and Row, 1978.

Hill, R. Decision making and the family life cycle. In E. Shanas & G. Streib (Eds.), *Social structure and the family: Generational relations.* Englewood Cliffs, N.J.: Prentice-Hall, 1965.

Hill, R. *Family development in three generations.* Cambridge, Mass.: Schenkman, 1970.

Hobbs, D. F., Jr., & Cole, S. P. Transition to parenthood: A replication. *Journal of Marriage and the Family,* 1976, *32,* 723–731.

Hoffman, L. W., & Manis, J. D. Influences of children on marital interaction and parental satisfactions and dissatisfactions In R. M. Lerner and G. B. Spanier (Eds.), *Child influences on marital and family interaction.* New York: Academic Press, 1978.

Hoffman, L. W., & Manis, J. D. The value of children in the United States: A new approach to the study of fertility. *Journal of Marriage and the Family,* 1979, *40,* 583–596.

Houseknecht, S. K. Voluntary childlessness. *Alternative Lifestyles,* August 1978, *1*(3), 379–402.

Houseknecht, S. K. Childlessness and marital adjustment. *Journal of Marriage and the Family,* 1979, 259–266.

Houseknecht, S. K., & Macke, A. S. Combining marriage and career: The marital adjustment of professional women. *Journal of Marriage and the Family,* 1981, *43,* 651–661.

Kahana, B., & Kahana, E. Grandparenthood from the perspective of the developing grandchild. *Developmental Psychology,* 1970, *3,* 98–105.

Kelleher, C. H. Second careers—a growing trend. *Industrial Gerontology,* 1973, *17,* 6–14.

Kim, S., & Stinner, W. F. Social origins, educational attainment, and the timing of marriage and first birth among Korean women. *Journal of Marriage and the Family,* 1980, *42,* 671–679.

Kinkead, G. On a fast track to the good life. *Fortune,* April 7, 1980, pp. 74–84.

Kitson, G. C. Attachment to the spouse in divorce: A scale and its application. *Journal of Marriage and the Family,* 1982, *44,* 379–393.

Kron, J. The dual career dilemma. *New York,* October 25, 1976, pp. 38–39.

Kulka, R. A., & Weingarten H. The long-term effects of parental divorce in childhood on adult adjustment. *Journal of Social Issues,* 1979, *35,* 50–78.

Lamb, M. E. Influence of the child on marital quality and family interaction during the prenatal, perinatal, and infancy periods. In R. M. Lerner & G. B. Spanier (Eds.), *Child influences on marital and family interaction.* New York: Academic Press, 1978.

Larson, L. E. The influence of parents and peers during adolescence: The situation hypothesis revisited. *Journal of Marriage and the Family,* 1972, *34,* 67–74.

Lerner, R. M., & Weinstock, A. Note on the generation gap. *Psychological Reports,* 1972, *31,* 457–458.

Levinger, A. A social psychological perspective on marital dissolution. *Journal of Social Issues,* 1976, *32,* 21–47.

Locksley, A. On the effects of wives' employment on marital adjustment and companionship. *Journal of Marriage and the Family,* 1980, *42,* 337–346.

Lopata, H. Z. *Widowhood in an American city.* Cambridge, Mass.: Schenkman, 1973.

Lopata, H. Z. Widowhood in social norms and social integration. In H. Z. Lopata (Ed.), *Family factbook.* Chicago: Marquis Academic Media, 1978.

Lowenthal, M. F., & Chiriboga, D. Transition to the empty nest: Crisis, challenge, or relief? *Archives of General Psychiatry,* 1972, *26,* 8–14.

Masnick, G. & Bane, M. J. *The nation's families: 1960–1990.* Boston, Mass.: Auburn House Publishing Co., 1980.

Mead, M. On grandparents as educators. In H. J. Leichter (Ed.), *The family as educator.* New York: Teachers College Press, 1975.

Murdock, G. P. World ethnographic sample. *American Anthropologist,* 1957, *59.*

Neugarten, B. L., & Weinstein, K. K. The changing American grandparent. *Journal of Marriage and the Family,* 1964, *26.*

Newman, B., & Newman, P. *Development through life: A psychosocial approach* (2nd ed.). Homewood, Ill.: Dorsey, 1979.

Nock, S. L. The family life cycle: Empirical or conceptual tool? *Journal of Marriage and the Family,* 1979, *41,* 15–26.

Nye, I. *Role structure and analysis of the family.* Beverly Hills: Sage, 1976.

O'Leary, V. E. The widow as female household head. Paper presented at the American Psychological Association Meetings, San Francisco, 1977.

Papanek, H. Men, women, and work: Reflections on the two-person career. *American Journal of Sociology,* 1973, 78, No. 4, 857–72.

Pope, H. & Mueller, C. W. The intergenerational transmission of marital instability: Comparisons by race and sex. *Journal of Social Issues,* 1976, *32,* 49–66.

Rapoport, R., & Rapoport, R. N., with Bumstead, J. M. *Working couples.* New York: Harper and Row, 1978.

Reiss, I. L. *Family systems in America* (3rd ed.). New York: Holt, Rinehart and Winston, 1980.

Rossi, A. S. Aging and parenthood in the middle years. In P. B. Baltes & O. G. Brim, Jr. (Eds.), *Life span development and behavior* (Vol. 3). New York: Academic Press, 1980.

Ryder, R. G. Longitudinal data relating marriage satisfaction and having a child. *Journal of Marriage and the Family,* 1973, *35,* 604–607.

Schlesinger, B. One parent families in Great Britain. *The Family Coordinator,* 1977, *26*(2), 139–141.

Shanas, E. Older people and their families: The new pioneers. *Journal of Marriage and the Family,* 1980, *42,* 9–15.

Silka, L., & Kiesler, S. B. Couples who choose to remain childless. *Family Planning Perspectives,* 1977, *9* 16–25.

Smith, P. C., & Karim, M. Urbanization, education, and nuptiality transition in four Asian societies. Paper presented at the Conference on Comparative Fertility Transition in Asia, Tokyo, March 1978.

Spanier, G. B., Sauer, W., & Larzelere, R. An empirical evaluation of the family life cycle. *Journal of Marriage and the Family,* 1979, *41,* 27–38.

Stephens, W. M. *The family in cross-cultural perspective.* New York: Holt Rinehart & Winston, 1963.

Troll, L. Grandparenting. In L. W. Poon (Ed.), *Aging in the 1980s.* Washington, D.C.: American Psychological Association, 1980.

Troll, L., & Bengtson, V. Generations in the family. In W. Burr, R. Hill, F. I. Nye & I. Reiss (Eds.), *Contemporary theories about the family.* New York: Free Press, 1979.

U.S. Bureau of the Census. *Social Indicators III.* Washington, D.C.: U. S. Government Printing Office, 1980.

U.S. Bureau of the Census. Current Population Reports, Series P–20, No. 363. *Population of the United States: 1980.* Washington, D.C.: U.S. Government Printing Office, 1981.

U.S. Bureau of the Census, Current Population Reports. Series P–20, No. 307, *Population profile of the United States: 1976.* Washington, D.C.: U. S. Government Printing Office, 1977.

Veroff, J., Douvan, E., & Kulka, R. A. *The inner American: A self-protrait from 1957 to 1976,* New York: Basic Books, 1981.

Waldman, E., Grossman, A. A., Hayghe, H., & Johnson, B. L. Working mothers in the 1970s: A look at the statistics. *Monthly Labor Review,* October 1979, *102*(10), 39–49.

Waldron, H., & Routh, D. K. The effect of the first child on the marital relationship. *Journal of Marriage and the Family,* 1981, *43,* 785–782.

Weinstock, A., & Lerner, R. M. Attitudes of late adolescents and their parents toward contemporary issues. *Psychological Reports,* 1972, *30,* 239–244.

9 Work

People do have to work with others, yes; the well-functioning team is a whole greater than the sum of its parts, yes—all that is indeed true. But is it the truth that now needs belaboring? Precisely because it is an age of organization, it is the other side of the coin that needs emphasis. We do need to know how to co-operate with The Organization but, more than ever, so do we need to know how to resist it.

William H. Whyte, Jr., *The Organization Man,* 1956, p.13

How can we understand the place of work in adult development? Work, like family, is a general concept that refers to varied situations. The Department of Labor's *Dictionary of Occupational Titles* describes 20,000 different jobs, each with its own pattern of skills, demands, products or services, and related forms of organization. The person who works as a mailman has a different work life than the grocer, the teacher, the airline pilot, or the professional athlete does. Even within a single profession, work experiences differ depending on the location of the work setting, the organization of the work setting, the nature of one's supervisor, and the level of responsibility one has. Any general statements about the impact of work must be interpreted in light of this variability of work environments.

Not only do work settings differ, but so do workers. Adults come to the world of work with varying needs and aspirations. Workers differ in their talents, their background and training, their personalities, and their ability to learn new skills. Workers also differ in the priorities they give to work in comparison with other life roles, including son or daughter, spouse, parent, and community member. In order to fully understand the psychological growth that adults experience as a result of their work experiences, it is necessary to consider the interaction of individuals and their work settings.

J. L. Holland (1966, 1973) has proposed that individual personality types and specific work environments can be described according to similar characteristics. A good person-environment fit would tend to lead to healthy personal development. The six types Holland describes are the realistic, social, conventional, intellectual, artistic, and enterprising.

The *realistic type* is aggressive, strong, well coordinated, not very verbal or interpersonally skilled, practical, a concrete thinker, and politically and economically conventional. The *realistic environment* requires well-coordinated, physically active, aggressive behavior. Work problems are practical and concrete. The setting is task-oriented and does not demand skillful interpersonal behavior. These settings reward conventional values. Some example occupations are surveyor, power-shovel operator, plumber, electrician, airplane mechanic, and gas station attendant.

The *social type* is sociable, responsible, verbal, and interpersonally skillful. This person does not like logical problem-solving and physical activity. A *social environment* requires sociable behavior. The work setting generates social activity and demands workers who are cooperative, flexible, verbal, and interpersonally skilled. Some example occupations are high school teacher, marriage counselor, and foreign service worker.

The *conventional type* likes well-structured tasks, material possessions, and status. This person is a conformist and prefers subordinate positions. Conventional types often are efficient, orderly, and well controlled. They do not like interpersonal problems. The *conventional environment* provides structured tasks that require orderliness and efficiency. It demands worker loyalty and offers a well-defined power structure. Some example occupations include bank teller, bookkeeper, payroll clerk, and accountant.

The *intellectual type* likes to think through problems. He or she is task-oriented, is introverted, likes ambiguous tasks, and tends to have unconventional values. The *intellectual environment* requires complex intellectual problem-solving. The environment is pervaded by unsolved intellectual problems that stimulate curiosity. It encourages people to be independent and scientific. Some example occupations include astronomer, design engineer, chemist, and scientific writer or editor.

The *enterprising type* has excellent verbal skills. He or she likes to lead, dominate, and persuade. This person is extroverted, prefers ambiguous social tasks, and gains power and prestige through verbal aggressiveness. The *enterprising environment* requires verbal problem-solving and selling. It is filled with complex interpersonal situations. It rewards people for dominance, leadership, and influence. Some example accupations are business management, salesmen, and political campaigner.

The *artistic type* is not very sociable. He or she is emotional and imaginative, generally needing some concrete outlet for personal expression. The *artistic environment* requires artistic competence and personal expression. It rewards people for being unconventional. Some example occupations include author, composer, musician, and painter.

It would be nice if this kind of person-environment fit could explain personal development as a result of work. Things are not quite this simple. Individuals do not fit easily and precisely into the type categories. Neither do occupations. Most people and occupations tend to represent a mixture of the characteristics described above.

Both the person and the work situation are dynamic, changing realities. Each influences the other. Workers adjust to the certain realities of their work. They create a pattern of daily activities to suit their work schedule. They develop skills, engage in social interactions, and choose a home in a particular community in order to accommodate demands of their work. Work situations are also modifiable. They respond to the ideas, the needs, and the vulnerabilities of workers. Adults can achieve a real sense of creativity and effectiveness by influencing the functioning or the products of their work.

Given the fact of variability among work settings and among workers, what can we say that is generalizable to the topic of adult development? This chapter uses three different approaches to understand this question. First, we examine areas of the world of work that can be considered sources of satisfaction and sources of stress for workers. They can be viewed as ecological variables of a work environment. They are the resources, barriers, and threats that individuals encounter in the work setting. These characteristics are the environmental stimuli that trigger adaptation. Adults who operate in an environment will be required to respond to its characteristics. They will have the opportunity to develop as they encounter, overcome, or benefit from the resources and hazards of the setting.

Second, we analyze the development of work life. We see work life as passing through three phases: work search, management of a career, and preparation for retirement. Two special cases that can disrupt this developmental pattern are unemployment and midlife career change. Both are discussed against a background of the kinds of learning and concerns that accompany the usual transitions from one phase of career development to the next.

The last approach emphasizes the ways that men and women experience their work activities. Here, our concern is for differences in the ways that men and women approach work roles and for differences in the expectations that people have for the behavior of male and female workers. These factors, reflecting both cultural stereotypes and individual preferences, strongly influence the meaning of work and its contribution to adult development for men and women.

An Analysis of Work: Satisfactions, Demands, and Hazards

Satisfactions

There are several approaches to describing the sources of satisfaction that characterize a work environment. At a very concrete level, there are objective sources of satisfaction including salary, fringe benefits, hours of employment, and the quality of the physical work environment. At another level, one can describe more abstract job outcomes as sources of satisfaction. These might include receiving praise and recognition, working on challenging projects, having opportunities to exercise competence, or being given new responsibilities based on previous performance. Finally, one might talk about psychosocial sources of satisfaction. These satisfactions reflect the ways that work relates to the total development of the person. Gardell (1977) has suggested six areas where work can either enhance or frustrate individual growth:

1. The individual's influence in the job world.
2. The individual's autonomy over work pace and working methods.
3. The individual's perception that his or her job connects with a larger, meaningful whole.
4. Opportunities to tap and to develop personal resources to their fullest.
5. Interest in cooperating and developing fellowship with other people.
6. Opportunities for satisfying the claims for involvement coming from other life roles and situations, including family, leisure, and civic affairs.

In this sense, one can see the potential of work for promoting the development of a sense of generativity. Through one's work efforts, one can contribute to the quality of life for others. Work brings the talents and commitments of many individuals to bear on the challenge of meeting a society's human needs. Of course, much of this type of satisfaction depends on the importance that an individual gives to the worker role. An old story is told about a traveler who comes across three men at work laying bricks at the side of the road. When the stranger asks the first man what he is doing, the man replies "I am laying bricks." When the second man is asked, he replies "I am building a wall." When the third man is asked, he smiles and replies, "I am building a church." Psychosocial sources of satisfaction can be found in almost any work environment if the worker is inclined to identify and value them.

One approach to the study of job satisfaction is to ask people to respond to the overall experiences of satisfaction or happiness associated with their work. Rather than specifying individual dimensions that might account for satisfaction, this approach measures a global sense of whether or not people feel that their job is meeting their needs. Seashore (1978) has found that in recent national surveys, close to 90 percent of those interviewed say they are satisfied with their work. Many adults say they would continue to work even if they did not need the money, or if they were guaranteed a lifelong annuity.

In 1957 and again in 1976, researchers at the Survey Research Center of the Institute for Social Research at the University of Michigan conducted a national survey on adjustment and mental health (Gurin, Veroff, & Feld, 1960; Veroff, Douvan & Kulka, 1982). A sample of 2,000 Americans who were 21 years old or older were asked to discuss sources of life satisfaction and conflict associated with significant life roles, especially marriage, parenthood, and work.

In comparison to marriage and parenthood, jobs were a less important source of personal happiness. Fourteen percent of the respondents mentioned their jobs as a reason for their happiness, and 11 percent mentioned them as a reason for their unhappiness (Gurin et al., 1960, p. 24). It is interesting to note that while work was less important as a contributor to personal happiness, it was also less important as a source of personal problems than marriage or parenting.

People who were interviewed differentiated their material and economic status from their jobs. A great many found economic considerations to be a source of both happiness and unhappiness. They were not seeking great luxury or riches, but a form of economic security that would protect them from debts, ill health, or inadequate housing. They appeared to be able to differentiate sources of job satisfaction from the economic contributions of their jobs to their life-styles. Three distinct sources of job satisfaction were identified: (1) ego satisfactions, or personal satisfaction with the job; (2) extrinsic satisfactions, which included financial benefits

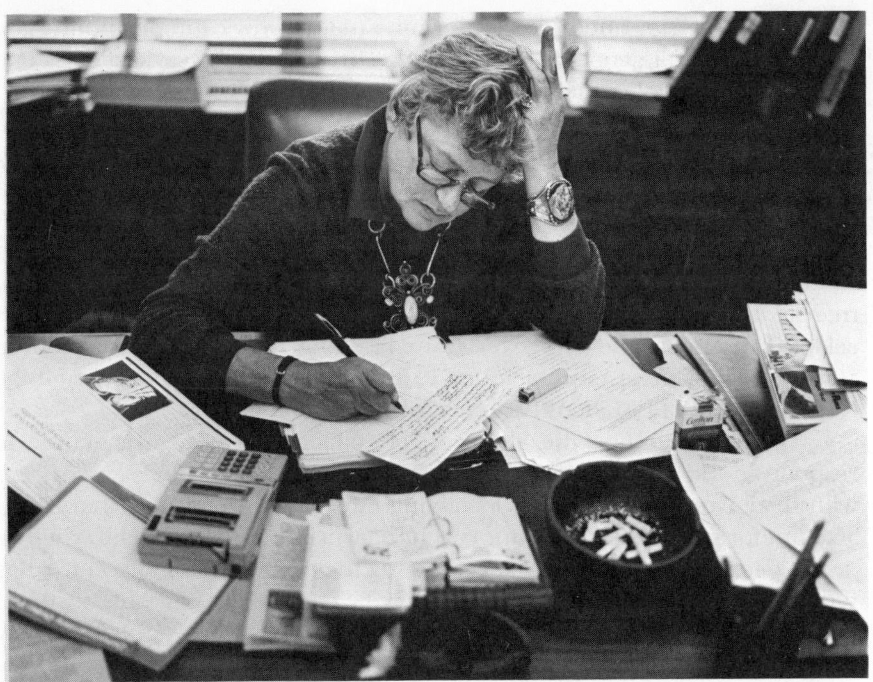

Many white-collar workers expect a high degree of personal involvement from their work.

and working conditions; and (3) the combination of ego and extrinsic sources of satisfaction. The greatest job satisfaction was associated with ego rather than extrinsic sources. This pattern has been confirmed in other national surveys. People evaulate the meaning they find in their work and the opportunities for advancement to be of greater importance to them than income, job security, and short working hours (U.S. Bureau of the Census, 1980). Individuals who seek personal gratification are likely to experience both greater satisfaction and greater problems in their work settings. This suggests that personal involvement in work is likely to lead an individual into some conflict in an effort to attain self-expression and creative productivity.

In the Survey Research Center survey, occupational status was divided into eight categories: (1) professionals and technicians, (2) managers and proprietors, (3) clerical workers, (4) sales workers, (5) skilled workers, (6) semiskilled workers, (7) unskilled workers, and (8) farmers. The majority of people at all occupational levels were quite satisfied with their jobs. Respondents in higher-status jobs derived greater ego gratification from their jobs, but they also demanded more ego involvement. Those in higher-status occupations expressed greater dissatisfaction about ego gratifications that were not perceived as forthcoming in their jobs. The clerical workers and sales workers expressed greater dissatisfaction than any other group except the unskilled worker. These groups also reported a high percentage of problems in the work setting (37 to 38 percent had experienced problems). This combination of dissatisfaction and problems suggests that middle-class or lower-middle-class white-collar workers are seeking a great deal more personal gratification than they are actually finding in their work.

Smith and Nock (1980) took a somewhat different approach to studying the relation between kinds of work and workers' satisfactions. They divided respondents into four categories: blue-collar public sector (example: bus driver for public transportation company); blue-collar private sector (example: taxi driver); white-collar public sector (example: government licensing agent); and white-collar private sector (example: secretary for a private law firm). They found that job satisfaction and social alienation were different depending on the occupational level, but also depending on the public-private sector distinction.

Public-sector white-collar workers were very satisfied with the material aspects of their work, including salary, hours, and job security. They were quite dissatisfied with the intrinsic or ego-related aspects of their work. They were least likely to see their superiors as helpful. They did not perceive their co-workers as interested in them. They felt they had few opportunities to see the results of their work or to develop their abilities.

The most dissatisfied workers were the private sector blue-collar group. These workers were less satisfied with extrinsic factors such as fringe benefits and job security, and intrinsic factors such as interest level in the work or opportunity to develop new skills. The study showed different profiles of work satisfactions and dissatisfactions for each of the four groups. The implication is that both the public-private sector distinction and the work category are important dimensions in conceptualizing adaptation to work during adult life.

Changes in the Perception of Work-Related Satisfactions with Age

Job satisfaction appears to increase with age. In both the 1957 and 1976 surveys, older adults reported fewer problems in their work and greater feelings of adequacy on the job. They expressed very little desire to do some other kind of work. Only 25 percent said they wanted to change jobs, whereas 52 percent of the younger group wanted to change jobs (Gurin et al., 1960, p. 109). It appears that after a period of job experimentation and training, the individual makes a commitment to the work setting and attempts to adjust to the setting rather than to leave it. This may also reflect a realistic adjustment to the difficulty of finding a new job at older ages.

The importance of certain work-related satisfactions and demands appears to change over the course of adult life. Breaugh and DiMarco (1979) asked engineers in five age groups to rate the desirability of 17 job outcomes. The subjects' responses could range from −4, highly undesir-

TABLE 9.1 Mean Ratings of Desirability of Job Outcomes for Five Age Groups

	Age Group				
Job Outcome	**20–29**[1]	**30–39**	**40–49**	**50–59**	**60–69**
1. Pay increase	3.41	3.60	3.51	3.46	3.15
2. Feeling a sense of accomplishment	3.56	3.59	3.61	3.64	3.80
3. Receiving praise	2.50	2.52	2.34	2.36	2.00
4. Working on challenging projects	3.30	3.18	3.15	3.30	3.00
5. Working autonomously	1.55	1.81	1.59	1.44	1.64
6. Having more responsibility	2.72	2.60	2.40	2.44	2.24
*7. Being promoted	3.14	3.15	2.72	2.49	2.20
*8. Receiving recognition	2.64	2.97	2.65	2.72	3.12
*9. Opportunity for professional development	2.76	2.61	2.22	1.99	1.80
*10. Opportunity for personal development	2.88	2.62	2.34	2.05	1.84
11. Better work facilities	2.88	2.62	2.34	2.05	1.84
12. Being under increased pressure	−1.02	−.94	−1.01	−.90	−.84
*13. Expected to do more in the future	.63	.37	.02	−.04	.12
*14. Having to move to a new city	−1.17	−1.25	−1.90	−1.88	−2.24
15. Being required to travel	−.26	−.54	−.43	−.71	−.64
16. Good working relations with supervisor	3.13	3.17	3.19	3.23	3.68
17. Job security	2.55	2.61	2.77	2.69	3.16

[1]Mean rating for age group (−4 = highly undesirable ... +4 = highly desirable)

*Statistically significant differences.

Source: "Age differences in the Rated Desirability of Job Outcomes" by J. A. Breaugh and N. DiMarco, Paper presented at the American Psychological Association meetings, New York City, 1979.

able, to +4, highly desirable. Table 9.1 shows the mean desirability rating for each age group. There were significant differences across age groups on six variables: being promoted, receiving recognition, opportunity for professional development, opportunity for personal development, expectations to do more in the future, and expectations to move to a new city. Although job security was not significantly more desirable for older than younger workers, it did rank among the top four most desirable outcomes for the oldest age group.

The pattern of responses also highlights some common perceptions of satisfactions and demands for this particular group of workers in this particular organization. Pay increase, a feeling of accomplishment, work on challenging projects, and good working relations with the supervisor were consistently viewed as important outcomes of the job. This suggests a blend of material needs with needs for psychosocial growth in the world of work.

There appears to be some conflict between positive ratings given to work on challenging projects and having more responsibility, and the negative rating for being under increased pressure. Here we see the dynamic tension of much of adult experience clarified in terms of job outcomes. The desire for growth leads the person to take on new, more difficult tasks and to assume greater leadership and decision-making responsibility. At the same time, these changes inevitably put the person under greater pressure. Decisions effect a broader range of people. Contributions to work become increasingly visible. Successes and failures "count" more. The tension between wanting to contribute and not wanting to let others down is a major source of developmental anxiety that prompts growth during the middle-adult years.

Another approach to the question of how adults change in their evaluation of the satisfactions and demands of work was taken by Powers and Goudy (1971). Subjects were men 50 years old and older. They were employed in five job categories: farmer, factory worker, owner-merchant, salaried professional, and self-employed professional. Each person was asked the following question:

"Assume you were offered an annuity that would provide a comfortable living equal to what you have now for the rest of your life, with no strings attached except that you had to quit doing work for pay or profit, would you take it?"

Table 9.2 shows the percentage of adults in four age groups that would quit work and the percentage that would continue to work. In each age group except those over 65 more men would quit work than remain working. The oldest category (65+), men who were already past the age of retirement but who had continued to work, not surprisingly responded in favor of continued work. When asked why they would or would not accept the annuity, the meaning that the workers placed on work became clear. Close to 30 percent of those who said they would accept the annuity said it would give them security and freedom from financial worries. There were just as many workers who saw this advantage in the younger, middle, and older age ranges. The second most frequently cited reason to accept the annuity was that it would give them freedom to do what they wanted.

TABLE 9.2 Percentages of Men Choosing To Remain Working or Take an Annuity

Age:	50–54	55–59	60–64	65+	Total
Quit working and take an annuity	58.2	61.2	58.1	48.7	57.3
Remain working and not take an annuity	41.8	38.8	41.9	51.3	42.7
Number of Respondents	591	551	408	343	1893

Source: "Examination of the Meaning of Work to Older Workers" by E. A. Powers & W. J. Goudy, *International Journal of Aging and Human Development*, 1971, 2, 38–45, Table 1.

Twenty-four percent gave this response. Of 1,085 men, about one-fourth had things they would rather do and interests they would rather pursue than the ones that were demanded by their work.

Of those workers who would not accept the annuity, 40 percent said they just couldn't accept something for nothing. They did not believe this kind of arrangement would be fair. This large group could not suspend their involvement in the world of reality long enough to fantasize about a world without the demands of work. The next largest group, 22 percent, said they really enjoyed their work. Eighteen percent gave a third reason to continue working. They said that work gives meaning to life. This dimension showed clear age differences. About 21 percent of the younger men (50–54, 55–59) believed that their work gave their life meaning. Only 12 percent of the older men (60–64, 65+) saw work in this light. For many of those under 60, the decision to continue to work is motivated by the feeling that work is an avenue for achieving a sense of purpose in life. We would suggest that for older workers, a sense of purpose exists independent of the world of work. As workers approach the age of retirement, they search for a personal philosophy that gives their life meaning at an individual level, one that is not so strictly tied to a role that will soon be ending.

Demands

Demands of a work environment vary along at least three dimensions: (1) demands for strong identification with the organization versus a sense of impersonal alienation; (2) demands for continued skill development versus tedium; and (3) demands for high-pressure performance versus self-governed, open-ended criteria for performance. As the criteria suggest, for each dimension both extremes can be experienced as sources of problems or conflicts about the job.

We referred to the demand for identification in Chapter 8 in our discussion of greedy occupations. For some adults, the work setting expectations require a very high level of personal commitment. Leisure time, family activities, and political or community roles are all influenced by the person's identification with the role of worker. At the other end of this dimension, there are some organizations in which workers feel totally alienated. The sabotage of automobiles by assembly-line workers is an expression of the frustration that can be caused by feeling depersonalized in the work setting. Typist, file clerk, factory worker, and telephone operator are some examples of jobs that can lead to feelings of alienation, especially when large numbers of workers are grouped together in one area, all doing the same kind of work.

The second dimension refers to demands for continued high-level competence. In some occupations, new information, new technology, and new problems require continued updating of knowledge or skills. Physicians, scientists, teachers, accountants, and engineers all need to be involved in continuing skill development. They attend seminars and conferences, they read technical journals, or they return to school in order to keep up with the growth of knowledge in their fields. In these professions, the passage of time and the accumulation of experience is a double-edged sword. Experience provides information about the application of the worker's initial training. However, the worker is constantly confronted with the fear of becoming outdated or obsolete because of new ideas or new techniques.

In direct contrast are jobs in which routine performance of tasks is repeated day after day. Jobs with standardized motion patterns, jobs which require constant repetition of short cycles of behavior, and jobs in which each step is predetermined lead to a sense of monotony, fatigue, general disinterest, high turnover, and even personal anxiety. The demands of this type of work require that people resist any attempts at self-expression, individuality, or imagination. The tasks require the careful focusing of attention on a very limited array of behaviors. We really do not know the costs of adapting to tedium, especially the costs in terms of cognitive development during adulthood.

The third dimension refers to the extent to which demands of the work situation impose performance pressures on the worker. These pressures can come in the form of constant supervision, salary determined by piece work or commission, or demands for long or extremely strenuous performance. In each of these instances the worker is always under very clear pressures to achieve a standard of excellence as it is defined by some external source.

At the other extreme are those kinds of work that are very open-ended. Being a poet, a novelist, or a sculptor requires imposing one's own work schedule, one's own standards of excellence, and one's own expectations for productivity. What might be viewed as a more authentic, self-determined pace by some can be a frustrating challenge to self-discipline for others. When structure and performance pressures are imposed from within they are subject to the influences of self-doubt, self-indulgence, and

FIGURE 9.1 Three Dimensions of Demands in the Work Setting

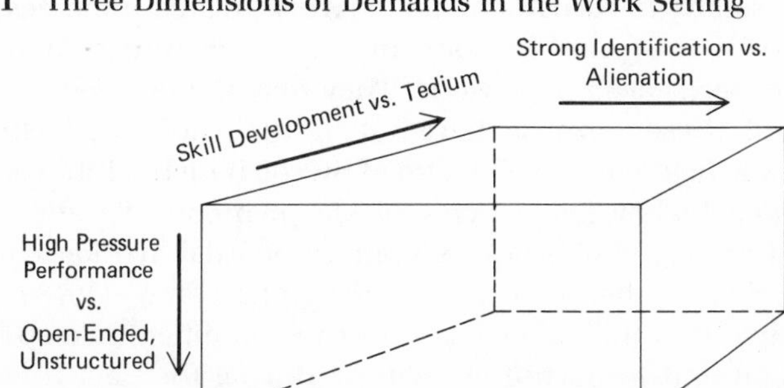

demands to attend to the needs of others. One does not have the firm expectations of some authority figure or organization to lean on. There is not even the clear promise of a commission at the completion of each piece unless one is already very well established. The push to perform must be highly internalized. In some cases it can totally dominate the person. In other cases it can be overshadowed by the competing structures of an active adult life.

Figure 9.1 summarizes the dimensions that represent demands of the work setting. The model suggests that the three dimensions are separate. Each one can be present to some degree in any work situation. The extremes of each pole are viewed as potential sources of conflict or challenge. Depending on one's temperament and talents, these conflicts can lead either to creative adaptations or to chronic feelings of ambivalence or even despair about one's work.

Hazards

As a friendly teacher once pointed out, every line of work has its "chalk dust." The notion of occupational hazards encompasses a broad range of risk factors, including risks to personal safety, to health, to psychological adjustment, and to subsequent employability. Steel workers who inhale the dust and chemicals of the plant, construction workers who work on the tops of tall apartment buildings, and miners who risk explosions, cave-ins, and blasting injuries are workers in hazardous occupations. Some hazards of the work world are obvious, and they are compensated for directly through high wages and fringe benefits.

In a 1977 Quality of Employment Survey, 78 percent of respondents said they were exposed to at least one health or safety hazard. The most frequently mentioned hazards were air pollution (40 percent), danger of fire or electric shock (30 percent), noise (30 percent), and exposure to dangerous chemicals (29 percent) (Quinn & Staines, 1979). Even in careers in which one might expect hazards to be minimal, working conditions may impose risks to workers. For example, in a study of the working conditions of teachers in southeastern Michigan, 29 percent said they were exposed to health and safety hazards, including work-related illnesses, personal attack, excessive noise, and indoor temperature extremes (Materka, 1980).

Other hazards are less obvious. They may not even be recognized by workers until these hazards have taken their toll. Levi (1978a,b) has reported on the health and well-being of Swedish night-shift workers. "The results showed higher frequencies of sleep, mood, digestive and social disturbances among shift workers than among day workers. Complaints about well-being reached their peak during night shift" (1978a, p. 22).

Levi found that the endocrine system is modified to keep the person awake at night and to permit sleep time during the day. However, even after three weeks of shift work, the normal day-night circadian rhythms persisted. When a group of steel workers were switched to a shift system that did not require night work, there were marked improvements in physical, mental, and social dimensions of well-being.

Another relatively subtle hazard is a pheonomenon described as "burnout." People whose work involves intense emotional interactions with others over a prolonged period are likely to experience a loss of concern for the people whom they serve. Burnout can involve physical exhaustion, a cynical and dehumanizing view of clients, and a loss of the capacity for empathy or respect for clients. Consequences of burnout may include high absenteeism, frequent job changes, increased use of alcohol and drugs, and increased conflict with family and friends. The person who has "burned out" usually blames himself or herself for becoming an ineffective professional.

Careers where burnout is likely to occur include many human-service occupations in which people seek help for problems that are especially embarrassing, conflictual, or highly emotional. The helping professions in which this problem can arise include "social welfare workers, physicians, psychiatrists, clinical psychologists, poverty lawyers, child care staff, police officers, psychiatric nurses, prison personnel, teachers, counselors, and ministers" (Maslach, 1978). Situations that can promote burnout include the demand to provide care to a large number of people, long working hours with continuous client contact, little access to a social support system, and the absence of training in the specific interpersonal dimensions of the job.

Career Development

Defining Career

A career can be thought of as any set of work experiences that permits a person to make productive use of talents and skills. The career of an artist, for example, may involve work in many media, including oil painting, sculpture, ceramics, sketching, collage, watercolor, and pen and ink. It is not the medium, the project, or the theme of the work that defines the career. It is the artist's personal definition of all these activities as the expression of a unique set of talents and goals. In the same way, one might think of an entrepreneur's career as a series of involvements in a number of small businesses. A salesperson's career may be selling many different products.

Wilensky defined a career as follows: "A career is a succession of related jobs, arranged in a hierarchy of prestige, through which persons move in an ordered (more-or-less predict able) sequence" (1961, p. 523). In this definition the career is recognized by the society as well as by the person as an enduring work pattern. People can train for, plan, and anticipate the continuity of such a career. Using this definition, Wilensky found that only 30 percent of a sample of over 600 working-class men showed an orderly career pattern for more than half of their work life.

Two indications of the fluctuation or disorder in work experiences are mobility rates and job tenure. The mobility rate is defined as the percentage of people who were employed in two consecutive years but who were in a different job each year. For 1978, the overall mobility rate was about 12 percent. This ranged from 36 percent for workers aged 16 to 19 to 3 percent for workers over 55 (U.S. Bureau of the Census, 1980). Job tenure is the number of years one has been in one's current job. In 1978, over 50 percent of all employed men had been in their current jobs for less than

FIGURE 9.2 Current Job Tenure of Employed Workers 35 Years Old and Over, by Age, Sex, and Race: 1978

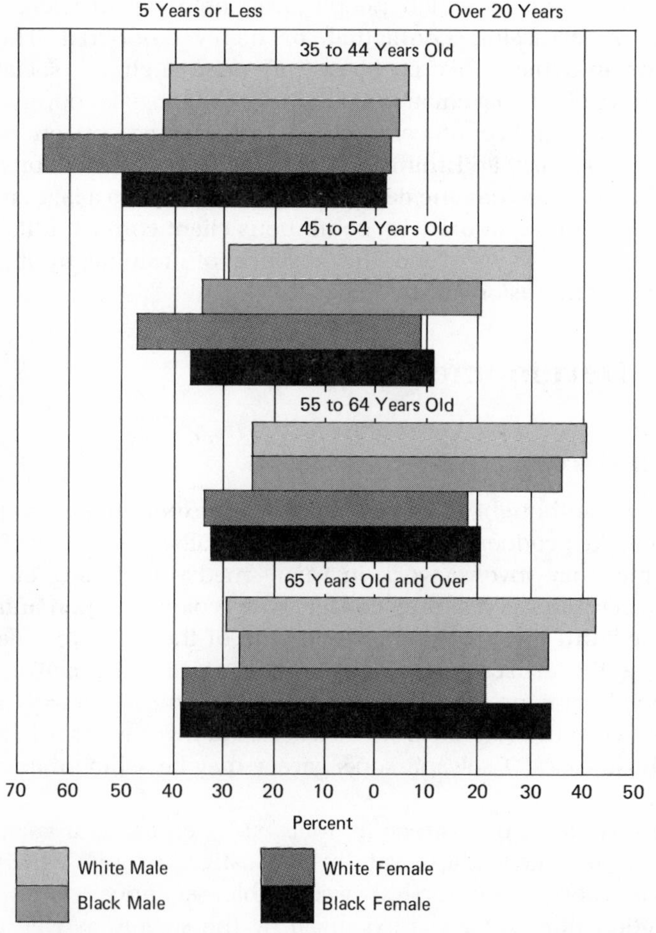

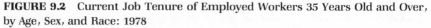

Source: U.S. Bureau of the Census. *Social Indicators III* (Washington, D.C.: U.S. Government Printing Office, 1980), 339.

five years. Over 60 percent of all employed women had been in their current job for less than five years (U.S. Bureau of the Census, 1980). These indices suggest a high rate of movement from one job to another, especially during adolescence and early adulthood (see Figure 9.2).

It makes sense to consider occupational career in a more loosely defined way than Wilensky does. Occupational career is a person's life pattern of work activities. If a person continues to work and to have work-related attitudes, he or she has an occupational career. Changes in work activities cause changes in the life structure. They may also result from changes in the life structure. Activities that were once satisfying may cease to provide satisfaction. The lifelong occupational career is a changing set of activites. These activities lead to changing competences, new goals, and a changed appreciation of the meaning of types of work and types of reward. From this point of view, it does not make sense to expect that a career decision that is made during adolescence will remain unchanged throughout life. Even if the decision is made in a rational, planned way, a good decision may not be a permanent one. As adults grow and change, their awareness of options and their understanding of their own skills change. The phases of decision-making and career choice that occur during later adolescence must help the person anticipate the likelihood of change. In fact, we expect that a person's career will be the subject of constant attention and adjustment throughout adulthood (Newman & Newman, 1979).

We will consider four phases of career development: career decision-making, work search, management of a career, and retirement. In each of these phases adults seek to match their own needs and talents with available opportunities. Over time, there is also a continuous interplay between the efforts of the work setting to socialize and train the worker and the efforts of the worker to influence and shape the world of work (Schein, 1971). Of course, the pattern of work and career development is not the same for all adults. Separate discussions of midlife career change and unemployment illustrate two potentially abrupt transitions in the unfolding of one's occupational career.

Career Decision-Making

Career choice refers to the purposeful choices and decisions that individuals make in guiding their careers. Career-related choices may include a decision to attend college, a decision about a major, or a decision about an occupation. Career decisions are made by a process of logical thought that considers the consequences of specific career choices. They require the ability to consider the suitability of career choices and work activities. Planning for career choice is also necessary.

Phases of Career Decision-Making Tiedeman has proposed a model of career decision-making. With effective problem-solving, the person gains increased control over life events. The person is better prepared to meet the challenges of each new decision. Tiedeman's theory offers seven phases in the career decision-making process. The phases of decision-making are exploration, crystallization, choice, clarification, induction, reformation, and integration. In the *exploration phase* the person becomes aware of the fact that there is a decision to be made. A need to learn more about oneself and the occupational world results. The person begins to generate alternatives for actions. There are feelings of anxiety and uncertainty about the future.

In the *crystallization phase,* the person becomes more aware of alternatives for action and their consequences. Some alternatives are discarded. Conflicts between alternatives are recognized. The rewards and costs of various decisions are evaluated. The person devlops a strategy for making the decision.

In the *choice phase,* the person decides which alternative for action will be followed. The decision is solidified in the person's mind as he or she elaborates reasons why the decision is beneficial. There is a sense of relief and optimism. The person develops a commitment to executing the decision.

In the *clarification phase,* the person more fully understands the consequences of commitment to the decision that has been made. Planning of action steps occurs. Execution of actions may occur in this phase or may be delayed until the appropriate time. The self-image is prepared to be modified by the decision.

During the *induction phase,* the person encounters the new environment for the first time. The individual wants to be accepted and looks to others for cues about how to behave. The individual identifies with the new group and seeks recognition for his or her unique characteristics. Gradually the self-image is modified. He or she learns to believe in the values and goals of the new group.

In the *reformation phase,* the individual is very much involved with the new group. He or she becomes more assertive in asking that the group perform better. The person also tries to influence the group to accommodate some of his or her values. The self is strongly committed to group goals. During this phase the group's values and goals may be modified to include the orientation of the new member.

In the *integration phase,* group members react against the new member's attempts to influence the group. This leads the new member to compromise. In the process the new member attains a more objective understanding of self and group. A true collaboration between the new member and the group is achieved. The new member feels satisfied and is evaluated as successful by self and others.

These phases are summarized in Table 9.3. This model emphasizes continuous interaction and feedback between the person and the work

TABLE 9.3 Seven Phases of Career Decision-Making

Phase	Characteristics
1. Exploration	Awareness of decision Generate alternatives Learn more about self and occupational world Feelings of anxiety and uncertainty about the future
2. Crystallization	Increasing awareness of alternatives and the consequences Disregard some alternatives Evaluate conflicts, rewards, and costs Develop a strategy for making the decision
3. Choice	The decision is made Elaboration of further reasons for its soundness Feelings of relief and optimism Commitment to executing the decision
4. Clarification	Full understanding of consequences of decision Planning action steps Execution of action or delay until appropriate time Preparation for modification of self-image
5. Induction	First encounter with new environment Desire for acceptance and cues for valued behavior Identification with new group Modification of self-image to include values and goals of the new environment
6. Reformation	Demands that the group perform better Attempts to get the group to accept values and goals Self acts in the interests of the group Group's goals and values are modified
7. Integration	Members react against influence attempt Compromise More objective understanding of self and group Collaboration Feelings of satisfaction and success

context. At first this interaction is necessary in order to clarify the person's talents and the choice of a career. Later, the interaction is necessary in order to achieve a satisfactory level of adaptation to the work environment. For each career-related decision, including the decisions about college major, occupation, job change, and career redirection, effective decision-making would involve all seven phases (Tiedeman & O'Hara, 1963; Miller & Tiedeman, 1972). You might think about the decision-making process that has led up to your own choice of major or occupation and try to identify how many of Tiedeman's phases have been involved.

Styles of Career Decision-Making The phases of decision-making are probably encountered by every person in the process of choosing a career. However, people use different decision-making styles that determine how they make use of information and how much responsibility they take for the decisions they reach (Dinklage, 1969; Harren, 1976; Lunneborg, 1977).

Harren (1976) has described three categories of decision-making styles. The *planning style* is the most rational. Planners assume personal responsibility for a decision. They seek out information to assess both personal competences and the qualities of the situation. The *intuitive style* makes primary use of fantasy and emotion. A decision is reached without much information-seeking. It is based on what feels right or best at the time. The *dependent style* is influenced by the expectations and evaluations of others. Dependent decision makers take little responsibility for their decisions. They see circumstances as forcing their decision or limiting the options.

Harren and Kass (1977) studied the progress of 578 college undergraduates in choosing a career. Their decision-making progress was determined by three tasks: the decision to come to college; the decision about a major; and the decision about a future occupation. Both academic class standing and having made a satisfying decision about one's major or future occupation were closely related to the career decision-making score.

Students identified the intuitive style as most like their decision-making process. Students responded favorably to items that reflected an instinctive sense of what would be a good career decision. They preferred this strategy to the more tedious activities of the planning style. Nevertheless, the intuitive style was not related to decisiveness, to the formation of a vocational self-concept, or to work values. Fantasy, awareness of feelings, and a sense of one's inner states may be highly valued as a path toward personal adjustment, but they are not the most effective coping strategies for career decision-making.

The great diversity of career directions and the need to choose among them has increased the importance of decision-making skills in career development. At every phase of career development, people need to be aware of the alternatives that are open to them and to evaluate those alternatives in light of their values and goals. Complex computerized career guidance systems have been developed to give people access to the variety of career opportunities and their consequences. One system called SIGI (System for Interactive Guidance and Information) is a flexible, interactive process (Educational Testing Service, 1974–1975). It permits the person to raise questions, seek additional information, and reconsider his or her decisions at various phases of the program. Table 9.4 shows the subsystems included in SIGI. The assumption is that through interactions with SIGI the person begins to develop decision-making skills that will contribute to other aspects of career development.

Work Search

Because many occupational choices are possible, young people are not usually prepared for a specific occupational role during childhood and adolescence. Most jobs require a period of training for the new employee. The training period may last from a few weeks, in the case of an assembly-line worker, to ten years, in the case of a physician. For some people, young adulthood has passed before training is completed. During the

TABLE 9.4 SIGI at a Glance: Subsystems of Computer-Based System of Interactive Guidance and Information

Subsystem	What the Student Does	Questions Answered
Introduction	Learns concepts and uses of major sections listed below.	Where do you stand now in your career decision-making? What help do you need?
I. Values	Examines 10 occupational values and weighs importance of each one.	What satisfactions do you want in an occupation? What are you willing to give up?
II. Locate	Puts in specifications on 5 values at a time and gets lists of occupations that meet specifications.	Where can you find what you want? What occupations should you look into?
III. Compare	Asks pointed questions and gets specific information about occupations of interest.	What would you like to know about occupations that you are considering? Should you reduce your list?
IV. Prediction	Finds out probabilities of getting various marks in key courses of preparatory programs for occupations.	Can you make the grade? What are your chances of success in preparing for each occupation you are considering?
V. Planning	Gets displays of program for entering each occupation, licensing or certification requirements, and sources of financial aid.	How do you get from here to there? What steps do you take to enter an occupation you are considering?
VI. Strategy	Evaluates occupations in terms of the rewards they offer and the risks of trying to enter them.	Which occupations fit your values best? How do you decide between an occupation that is highly desirable but risky and one that is less desirable but easier to prepare for?

Source: Educational Testing Service, *SIGI: A Computer-Based System of Interactive Guidance and Information* (Princeton, N.J.: 1974–1975).

training period, workers are taught the norms and goals of the work setting. This involves learning the technical skills, interpersonal behaviors, and authority relations that are needed in this job.

Brim discusses the "occupational search phase" of this period:

> Thus the typical adult during his first years in the labor force experiments with various jobs and passes through his trial work period. People become differentially attracted to occupations on the basis of income, accessibility, and the fit of the job to their skills and their personalities (Inkeles & Smith, 1964), so that an individual's discovery of a compatible occupation is a result of his shifting from one line of work to another until he finds work that he likes. Often the individual leaves jobs which he does not like until he stumbles upon something better. It is during this period that he acquires the knowledge and skills suitable for his more mature occupational choice (Form & Miller,1960) and enters that phase of his occupational history in which he is likely to continue in the same general line of work for the next 30 years. (1968, p. 197)

Many factors may limit which occupations are open to a person during the work search phase. The most obvious include education level, talent, and location. Other social and psychological factors may limit a person's work goals or chance to do certain kinds of work. Let us offer some examples. First, some occupations are sex-labeled. Females are more likely to think of nursing, teaching, or library work as suitable careers. Men are more likely to see administration, engineering, or management as fitting them (Oppenheimer, 1968).

Second, women's career goals depend on whether or not they expect to marry and to have children. In a study of a national sample of women, results showed that the higher their occupational achievement, the more likely they were to remain single (Havens, 1973; Mueller & Campbell, 1977). In contrast, the more a woman is committed to the family roles of wife and mother, the more likely she is to interrupt her career, to choose a lower-status occupation, or to reject graduate training (Astin, 1977; Cartwright, 1977).

Third, racial discrimination continues to affect the participation of white and black men in the labor force. There continue to be limits on school achievement, work status, and income level of blacks that are the consequences of racial discrimination (Hauser & Featherman, 1974).

There is also a need to make a distinction between occupational choice and job choice. The choice of an occupation is likely to be a prolonged process. The decision to accept a specific job takes place in a shorter time and probably involves a review of fewer interrelated considerations. O'Reilly and Caldwell (1980) studied the impact of the kinds of factors that influenced job choice and subsequent job satisfaction. Subjects were graduates of a master's program in business administration. Two groups of factors influenced job choice. *Intrinsic factors* included interest in the job, personal feelings about the job, responsibility on the job, and opportunities for advancement. *Extrinsic factors* included family or financial pressures, advice of others, the job location, and the salary. Six months after taking the job, the subjects' satisfaction with the job and their commitment to remaining in that job were positively related to the strength of the intrinsic factors that influenced job choice. However, two extrinsic factors were also positively related to job commitment and satisfaction. They were salary and job location. One extrinsic factor, pressure from family or financial need, was associated with lower satisfaction and lower commitment to remain in the position. This study suggests that the basis upon which a job is chosen may influence future job attitudes and satisfaction.

In summary, we see early years of adulthood as the time for training, seeking information, engaging the world of work, and examining one's own talents and values. By working in several settings, young adults learn about the requirements of specific occupations and environments. They also begin to imagine themselves moving into the future through a particular work role. They begin to weigh the costs and rewards of their chosen occupation. The work search is limited by the kinds of work individuals are willing to consider and by the responses of the work world to the diversity of potential employees.

Management of a Career

Understanding Skills The management of one's occupational career is one of the tasks of adulthood. There are 44 characteristics that are used in the *Dictionary of Occupational Titles* to describe the unique blend of aptitudes and temperament required for each type of work. These 44 variables have been condensed to six basic factors: substantive complexity, motor skills, physical demands, management, interpersonal skills, and undesirable working conditions (Cain & Treiman, 1981). The characteristics of the occupation and the work setting will determine the kinds of work-related skills that will dominate the energies of the adult. If the demand for technical skill or subject-matter expertise is very great, for example, then individuals will be likely to spend considerable time keeping up to date in their field. They will have to practice their skills, attend special seminars, read technical journals, and, in general, think about the technical aspects of their work. If the demand for technical skill is low, then individuals are likely to learn all they need to know about their work in the first few months of employment. Their time and energy may be devoted to other aspects of their work or to life outside the work setting. A successful career in an occupation that does not require a great deal of technical skill may depend on tenure, administrative abilities, or success at interpersonal relationships.

Two other aspects of the work setting that have implications for career management are the degree of emphasis on interpersonal relations and the kinds of authority relations that exist. Both of these areas of relationships require an analysis of the patterns within the work setting and the development of skills that lead to adaptation in these settings.

Understanding Interpersonal Relationships Some occupations place a great deal of emphasis on the development and utilization of interpersonal skills. Success in these occupations may require the ability to influence others, to appear credible, to develop a fluent conversational style, or to learn to work effectively in groups or teams. People in these occupations must devote some thought to their social presentation and must work on acquiring the interpersonal skills that will increase their value in their work setting. People who value interpersonal skills as part of their occupational role are also likely to bring these skills to bear in family and other social relationships. People whose occupational roles require interpersonal skill development may find that at retirement they can more easily make the transition from a structured work life to a leisure life-style

In many kinds of work, interpersonal skills are central to success.

than those whose jobs are characterized by a great deal of emphasis on technical skills.

Individuals also must be able to understand the demands that are made on them for interpersonal behavior in their work setting. They must be able to identify and distinguish between a competitive and a cooperative situation. In a highly competitive situation some of the interpersonal demands may be nothing more than gamesmanship ploys designed to produce a decrement in performance. In order to succeed in this type of situation, individuals must learn to ignore some of these demands and retain their productivity. In a highly affiliative work setting they must be very tactful so as not to appear to be in competition with peers. They might also find it necessary to comply with certain interpersonal requests even though the requests may slow their performance. In some work settings, work norms are developed that may enhance or limit the productivity of the entire work staff. Once individuals are accepted into the work setting by virtue of their ability to comply with work norms and to get along with co-workers, they may have an opportunity to influence these norms. At that point they may alter their work environment so as to meet their own needs for stimulation, productivity, and interpersonal relationships more adequately.

We have discussed differences in work settings that are characterized by either a competitive or a cooperative interpersonal style. In fact, most work settings require some blend of both competitive and cooperative behaviors. The task for the individual in these kinds of settings is to be able to assess individual interpersonal demands as competitive or cooperative in nature and to respond appropriately. In the process of establishing an interpersonal work style, individuals will probably form temporary alliances from time to time, some lasting friendships, and some animosities that also endure (Argyle, 1972).

Understanding Authority Relations In addition to work relationships with colleagues there are a wide variety of authority relations in the world of work. Initially the individual must identify the authority structure that operates in the work setting and begin to establish a position in that structure. Advancement in a career inevitably involves some increase in the sphere of responsibility and decision-making power. One cannot hope to advance without assuming some increased authority. Thus, career management eventually involves the ability to assume the authority role as well as to respond to higher authorities.

Jobs vary in the patterns of advancement they offer the individual. Some careers begin with a long period of subordinance, which gradually gives way to increased authority. Some careers place new employees in positions of authority quite early and continue to move them up a ladder of authority at a fairly steady pace. Still other careers find the new worker established at the very beginning in a position of authority which never really changes much. The task is to identify the authority pattern and to assess which skills will be needed for advancement in the hierarchy.

Some people do not choose to advance beyond a given point in the authority structure. They find a position in which the degree of responsibility and the degree of subordination are both comfortable, and they choose to remain at that level. Others find that if they do not choose to advance, their careers suffer. Still others discover that achievement is not possible and that they have attained some peak in status beyond which they cannot rise.

It is the ability of individuals to understand the nature of the authority relationships and the quality of the authority figures in their work setting that will in large part determine their success at work. Success in this sense means not only advancement or movement toward material goals, but freedom from the arbitrary demands or the needs for advancement of other people. The individual must be able to separate the demands that are necessary for successful, coordinated labor from those that are characteristic of individuals who merely seek power and dominance over others.

In institutions in a democratic country, the need for efficient organization and division of labor is recognized. At the same time, the need for workers to participate in the processes of influence and decision-making in the work setting is also recognized. Workers should be allowed to have strong and firmly developed opinions about how the people in positions of authority are doing their jobs, and they should be allowed to express those opinions without fear of retribution. In this way they are able to contribute to the work process, to check the corruption of individuals in positions of power, and to facilitate the appropriate placement of people in positions that best meet their skills.

As individuals settle into a career, they begin to set out a timetable for their expectations about the progression of their work life. They decide when they should be at the peak of their productivity, when they will seek advancement to positions of greater authority, when they expect to reach their greatest earning power, and when they expect to retire. This "work clock" serves as a motivator which is separate from the external rewards of the career itself and as a standard of evaluation of one's progress as one moves through the career cycle (Brim, 1975).

In addition to the conceptualization of a plan for progress in one's career, the individual may attempt to plan for both vertical and horizontal movements. Vertical movements are considered to be promotions, the attainment of higher positions, or changes to more prestigious organizations or institutions. Horizontal movements are changes that represent the same level of attainment in a more personally comfortable work setting.

Other aspects of career management are determined by whether one works for oneself or for someone else and whether one works in the private or in the public sector. The goals of work in one setting are different from the goals of work in the other. The individual who can produce a good fit between personal needs and the expectations of the work setting will be aided in career management. Motives for work also vary from person to person. People may seek security, monetary gain, or prestige, or they may work because they enjoy it. Once again, the individual who is able to assess personal needs and the requirements of the work setting will facilitate management of a career.

The discussion above has been concerned with the management of a career for individuals who are involved in their work life. The degree of involvement varies greatly from individual to individual. There are some people who, by the end of the work-search phase, are alienated from work. They withdraw their emotional investment in work, lower their standards, and become uninterested (Argyris, 1964). These are people who find little source of satisfaction in the work setting and little opportunity for meaningful labor. If these people do work, they are probably not very involved in their work settings and therefore do not learn much about the interpersonal relations, the authority relations, or the skill-related tasks that are sources of challenge to the management of a career. They have little opportunity to develop competence within the context of work.

Because of the cultural emphasis on productive work, these individuals are likely to experience some degree of guilt about being unable to work. They may become the "invisible men" who disappear from the census rolls. They may also find it hard to direct their energy toward creative solutions to life problems if they feel alienated from the work role.

By the time they reach adulthood, some young people are quite alienated from the world of work.

The inability to work could become a serious barrier to a positive resolution of the psychosocial conflict of generativity versus stagnation.

Clearly, management of a career does not occur independently of commitments to one's spouse and one's children. Decisions about assuming more authority, working longer hours, accepting an offer with another company, quitting one's job, and accepting a transfer to a new location are

BOX 9.1 Midlife Career Change

Simeon Wooten

Simeon Wooten, Jr., at 52, gave up his comfortable life as president of the Southeast Everglades Bank of Fort Lauderdale to embark on a new career in teaching. Wooten, who calls himself a "new conservative," is worried that the drift toward egalitarianism in the United States is eroding the foundations of capitalism, and he blames this partly on the U.S. educational system. As he put it: "If I have a voice that has any impact at all, it will be in that system. I'm a very concerned citizen, and I no longer want to be among the silent majority."

Wooten's first stint at teaching came when he was recalled during the Korean War and taught leadership to noncoms. The satisfaction of that experience stayed with him. Once financial commitments to the education of his own three children were taken care of, he began to think about changing careers. After a year as a college instructor, to make sure he still enjoyed teaching, Wooten enrolled in the fall of 1976 in the doctoral program at the University of Virginia's Darden Graduate School of Business.

Shifting gears hasn't been easy. "If you really want a course in humility, come back to school after 30 years," Wooten remarks. He's found one of his biggest problems to be acquiring the quantitative skills necessary to use computers. And he has had to redevelop the habit of concentrating for hours on a problem. "It's not retirement," he notes. "I thought I would have a nervous breakdown the first year."

Wooten has traded the sailing club for the library, and his wife, Marion, has traded the Junior League for real estate brokerage. "Obviously our living standard is lower in a material way," says Wooten, who doesn't seem to mind because "in an intellectual way, life is much more stimulating."

Source: "Reassessment Time for the Forty-Niners" by M. Wellemeyer, *Fortune,* May 21, 1979, p. 120.

all decisions that will touch the lives of other family members. One of the most draining aspects of career management is the effort to meet conflicting expectations of one's marital, parental, and work roles.

Patterns of Midlife Career Change The development of a career does not necessarily mean doing the same job or even the same kind of work. There are many reasons to change one's work goals during midlife. Here, we will consider four different patterns.

First, some careers reach an end during middle adulthood. One obvious example is the professional athlete. Work roles that require physical strength, speed of reaction, or endurance may force a midlife career change when these abilities are diminished.

Second, some adults cannot resolve conflicts between job demands and personal goals. Here we think of the young Chicago executive who decides to buy a farm in Arkansas (Terkel, 1974) or the public relations aide to a senator who leaves Washington to return to Maine to sell real estate (Sheehy, 1976). The case of Simeon Wooten, Jr., illustrates this kind of career change. It is guided by careful study and decisions about what is important (see Box 9.1). Wooten was one of the graduates of the Harvard Business School class of 1949. Affectionately called the 49ers, this class met with unusual business success. Sixteen percent of those who responded to a *Fortune* survey in 1974 were millionaires. Thirty years after graduation, Wooten shows a common pattern of personal understanding and change (Wellemeyer, 1979).

Third, some workers recognize that they have succeeded as much as they can in their work. Their career change reflects a realization that they are not going to achieve their aspirations for their career. It may take a person several years to reach this understanding. Many adults decide to stick it out in a secure position, even when it falls short of their goals. Others decide to retrain, return to school, or begin in a new field.

Fourth, there are women who have been in and out of the work force who decide to make a greater commitment to career once their children are in high school or college. These women often begin by returning to college to complete a degree or to pursue a new degree. Nearly 40 percent of women who leave work while their children are young and 60 percent of those who have never worked but want to state a need for more education or training before entering the job market. At every age range women look for an employment pattern that allows them to stay home while their children are young. They want to combine career and homemaking before children are born and after the children are older (Market Opinion Research, 1977). Many women actually desire a life-style that would have a built-in midlife career change.

In contrast to the midlife career change, some adults are "locked-in" to their career choice. In a national survey of people 16 years or over who were employed for 20 hours a week or more, almost 42 percent felt it would not be at all easy to find another job with a similar salary and fringe benefits. What is more, 62 percent of the sample said they would not be willing to move 100 miles away in order to get a much better job. In fact 26 percent were not willing to move that far for another job even if they were out of work. The risks of trading certainty, even an unpleasant or unfulfilling certainty, for uncertainty are not very appealing to many adult workers (Quinn & Staines, 1979).

Retirement

Retirement refers to one's status with respect to the paid labor force. One definition of retirement requires that the person work less than full-time year-round and receive income from a retirment pension earned during earlier periods of employment (Atchley, 1977). Some people define retirement as the time at which people begin to receive a social security pension or some other national retirement pension (Horn, 1980). However, retirement also refers to a psychological state, a sense of psychological withdrawal from a job or organization and entry into a new orientation toward work.

Let us note here that some people never retire; they never face this part of career development. Individuals who are self-employed or who are in a profession in which advanced age is not a deterrent to productivity may continue at their work until death. They may discover new skills; they may redefine their work goals or their standards of success. They never abandon their occupational role (Dennis, 1966; Simonton, 1977).

Retirement is a relatively new historical opportunity. At the turn of the century, slightly more than 30 percent of men over age 65 were *not* in the paid labor force. By the year 2000, it is estimated that 90 percent of men over age 65 will not be in the paid labor force (see Figure 9.3). What is more,

FIGURE 9.3 Percent U.S. Males over Age 65 Not in the Labor Force in Each Decade of 20th Century

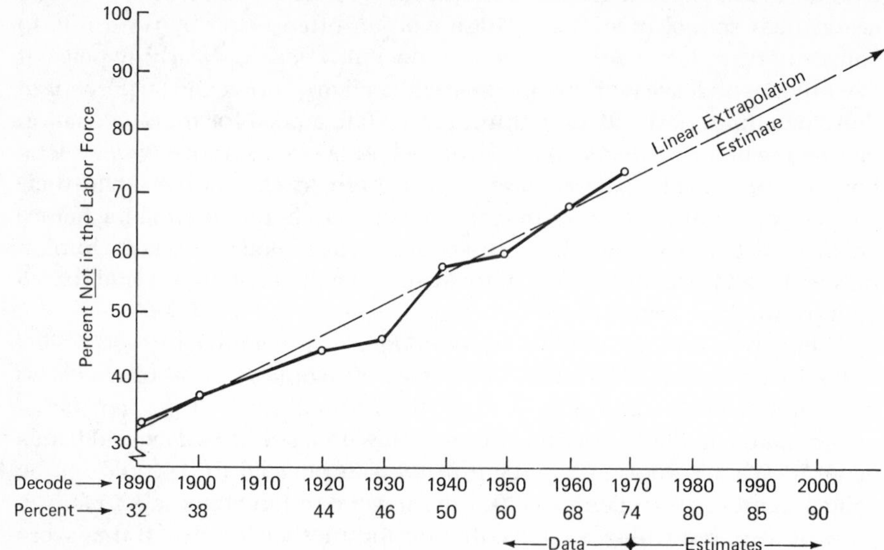

Source: Adapted from R. Atchley, *The Sociology of Retirement* (Cambridge, Mass.: Schenkman, 1976), p. 17.

as the age for eligibility for receiving retirement pensions declines, more and more adults are retiring in their late fifties and early sixties.

There is evidence that younger cohorts are more accepting of retirement than cohorts who reached retirement age during the 1940s and 1950s. At that time, most adults had not come to expect retirement as an appropriate end to their work life. They expressed guilt and even dread of retirement. Today, more workers see retirement as something to which they are entitled (Atchley, 1976).

The extent to which retirement is viewed as a positive life transition is supported by studies of pre-retirement and retirement-aged adults. Retirement is *not* associated with high levels of depression, declines in self-esteem or optimism, or dramatic drops in social participation. People whose post-retirement income is very low or who encounter ill health or widowhood in retirement perceive retirement as a greater loss. However, retirement itself is not the major factor that accounts for this view. Rather, it is a nostalgic longing for a time when one's spouse was alive or when one's health was better that makes the earlier working days appear more desirable (Cottrell & Atchley, 1969; Levy, 1981).

Adjusting to Retirement Some people have more difficulty adjusting to retirement than others. There are at least three reasons for this. First, some people do more planning for their retirement, and this seems to promote better adjustment during retirement itself. Retirement preparation includes some financial plan and anticipation of one's financial resources after retirement. Retirement preparation includes anticipation of changes in physical health and resilience that may influence daily activity. Retirement preparation also includes anticipation of changing family roles and household responsibilities (Schafer & Keith, 1981).

Second, some people are reluctant to retire. They view retirement as bad for people. When they are at retirement age, they are still strong, energetic, and involved. Work gives their lives structure and meaning. Their salary permits them to live independently and to maintain their sense of personal competence (Powers & Goudy, 1971; Shapiro, 1977). These people may not be ready to retire. They may feel discouraged by feelings of uselessness that accompany not working (Streib & Schneider, 1971). For these people, introspection is more likely to focus on injustices of the retirement regulations, anxiety about how to maintain a certain financial level, and regrets about a lack of personal control over one's life. Those who do not feel content about this new phase of their lives are unlikely to find sources of satisfaction in their own introspective thinking. Retirement may facilitate the development of a sense of despair (Atchley, 1976).

Third, adjustment to retirement is especially difficult for those who must live on a dramatically reduced or minimal income. Retirement usually brings about a 50 percent reduction in income. In 1979, 15 percent of all people 65 years old and over reported income below the poverty level. Thirty-five percent of blacks and 13 percent of whites over age 65 were below the poverty level. Table 9.5 shows three levels of budgeting for retired couples in 1977. In thinking about retirement, costs for work-related expenses, taxes, and child-care expenses are reduced. However, health care and recreational expenses may rise. In 1976, the median income of persons 65 years old and over was about $7,600 if they were members of a married

TABLE 9.5 Annual Budgets for Retired Couples at Three Levels of Living, Urban United States, Autumn 1977

	Level of Living		
Budget item	**Lower**	**Intermediate**	**Higher**
Total budget	5,031	7,198	10,711
Total family consumption	4,815	6,765	9,898
Food	1,535	2,035	2,554
Housing	1,745	2,518	3,936
Transportation	337	658	1,215
Clothing	214	360	555
Personal care	146	214	313
Medical care	628	632	637
Other family consumption	209	347	687
Other items	217	433	813

Source: "Medical Care Costs Lead Rise in 1976–77 Family Budgets" by M. Louise McCraw, *Monthly Labor Review 101,* November 1978, *101,* 33.

couple, but only $3,800 for an unmarried male, and $3,200 for an unmarried female. This compares to an overall median family income of about $16,000 for all American families (U.S. Bureau of the Census, 1980).

As adults get close to retirement, many turn to leisure activities to fill their time. Some people decide that tennis, golf, fishing, cards, boating, or administrative work related to these activities will occupy the remainder of their lives. Investment in leisure activities is not exactly a new role. The retired businessman does not think of himself as a golfer. However, the energy spent in these sports can be quite intense. Satisfactions with the range of leisure activities can contribute significantly to life satisfaction after retirement (O'Brien, 1981). Adults may choose a retirement community that helps them satisfy their leisure interest. They may plan vacations to allow new experiences related to their favorite sport. As the case of Ivy Wood illustrates, involvement with a leisure activity can actually become like a full-time job.

> At one time, when she was 18 and excited by courses she had taken in applied design, Ivy Wood wanted to be an art teacher, but the Depression came and, she said, "I couldn't, I had to go out and work."
>
> Work for her was many years as a cashier in the New York State Department of Motor Vehicles, during which time she married and raised children and, except for a few occasional classes in life drawing at Pratt Institute, art became for Ivy Wood a distant, recurring and unsatisfied interior ache.
>
> Then, nine years ago, her husband died, and in 1978, when she retired, her son suggested that she take up painting at the Springfield Gardens-St. Albans Senior Center near her Queens home. Three years later Ivy Wood, at 70, is somewhat of a cultural cottage industry, whose apartment house kitchen doubles as a painting studio, who teaches and conducts painting workshops at the center, and who has begun to sell her paintings even though, she says, "they're like children, you hate to see them go." (Ferretti, 1981, p. 28)

A growing new interest among many older adults is continuing education. Community colleges as well as four-year schools have begun to respond to the educational interests of the adult population. Older adults are returning to complete bachelor and advanced degrees, to develop new skills, or simply to share interesting times with other students (Stetar, 1975).

An interesting new role that has begun to emerge for people who have ended their life work activity is that of retiree. Current publications such as *Modern Maturity* define an older age group with common interests in much the same way as *Seventeen* defines early adolescence as an age role. There are groups of older people who form active voting blocks and maintain lobbies which attempt to promote the passage of legislation in their interest. Some examples are the American Association of Retired Professionals (AARP) and the National Retired Teachers Association (NRTA). Within many companies there are groups of retirees who, as former

Older adults are becoming an active political voice for the rights and welfare of the aged.

employees of that company, attempt to administer pension plans and influence company policy. The presence of these groups is evidence of the continued vigor of older adults. It is also evidence of their ability to identify and promote issues related to their own welfare (Ragan & Dowd, 1974).

A Look toward the Future of Retirement The ongoing dialogue between older workers, retirees, and organizations is likely to result in the formulation of more varied, more flexible alternatives to full retirement. More and more businesses are eliminating a mandatory retirement age. Pre-retirement plans, including phased retirement, part-time work, and reduced or redefined job expectations, are being devised. There seem to be two directions of exploration occurring at the same time. One looks at the ways to retain older workers in meaningful work roles. The other looks at ways to permit more flexible, early retirement (Gonda, 1981).

There are several long-range concerns that suggest a need to reexamine the "right to retirement" concept. First, a longer healthy adulthood means that a large proportion of the population would be out of the labor force for nearly one-third of their adult lives (from 60 to 80). With a reduced fertility rate there may not be a number of younger workers available to support this large nonworking population. Second, older adults who are well educated and who have enjoyed their work life will want to continue some of the positive experiences of their work life through constructive labor participation. Third, people who reenter the labor force during midlife or who make a major midlife career change will want to persist at that new career activity in order to fulfill both personal and societal expectations for achievement (Horn, 1980; Ragan, 1980). Thus, just as the past few generations have begun to grow accustomed to retirement the next generations of older adults may be finding ways to prolong their productive labor involvement.

Unemployment

The first thing to take into account in discussing the topic of unemployment is that it is a concept that exists in people's minds as well as an objective state of being. One wonders whether hundred of years ago the concept was as firmly established in people's minds. Did a peasant think of himself or herself as "employed"? Was a guildsman "employed"? Was a farmer of biblical times "employed"? These people probably did not have the concept of employment in their minds in the same way that the modern person does.

What does the concept of unemployment mean? This question is not as simple to answer as one might think. One definition would be that the person does not hold a job working for someone or some institution. Another definition would be someone who does absolutely no work at all of any kind. In its simplest form, this is equating unemployment with doing nothing. A third definition would be someone who collects checks from the state government Worker's Insurance Fund. These checks are often referred to as "unemployment checks." These people have been employed by someone or some institution but they are no longer employed. Is the woman who cares for children and maintains the family household unemployed? Is the man or woman who runs a business and therefore does not receive a salary from someone else unemployed? Is the person who lives on the income from capital investments and does little else unemployed? These questions lead one to the realization that the sense of being unemployed and the associated feelings or meanings attached to that status will vary depending on the person's point of view.

The total unemployment rate for 1980 was 7.1 percent of the labor force. This compares to a low rate of 5.5 percent in 1960 and a high rate of 8.5 percent in 1975. Over the past 20 years, the unemployment rate has been highest for adolescents between the ages of 16 and 19 (17.7 percent in 1980) and lower for older workers in their fifties (about 3 percent) (see Figure 9.4). Whites consistently have a lower unemployment rate (6.3 percent in 1980) than nonwhites (13.2 percent in 1980) (U.S. Bureau of the

FIGURE 9.4 Unemployment of Persons 16 Years Old and Older by Duration, 1948–1979

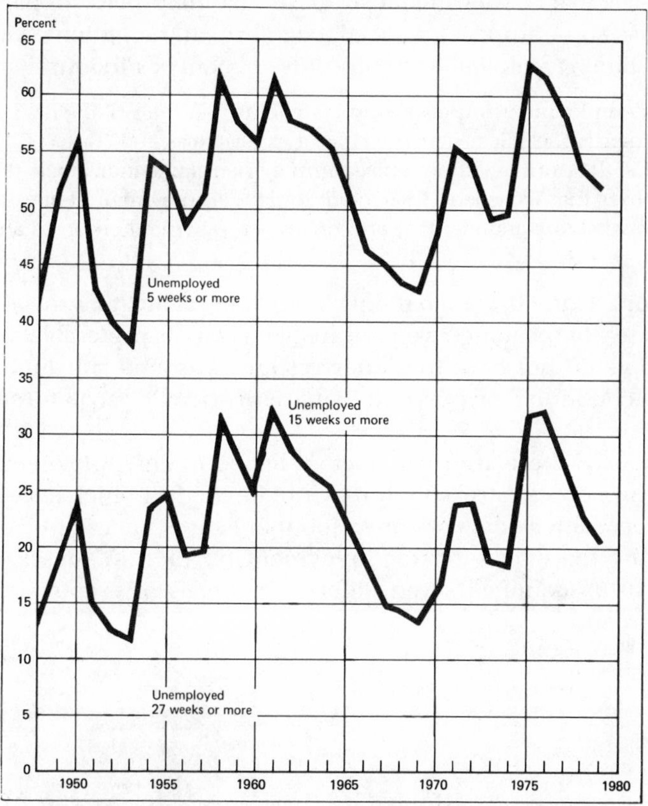

Source: U.S. Bureau of the Census. *Social Indicators III* (Washington, D.C.: U.S. Government Printing Office, 1980), 333.

Census, 1981). These rates reflect annual estimates of people who are looking for work. They do not tell about the duration of unemployment or the number of people who are discouraged from looking for work because they know unemployment is high.

Unemployment and Stress

It is commonly assumed that unemployment is a source of life stress. Brenner (1973) has traced the relationship between national economic activity and patterns of physical and mental health. He has argued that there is a direct link between fluctuations in unemployment and such health indicators as homicide rates, suicide rates, and certain disease rates, especially liver disease, kidney disease, and cardiovascular disease.

The psychological consequences of unemployment are linked to the underlying satisfactions of work. Even if we assume that people must work to meet basic needs, we can still suppose that the process of participating in work has some important social, cognitive, and emotional benefits for adult functioning. Jahoda describes those benefits as follows:

> First, employment imposes a time structure on the waking day; second, employment implies regularly shared experiences and contacts with people outside the nuclear family; third, employment links individuals to goals and purposes that transcend their own; fourth, employment defines aspects of personal status and identity; and finally, employment enforces activity. (1981, p. 188)

We see work as the bridge that links people to reality, to a social network, and to a sense of meaning. Even unsatisfying work is preferable to no work. Many people do not have the inner resources to find substitutes for the structure, continuity, or purpose that are provided by structured employment.

Obviously, there are many factors linked to unemployment that can make it more or less stressful. It may not be the fact of job loss per se but what happens after one loses one's job that causes uncertainty or anxiety. In analyzing the effects of unemployment on men in the Detroit area, Ferman (1979) identified seven different patterns of events surrounding unemployment:

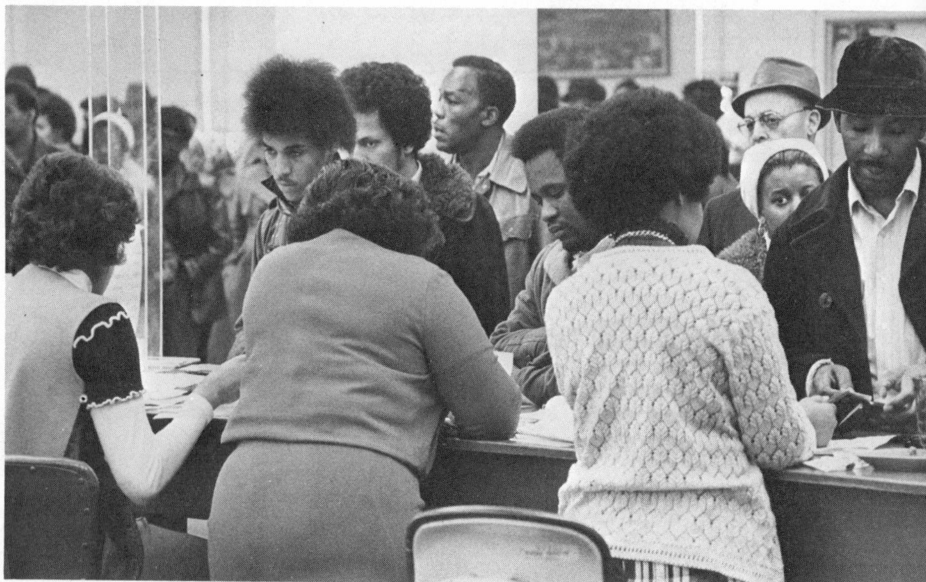

The stress of unemployment is determined in part by what happens after people lose their jobs.

1. Those who remain unemployed after job loss.
2. Those who return to their former employer and remain on the job.
3. Those who find new jobs and remain working there.
4. Those who continue to be in and out of work with their former employer.
5. Those who are periodically in and out of work with one new employer.
6. Those who are in and out of work with more than one employer.
7. Irregular patterns including changing professions, enjoying a period of unemployment and then returning to work, or voluntary early retirement.

Ferman has argued that it is the post-unemployment events that will determine just how stressful the experience is. We would add that it is the person's perception of the unemployed status and his or her coping skills for dealing with this new uncertainty that mediate its stressfulness. People who can see advantages to a break in employment or who are very optimistic about returning to a job will undoubtedly be less anxious about temporary unemployment. Older workers who are depending on a retirement pension, high-status workers who are fired suddenly, and workers with long years of service for a single firm seem to adapt less readily and to retain bitterness over their job loss. Workers who return to work only to be fired again or who return to a level of work that is less demanding and less prestigious than their former position can become very cynical about their own worth and the value of work.

In a study of the experiences of unemployment, Dorothea and Benjamin Braginsky (1975) interviewed 43 jobless men and a comparison group of employed men. Many of the men had college degrees. They had been in managerial or engineering positions. Eighty percent were experiencing their first unemployment in 20 years of work. The unemployed men felt unwanted, insignificant, and bitter. They were experiencing dramatic reevaluation of long-held values. They expressed a sense that their college years had been wasted, that hard work and skill were not as important as "brown-nosing the boss," and that their friends shunned them after they lost their jobs. Believing that society should judge each person by his or her labor was a costly value for these unemployed men. It resulted in a sense of worthlessness and low self-esteem that persisted for many even after they were reemployed.

Two factors that influence the impact of unemployment are kin support and income loss. The impact of unemployment can intensify conflict at home. Men may feel sensitive about performing household chores. They may equate job loss with a loss of masculinity. Their physical presence in the home after a pattern of daily absence may in itself lead to more disruptive interactions. However, family members, especially wives, can also provide the kind of support and encouragement that prevents intense feelings of alienation or worthlessness. Where a marriage is already strong, a couple can enjoy more time together. They can solve the problem of unemployment as they have solved other difficult life challenges, and feel closer as a consequence.

Income loss is a very real consequence of unemployment. Ferman (1979) found that when weekly income was reduced by $150 or more, other indices of trauma were also high. In families where there is more than one worker, the impact of job loss can be buffered by the continued income of other family members.

Men and Women in Their Work Activities

In recent years, more and more women have entered the paid labor force. Many women hold the roles of wife, mother, and worker. There is no sign that this trend toward increased employment of women is going to decline in the near future. In fact, the census data show that women are delaying marriage and childbearing longer and that more women are voluntarily childless (U.S. Bureau of Census, 1981). These data suggest a growing involvement in work and a decision to limit the demands of competing roles.

Despite the fact that more women are entering the labor force, men and women do not participate equally in areas of employment (Bernard, 1971; Parsons, 1977). Even though women do as well as men in college, fewer women plan for graduate training (Astin, 1977; Baird, 1976). Women continue to enter a few traditional careers, and many women are "underemployed," considering their level of ability and education (Tangri, 1972; Severance & Gottsegen, 1977). Table 9.6 shows the percent of men and women in the labor force in eight occupational categories. The data compare the years 1958, 1968, and 1978. In five categories, managerial and administrative, clerical, crafts, other blue-collar workers, and service workers, men and women have been differentially involved. The patterns have not changed very dramatically in any category except farm workers, where 6 percent fewer males are involved than was the case in 1958.

Several explanations have been offered to account for these differences in participation. Four explanations are presented along with supporting or qualifying evidence.

1. Men and women use different cognitive styles to make career choices. Women use the intuitive style, and men use the planning style. As we discussed above, the intuitive style is a less effective coping strategy. It would, therefore, lead to less carefully planned or less mature career decisions. However, studies do not support this explanation. Comparisons of male and female college students do not find differences in decision-making styles (Barrett & Tinsley, 1977; Lunneborg, 1977; Harren & Kass, 1977).

2. Men and women understand specific careers in different ways. Baird (1977) asked a national sample of college seniors to evaluate five careers: medicine, law, college teaching and research, elementary and senior school teaching, and business. Except for business, men and women

TABLE 9.6 Occupational Distribution of Employed Workers by Sex: 1958, 1968, and 1978

Year, Sex	Number Employed (thous.)	Occupational Distribution (percent)								
		Total	Professional and Technical Workers	Managerial and Administrative Workers'	Sales Workers	Clerical Workers	Crafts Workers	Other Blue-Collar Workers	Service Workers	Farm Workers
1958										
Total	63,036	100.0	11.0	10.8	6.3	14.5	13.4	23.6	11.9	8.5
Male	42,423	100.0	10.4	13.6	5.7	6.9	19.4	27.4	6.4	10.4
Female	20,613	100.0	12.3	5.0	7.6	30.1	1.1	16.0	23.2	4.7
1968										
Total	75,920	100.0	13.6	10.2	6.1	16.9	13.2	23.1	12.4	4.6
Male	48,114	100.0	13.4	13.6	5.7	7.1	20.2	27.2	6.9	6.0
Female	27,807	100.0	13.9	4.5	6.9	33.8	1.1	15.8	21.8	2.1
1978										
Total	94,373	100.0	15.1	10.7	6.3	17.9	13.1	20.3	13.6	3.0
Male	55,491	100.0	14.7	14.0	5.9	6.2	21.1	25.3	8.7	4.1
Female	38,881	100.0	15.6	6.1	6.9	34.6	1.8	13.0	20.7	1.3

Source: U.S. Bureau of the Census, *Social Indicators III* (Washington D.C.: U.S. Government Printing Office, 1980), adapted from Table 7/12.

saw different advantages and disadvantages in these careers. For example, more women than men thought that law provided challenge and interest, that it required a high level of intelligence, and that it offered avenues to contribute to the advancement of knowledge. More women than men saw success in law as affected by one's political views. Women saw law as a high-pressure profession requiring hard work, long hours, and a lot of time away from one's family. In this sense, women may see law as a less desirable career, particularly if they have already made a strong commitment to marriage and family.

3. The absence of female models in certain industries or in highly visible leadership positions contributes to differences in the career aspirations of men and women (Severance & Gottsegen, 1977). Table 9.7 shows the percentage of women in selected power roles. Following the hypothesis

TABLE 9.7 Percent of Women in Selected Principal Power Processes: 1978

Position	Percent	Number	Office
Local office	7.8		
State legislator	9.3		
School board member	25.0		
County commissioner	3.0		
Mayor or councilor of municipality or township	8.0		
Congress[1]	3.6	16	96th Congress
		1	Senate
Statewide office[2]	10.7	10	Secretary of State
		6	Lt. Governor
		6	State Treasurer
Federal judgeship	1.1		
State appellate court	1.8		
Executive branch			
Federal level,			
GS15–18	16.6		
GS 15	4.8		
GS 16	3.7		
GS 17	3.2		
GS 18	4.9		
Party office[3]			
Democratic State chair	12		
Republican State chair	8		
Trade unions—AFL-CIO			
Governing boards	8.7		
Voter turnout (1978)[4]	45.3		

[1]103 women and 11,400 men have served in Congress.

[2]1977.

[3]1979.

[4]Women of voting age.

Source: U.S. Bureau of the Census, *Reflections of America: Commemorating the Statistical Abstract Centennial* (Washington, D.C.: U.S. Government Printing Office, 1980), Table 6, p. 188.

that a lack of models leads to lower career aspirations, Tidball (1973) found a correlation of +.95 between the number of women faculty at an undergraduate college and the number of women graduates who followed successful careers. In the Soviet Union, where there is an attempt to make full use of women in the labor force, 36 percent of the engineers and 45 percent of the scientific workers are women (Chabaud, 1970). Russian girls are more likely than American girls to have mothers who are in professional roles and to hear about professional women who are in positions of responsibility.

4. Career aspirations are determined by attitudes, personality, and childrearing experiences. Women who are most committed to the roles of wife and mother will have less innovative career aspirations. Tangri (1972) reported that female college students who choose occupations which few women choose are likely to have educated, working mothers. These women are autonomous and internally motivated. They have well-developed self-concepts. They have a strong career commitment. They are likely to have support for their career goals from faculty, female friends, and a boyfriend. In a study of female college students, a number of attitudes were important to high career aspirations (Parsons, Frieze, & Ruble, 1975). These attitudes included:

1. A belief that women's demands for equality are justified.
2. A sense that men think women's demands for equality are justified.
3. A belief that career and family roles are not in direct conflict.

A woman with high aspirations was likely to have a mother who had a career or a mother who was dissatisfied with her work. In this analysis, the strength of the woman's commitment to her own career was greater when she understood the ways that discrimination had influenced the problems of women in careers.

In summary, men and women bring the same intellectual skills to career decision-making. Women do not use a less effective cognitive style than men. Women do tend to have different views than men about the desirability of certain careers. This is probably due to past differences in the participation of men and women in various professions. The absence of female models reduces the likelihood that women will aspire to some careers. The more women understand how these patterns have come about and the more support they have from parents, faculty, and peers, the more likely they are to seek more innovative careers.

As we pointed out in Chapter 8, the two-earner family places different stresses on men and women. Most couples see child care and certain household tasks primarily as the job of the wife (Hoffman, 1974; Stafford, Backman, & Dibona, 1977). When both the husband and the wife are working, the woman may experience a lot of stress as she tries to meet work demands and still have the time to spend with her children. In a study of 200 professional couples, women were more likely to have greater responsibility for the home and family and to put their husband's career ahead of their own (Heckman, Bryson, & Bryson, 1977). Some women handle the conflict between career aspirations and family commitment by limiting their competitive achievement strivings.

For other women, the work setting may limit achievement through assumptions employers make about a woman's commitment to her family role. Women do not tend to be promoted to high-level administrative or managerial positions where work demands would begin to interfere with family needs (Blaxall & Reagan, 1976). Companies do not like to put women in positions where they may have to be transferred. They assume that the husband will not make the move (Gallese, 1978). What is more, companies can be noticeably affected when management-level women take maternity leaves. In a recent *Wall Street Journal* article, the headline read as follows: "Maternity Leave: Companies Are Disrupted by Wave of After–30 Pregnancies Among Middle Managers." Many women find that after they have had a child they cannot or do not want to work the long hours or experience the hectic travel schedules of an executive-level position. Other women discover ways to modify their careers to incorporate the mother role.

> Carol Brown, 40, a Manhattan computer consultant, was able to alter her job so she could do most of her work at home. A partner with her husband

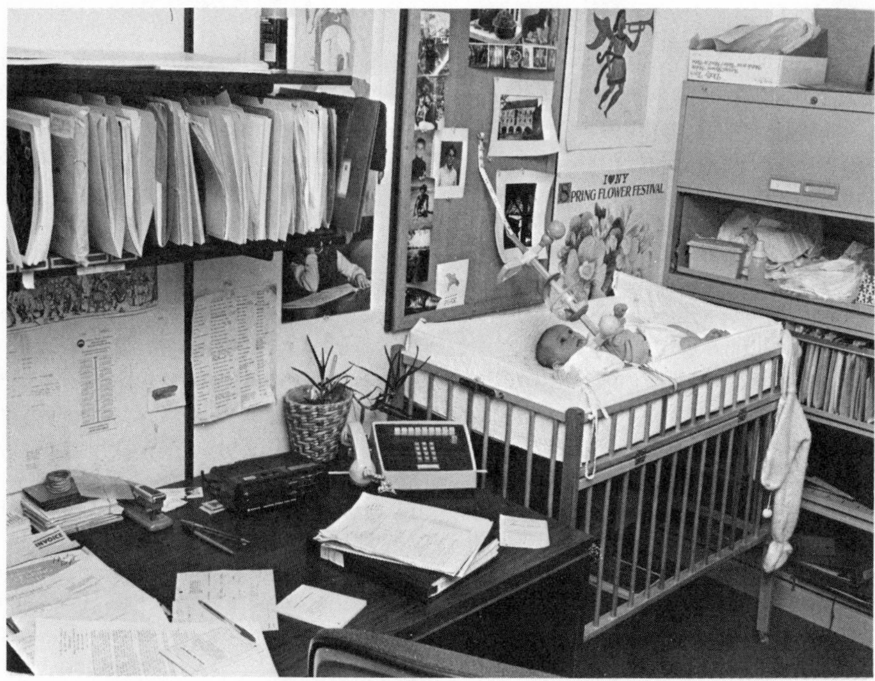

Some women are creating innovative strategies for combining their work and parental roles.

> in a New York investment-counseling and minicomputer-consulting concern, Mrs. Brown switched her job emphasis from consulting with businesses on how to adapt minicomputers to their operations, to writing software programs for clients.
>
> She had a computer terminal installed in her home, and she uses it to communicate and give instructions to one of her clients, a Manhattan architectural firm. She can pick up her telephone, attach it to her computer, and make changes in the programs for the firm. She admits she could have made more money by staying in the office, but she enjoys working at home and taking care of her daughter at the same time. (Gottschalk, 1981, p. 8)

In spite of the stresses and conflicts that confront working women, career development appears to be well worth the effort in the long run. Low-income women who do not have a husband are more confident and more independent if they are employed than if they are not. In a study of women in middle adulthood, the self-esteem of career women was higher than the self-esteem of noncareer women (Birnbaum, 1975). Married women who are working are more independent, assertive, and self-assured than those who are not. They are more likely to have a more equitable decision-making role and to share more evenly in the power of the family than women who are not employed outside the home. As productive workers, women have the security of their income and their social network of coworkers as sources of self-esteem and well-being (Dunlop, 1981).

If women are going to become more involved in the labor force, what can we expect to be the changes in life-scheduling for men and women? How will men, women, and work settings coordinate the simultaneous demands of the worker, spouse, and parent roles? Best (1981) explored this question by asking working men and women about their preferences for certain time/income/life-scheduling trade-offs. The kind of life-scheduling that was desired depended on the sex of the respondent, the traditional or nontraditional sex-role attitudes of the respondent, and the family life stage of the respondent. For example, options for exchanging portions of current income for more vacation time were presented. About 50 percent of the sample would not forego current income for more vacation. However, 8 percent of men and 4 percent of women were willing to trade 20 percent of their income for 50 vacation days. A much greater proportion of those who described their sex-role attitudes as flexible were interested in making money-vacation trade-offs in comparison to those who held traditional sex-role attitudes.

The family-life-stage factor seemed to operate differently for men and women. Overall, both men and women were more likely to prefer five more days of vacation as a desirable trade-off for a 2 percent raise in income. However, at the birth of the first child, 27 percent of men expressed a need to emphasize money over free time or more vacation. Women expressed greater preference for time over money at that life stage. In families with older children, men expressed greater willingness to trade income for time whereas women increased their preference for money over time. We are clearly in a period of experimentation. As the needs of adults in various phases of their personal and family development interact with the needs of organizations, we will begin to see some creative problem-solving. The more essential the worker is to the organization and the more costly high turnover and alienation are, the more the work place will accommodate to changing family and personal needs. There are many indications that we are moving toward a more cyclic work pattern in which both men and women alternate time on the job, time in educational settings, and time devoted to parenting throughout the occupational career.

Chapter Summary

Through experiences in work, adults learn more about their own temperament, talents, aspirations, and vulnerabilities. They may be "shaped" to some extent by the regular and persistent demands of the work setting. They also come to appreciate the complexity of any work effort. The inherent conflicts among role groups, norms for productivity and for social relationships, and the unpredictable fluctuations in economic conditions all influence the consciousness of adults as they engage in their roles as workers.

Work settings and occupations are quite varied. So are the characteristics and expectations of individual workers. In order to appreciate the contribution of work to adult development it is necessary to consider some of the dimensions of work that have a potential impact. Three dimensions were described: satisfactions, demands, and hazards. Satisfaction accounts for the persistence, the identification, and the conscientiousness with which workers carry out their responsibilities. The demands can be seen as dimensions of challenge with which workers cope. Meeting work demands may be difficult, but it may also foster new growth. For some workers, the demands or challenges of work are a source of satisfaction. Hazards refer to the dangers of a work setting. All forms of work expose workers to physical or psychological risk. As adults identify and anticipate those risks, they may become disenchanted with the world of work. Much adult effort to change work environments is directed toward reducing the hazards and increasing opportunities to achieve satisfaction.

Occupational careers are not static. They change because of new demands from the world of work as well as new needs and abilities of workers. With each new phase of career development adults have opportunities to discover aspects of their competence. Career changes help an adult to clarify the relationship between sense of worth as a person and sense of worth as a worker. The seven phases of career decision-making offered by Tiedeman actually reflect this dynamic reciprocal process of clarification of the work setting and clarification of personal values and needs. The process continues to operate through the phases of career choice, work search, management of a career, and retirement. As a result of participation in the world of work, adults have many opportunities to explore the relationship between life satisfaction and productive labor.

Career change can be experienced as a smooth progression over time or as dramatic shifts and disruptions. It is difficult to determine the extent to which abrupt changes have negative consequences for adults. Much depends on the person's outlook and on the sense of control he or she has about future work opportunities. In many cases, shifts in career direction reflect a clarification of personal values that dictates a change. Even when the change is brought about by job loss, subsequent retraining can lead to a more adequate fit between personal needs and work demands.

Men and women do not yet approach the world of work in the same ways. Women continue to enter a more limited range of careers. They are more likely to have part-time employment and to earn lower salaries than men. Many women are underemployed, given their educational background. The more traditional a woman's value system, the less likely she is to seek an "innovative" career. Even in two-earner families, it is not uncommon for the husband's career to take priority. Women continue to expect to assume major responsibility for home and child care, even when they are employed. On the other hand, as we look ahead to the older woman, involvement in the world of work, with all its stresses and conflicts, appears to contribute significantly to a sense of personal fulfillment. As women continue to increase their lifelong participation in the paid labor force, we can expect the pattern of involvement in work to become more varied for both men and women.

References

Argyle, M. *The social psychology of work.* Harmondsworth, England: Penguin, 1972.

Argyris, C. *Integrating the individual and the organization.* New York: Wiley, 1964.

Astin, A. W. *Four critical years.* San Francisco: Jossey-Bass, 1977.

Atchley, R. C. *The sociology of retirement.* Cambridge, Mass.: Schenkman, 1976.

Atchley, R. C. *The social forces in later life.* Belmont, Calif.: Wadsworth, 1977.

Baird, L. L. Entrance of women to graduate and professional education. Paper presented at the American Psychological Association Meetings, Washington, D.C., 1976.

Baird, L. L. Men and women college seniors' images of fine careers. Paper presented at the American Psychological Association Meetings, Washington, D.C., 1976.

Barrett, T. C., & Tinsley, H. E. A. Vocational self-concept crystallization and vocational indecision. *Journal of Counseling Psychology,* 1977, *24,* 301–307.

Bernard, J. *Women and the public interest.* Chicago: Aldine-Atherton, 1971.

Best, F. Changing sex roles and worklife flexibility. *Psychology of Women Quarterly,* 1981, *6,* 55–71.

Birnbaum, J. A. Life patterns and self-esteem in gifted family oriented and career committed women. In M. T. S. Mednick, S. S. Tangri, & L. W. Hoffman (Eds.),

Women and achievement: Social and motivational analyses. New York: Halstead, 1975.

Blaxall, M., & Reagan, B. *Women and the workplace.* Chicago: University of Chicago Press,1976.

Braginsky, D. D., & Braginsky, B. M. Surplus people: Their lost faith in self and system. *Psychology Today,* August 1975, 68–72.

Breaugh, J. A., & DiMarco, N. Age differences in the rated desirability of job outcomes. Paper presented at the American Psychological Association Meetings, New York City, 1979.

Brenner, M. H. *Mental illness and the economy.* Cambridge, Mass.: Harvard University Press, 1973.

Brim, O. Adult socialization. In J. Clausen (Ed.), *Socialization and society.* Boston: Little, Brown, 1968.

Brim, O. Life span development of the theory of oneself. Invited address to the Biennial Conference of the International Society for the Study of Behavioral Development, University of Surrey, Guilford, England, July 1975.

Cain, P. S., & Treiman, D. J. The *DOT* as a source of occupational data. *American Sociological Review,* 1981, *46,* 253–278.

Cartwright, L. K. Continuity and non-continuity in the careers of a sample of young women physicians. *Journal of the American Medical Women's Association,* 1977, *32,* 316–321.

Chabaud, J. *The education and advancement of women.* Paris: UNESCO, 1970.

Cottrell, F., & Atchley, R. C. *Women in retirement: A preliminary report.* Oxford, Ohio: Scripps Foundation, 1969.

Dennis, W. Creative productivity between the ages of twenty and eighty years. *Journal of Gerontology,* 1966, *21,* 108.

Dinklage, L. B. *Student decision-making studies: Studies of adolescents in the secondary schools.* Report No. 6. Cambridge, Mass.: Harvard Graduate School of Education, 1969.

Dunlop, K. H. Maternal employment and child care. *Professional Psychology,* 1981, *12,* 67–75.

Educational Testing Service *SIGI: A computer-based system of interactive guidance and information.* Princeton, N.J.: ETS 1974, 1975.

Ferman, L. A. Family adjustment to unemployment. In E. Corfman (Ed.), *Families Today: A research sampler on families and children,* Vol. 1, (NIMH Science Monograph No. 1). Washington, D.C.: U.S. Government Printing Office 1979.

Ferretti, F. Elderly find second careers on canvas. *New York Times,* August 21, 1981, p. 28.

Form, W. H., & Miller, D. C. *Industry, labor, and community.* New York: Harper, 1960.

Gallese, L. R. Women managers say job transfers present a growing dilemma. *Wall Street Journal,* May 4, 1978.

Gardell, B. Psychosocial aspects of the working environment. *Working Life in Sweden,* October 1977, No. 1.

Gonda, J. Convocation in work, aging and retirement: A review. *Human Development,* 1981, *24,* 286–292.

Gottschalk, E. C. Maternity leave: Firms are disrupted by wave of pregnancy at the manager level. *Wall Street Journal,* July 20, 1981.

Gurin, G., Veroff, J., & Feld, S. *Americans view their mental health.* New York: Basic Books, 1960.

Harren, V. A. An overview of Tiedeman's theory of career decision making and a summary of related research. Unpublished manuscript, Southern Illinois University—Carbondale, 1976.

Harren, V. A., & Kass, R. A. The measurement and correlates of career decision making. Paper presented at the American Psychological Association Meetings, San Francisco, 1977.

Hauser, R. M., & Featherman, D. L. Socioeconomic achievement of U.S. men, 1962 to 1972. *Science,* 1974, *185*(4148), 325–331.

Havens, E. M. Women, work, and wedlock: A note on female marital patterns in the United States. *American Journal of Sociology,* 1973, *78,* 975–981.

Heckman, N. A., Bryson, R., & Bryson, J. B. Problems of professional couples: A content analysis. *Journal of Marriage and the Family,* 1977, *39*(2), 323–330.

Hoffman, L. W. Effects of maternal employment on the child. In L. W. Hoffman, & F. I. Nye (Eds.), *Working mothers.* San Francisco: Jossey-Bass, 1974.

Holland, J. L. *The psychology of vocational choice.* Lexington, Mass.: Ginn/Blaisdel, 1966.

Holland, J. L. *Making vocational choices: A theory of careers.* Englewood Cliffs, N.J.: Prentice-Hall, 1973.

Horn, J. L. On the future of growing old. Paper presented for a university lecture, University of Denver, May 15, 1980.

Inkeles, A. & Smith, D. H. *What is sociology?* Englewood Cliffs, N.J.: Prentice-Hall, 1964.

Jahoda, M. Work, employment and unemployment: Values, theories, and approaches in social research. *American Psychologist,* 1981, *36,* 184–191.

Levi, L. Quality of the working environment: Protection and promotion of occupational mental health. *Working Life in Sweden,* November 1978, No. 8.(a)

Levi, L. An international research center on psychological factors and health. *Working Environment,* 1978, pp. 22–23.(b)

Levy, S. M. The aging woman: Developmental issues and mental health needs. *Professional Psychology,* 1981, *12,* 92.

Lunneborg, P. W. Sex and career decision-making styles. Paper presented at the American Psychological Association Meetings, San Francisco, 1977.

Market Opinion Research. *American women today and tomorrow.* National Commission on the Observance of the International Women's Year. Washington, D.C.: U.S. Government Printing Office, 1977.

Maslach, C. Burnout: A social psychological analysis. Paper presented at the American Psychological Association Meetings, Toronto, 1978.

Materka, P. Teachers and stress: An unsatisfactory duo. *Rackham Reports,* 1980, *6*(1), 5–6.

McCraw, M. L. Medical care costs lead rise in 1976–77 family budgets. *Monthly Labor Review,* 1978, *101,* 33.

Miller, A. L., & Tiedeman, D. V. Decision making for the 70's: The cubing of the Tiedeman paradigm and its application in career education. *Focus on Guidance,* 1972, *5*(1).

Mueller, C. W., & Campbell, B. G. Female occupational achievement and marital status: A research note. *Journal of Marriage and the Family,* 1977, *39*(3), 587–593.

Newman, P., & Newman, B. *Development through life: A psychosocial approach.* Homewood, Ill.: Dorsey, 1979.

O'Brien, G. E. Leisure attributes and retirement satisfaction. *Journal of Applied Psychology,* 1981, *66,* 371–384.

Oppenheimer, V. K. The sex-labeling of jobs. *Industrial Relations,* 1968, *7,* 187–248.

O'Reilly, C. A., & Caldwell, D. F. Job choice: The impact of intrinsic and extrinsic factors on subsequent satisfaction and commitment. *Journal of Applied Psychology,* 1980, *65,* 559–565.

Parsons, J. E. Attributional factors mediating female underachievement and low career aspirations. Paper presented at the American Psychological Association Meetings, San Francisco, 1977.

Parsons, J. E., Frieze, I. H., & Ruble, D. N. Intrapsychic factors influencing career aspirations in college women. Unpublished paper, 1975.

Powers, E. A., & Goudy, W. J. Examination of the meaning of work to older workers. *International Journal of Aging and Human Development,* 1971, *2,* 38–45.

Quinn, R. P., & Staines, G. L. *The 1977 quality of employment survey.* Ann Arbor, Mich.: Institite for Social Research, 1979.

Ragan, P. K. *Work and retirement: Policy issues.* Los Angeles: Andrus Gerontology Center, University of Southern California Press, 1980.

Ragan, P. K., & Dowd, J. J. The emerging political consciousness of the aged: A generational interpretation. *Journal of Social Issues,* 1974, *30,* 137–158.

Schafer, R. B., & Keith, P. M. Equity in marital roles across the family life cycle. *Journal of Marriage and the Family,* 1981, *43,* 359–367.

Schein, E. H. The individual, the organization and the career: A conceptual scheme. *Journal of Applied Behavioral Science,* 1971, *7,* 401–426.

Seashore, S. E. On the quality of working life. *LSA,* Spring 1978, *1*(5), 6–7, 15–17.

Severance, L. J., & Gottsegen, A. J. Modeling influences on the achievement of college men and women. Paper presented at the American Psychological Association Meetings, San Francisco, 1977.

Shapiro, H. D. Do not go gently. . . . *New York Times Magazine,* February 6, 1977, pp. 36–54.

Sheehy, G. *Passages: Predictable crises of adult life.* New York: Dutton, 1976.

Simonton, D. K. Creative productivity, age, and stress: A biographical time period analysis of 10 classical composers. *Journal of Personality and Social Psychology,* 1977, *35,* 791–804.

Smith, M. P., & Nock, S. L. Social class and the quality of work life in public and private organizations. *Journal of Social Issues,* 1980, *36,* 59–75.

Stafford, R., Backman, E., & Dibona, P. The division of labor among cohabiting and married couples. *Journal of Marriage and the Family,* 1977, *39*(1), 40–47.

Stetar, J. M. Community colleges and educational needs of older adults. *Education Digest,* April 1975.

Streib, G. F., & Schneider, C. J. *Retirement in American Society.* Ithaca: Cornell University Press, 1971.

Tangri, S. S. Determinants of occupational role innovation among college women. *Journal of Social Issues,* 1972, *28*(2), 177–179.

Terkel, S. *Working: People talk about what they do all day and how they feel about what they do.* New York: Pantheon, 1974.

Tidball, M. F. Perspective on academic women and affirmative action. *Educational Record,* 1973, *54,* 130–135.

Tiedeman, D. V., & O'Hara, R. P. *Career development: Choice and adjustment.* New York: College Entrance Examination Board, 1963.

U.S. Bureau of the Census. Current Population Reports, Series P–20. No. 363, *Population Profile of the United States; 1980.* Washington, D.C.: U.S. Government Printing Office, 1981.

U.S. Bureau of the Census. *Reflections of America: Commemorating the Statistical Abstract Centennial.* Washington, D.C.: U.S. Government Printing Office, 1980.

U.S. Bureau of the Census. *Social Indicators III.* Washington, D.C.: U.S. Government Printing Office, 1980.

U.S. Department of Labor. *Dictionary of occupational titles* (4th ed.). Washington, D.C.: U.S. Government Printing Office, 1977.

Veroff, J., Douvan, E., & Kulka, R. *The Inner American: A self-portrait from 1957 to 1976.* New York: Basic Books, 1982.

Wellemeyer, M. Reassessment time for the Forty-Niners. *Fortune,* May 21, 1979, pp. 118–122.

Whyte, W. H. *The organization man.* New York: Doubleday, 1956.

Wilensky, H. L. Orderly careers and social participation: The impact of work history on social integration in the middle mass. *American Sociological Review,* 1961, *26,* pp. 521–539.

10 Adulthood and Society

Riders

by Robert Frost

The surest thing there is is we are riders,
And though none too successful at it, guiders,
Through everything presented, land and tide
And now the very air, of what we ride.

What is this talked-of mystery of birth
But being mounted bareback on the earth?
We can just see the infant up astride,
His small fist buried in the bushy hide.

There is our wildest mount—a headless horse.
But though it runs unbridled off its course,
And all our blandishments would seem defied,
We have ideas yet that we haven't tried.

There is no way to separate the experiences of adulthood from the society in which one lives. As a product of socialization in the family, the school, the work place, and the community, each adult carries a complex set of values and beliefs. These values and beliefs reflect what has been emphasized as critical to the society's definition of maturity. They provide an inner guide, an internalized map of what the culture has defined as ideal or undesirable. The map extends across many domains. The internal code has content that may guide behavior as a worker, a spouse, a parent, a friend, a religious believer, or a citizen of a community. It may influence what and how one thinks, especially what is permissible to think about, what questions appear to be answered, what methods are available for seeking answers to questions, and what kind of answers are satisfying.

Keep in mind, however, that adults are not only the product of their socialization. They are also the socializers of others. They are the parents, the lovers, the husbands and wives, the workers and bosses, the religious leaders, the political leaders, the healers, the scholars and inventors, and the builders of the society. In these varied roles they integrate the messages of their own socialization with the realities of their historical period and the nature of their own personalities. They must build with the materials available or create new materials. They may support the existing political or religious or social values. They may also choose to revise or revolutionize those values. Continuity or change of a culture is a product of the adaptations of adults to their immediate present reality and to their vision or aspirations about a possible future. In this sense, an understanding of adulthood in any society provides an avenue for analysis of the evolution of the society as a whole.

Adulthood is not a constant experience. It is not the same from culture to culture or from generation to generation. The more rapidly the society changes, the more we can expect the experiences of adult life to change. Think, for a moment, of the way of life in the United States 40 years ago, in the 1940s. No television, no space program, no transistors, no paper diapers, no microwave ovens, few frozen food products, many homes without electricity or indoor plumbing. It was wartime. Many men and women were in the military service. Many women who had been housewives and mothers went to work. The Russians were our allies and the Japanese were our enemies. Americans believed they were the force of good fighting evil, and the soldiers of the war returned home as proud heroes. Doors were flung open to them as veterans.

It was a time of idealism and cultural naivete. America had not yet been called to task for its imperialism, its racism, its social violence, its pockets of deep poverty, or its inability to provide meaningful employment for its people. Most Americans believed in the ethic of success through hard work and competence. We had not yet begun to expose the deception, the manipulation, and the scandal that thrived in government and in big business. Past heroes and present heroes had not yet been scrutinized to

America welcomes her soldiers returning from World War II. It was an era of victory and confidence.

reveal their human frailties. The adult American of 40 years ago lived in a world more clearly demarcated as good and evil, valued and worthless, sacred and profane. Those who were oppressed by this system had not yet developed the power to change it. Many of the oppressed lived an adulthood of outward compliance and muffled rage. It would be another generation before the children of those oppressed would find the cracks in the armor of national self-righteousness and burst out with a new vision of society.

The impact of contemporary society on adult development is explored in the remainder of this chapter. Three major factors are discussed for their contributions to biological, intellectual, social, and emotional development. These factors are the rapid growth of technology, the expansion of the healthy adult years, and the dramatic increase in information available to adults. These three factors play a major role in our conceptualization of adult life as we work to help adults cope with their own life choices and as we struggle to understand the processes underlying development.

Adulthood in a Technological Era

Our contemporary society can be characterized by a rapidly expanding technology; a vast array of products competing for the consumer market; a complex bureaucratic organization in most institutions, including government, business, health care, and education; and a large population of diverse racial, cultural, economic, and educational backgrounds. Diversity and change appear to be the constants in our daily experience. Let us consider some of the possible influences of these characteristics of our own society on the experience of adulthood and the psychological growth that may take place during this phase of life. We begin with a bold admission of the speculative nature of this discussion. Only historical comparisons with past or future generations will confirm or refute our speculations. Yet in reviewing the literature we find suggestions that adaptation to contemporary society should have some predictable impact on the present adult generation.

Education

Along with technology has come an increasing emphasis on education. Children are beginning school younger with almost 30 percent attending some kind of preschool, and they are continuing their education longer. Approximately 11 million students were enrolled in degree-granting postsecondary institutions in 1980 as compared to 7.9 million in 1970 and 5.5 million in 1965 (Grant & Lind, 1976; U. S. Bureau of the Census, 1981). We have some indication that there are long-range consequences of each

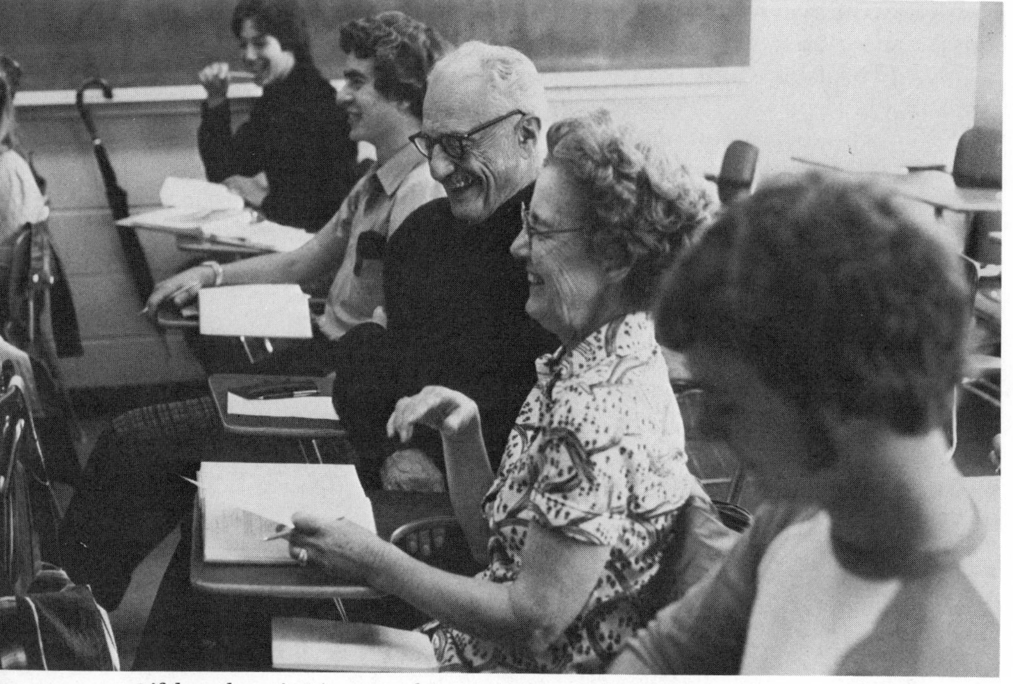

Lifelong learning is a trend in contemporary society.

higher level of education. First, education influences employability. Second, education is associated with more democratic, responsive parenting. Third, education relates to a person's ability to seek out, find, and make use of new information.

Hyman, Wright, and Reed (1975) reviewed survey data that were collected in the early 1950s, the late 1950s, the early 1960s, and the late 1960s. For each period, they evaluated the responses of subjects in the age ranges 25–36, 37–48, 49–60, and 61–72. At each period, the less-educated subjects had less knowledge than the more highly educated subjects in the areas of civics, domestic policy, foreign affairs, science, geography, history, and the humanities. Comparing subjects who had completed college with subjects who had completed high school and subjects who had completed elementary school, it was found that each successive level of education was associated with a broader range of knowledge and with greater involvement in seeking new information.

Norms also are changing about the best age to attend college. Even though it is difficult to start back to school after a period of non-school-oriented life, many adults are choosing to do just that. In 1980, 10 percent of students in 2-year colleges and 5 percent of students in 4-year colleges were in the age range 30–34 (U.S. Bureau of the Census, 1981). In preparation for a career change, in anticipation of entering the labor market, or in an effort to upgrade their earlier training, adults are returning to school. For some adults, school is the best way to keep abreast of technological change. Through enrollment in summer programs, televised courses, evening programs, and correspondence courses, adults are expressing a desire to expand their information and skills.

Values

With rapid technological change, adults encounter diverse and changing values. Expressions such as "do your own thing," "laid-back," and "uptight" reflect a preoccupation with our sense of the relativity of values. Much of the experimentation in intimate relationships, in marital and parental roles, and in career management reflect a loosening of commitment to one way of life. Even within socioeconomic groupings, where we might expect that resources and education would determine the expression of values and preferences, we see diverse life choices being expressed. Homosexual relationships, single-parenting, communal living, and two people sharing one job all have been looked upon at an earlier time as deviant adult life-styles. Now we consider them "alternative life-styles" or simply options of adult life (Zablocki & Kanter, 1976).

Let us consider two aspects of the interaction between technology and adult development. The first technological advance is the automobile. When cars were first introduced in the United States, people argued that they would never replace the horse—that they were "a passing fancy" that would never sell. Today the automobile industry and its related industries—steel, oil, tires, and molded plastics, are the major employers of the nation. In 1977, Americans used motor vehicles to travel 1.477 billion miles. They spent $152,730,000,000 on cars, gasoline, maintenance, insurance, and other costs. There were over 49,000 deaths and almost 2 million disabling injuries in the over 17 million automobile accidents (U.S. Bureau of the Census, 1980). The automobile has become a necessity of life. Over 50 percent of people responding to a national transportation survey could not get along with only one family car. People spend 7 percent of their annual expenditures on cars and another 3 percent on gasoline and oil (U.S. Bureau of the Census, 1980). The availability of the automobile has led to the establishment of sprawling cities where people may live long distances from their place of employment. Driving a car has become a "rite of passsage" into adulthood. The inability to drive is one of the painful losses that accompany impaired vision in later life.

With the increased doubts about energy availability and rising energy costs, adult dependence on automobile travel has become a major source of concern. Funds for alternative modes of public transportation have been markedly reduced from the 1960s to the 1970s. Today, people are dissatisfied with public transportation and reluctant to depend on it. However, those who cannot drive, including those who have no car, the young, the visually impaired, and the elderly, must endure a severely restricted range of movement in most communities where public transportation is limited. As the cost of energy rises, people will be challenged to give up some of their deep investment in personal autonomy in order to arrive at a community solution to transportation needs.

The second technological advance is the birth-control pill. Effective contraception has had a broad impact on sexual behavior, decisions to marry, family planning, involvement of women in the world of work, and values about sexual behavior. Studies of sexual behavior and attitudes about sex during the college years suggest that young adults enter the process of building an intimate relationship with a changing moral stance toward sexuality. When attitudes and behaviors are studied over the four years of college, males and females become increasingly "single standard." That is, they do not differentiate between the sexual behaviors that are appropriate for males and those that are appropriate for females. What is more, this single standard becomes increasingly permissive over the college years. Students move from a standard that emphasizes restraint or abstinence to a standard that endorses sexual expression for both sexes (Ferrell, Tolone, & Walsh, 1977).

Robinson and Jedlicka (1982) compared the responses of university students in 1965, 1970, 1975, and 1980 to questions about sexual behavior and attitudes about sex. Table 10.1 compares the percentage of students who had experienced intercourse and the percentage who had experienced heavy petting at the four time periods. These data suggest that there has been increasing participation in intense sexual activity by both males and females, but markedly more involvement by females. As sexual experience has increased, there has been an accompanying change in the permissiveness of attitudes toward sex. From 1965 to 1975, fewer students viewed premarital sex as immoral and fewer students felt that having sexual intercourse with a number of different people was sinful or immoral. However, in 1980, even though sexual behavior continued to increase, attitudes about premarital sex moved toward a more conservative position. The 1980 attitudes are not as restrictive as they were in 1965. The

TABLE 10.1 Percentage of Students Experienceing Sexual Intercourse and Heavy Petting at Three Time Periods: 1965, 1970, and 1975.

	Sexual Intercourse		Heavy Petting[1]	
	Male	Female	Male	Female
1965	65.1	28.7	71.3	34.3
1970	65.0	37.3	79.3	59.7
1975	73.9	57.1	80.2	72.7
1980	77.4	63.5	84.9	72.9

[1]Manual and oral manipulation of genitals

Source: Adapted from "Change in Sexual Attitudes and Behavior of College Students from 1965 to 1980: A Research Note" by Ira E. Robinson and Davon Jedlicka, *Journal of Marriage and the Family*, 1982, *44*, p. 238.

TABLE 10.2

	Premarital Sexual Intercourse	Homosexual Relations	Extramarital Sexual Relations
Always wrong	31	72	73
Almost always wrong	9.5	6	14
Only sometimes wrong	23	7.5	10
Not wrong at all	36.5	15	3
	(N=1,481)	(N=1,453)	(N=1,510)

Source: National Opinion Research Center, *Cumulative Codebook for the 1972–1977 General Social Surveys* (Chicago: University of Chicago Press, 1977), pp. 131,132.

implication is that young people in the '80s may be in greater conflict about the appropriateness of their sexual behavior.

If attitudes toward premarital sex have become more permissive, attitudes about extramarital sex remain conservative. Table 10.2 shows attitudes of a national sample of adults toward premarital intercourse, homosexuality, and extramarital relations. The sample expressed greater rejection of extramarital relations than of homosexual relations. This attitudinal restrictiveness must be appreciated in contrast to actual behavior. Kinsey (Kinsey, Pomeroy, & Martin, 1948; Kinsey, Pomeroy, Martin, & Gebhard, 1953) reported that 28 percent of husbands and 17 percent of wives had experienced extramarital intercourse by the age of 40. *Redbook study* (Tavris & Sadd, 1977) reported that 40 percent of women had extramarital relations by age 40. The implication is that today's generation is encountering greater conflict between attitudes and behavior. Perhaps the high divorce rate is in part a reflection of that conflict.

Bureaucratization

The third consequence of increasing technology is the growing bureaucratization of the world of work. Our postindustrial society is composed of thousands of interconnecting bureaucracies. We expect any institution to be characterized by a hierarchy of authority, division of roles and responsibilities, and a complex decision-making network. As children, we are taught to adapt to the conditions of these institutions through our attendance in schools. As we enter the world of work, the importance of understanding authority relations, reading the norms of the setting, complying with expectations about performance, and enacting one's proper role all become evident.

Participation in a bureaucracy has its impact on adult development. First, it promotes a more complex view of reality. Just as games require players who take different parts, so bureaucracies require compartmentalization. One learns that many elements are involved in the final outcome. These elements may even be in opposition to one another. Management

Bureaucracy can create a sense of replaceability.

and labor, sales and research and development, administration and professional staff may bring opposing needs and goals to an organization. One begins to recognize the inevitability of opposition and perhaps even to appreciate the positive consequences of this tension.

Bureaucratization may also breed interactions that are dominated by role demands rather than personal needs. We expect the bureaucrat to exercise his or her function regardless of personal views. The bureaucrat upholds the rules or guidelines and passes on questions that create uncertainty to another level of decision-making. One might expect adults to be less confident of their own decision-making abilities to the extent that they are expected to enact institutional regulations rather than to use their own judgment.

The bureaucracy also creates a sense of replaceability. If the functions of a role are clearly defined, many people could enact them equally well. The less a person's individual talents are valued or given a legitimate place in the work role, the more he or she will sense replaceability.

There is some evidence that increased exposure to the bureaucratic environment produces stress in related roles. Recall that in Chapter 9 data on life satisfaction were compared for Americans 21 years old and older in 1957 and 1976 (Gurin, Veroff & Feld, 1960; Veroff, Melnick, & Kulka, 1977). Over the 20-year period, there have been clear changes in adults' overall sense of life satisfaction and in their perceptions of what causes their problems. Unhappiness with personal life rose from 3 percent to 13 percent. People expressed a sense of being out of tune with their world and more uncertain about their social relationships.

The Expansion of the Healthy Adult Years

One by-product of an advanced medical technology combined with rich food-producing resources and access to health services is expanded life expectancy. Currently, 11.3 percent of the people in the United States are over 65. Over 2 million adults are over 85. Medical advances have significantly increased the life span for those who are over 75. In fact, the population is growing faster in the 75-and-over group than in the 67–75 group (U.S. Bureau of the Census, 1981).

In the last century, the life expectancy has increased by 30 years. A major factor in this increase has been the reduction of infant mortality. Equally important, are the medical advances that have reduced the deaths from heart disease during the period from 40 to 65. People born in the early 1900s never anticipated this expanding adulthood. They grew up thinking of people who were 50 or 60 as old. Today, in their seventies and eighties they are facing the demand to define a period of old age for which most older adults had no models.

Today's adults have far greater opportunity to anticipate the possibility of a competent later-adult period. They live in a period when they can observe the life-styles of older adults as they encounter the demands of later adulthood. The question is whether adults will come to look upon the increase in life expectancy as a blessing or a curse.

Right now there appears to be a gap between the perceptions Americans hold about the aged and the concerns of the aged themselves. In a Harris poll, a national sample of adults were asked what they thought were serious problems for the elderly. These expectations were compared with the concerns expressed by older adults. Figure 10.1 shows the discrepancy between experiences of older adults and expectations of others. Harris concluded that one of the biggest problems of aging is the confusion and lack of understanding about just what the experiences of aging adults are (Moore, 1975).

Today, more and more adults experience the reality of aging through interactions with their own aging parents. In one large survey, 90 percent of older adults had talked to their adult child within the past 24 hours (Lieberman, 1978). Approximately 4 percent of men and 50 percent of women over 65 are living as a member of a family in which they are not the

FIGURE 10.1 "Serious" Problems of Older People: Public Expectation versus Personal Experience

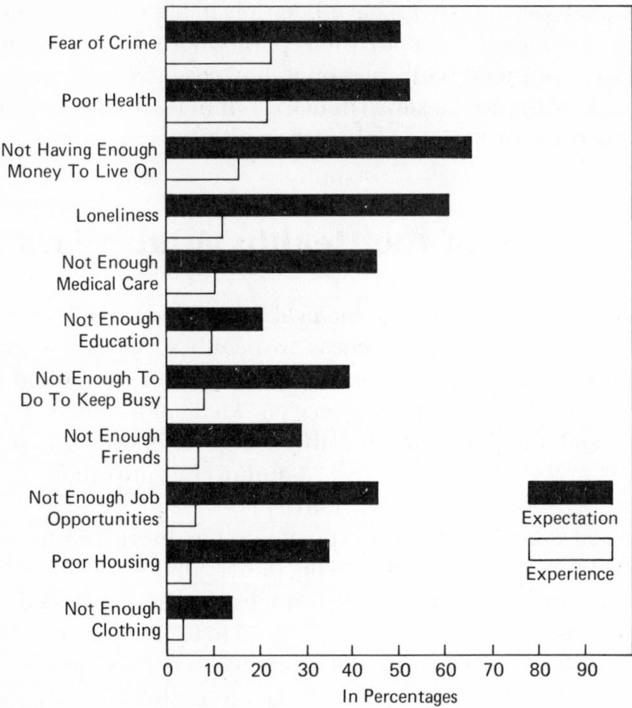

Source: "Attitudes: What We Expect and What It's Like" by P. Moore, *Psychology Today,* August 1975, pp. 29–30.

head of the household. The vast majority of these living arrangements involve adult children, their parents, and their own children. The challenge for these families is to achieve a relationship in which the needs of all generations are accurately perceived and met. This means a reworking of the parent-child relationship for the older adults, an extension of nurturant motives toward the older as well as the younger generations, and an accurate assessment of the competences of each generation.

One area in which today's adults can benefit from the lesson of today's elderly is prevention of the waste of the skills and information that the older adults command. At present, the focus of most programs for the elderly has a service emphasis. Health care, food services, housing, activity centers, and transportation are all very real needs that must be met. However, very little attention has been given to what older adults know. After a long period of functioning as parents, household managers, workers, teachers, or advisers, the older generation finds that its resources are quickly exchanged for the new skills and education of the young adult generation. Older adults, like adolescents, are a wasted resource (Hamlin,

1977). Today's adults are recognizing this. They have no intention of being disregarded at age 65 or 70. They expect to remain vital, informed, and involved. They expect to continue to be able to direct their life choices and to make meaningful contributions. By changing their orientation toward the aged, they are ensuring their own sense of worth in their later-adult years.

Today's elderly are being supported by a large pool of younger adults. Not only their own children but the children of their entire generation are engaged in a vast array of human-service activities that support the lives of aging adults. As we look ahead to the future of our own later adulthood, we will not have this luxury. The boom generation of the 1940s and 1950s did not share the enthusiasm for large families that was modeled by their parents. Our birth rate is declining. Today's adult women are anticipating smaller families than was true 20 years ago. In 40 years, when today's 30-year-olds are 70, there will probably be more healthy older adults than there are today, but fewer middle adults to care for their needs.

A challenge to today's adults is to anticipate this discrepancy and plan for it. Will we create more adequate and efficient delivery of services? Will we offer higher rewards to human-service professionals? Will we make greater use of older adults as resources for meeting community needs? Or will we ignore this reality until the needs of the first wave of older adults go sorely unmet? Psychological growth during adulthood involves adaptation to the demands of the present, but it also requires the capacity to anticipate future events. In order to meet the needs of younger generations, older generations, and one's own future life needs, one must begin to formulate hypotheses about the changing structure of society.

An Expansion of the Realm of Consciousness

We are all part of the process of psychosocial evolution. Each generation adds to the knowledge and reinterprets the norms of the society. Some adults, like Thomas Edison or Albert Einstein or Mahatma Gandhi, move a culture in breathtaking new directions. Through their inventions or their ideas or their leadership, they bring their civilization to a new level of functioning. Even those adults who do not contribute major innovations are part of the evolution of culture. They adapt to change and communicate that change to the next generation.

In a society such as ours, characterized by diverse settings, climates, values, ethnic groups, and life-styles, the experience of adulthood is bound to be mind-expanding. The more fully one explores the culture, the more one is likely to encounter diversity. In order to understand and organize that diversity, one must modify familiar thoughts and orientations in order to accommodate the unique elements of the novel experience. Alternatives in life-style, in consumer preference, in living area, in choice of marital partner, in career, and in educational attainment all require decision-making. To the extent that alternatives are evaluated, awareness increases. As adults strive to meet their own needs, they are confronted by the profusion of information and options. Alternatives complicate decision-making. They also require a new level of complexity of thought.

Adulthood also brings the demands of meeting the needs of others. As a parent, one is drawn into an assessment of the talents and weaknesses of one's children. One begins to seek those experiences that will complement or enhance each child's potential. As a socialization agent, one also strives to teach those values that have enduring value and to prepare each child for a changing future. Parenting, with its deep emotional commitment to one's offspring, calls forth an expanded consciousness.

Finally, looking ahead to one's later adulthood, adults begin to sense the urgency of formulating a meaningful philosophy of life, a code that will give a sense of purpose to existence. The formation of this philosophy is mind expanding. It poses basic ethical, religious, and philosophical questions which each person struggles to answer. Why did I live? What is a good life? What am I striving for? Adulthood, more than any earlier time, is a period when it becomes imperative to arrive at answers to these questions. In order to cope with the anxiety of death, in order to direct decision-making efforts of the present, and in order to advise, teach, or parent others it becomes essential to establish a personal philosophy.

In sum, through encounters with diversity, decision making, parenting, and efforts to formulate a personal philosophy, adults reach a new level of conscious thought. Adults are more aware of alternatives. They can look deeply into past and future. They recognize that opposing forces can exist side by side. In the case of Rabbi Shlomo Riskin we see the struggle to bring orthodox religious views into harmony with deeply pressing and challenging contemporary issues. A choice can be both good and bad. A person can be both kind and cruel. A relationship can be both productive and destructive. Adults are aware of the interplay of planning and fate. They can see from their experience that their life is an outcome of the many choices and plans they have made as well as the circumstances of fortune that bring opportunities or hardships. A sense of life's uncertainties, its wonders, and its pain is what draws out the religious and philosophical elements of adult thought.

BOX 10.1 Rabbi Shlomo Riskin: Adulthood and Society

The case of Rabbi Shlomo Riskin illustrates the challenging task of adult life to find ways to express one's values and beliefs in the daily life of contemporary society. Rabbi Riskin, along with many other religious leaders of all faiths, is struggling to preserve the essence of his religious identity by connecting it to the concerns of modern life.

Whether chaining himself to the White House gates to protest an arms sale to Saudi Arabia, battling with the local community board last month for permission to erect a menorah at 72nd Street and Broadway, or lecturing at his Lincoln Square Synagogue on the Jewish attitude toward war, Rabbi Shlomo Riskin sees as his mission the bridging of Orthodox Judaism and the modern world. To further this, he founded two yeshiva high schools in Riverdale; they now draw students from the entire world.

In the 1960s a new brand of Orthodox rabbi appeared on the American scene, stressing the relevance of Jewish law for modern life, and willing to take to the streets when Jewish interests seemed at stake. As the leading figure of this "reach out" school of Orthodoxy, the 39-year-old Rabbi Riskin serves as a model for scores of rabbis and rabbis-to-be. He draws inquiries from intellectually inclined Jewish youth on such subjects as business ethics and homosexuality, and he has awakened other rabbis to the educational needs of women. "There are two types of Jews," says Rabbi Riskin, "the religious and the not yet religious. Every Jew owes it to himself to study his tradition as it has been studied for thousands of years."

Rabbi Riskin is entitled to kvell over his revitalization of Jewish life on the West Side—four different Sabbath services attract 1,000 people, half of whom are under 30, and an adult-education program draws 1,200 students weekly. The synagogue also runs two yeshivas for college students and graduates who have never studied Torah before.

Yet the rabbi despairs for the future of Judaism in America. "More and more the axioms of American society are not in accord with our own," he says. "The family is in disarray, sexual conduct is not governed by moral standards, and any sort of restraint, whether in print or on the TV screen, is rapidly disappearing."

As a result, he plans in the near future to spend six months a year in Israel building a model community, Efrat, where he hopes 5,000 familes will live by 1999.

Source: "The Most Powerful Rabbis in New York" by R. I. Rubin, *New York,* January 22, 1979, p. 42.

The expansion of consciousness in adulthood is a primary factor in the continuation of psychosocial evolution. Each new generation assimilates the information passed to it by a parent generation. Through written records and oral history, children, adolescents, and adults encounter the experiences and ideas of past cultures. They select those elements of the past that appear most salient to immediate circumstances. Through a process of creative coping, adults in each generation blend the salient parts of their history with the demands of the reality of which they are aware. The results are new modes of interaction, new inventions, new types of work, new family forms, new cultural values, or new visions of the future.

Chapter Summary

Throughout this book we have focused on the promise of continued growth in adulthood. In our society, the life patterns of adults are diverse. What is more, we are in the process of redefining some of the central adult roles—those of male and female—mother and father—parent and child—grandparent and grandchild—employer and employee. Even some of the factors that were thought to be "givens" of aging, such as slowed reaction time and social disengagement, are coming under the scrutiny of new research and new interpretation. The importance of the historical era and the generational cohort are becoming increasingly appreciated as factors that dramatically color the experiences of adult life. Nevertheless, the power of the individual will and the motive of personal competence continue to be impressive. People take a stance toward their own lives. They define and redefine events to converge with their aspirations. We see each adult life as an integration of the biological forces that foster growth, vigor, illness, and death; the social forces that transmit the rules and goals of the culture; and the creative psychological forces that interpret and express the self through unique ideas, social commitments, loving relationships, and productive work.

References

Astin, A. W. *Four critical years.* San Francisco: Jossey-Bass, 1977.

Ferrell, M. Z., Tolone, W. L., & Walsh, R. H. Maturational and societal changes in the sexual double-standard: A panel analysis (1967–1971, 1970–1974). *Journal of Marriage and the Family,* 1977, *39,* 255–271.

Frost, R. *Complete poems of Robert Frost.* New York: Holt, Rinehart and Winston, 1964.

Grant, W. V., & Lind, C. G. *Digest of educational statistics.* Washington, D. C.: U.S. Government Printing Office, 1976.

Gurin, G., Veroff, J., & Feld, S. *Americans view their mental health.* New York: Basic Books, 1960.

Hamlin, R. M. Restrictions on the competent aged. Paper presented at the American Psychological Association Meetings, San Francisco, 1977.

Hyman, H. H., Wright, C. R., & Reed, J. S. *The enduring effects of education.* Chicago: University of Chicago Press, 1975.

Kinsey, A. C., Pomeroy, W., & Martin, C. *Sexual behavior in the human male.* Philadelphia: Saunders, 1948.

Kinsey, A. C., Pomeroy, W., Martin, C., and Gebhard, P. *Sexual behavior in the human female.* Philadelphia: Saunders, 1953.

Lieberman, G. L. Children of the elderly as natural helpers: Some demographic differences. *American Journal of Community Psychology,* 1978, *6,* 489–498.

Moore, P. Attitudes: What we expect and what it's like. *Psychology Today,* August 1975, pp. 29–30.

National Opinion Research Center. *Cumulative codebook for the 1972–77 general social surveys.* Chicago: University of Chicago Press, 1977.

Robinson, I. E., & Jedlicka, D. Change in sexual attitudes and behavior of college students from 1965 to 1980: A research note. *Journal of Marriage and the Family,* 1982, *44,* 237–240.

Rubin, R. I. The most powerful rabbis in New York. *New York,* January 22, 1979, pp. 39–46.

Tavris C., & Sadd, S. *The Redbook report on female sexuality.* New York: Delacorte, 1977.

U.S. Bureau of the Census. *Social Indicators III.* Washington, D.C.: U.S. Government Printing Office, 1980.

U.S. Bureau of the Census. Current Population Reports, Series P–20, No. 363, *Population profile of the United States: 1980.* Washington, D.C.: U.S. Government Printing Office, 1981.

U.S. Bureau of the Census. Current Population Reports, Series P–20, No.336, *Population profile of the United States: 1978, population characteristics.* Washington D.C.: U.S. Government Printing Office, 1979.

U.S. Department of Health, Education, and Welfare. *Facts about older Americans,* 1976, DHEW Publication No. (OHD) 77–2006.

Veroff, J., Melnick, H., & Kulka, R. Personal, situational, and interpersonal attributions of causes of critical life problems. Paper presented at the American Psychological Association Meetings, San Francisco, 1977.

Zablocki, B. D., & Kanter, R. M. The differentiation of life-styles. *Annual Review of Sociology,* 1976, *2,* 269–298.

Glossary

Abortion The termination of pregnancy before the fetus is able to live outside the uterus. **(Ch. 4)**

Accommodation (1) In Piaget's theory of cognitive development, the process of changing existing schema or rules in order to account for novel elements in the object or the event. **(Ch. 5)**

Accommodation (2) The ability to adjust the focus of vision to objects near or far. **(Ch. 3)**

Acuity The ability to distinguish small details. **(Ch. 3)**

Acute Having a sharp onset, rising rapidly to a peak, and then subsiding after a brief duration. **(Ch. 3)**

Adaptation (1) The total process of change in response to environmental conditions. **(Ch. 5)**

Adaptation (2) The ability to adjust to changes in the level of illumination. **(Ch. 3)**

Adult-executive Family pattern in which all the adults in the household participate in decision-making. **(Ch. 8)**

Age norms Expectations that foster some behaviors and restrain others at specific ages. **(Ch. 2)**

Ancestry Line of people from whom an individual is descended; lineage. **(Ch. 8)**

Anticipation To expect and provide for some event beforehand. **(Ch. 5)**

Artistic type A personality type that is not very sociable. This person is emotional and imaginative, generally needing some concrete outlet for personal expression. **(Ch. 9)**

Assimilation In Piaget's theory of cognitive development, the process of explaining the environment in terms of rules and schema already established. **(Ch. 5)**

Associational relations Repeated encounters with certain people over the course of time. **(Ch. 5)**

Assumed Taken as true though not proven. **(Ch. 9)**

Asynchrony Simultaneous occurrence of demanding life events. **(Ch. 6)**
Attachment The tendency for an infant to seek closeness to a caregiver. **(Ch. 7)**
Behavioral slowing A change in adult functioning characterized by an increase in the time needed to respond to stimuli. **(Ch. 3)**
Bereavement The suffering that follows the death of a loved one. **(Ch. 8)**
Bisexuality A sexual orientation and attraction toward individuals of both sexes. **(Ch. 4), (Ch. 7)**
Blockbusting Technique for generating new solutions to problems by encouraging the problem solver to relinquish interferring orientations. **(Ch. 5)**
Bundling A colonial American courtship custom in which a couple would share a bed without undressing and/or with a board placed between them. **(Ch. 7)**
Bureaucratization The process of developing a system of administration characterized by specialization of functions under fixed rules and a hierarchy of authority. **(Ch. 10)**
Burn-out A work hazard that involves a state of depression and loss of interest in one's work. **(Ch. 9)**
Cautiousness The learned or habitual slowing of response time to avoid mistakes. **(Ch. 3)**
Central nervous system The brain and spinal cord. **(Ch. 3)**
Cerebral atrophy A shrinking of the brain mass. **(Ch. 3)**
Choice phase The career decision-making phase in which the person decides which alternative for action will be followed. **(Ch. 9)**
Chronic Having a long duration or a pattern of frequent recurrence. **(Ch. 3)**
Chunking Process of consolidating separate pieces of information into meaningful units. **(Ch. 5)**
Clarification phase The career decision-making phase in which the person more fully understands the consequences of commitment to decisions that have been made. **(Ch. 9)**
Classical conditioning A form of learning in which a previously neutral stimulus is repeatedly presented with a stimulus that evokes a specific reflexive response. After repeated pairings, the neutral stimulus elicits a response that is similar to the reflexive response. **(Ch. 2)**
Classification The capacity to group objects according to some specific characteristics they have in common, including all objects that show the characteristic and none that do not. **(Ch. 5)**
Climacteric Menopause; period of natural cessation of regular menstrual periods. **(Ch. 4)**
Cognition The process of knowing, organizing, and perceiving information. **(Ch. 2)**
Cohabitation A relationship in which a man and woman live together but are not married. **(Ch. 7)**
Cohort In research design, a group of subjects who are born during the same time period. **(Ch. 6)**
Coitus Sexual intercourse. **(Ch. 4)**
Colleaguial relations Interactions with others who are co-workers. **(Ch. 5)**
Collective unconscious In Jungian theory, the genetically transmitted impulses and images that are common to the human species. **(Ch. 2)**
Color discrimination The ability to distinguish among various hues and gradations of hues. **(Ch. 3)**
Commitment A criterion of identity status including the expression of personal

values and the demonstration of involvement in the areas of occupational choice, sexuality, religion, and political ideology. **(Ch. 6)**

Commune A contemporary form of experimental community in which emphasis is placed upon interpersonal relationships. **(Ch. 7)**

Compartmentalize Divide into separate sections. **(Ch. 10)**

Competence The sense that one is capable of exercising mastery over one's environment. **(Ch. 2)**

Concrete operational thought In Piaget's theory of cognitive development a stage in which rules of logic can be applied to observable or manipulatable physical relations. **(Ch. 2)**

Conventional type A personality type that likes well-structured tastes, material possessions, and status. This person is a conformist and prefers subordinate positions. **(Ch. 9)**

Coercive Drive, urge, or compel another to do something. **(Ch. 7)**

Conciliatory Appeasing; trying to gain another person's good will. **(Ch. 7)**

Conjugal duty Sex when viewed as an obligation the wife performs for her husband. **(Ch. 4)**

Conservation The concept that physical changes do not alter the mass, weight, number, or volume of matter. **(Ch. 5)**

Consistency The dimension of stability of personality. **(Ch. 6)**

Contextualism A view of responses that take into account setting and relational demands. **(Ch. 5)**

Contingent reinforcement Reinforcement that occurs following specific responses. **(Ch. 2)**

Continuity Refers to whether the meaning of a behavior and its function for the person remain the same at different times in life. **(Ch. 5)**

Conventional morality A stage of moral reasoning described by Kohlberg in which right and wrong are closely associated with the rules created by legitimate authorities, including parents, teachers, or political leaders. **(Ch. 5)**

Coping Active efforts to respond to stress. Coping behavior includes gathering new information, maintaining control over one's emotions, and preserving freedom of movement. **(Ch. 2), (Ch. 6)**

Couvade French term for ritual male response to his wife's "pregnancy;" literally means "hatching". **(Ch. 4)**

Crisis An interruption in the normal way of life resulting from the occurrence of an unexpected situation requiring active decision-making between alternative choices. **(Ch. 6)**

Crystallization phase The career decision-making phase in which a person becomes more aware of alternatives for action and their consequences. **(Ch. 9)**

Crystallized intelligence Skills and information that are acquired through education and socialization. **(Ch. 5)**

Cues Something that helps connect desired information with its location in long term memory; a hint. **(Ch. 5)**

Defense Act and method of protecting the integrity of the ego. **(Ch. 6)**

Denial A defensive process in which a stressful event is not accepted or allowed into awareness. **(Ch. 6)**

Dependency Reliance on another for support or to meet basic needs. **(Ch. 6)**

Dependent style A decision-making style in which a person takes little responsibility for decisions and is influenced by the expectations and evaluations of others. **(Ch. 9)**

Desensitization A technique for reducing anxiety about an event that is expected to be stressful by imagining the event beforehand. **(Ch. 5)**

Despair In Erikson's theory, feeling a loss of all hope and confidence. Those experiencing despair typically view their lives as fruitless and void of meaning. **(Ch. 1)**

Development A natural process of growth and gradual differentiation. **(Ch. 1)**

Developmental tasks Skills and competences that are acquired at each stage of development. **(Ch. 2)**

Dilation The gradual enlarging of the cervix during labor until wide enough for a baby to pass through. **(Ch.)**

Discrimination The ability of a person to perceive or detect differences between stimuli. **(Ch. 2)**

Disengagement theory A theory describing later adulthood that suggests that positive psychological adjustment is associated with withdrawal from social roles and social relationships. **(Ch. 6)**

DNA Deoxyribonucleic acid. The genetic material present in chromosomes that contains the sequences of coded information used in protein synthesis. **(Ch. 3)**

Down's Syndrome Mongolism; a form of mental deficiency produced by a genetic abnormality; an extra chromosome on pair 21. **(Ch. 4)**

Dual-worker The family life-style of a couple who are both involved in the labor force. **(Ch. 8)**

Effacement The shortening of the cervical canal during labor. **(Ch. 4)**

Egalitarian Marked by the treatment of others as peers and equals; guided by a belief in human equality. **(Ch. 7)**

Ego In psychoanalytic theory, the mental structure that experiences and interprets reality; differentiates between the inner world and the outer world and seeks appropriate gratification of needs and wishes. The ego includes most cognitive capacities, including perception, memory, reasoning, and problem-solving. **(Ch. 2)**

Ego satisfaction A personal source of job satisfaction. **(Ch. 9)**

Egocentrism The perception of oneself at the center of the world; the view that others and events base their behavior on or occur as a direct result of one's own perceptions. **(Ch. 5)**

Emotional inoculation Coping with a stressful event by anticipating the stressors and imagining how one will handle the problem. **(Ch. 6)**

Empty nest The time when children leave the home. **(Ch. 8)**

Encoding Changing sensory input into a form that can be processed by and held in the memory system. **(Ch. 5)**

Endocrine system System of glands which secretes hormones into the bloodstream. **(Ch. 9)**

Enterprising type A personality type that likes to lead, dominate, and persuade, and has excellent verbal skills. This person is extroverted, prefers ambiguous social tasks and gains power and prestige through verbal aggressiveness. **(Ch. 9)**

Enzyme A protein catalyst produced within a living organism that accelerates specific chemical reactions. **(Ch. 3)**

Estrogen The female sex hormone produced mainly by the ovaries. **(Ch. 4)**

Exploration phase The phase of career decision-making in which the person becomes aware of the fact that there is a decision to be made. **(Ch. 9)**

Extended family Three or more generations of a family. **(Ch. 7)**

External subjective culture The "man-made" part of the environment including norms, roles, and values as they exist outside the individual. The external subjective culture is internalized through socialization. **(Ch. 2)**

Extrinsic factors A group of factors that influence job choice. These include family or financial pressures, advice of others, job location, and salary. **(Ch. 9)**

Extrinsic satisfactions Job satisfaction resulting from financial benefits and working conditions. **(Ch. 9)**

False intimacy A false image of closeness generated by adults who encourage their children to express love, but never reciprocate that love and really view their children's needs as unimportant. **(Ch. 7)**

Family-executive A family pattern in which all people in the household participate in decision-making. **(Ch. 8)**

Family of origin The family in which one participates as a child. The family to which one is born. **(Ch. 8)**

Family of procreation The family one begins as an adult. **(Ch. 8)**

Family relations Associations with people within the same family. **(Ch. 5)**

Fantasy A form of symbolic thought that is not restrained by the limits of reality; imagination. **(Ch. 5)**

Fetal development The process of growth of a human embryo from the third to the ninth month. **(Ch. 4)**

Fluid intelligence The ability to inductively reason about essentially new problems. **(Ch. 5)**

Formal operational thought In Piaget's theory, the final stage of cognitive development characterized by reasoning, hypothesis generating, and hypothesis testing. **(Ch. 2)**

Friendship relations Interactions between people who like and support each other. **(Ch. 5)**

Fulfillment Total satisfaction. **(Ch. 2)**

Generalization The tendency for a conditioned response to be evoked not only by the stimulus to which the individual was conditioned, but also by other similar stimuli. **(Ch. 2)**

Generativity In Erikson's psychosocial theory, the capacity to contribute to the quality of life for future generations. A sense of generativity is attained toward the end of middle adulthood. **(Ch. 1)**

Gestation Pregnancy; incubation. **(Ch. 4)**

Heterosexual Interest in or attachment to a member of the opposite sex. A sexual orientation leading to a choice of sexual partners of the opposite sex. **(Ch. 4)**

Homeostasis The tendency to maintain uniformity or stability in the internal environment of the organism. **(Ch.)**

Homosexuality Attraction and sexual preference for someone of the same sex. **(Ch. 4)**

Id In psychoanalytic theory, the mental structure that is made up of drives, impulses, and wishes. Much of the content of the id is unconscious. **(Ch. 2)**

Identification A psychological mechanism in which people elaborate their own self-concept by incorporating some of the valued characteristics of important others. **(Ch. 6), (Ch. 2)**

Identity-achievement Individual identity status in which, after crisis, a sense of commitment to family, work, and political and religious values is established. **(Ch. 6)**

Identity foreclosure Individual identity status in which a commitment to family, work, political and religious values is established prematurely, without crisis. **(Ch. 6)**

Identity status The degree and direction of clarification of personal identity. **(Ch. 6)**

Immune system The system that produces antibodies which give the body the ability to resist infection. **(Ch. 3)**

Incest Sexual relations between people so closely related that they are forbidden by law to marry. **(Ch. 7)**

Induction phase The career decision-making phase in which the person encounters the new environment for the first time, gradually modifies their self-image and learns to believe in the values and goals of the new group. **(Ch. 9)**

Industry In Erikson's psychosocial theory, a sense of pride and pleasure in acquiring culturally valued competencies. The sense of industry is usually acquired by the end of the middle childhood years. **(Ch. 6)**

Infantile autism A childhood disorder resulting in an inability to participate in social relationships or to form attachments, marked by withdrawal. **(Ch. 7)**

Inferiority In Erikson's psychosocial theory, a sense of incompetence and failure which is built on negative evaluation and lack of skill. **(Ch. 6)**

Instrumental conditioning A form of associational learning in which the behaving organism emits responses that are shaped into the desired response by reinforcement. Once the desired response occurs it is strengthened by continued reinforcement. **(Ch. 2)**

Integration phase The career decision-making phase in which a synthesis is achieved between existing group norms and individual values. **(Ch. 9)**

Integrity In Erikson's theory, the ability to accept the facts of one's life and to face death without great fear. The sense of integrity is usually acquired toward the end of later adulthood. **(Ch. 1)**

Intellectual type A personality type that likes to think through problems. This person is task-oriented, introverted, likes ambiguous tasks, and tends to have unconventional values. **(Ch. 9)**

Intimacy In Erikson's theory, the ability to experience an open, supportive, tender relationship with another person without fear of losing one's own identify in the process of growing close. The sense of intimacy is usually acquired toward the end of early adulthood. **(Ch. 1)**

Intimate relations People who share strong emotional bonds and who understand each other. **(Ch. 5)**

Intrinsic factors The group of factors that influence job choice. These include interest, personal feelings, responsibility, and opportunity for advancement. **(Ch. 9)**

Introspection Deliberate self-evaluation and examination of private thoughts and feelings. **(Ch. 5)**

Intuitive style A decision-making style in which decisions are reached without much information seeking; makes primary use of fantasy and intuition. **(Ch. 9)**

Isolation In Erikson's theory, a crisis resolution in which situational factors or a fragile sense of self lead a person to remain psychologically distant from others. **(Ch. 1)**

Job tenure The number of years one has been employed in one's current job. **(Ch. 9)**

Life course Individual life pattern as it is expressed in a social and historical time period. **(Ch. 1)**

Life-events Experiences having significant influence or effect on one's life (for example, marriage or retirement). **(Ch. 1)**

Life review The life evaluation process through reminiscence and introspection. **(Ch. 5)**

Lipofuscin The pigment which accumulates in a cell and can be used to determine the age of an organism. **(Ch. 3)**

Living corpse A category of death characterized by the delaying of official death to make use of the healthy organs in the body by transplanting into a needy recipient. **(Ch. 3)**

Long-term memory A memory storage system that keeps memories for long periods and has a very large capacity. **(Ch. 5)**

Longitudinal study A research method in which the same group of subjects is observed at different points in time. **(Ch. 6)**

Menopause The ending of regular menstrual periods. **(Ch. 4)**

Mental images Representations or pictures in the mind. **(Ch. 5)**

Menstrual cycle The hormonally controlled monthly cycle of egg development, ovulation, and sloughing off of the uterine lining two weeks after ovulation when pregnancy does not result. **(Ch. 4)**

Metabolism The physical and chemical processes by which cells maintain life. **(Ch. 3)**

Metacognition Monitoring and directing thought toward thought itself. **(Ch. 5)**

Metamemory What you know about and how you manipulate (improve, create) your own memory system. **(Ch. 5)**

Mobility rate The percentage of people who were employed in two consecutive years, but who were in a different job each year. **(Ch. 9)**

Model In social learning theory, the person who is imitated. **(Ch. 2)**

Monogamy A family arrangement in which one male and one female marry. **(Ch. 7)**

Morality The thoughts and behaviors associated with issues of good and bad, justice and injustice, and right and wrong. **(Ch. 5)**

Moral reasoning Process of making rational judgments and decisions about moral behavior. **(Ch. 5)**

Mutuality Ability of two people to meet each other's needs and share each other's concerns and feelings. **(Ch. 2)**

Natural childbirth Delivery of a child by the mother without medication, making use of relaxation techniques and pushing; often with the help of the father and medical team. **(Ch. 4)**

Neurological tests Scientific studies performed on the nervous system. **(Ch. 3)**

Neurons Nerve cells, capable of transmitting and receiving impulses throughout the body. **(Ch. 3)**

Normative Conforming to a typical pattern. **(Ch. 1)**

Objective culture The "man-made" part of the environment including roads, tools, factories, etc. **(Ch. 2)**

Objective reality The way things really are outside and independent of the person's point of view. **(Ch. 1)**

Occipital cortex Visual projection area in occipital lobe of the brain. **(Ch. 3)**

Orgasm Sexual climax. **(Ch. 4)**

Ovulation The release of the egg from the ovary. **(Ch. 4)**

Partial brain death A category of death characterized by a loss of all capacity for consciousness while the brain stem continues to function and to maintain breathing. **(Ch. 3)**

Passivity The lack of assertiveness; submissiveness. **(Ch. 5)**

Personal identity An integration of past identifications, personal characteristics, and a commitment to future aspirations. **(Ch. 6)**

Personal philosophy A system of thought about the meaning and purpose of experience. **(Ch. 5)**

Personality The distinct set of characteristic thoughts, feelings, and behavior patterns that guide the organization of experience and the direction of new growth. **(Ch. 6)**

Planning style A rational decision-making style in which the individual assumes personal responsibility for a decision. **(Ch. 9)**

Polygyny Having more than one wife at the same time. **(Ch. 7)**

Post-industrial Our contemporary service-oriented society which focuses less on production of goods and machines, and more on the production of information and services. **(Ch. 10)**

Postconventional morality In Kohlberg's stages of moral reasoning, the most mature form of moral judgments. Moral decisions are based on an appreciation of the social contract which binds members of a social system and on personal values. **(Ch. 5)**

Pragmatism A practical approach to problems. **(Ch. 2)**

Preconventional morality In Kohlberg's stages of moral reasoning, the most immature form of moral judgments. Moral decisions are based on the consequences or rewards of an act. **(Ch. 5)**

Preoperational thought In Piaget's theory of cognitive development, the stage in which representational skills are acquired. **(Ch. 2)**

Private sector Business and work settings that are supported through individual investment or trade. **(Ch. 9)**

Procreation Reproduction, conceiving, bearing, and giving birth to children. **(Ch. 1)**

Progesterone A hormone produced by the ovaries which is secreted in largest amounts during the third week after ovulation. **(Ch. 4)**

Protein synthesis The process by which DNA and RNA determine the combination of amino acids to form proteins. **(Ch. 3)**

Psychosocial A way of looking at the person as an integration of inner competence and social demands. **(Ch. 1)**

Psychosocial crisis In Erikson's psychosocial theory, a predictable life tension that arises as people experience some conflict between their own competences and the expectations of their society. **(Ch. 2)**

Psychosocial evolution Julian Huxley's term for generational changes in thoughts, beliefs, and knowledge. **(Ch. 5)**

Psychosocial moratorium A period of free experimentation before a final identity is achieved. **(Ch. 6)**

Puberty The period of physical development at the onset of adolescence when the reproductive system matures. **(Ch. 4)**

Public sector Business or work settings that are supported by city, state, and federal funds. **(Ch. 9)**

Rationalization A process for defending self-esteem by replacing the real reason for unacceptable conduct or events with a series of arguments that appear to explain the conduct. **(Ch. 6)**

Reaction-time The interval of time it takes to respond to stimuli. **(Ch. 5)**

Realistic type A personality type that is characteristically aggressive, strong, well-coordinated, not very verbal or interpersonally skilled, practical, concrete in thinking, and politically and economically conventional. **(Ch. 9)**

Reality-testing The process of distinguishing between reality and fantasy. **(Ch. 3)**

Recall Searching for and producing a required memory item. **(Ch. 5)**

Recognition Identification of familiar stimuli. **(Ch. 5)**

Reconstructive memory Memory based on inferred knowledge as well as recall. **(Ch. 5)**

Reformation phase The career decision-making phase in which the individual is very involved and becomes more assertive with the new group. **(Ch. 9)**

Rehearsal Strategy for increasing short-term memory storage capacity through repetition of information. **(Ch. 5)**

Reinforcement In operant conditioning, the consequence of a response that increases the probability that the response will occur again. **(Ch. 2)**

Reminiscence Process of thinking and/or telling about past experiences. **(Ch. 5)**

Representational Serving to portray or depict ideas. **(Ch. 5)**

Repression A defensive process in which a stressful event or thought is simply removed from conscious awareness. **(Ch. 6)**

Responsiveness The ability to react relatively quickly and accurately to another person's needs. **(Ch. 7)**

Retrieval Process of finding information that was experienced or learned at an earlier time. **(Ch. 5)**

Rite of passage A ritual associated with a crisis or a change of status (for example, marriage for an individual). **(Ch. 1)**

RNA Ribonucleic acid. A compound that conveys the information in the DNA strands to the cytoplasm in order to stimulate the production of specific amino acids. **(Ch. 3)**

Role A set of behaviors that have some socially agreed upon functions and for which there exists an accepted code of norms, such as the role of teacher, child, or minister. **(Ch. 1)**

Role diffusion The negative pole of the psychosocial crisis of later adolescence in which the person cannot make a commitment to any unified vision of the self. **(Ch. 6)**

Schedules of reinforcement The frequency and regularity with which reinforcement is provided. **(Ch. 2)**

Self-acceptance Achievement of a sense of trust and feelings of worthiness in one's ideas and impulses. **(Ch. 2)**

Self-actualization In Maslow's theory, the highest of human motives, the motive for making the most of one's competences and for realizing one's potential. **(Ch. 2)**

Sensorimotor intelligence In Piaget's theory of development, the first stage of cognitive growth during which schema are built on sensory and motor experiences. **(Ch. 2)**

Sexual dysfunction The inability to react emotionally or physically to sexual stimulation in a way that is anticipated or expected of healthy persons. **(Ch. 4)**

Short-term memory A memory storage system that keeps material for short intervals and has a limited storage capacity (approximately 7 ± 2 units). **(Ch. 5)**

Single encounters A social relationship that does not go beyond a single interaction. **(Ch. 5)**

Single-adult executive Family pattern in which one adult in the household makes the major decisions. **(Ch. 8)**

Social clock Changes in social expectations that occur as individuals move from adolescence through adulthood and old age. **(Ch. 8)**

Social learning theory A theory of learning that emphasizes the ability to learn new responses through observation, imitation of others, and cognitive appraisal of oneself. **(Ch. 2)**

Social type A personality type that is sociable, responsible, verbal, and interpersonally skillful. Does not like logical problem solving and physical activity. **(Ch. 9)**

Solicitude Concern; interest. **(Ch. 4)**

Stage A degree of advance in development that is characterized by some qualitatively unique features. Most stage theories assume a hierarchical organization such that movement to later stages depends on adequate achievement of earlier and less complex levels of development. **(Ch. 1)**

Stagnation In Erikson's theory, a lack of psychological movement or growth during middle adulthood which may result from self-aggrandizement or from the inability to cope with developmental tasks. **(Ch. 1)**

Storage Capacity for accumulated information or experiences. **(Ch. 5)**

Subjective reality The way things appear from the individual point of view. **(Ch. 1)**

Sublimation Directing the expression of impulses toward socially or culturally acceptable ends. **(Ch. 2)**

Superego In psychoanalytic theory, the mental function that embodies moral precepts and moral sanctions. The superego includes the ego ideal, or the goals toward which one strives, as well as the punishing conscience. It operates primarily at an unconscious level. **(Ch. 2)**

Symbolic Pertaining to an object, image, or word that represents something such as "dove" represents the concept of peace. **(Ch. 2)**

Synapse The junction between the axon (impulse transmitter) of one neuron and the dendrite or cell body of the next neuron. **(Ch. 3)**

Technology The machines, tools, and information used to provide all the objects needed for daily life. **(Ch. 10)**

Testosterone The principal male sex hormone. **(Ch. 4)**

Theory A formulation of apparent relationships which have some degree of verification and supportive evidence. A plausible or scientifically acceptable general principle or body of principles offered to explain phenomena. **(Ch. 2)**

Total brain death A category of death characterized by unreceptivity and unresponsiveness, lack of movement, breathing, and reflexes, and a flat electroencephalogram. **(Ch. 3)**

Traditional family Family believing in a clear division of functions along sex lines. Husbands provide income and wives care for children and maintain the household. **(Ch. 8)**

Trait A persisting personality characteristic by which an individual can be rated or measured. **(Ch. 6)**

Transference The displacement of emotions and feelings (positive or negative) from one person or object to another. **(Ch. 2)**

Type A personalities People who interpret stressful events as a threat to their control and who react by becoming more hostile, competitive, and anxious to resolve the stress. **(Ch. 6)**

Type B personalities People who do not feel a sense of urgency in stressful situations, are confident of their abilities, and less preoccupied with proving themselves to others. **(Ch. 6)**

Unconscious In Freud's psychosexual theory, a reservoir of wishes, needs, and fantasies that influence behavior but of which we are not aware. **(Ch. 2)**

Vasectomy The surgical sterilization of a male by cutting the sperm-carrying ducts. **(Ch. 8)**

Vicarious expectation Anticipation of the rewards or status achieved by a model if one imitates the model's behavior. **(Ch. 2)**

Zygote A cell formed by the union of two gametes (male and female); the fertilized ovum or egg. **(Ch. 4)**

Name Index

Subject Index